Liberal Ideals and the Politics of Decolonisation

Liberal Ideals and the Politics of Decolonisation explores the subject of liberalism and its uses and contradictions across the late British Empire, especially in the context of imperial dissolution and subsequent state-building.

The book covers multiple regions and issues concerning the British Empire and the Commonwealth, in particular the period ranging from the late-nineteenth century to the late-twentieth century. Original intellectual contributions are offered along with new arguments on critical issues in imperial history that will appeal to a wide range of scholars, including those outside of history. *Liberal Ideals and the Politics of Decolonisation* exposes commonalities, contradictions and contexts of different types of liberalism that animated the late British Empire and its rulers, radicals, subjects and citizens as they attempted to forge new states from its shadow and understand the impact of imperialism.

This book examines the complexities of the idea and quest for self-government in the last stages of the British Empire. It also argues the importance of the political, intellectual and empirical aspects of liberalism to understand the process of decolonisation.

The chapters in this book were originally published in a special issue of *The Journal of Imperial and Commonwealth History*.

H. Kumarasingham is Senior Lecturer in British Politics and a Political Historian at the University of Edinburgh, UK. His research is especially concerned with the constitutional and political manifestations of decolonisation in multiple parts of the British Empire.

Liberal Ideals and the Politics of Decolonisation

Edited by
H. Kumarasingham

LONDON AND NEW YORK

First published 2021
by Routledge
2 Park Square, Milton Park, Abingdon, Oxon, OX14 4RN

and by Routledge
52 Vanderbilt Avenue, New York, NY 10017

Routledge is an imprint of the Taylor & Francis Group, an informa business

© 2021 Taylor & Francis

All rights reserved. No part of this book may be reprinted or reproduced or utilised in any form or by any electronic, mechanical, or other means, now known or hereafter invented, including photocopying and recording, or in any information storage or retrieval system, without permission in writing from the publishers.

Trademark notice: Product or corporate names may be trademarks or registered trademarks, and are used only for identification and explanation without intent to infringe.

British Library Cataloguing in Publication Data
A catalogue record for this book is available from the British Library

ISBN13: 978-0-367-51313-9

Typeset in Minion
by Newgen Publishing UK

Publisher's Note
The publisher accepts responsibility for any inconsistencies that may have arisen during the conversion of this book from journal articles to book chapters, namely the inclusion of journal terminology.

Disclaimer
Every effort has been made to contact copyright holders for their permission to reprint material in this book. The publishers would be grateful to hear from any copyright holder who is not here acknowledged and will undertake to rectify any errors or omissions in future editions of this book.

Contents

	Citation Information	vii
	Notes on Contributors	ix
	Introduction: Liberal Ideals and the Politics of Decolonisation H. Kumarasingham	1
1	The Plural Society: Labour and the Commonwealth Idea 1900–1964 Pippa Catterall	7
2	Imperial Citizenship or Else: Liberal Ideals and the Indian Unmaking of Empire, 1890–1919 Mark R. Frost	31
3	Written Differently: A Survey of Commonwealth Constitutional History in the Age of Decolonisation H. Kumarasingham	60
4	An Acutely Embarrassing Affair: Whitehall and the Indian-South African Dispute at the United Nations (1946) Lorna Lloyd	95
5	A Liberal Ghost? The Left, Liberal Democracy and the Legacy of Harold Laski's Teaching Brant Moscovitch	121
6	The Post-Colonial Constitutional Order of the Commonwealth Caribbean: The Endurance of the Crown and the Judicial Committee of the Privy Council Derek O'Brien	144

7 Primitive Liberals and Pirate Tribes: Black-Flag Radicalism and the
   Kibbo Kift   170
   Hana Qugana and Simon Layton

8 Imperial Liberalism and Institution Building at the End of Empire
   in Africa   195
   Sarah Stockwell

   Index   220

Citation Information

The chapters in this book were originally published in *The Journal of Imperial and Commonwealth History*, volume 46, issue 5 (October 2018). When citing this material, please use the original page numbering for each article, as follows:

Introduction
Liberal Ideals and the Politics of Decolonisation
H. Kumarasingham
The Journal of Imperial and Commonwealth History, volume 46, issue 5 (October 2018), pp. 815–820

Chapter 1
The Plural Society: Labour and the Commonwealth Idea 1900–1964
Pippa Catterall
The Journal of Imperial and Commonwealth History, volume 46, issue 5 (October 2018), pp. 821–844

Chapter 2
Imperial Citizenship or Else: Liberal Ideals and the Indian Unmaking of Empire, 1890–1919
Mark R. Frost
The Journal of Imperial and Commonwealth History, volume 46, issue 5 (October 2018), pp. 845–873

Chapter 3
Written Differently: A Survey of Commonwealth Constitutional History in the Age of Decolonisation
H. Kumarasingham
The Journal of Imperial and Commonwealth History, volume 46, issue 5 (October 2018), pp. 874–908

Chapter 4

An Acutely Embarrassing Affair: Whitehall and the Indian-South African Dispute at the United Nations (1946)
Lorna Lloyd
The Journal of Imperial and Commonwealth History, volume 46, issue 5 (October 2018), pp. 909–934

Chapter 5

A Liberal Ghost? The Left, Liberal Democracy and the Legacy of Harold Laski's Teaching
Brant Moscovitch
The Journal of Imperial and Commonwealth History, volume 46, issue 5 (O ctober 2018), pp. 935–957

Chapter 6

The Post-Colonial Constitutional Order of the Commonwealth Caribbean: The Endurance of the Crown and the Judicial Committee of the Privy Council
Derek O'Brien
The Journal of Imperial and Commonwealth History, volume 46, issue 5 (October 2018), pp. 958–983

Chapter 7

Primitive Liberals and Pirate Tribes: Black-Flag Radicalism and the Kibbo Kift
Hana Qugana and Simon Layton
The Journal of Imperial and Commonwealth History, volume 46, issue 5 (October 2018), pp. 984–1008

Chapter 8

Imperial Liberalism and Institution Building at the End of Empire in Africa
Sarah Stockwell
The Journal of Imperial and Commonwealth History, volume 46, issue 5 (October 2018), pp. 1009–1033

For any permission-related enquiries please visit:
www.tandfonline.com/page/help/permissions

Notes on Contributors

Pippa Catterall is Professor of History and Policy at the University of Westminster, UK. As well as publishing widely on British and imperial history, she co-founded and continues to edit the journal *National Identities*. Her latest publication is *Labour and the Free Churches 1918–1939: Radicalism, Righteousness and Religion* (2016) and her current research focuses upon Britain and Islam in the twentieth century.

Mark R. Frost is Senior Lecturer in Modern History and Head of Department at the University of Essex, UK. He is the author of the award-winning book *Singapore: A Biography* (2009) and articles in major historical journals such as *Past and Present*, *The American Historical Review*, *The English Historical Review*, *Modern Asian Studies*, and *The Journals of Southeast Asian Studies*.

H. Kumarasingham is Senior Lecturer in British Politics and a political historian at the University of Edinburgh, UK. His work has mainly been concerned with the political manifestations of decolonisation. His works include *A Political Legacy of the British Empire – Power and the Parliamentary System in Post-Colonial India and Sri Lanka* and he has edited the volumes *Constitution Maker – Selected Writings of Sir Ivor Jennings* (2015) and *Constitution-Making in Asia – Decolonisation and State-Building in the Aftermath of the British Empire* (2016). He is presently co-editing *The Cambridge Constitutional History of the United Kingdom* and is preparing a monograph on the legacy of the Crown in South Asia.

Simon Layton is Lecturer in Early Global History at Queen Mary University of London, UK. His research explores oceans and other transnational spaces of historical enquiry, considering questions pertaining to empire, exploration, violence and sovereignty in the early-modern and modern periods. His forthcoming monograph is entitled *Piratical States: British Imperialism in the Indian Ocean World*.

Lorna Lloyd is Senior Research Fellow in International Relations at Keele University, UK. Her research reflects her interest in diplomacy, international history, international law, international organisation, and the evolution of the

Commonwealth. Her publications include *Peace through Law: Britain and the International Court in the 1920s* (1997), and *Diplomacy with a Difference: The Commonwealth Office of High Commissioner, 1870–2006* (2007).

Brant Moscovitch researches global and imperial history at the University of Oxford, UK. He is also a postdoctoral fellow at the Max Weber Stiftung in New Delhi, contributing a module 'Critiques and Renewals of Democracy' for the project Metaphorphoses of the Political: Comparative Perspectives on the Long Twentieth Century.

Derek O'Brien is a Reader in Public Law at Oxford Brookes University, UK. He has written extensively on Caribbean constitutional history and is the author of the monograph *Constitutional Law Systems of the Commonwealth Caribbean*. He is a member of the editorial board of the *Caribbean Law Review*.

Hana Qugana recently completed her PhD at University College London, UK. Her thesis centres on the Kibbo Kift's role in British political culture and intellectual life, exploring youth oriented, civic education initiatives in the early twentieth century. Her current research looks at the colonial and postcolonial worlds of educational publishing in the Philippines and Southeast Asia.

Sarah Stockwell is Professor of Imperial and Commonwealth History at King's College London, UK. Her books include *The Business of Decolonisation: British Business Strategies in the Gold Coast, 1945–1957* (2000), *The British End of the British Empire* (2018), the edited collections *The British Empire. Themes and Perspectives* (2008), and with L. J. Butler, *The Wind of Change: Harold Macmillan and British Decolonization* (2013).

INTRODUCTION

Liberal Ideals and the Politics of Decolonisation

H. Kumarasingham

The twentieth century witnessed some of the British Empire's most creative and contradictory political manoeuvres. Creative in that it employed multiple reforms, policies and techniques to extend its influence while moulting power as its ability to impose itself shrank. Contradictory in that while it attempted to dismantle an empire and build a commonwealth of self-governing states it also wanted to maintain, if not strengthen, a liberally led and light-touch dominion over the world it once ruled. The rhetoric of Britain's political liberalism rung everywhere from legislative council chambers and Colonial Office memoranda to youth clubs and debating societies. Just as Britain's stance was perplexing and far from uniform in its political attitude towards the Empire and Commonwealth so indeed were the positions and feelings of the ruled. Could colonial masters become equals with those they once ruled united by political and liberal ideals? Or did political emancipation require political maturity, which could not be given, but only learned. Could the tenets of British liberalism be extended to regions and societies whose members would have been blackballed from the hallowed Reform Club? Responsible Government meant what and to whom? Could the guardianship of countless minorities be surrendered to the slick new sahibs? Would the political ideology and institutions of Westminster be sufficient, let alone appropriate, to the tasks facing governments and societies that were simultaneously familiar and removed from London?

At no time were these issues more apparent than in the drama of what became known as the decolonisation of the British Empire during the twentieth century. Questions arose that proved difficult to answer. Even when solutions might be found their reason and reach might give limited alleviation or even provoke political contretemps and violence. Political liberalism across the British Empire and Commonwealth drifted on an inclement sea uncertain of its bearings and often imprudent in its anchorage. However, political liberalism of the British variety in the Empire-Commonwealth, was no passing fad. Since at least the 1897 Diamond jubilee of Queen Victoria, an event Max Beloff believed trumpeted Britain's 'liberal empire',[1] the quest across the Empire was for political liberalism and to share in the responsibility and mantle of government – more often than not within the British orbit. Constitutions, institutions, royal commissions, memorials, treaties, ritual, travel, literature, art and the establishment of societies, clubs and educational centres all promoted the ideals of political liberalism. As the Conservative M.P. E. F. L. Wood (the future viceroy of India and Earl of Halifax) said in a 1922 report on political development in the Caribbean, which would have been gloomy reading for those seeking independence, the British territories in the region possessed 'not a few individuals of somewhat exceptional capacity and intelligence' despite there being 'Great blocks of it [which] are backwards and politically undeveloped'. Nonetheless he continued 'We shall be wise if, with these facts before us, we make steps to build upon the foundation of the remarkable loyalty to the Throne' and .....

> avoid the mistake of endeavouring to withhold a concession ultimately inevitable until it has been robbed by delay of most of its usefulness and of its grace.[2]

Fifty years later, just months before Jamaican independence in 1962, one of the island's leading political lights, Norman Manley proclaimed words which link with Wood's and with the association British political liberalism held for those like him.

> I make no apology for the fact that we did not attempt to embark upon any original or novel exercise in constitutional building..... Let us not make the mistake of describing as colonial, institutions which are part and parcel of the heritage of this country. If we have any confidence in our own individuality and our own personality, we would absorb these things and incorporate them into our own use as part of the heritage we are not ashamed of. I am not ashamed of any institution which exists in this country merely because it derives from England.[3]

Characteristic of such statements like Manley's is the sentiment that for political liberalism of the British variety to work effectively trust and delegation would need to be conceded to indigenous leadership. A way of advocating this path seen across the colonial world was to appeal to the 'Throne' of Wood's report and send into sharp relief the inadequacy or worse of the British administration and social presence in their territories. As ever, there was an eloquent demonstration to condemn the Colonial government's injurious propensity to abjure the principles local elites considered intrinsic to British governance and their rights as subjects of the Crown. In 1890 one of Ceylon's leading political grandees, Sir Ponnambalam Ramanathan, authored a memorandum to Queen Victoria, outlining in great detail on behalf of the Ceylon Political Association, the 'invasion of the rights of Your Majesty's Legislative Council on the Island on the part of some Governors'. Ramanathan believed that the Queen's local subjects deserved better and

> should be allowed to at least enjoy the privileges of the existing constitution according to the intention of its beneficent founders without interference on the part of some Governors who believe in the expediency of mild despotism.[4]

Civis Britannicus sum was something that fuelled such beliefs. It was not just for the English. Instead national leaders from General Hertzog to Mahatma Gandhi believed, when it suited their aims, that their position and community should not be regarded as, or reduced to, second-class vis-à-vis the English within the British Empire. As late as 1954 a Conservative Minister at the Colonial Office, would tell the House of Commons: 'we can still take pride in the fact that a man can say *Civis Britannicus sum* whatever his colour may be, and we take pride in the fact that he wants and can come to the Mother country'.[5] However, there lingered, all over a suspicion, often justified that reality meant something else. Liberal political principles did not necessarily mean liberal realities. Harry Hopkinson, the same Colonial Office Minister, who trumpeted the liberalism of Civis Britannicus sum had only months earlier in July 1954 had unguardedly voiced in the House of the Commons that some parts of the Empire 'can never expect to be fully independent'. An utterance that had direct violent and political ramifications in Cyprus.[6] In this era, as before, countless cases abounded that eroded the constitutional confidence of British and Commonwealth law to protect rights most held as inviolable. Liberal ideals suffered in the face of disenfranchisement of indentured labourers in Asia, Africa, Caribbean and Pacific; miserly and lethargic extension of civil rights across the 'old' Dominions; banishment of local leaders from Botswana to Burma; the use of state sanctioned torture in East Africa and South East Asia; and of course, statutory racial discrimination most obviously manifested in Apartheid, but also across the Commonwealth from Canada to Ceylon. The New Zealand head of external affairs, Sir Alastair McIntosh, when asked to support a republican India within the Commonwealth by a visiting British Cabinet minister stated that it was 'too great a sacrifice' since the 'whole conception of the Commonwealth seemed to be based on the fact of European decent'.[7] In Britain itself, less than a decade after the minister extolled the virtues of British rights across the Empire-Commonwealth in 1954 his government curtailed those principles and circumscribed *civis* with the Commonwealth Immigrants 1962, which the Leader of Opposition called 'cruel and brutal anti-colour legislation'[8] – though Labour when in government two years later went on to add further restrictions. Liberalism was always a selective tool. For example, liberalism, like all ideals, could also imply an impatience with many attributes of freedom such as a critical press. General Templer in 1953 was perturbed by the media's potential for 'undesirable influence' on local students in Malaya along with the invasive bogey of communism. Templer

> raised the wider question of the influence of the Press on the political development of Malaya. He deplored the influence of the 'Singapore Standard' with its doctrinaire left-wing views. What the country needed was a newspaper that would preach the gospel of decent Liberalism and good government.[9]

Liberalism, of course, could be used as an evocation by those who were acting contrary to the conception being extended to crucial segments of the population. In late 1947 another British solider, Field Marshal Bernard Montgomery, wrote that Africa was a continent full of exciting opportunity, but could not be left to the African who was 'a complete savage'. Instead tough liberalism meant policies were required over the objections of those in Britain who will think 'that the African will suffer in the process'. British interests and imported 'brains and go-getters' were required to develop the region. Invoking Cecil Rhodes he stated

> We must face up to the problems now; they will be far more difficult if left for our children. The plain truth is that these lands must be developed in order that Britain may survive.[10]

To such statements, which were common, can be what C.A. Bayly called a different liberalism – that of contradicting Britain. Indians (but applicable to other non-Britons within the Empire), 'refused to accept that the principle of liberty did not apply to them because they were "barbarians" and consequently, like children, in need of direction by benign imperial authority'. Instead they drew not only on British political liberalism as evidently within their capability, but also their own civilisational values that asserted India's manifest liberal character and consequent candidature for self-government.[11] The post-independence period would challenge these ideals too.

This special issue probes these concerns surrounding the politics and culture of liberalism in the Empire-Commonwealth during the twentieth century, especially concerning decolonisation. While there has been growing interest in liberalism and empire there still remains more to be investigated. This special issue is especially interested in the political historical and constitutional elements of liberalism. Pippa Catterall explains the Labour Party's difficulty to adjusting from Empire to Commonwealth in those critical years following the end of the Second World War. For many being a citizen of empire was the highest liberal honour, for others still it was a mark of servitude to a foreign power. Using the crucial period around the end of the nineteenth century and the beginning of the twentieth, Mark Frost looks at 'loyal dissent' and the frustrations of waiting for liberal ideals to translate into political realities. It has been considerable time since a constitutional analysis of the decolonisation of the British Empire has been undertaken. H. Kumarasingham surveys and defines the importance of Commonwealth constitutional history to the discipline of history and to the liberal political project that underwrote much of it. A common theme throughout this issue is the importance of personal factors and relations to the reception and style of political liberalism. Lorna Lloyd explores Britain's response to India's attack on South Africa's racial policies at the United Nations, the outcome of long-anxious relations between South Africa and India whose respective liberal and political visions were often in conflict, but also full of nuance and paradox. Brant Moscovitch examines the educational and the ideological impact of socialism on liberal ideals for those seeking to break the imperial yoke while Derek O'Brien examines the historical and legal aspect of the Caribbean's relationship with the Crown and Courts and how this has affected political options and discourse. Hana Qugana and Simon Layton search for the essence of social groups that challenged the cultural and liberal pretensions of the British Empire such as the Kibbo Kift and finally Sarah Stockwell looks at the contradictions and causes of the British liberal tradition using key institutions during the decolonisation of Africa – a continent that experienced a bewildering array of liberal and illiberal policies. Together this special issue attempts to emulate C.A. Bayly and explore aspects of the liberal ideal and political experiences in areas either previously unfamiliar or overlooked. The twentieth century British Empire-Commonwealth holds a captivating period to traverse the many roads and ravines that liberal ideals ran, and stunted, with enduring consequence.

Notes

1. See Beloff, *Imperial Sunset, 1897–1921*.
2. 'Report of the Hon. E. F. L. Wood, M. P., on His Visit to the West Indies and British Guiana, December 1921 to February 1922', HMSO: Cmnd. 1679/1922.
3. As quoted in Girvan, "Assessing Westminster in the Caribbean," 97.
4. 'Memorandum on the Reform of the Constitution, presented to Her Majesty Queen Victoria on 10 February, 1890, by the Honourable P. Ramanathan, C.M.G., M.L.C.', Appendix in Vythilingam, *The Life of Sir Ponnambalam Ramanathan*, 587–88.
5. Henry Hopkinson quoted in Thompson, "Empire and the British State," 55.
6. See Holland, "Never, Never Land," 148–176.
7. Kumarasingham, *Onward with Executive Power*, 26–27.
8. Horne, *Macmillan 1957–1986*, 423.
9. Templer had been accused in the British Press of running a 'Police State'. 'Minutes by R. L. Baxter and T. C. Jerrom on discussions with Sir G. Templer and Sir D. MacGillivray on 11 and 14 November 1953', CO 1022/85, no 36, 18 November 1953, document 309 in Stockwell, *British Documents on the End of Empire (BDEEP)*, 13–16.
10. 'Memorandum by Field Marshal Lord Montgomery, "Tour in Africa, Nov-Dec 1947", December 19, 1947, DO 35/2380, no. 1, document 104, in Hyam, *BDEEP, The Labour Government and the End of Empire*, 188–93.
11. Bayly, *Recovering Liberties*,13–18.

Acknowledgements

The articles in this special issue 'Liberal Ideals and the Politics of Decolonisation' are the result of a workshop held in Colombo in December 2015. I wish to record thanks to Dr Paikiasothy Saravanamuttu, Dr Asanga Welikala and their colleagues at the Centre for Policy Alternatives for helping make possible a stimulating academic and social event. Sir

Christopher A. Bayly was to have delivered the keynote for the workshop comparing the liberalism and politics of the independence leaderships of South Asia and East Africa. His death in April 2015 robbed us of a mentor, scholar and friend. This special issue which has his ideas weaved, naturally, within it is dedicated to his lasting memory with gratitude for his timeless work and scholarly span, which has influenced us all.

Disclosure statement

No potential conflict of interest was reported by the author.

ORCID

H. Kumarasingham http://orcid.org/0000-0001-7424-6626

References

Bayly, C. A. *Recovering Liberties – Indian Thought in the Age of Liberalism and Empire*. Cambridge: Cambridge University Press, 2012.

Beloff, M. *Imperial Sunset, Vol. 1. Britain's Liberal Empire 1897–1921*. London: Methuen, 1969.

Girvan, N. "Assessing Westminster in the Caribbean: Then and now." *Commonwealth & Comparative Politics* 53, no. 1 (2015): 95–107.

Holland, R. F. "Never, Never Land: British Colonial Policy and the Roots of Violence in Cyprus, 1950–54." *Journal of Imperial and Commonwealth History* 21, no. 3 (1993): 148–176.

Horne, A. *Macmillan 1957–1986, Vol. II*. London: Macmillan, 1989.

Hyam, R., ed. *British Documents on the End of Empire (BDEEP), The Labour Government and the End of Empire 1945-1951, Part II*. London: HMSO, 1992.

Kumarasingham, H. *Onward with Executive Power – Lessons from New Zealand 1947-57*. Wellington: Victoria University of Wellington/Institute of Policy Studies, 2010.

Stockwell, A. J., ed. *British Documents on the End of Empire (BDEEP), Malaya, Part III*. London: HMSO, 1995.

Thompson, A. "Empire and the British State." In *The British Empire – Themes and Perspectives*, edited by S. Stockwell, 39–62. Oxford: Blackwell, 2008.

Vythilingam, M. *The Life of Sir Ponnambalam Ramanathan, Vol. 1*. Colombo: Ramanathan Commemoration Society, 1971.

The Plural Society: Labour and the Commonwealth Idea 1900–1964

Pippa Catterall

ABSTRACT
The Labour Party founded in 1900 necessarily confronted the imperial nature of the British state, the empire as an economic and military entity, and the inequalities it contained. Yet Labour initially thought on the subject primarily in terms of the liberal objective of the advancement of self-government. It was only in the 1930s, in the writings of Lansbury and Attlee, that more systematic thinking about the empire in terms of global divisions of labour of which the British working class were among the beneficiaries, began to emerge. Tensions between the perceived interests of these beneficiaries and of the working classes of the empire as a whole remained in Attlee's postwar government. It did, however, begin to develop a reconceptionalisation of the empire as a multi-racial Commonwealth. This facilitated a Labour patriotism around the Commonwealth that reached its apogee in Gaitskell's weaponising of it as a means of resisting European entry in 1962. Yet the economic and military relations he evoked were already out of date, leaving his successor, Harold Wilson, to adjust to a multi-racial partnership.

When the British Labour Party was founded in February 1900, it emerged in the metropole of an imperial state and in the midst of the first imperial war to be fought as an empire. Imperialism was thus one of the central political realities confronting the new party, whether in the form of the projection of power at the imperial frontier, the role of the empire in providing the raw materials for Britain's industries and foodstuffs, or in the politics of oppression across its vast extent. The latter – in the form of Chinese indentured labour in South Africa – was indeed a major issue in the 1906 election which saw Labour's breakthrough to 30 seats in parliament. The empire thus raised, in more extreme and racially varied forms, similar issues about exploitation, oppression and inequality to those the party had been created to confront in Britain. To this can be added the duty these newly elected Labour politicians had to hold to account those British ministers who were responsible for administering the empire, a responsibility that Labour ministers were themselves to exercise in 1924, 1929–1931 and 1945–1951.

The party thus emerged at a point when thinking about empire more generally within British society was arguably in transition. A year before Kipling had, in the context of American imperialism, identified and popularised the "White Man's Burden'; the *Mission Civilisatrise* of imperial development. The contemporary Boer War was, however, also to raise in the mind of J. A. Hobson the idea of empire as economic exploitation and, in that of Joseph Chamberlain – faced with intimations of British imperial decline – the need for closer military and economic co-operation across the empire.[1] As C. Delisle Burns observed in an official Labour publication in 1925, without quite capturing these complex nuances, modern empires were thus economic rather than military: 'Imperialism was the faith of those who believed that this expansion of their nation was for the good of the peoples governed as well as for the development of the whole world'. It was thus also an idea, as Burns noted, actively promoted throughout the empire through the innovation of Empire Day from 1902, through school textbooks and indeed through the spread of tropes of Britishness and of British forms of Christianity across its length.

Empire, as Burns acknowledged, thus posed a number of challenges to the new party. There was the electoral problem of the conflation of imperialism with patriotism given that 'Imperialism is necessarily opposed to Socialism, not only because Socialism looks towards international peace, but also because Socialism is opposed to private advantages gained at the expense of the common good'. Empire at the same time raised the policy issue of responding to the needs of the 'common men of other lands'.[2]

This posed the challenge of thinking of the empire as an interconnected system in which the British working classes were among the beneficiaries. In the process it therefore raises the question of whether, when Labour writers waxed lyrical – as they were wont to do until the 1940s – on the Socialist Commonwealth that was to come, did they also include in that the Commonwealth that already existed as an appellation for those parts of empire which had been given some form of self-governing autonomy, let alone the imperial whole? Often the answer appears to be no. Consider G. D. H. Cole, one of the leading left-wing thinkers and populariser of the inter-war years. His 1918 tome, *Labour in the Commonwealth*, attempted to think through how Labour could achieve its place in a state – specifically the British one – rather than the wider issue of the place of labour across the vaster realms of the empire.[3] It has also been suggested that at the official level the new party's references to Commonwealth similarly tended to be concerned with the Socialist, rather than the imperial, variety.[4] Take, for instance, the statement of *The Aims of Labour*, published the year before Cole's work by Arthur Henderson, the Labour Party's general secretary, as part of the re-launch of the party he and Sidney Webb masterminded to prepare it for the world emerging after the

Great War.[5] The empire may have been heavily involved in supporting Britain's war efforts militarily, commercially and financially (for instance, George Lansbury claimed in 1935 that India contributed £100m to the British war effort, spent £207.5m on its own military campaigns and contributed greatly to saving the Channel ports in 1914–1915),[6] and it was to reach its greatest extent in its immediate aftermath. It was, however, passed over in silence by Henderson.

The limited attention Labour paid to imperial matters before 1914 was understandable given that it remained a small party which could influence the governing Liberals but not yet aspire to replace them. For instance, in 1906 it joined the Liberals in condemning 'Chinese Slavery'. In general, however, the essence of Labour's thinking about the empire in the Edwardian era was expressed in the aspiration contained in party's first election manifesto in 1900 for 'Legislative Independence for all parts of the Empire'.[7] This would thus extend throughout the dependent empire the legislative autonomy already achieved by then in the 'White' Dominions of Australia, Canada, New Zealand and Newfoundland, to be shortly joined by the Union of South Africa in 1910.

The problems with such an approach became apparent to the party when, in April 1914, the Labour MP Frank Goldstone initiated a debate in the Commons on the applicability of Magna Carta, *Habeas Corpus* and the Petition of Right across the empire, calling for their inviolability to be assured in every self-governing Dominion.[8] This is an early example of thinking about the empire systematically, rather than imperial wrongs in particular territories, notably India, Ireland, and South Africa. In calling this debate in light of the alarming handling and aftermath of the mines dispute in South Africa in 1913, Labour clearly were expressing a sense of responsibility for the empire as a whole. This was even more apparent when Henderson (notwithstanding his silence on such issues three years later) in seconding the motion noted:

> It seems to me that if we were indifferent to this situation, especially we on the Labour benches, we would be false to the trust that has been reposed in us, not only by our constituents, but by crowds of organised workers, whom, to some extent, we represent in this House.[9]

South Africa's legislative independence, however, meant that Labour's attempt to invoke a standard of liberty across the empire proved to be a dispiriting experience. Disconsolately, the Labour MP Stephen Walsh observed:

> I have been under the impression that there were certain fundamental principles of British law upon which all these self-governing institutions were to be based....In the ignorance under which we labour upon these benches we really thought that that fundamental condition would exist just as much in the South African Dominions as in our own country, that there should be no person outlawed or exiled, that justice should not be sold and should not be deferred, that no man should be deprived of his fundamental liberties, except through trial by his peers.[10]

Such difficulties seem to have been largely overlooked when Labour for the first time included a substantial passage (albeit only two pages long) on empire and Commonwealth policy in an official party publication. This was *Labour and the New Social Order*, a statement of post-war aims largely drafted by Henderson and Webb and revised at the party conference in June 1918. The aspirations of Joseph Chamberlain and his later acolytes such as Lionel Curtis for some kind of imperial federation were roundly condemned as implying a dangerous subjection to a common imperial legislature coercing tax and military services, invading the autonomy of the Dominions and – by the imposition of imperial duties – undermining the democratic freedom of choice in the United Kingdom itself. Labour, the publication proclaimed, did not want parliament to become an imperial senate representing the plutocracies of the empire. Instead:

> With regard to that great Commonwealth of all races, all colours, all religions and all degrees of civilisation, that we call the British Empire, the Labour Party stands for its maintenance and its progressive development on the lines of Local Autonomy and 'Home Rule All Round'; the fullest respect for the rights of each people, whatever its colour, to all the Democratic Self-Government of which it is capable, and to the proceeds of its own toil upon the resources of its own territorial home, and the closest possible co-operation among all the various members of what has become essentially not an Empire in the old sense, but a Britannic Alliance.

There are certain omissions and contradictions here. The prime omission relates to what was arguably the most obvious manifestation of the empire as a political entity, particularly at the end of a war in which its resources had been massively deployed to the waging of it: the core military functions. On this Labour had seemingly nothing to say.

Labour and the New Social Order had a little more to say on the economics of empire. Its disavowal of all claims for territorial or economic gain is clear. Yet there was no attempt to think through the challenges of the power disparities raised by the mention of plutocracy. Pre-war thinking about cross-national class alliances against economic or other forms of oppression, as exemplified by the Second International's failed pledge to hold a general strike in the event of war, is conspicuously absent. That Labour might have a responsibility, even if only a paternalistic one, to assist the development of labour movements in the Dominions and colonies and unite with them in common witness against economic exploitation is also missing.

Furthermore, there is a potential contradiction between the stated objection to all protective tariffs and the principle that nonetheless 'we hold that each nation must be left free to do what it thinks best for its own economic development, without thought of injuring others'.[11] If all parts of empire could autonomously pursue what was locally in their perceived economic interests, including the UK, then avoiding competitive economic nationalism would likely prove challenging. A consequence was the regrettable effect of Indian tariffs on the Lancashire cotton industry noted and accepted by Burns.[12] Oddly, and notwithstanding Goldstone's initiative in 1914, Labour does not in 1918 even seem to think about this in terms of minimal labour regulation. There is plenty on this subject in the rest of the document, but nothing in the section on empire, despite Labour's contemporary role in the creation of the International Labour Office [ILO] as a key organ of the League of Nations.

The other dimensions of empire that emerge in *Labour and the New Social Order* are as a social and constitutional entity. In terms of the former there is a clear appreciation of social and cultural variety and a commitment to inclusive respect for rights. There is, however, a vagueness about what this entails, particularly given the problem of how this respect for rights can be imposed on autonomous Dominions like South Africa. This reflects the fundamental contradictions within Labour's approach to the empire as a constitutional entity. The aspiration is for local autonomy, which clearly should include India, where Labour favoured a democratic transition far in advance of the contemporary Montagu-Chelmsford plans being formulated by the Lloyd George Coalition. The document is, however, ambiguous about how far this might extend to the dependent parts of empire more generally.

How this local autonomy is consistent with at the same time seeking 'the closest possible co-operation' among the members of empire is studiously unclear. In these circumstances how could such co-operation be secured? Labour's suggestion herein is to transform the imperial conferences which had developed among the Dominions since the 1880s into annual Imperial Councils, which would consult on matters of common interest and make recommendations for simultaneous consideration across the legislatures of what would be constituted as an 'Alliance of Free Nations'.[13] Its understanding of how this Alliance might work as a system thus seems to rest on a weak confederalism, united only by unmentioned ties of sentiment and the equally unmentioned symbol of the Crown. In this a liberal parliamentarianism appears to have trumped a wider commitment to socialistic raising of the well-being of the workers as a class spread across the empire. Indeed, this parliamentarianism was apparently dominant over the aspiration even for minimal liberal standards of equality before the law across the empire that Labour had voiced in the Goldstone debate. The Socialist Commonwealth Labour dreamt of seemingly then did not extend across the seas.

This liberal parliamentarianism is marked in the first reference to the term 'Commonwealth' in connection with empire in a Labour manifesto in 1918, when the party promised to 'extend to all subject peoples the right of self-determination within the British Commonwealth of Free Nations'.[14] How far party figures really thought that this aspiration could actually be achieved remains, however, a matter of conjecture. Sidney Webb, who went on to serve as the party's first Dominions Secretary in 1929–1930, certainly seems to have been dubious. In 1913 he noted that in many parts of the empire 'it would be idle to pretend that anything like effective self-government, even as regards strictly local affairs, can be introduced for many generations to come – in some cases conceivably never'.[15] Thus although there was certainly a desire in Labour to transform the empire into a commonwealth of free nations (not peoples, given the tendency to overlook the oppression of indigenous populations in White Dominions other than South Africa) this was not necessarily considered practical politics.

The other facet of the development of Labour's thinking about the empire that might be remarked upon is the way that it was then compartmentalised. Unlike the Tories, Labour did not overtly recognise empire as a central characteristic of the British state and its economic and political order.[16] It also tended to compartmentalise empire in a racialised hierarchy.[17] Burns commented in 1925: 'The Labour Movement had always a vague affection for all members of the British race beyond the seas, but was hardly aware of the problems of the tropics before the Labour Party came into existence'.[18] In many ways the same prism of Britishness seems still very much present in his thinking in the 1920s. Consider Burns' comment about South Africa: 'No one, of course, wants the white civilisation to be swamped by barbarism, but a real native civilisation can be developed side by side with the European'.[19] In 1928 a memorandum to the second Commonwealth Labour conference divided the empire along similar civilisational lines into European (including the West Indies), Oriental and primitive.[20] This mindset derived from nineteenth century racial hierarchies ensured that the empire thus remained external and paternal.

Nor was the empire integrated into Labour thinking on Britain's international role. Empire played no part, either as a military or a geopolitical entity, in the discussion of Labour's foreign policy set out by Ramsay MacDonald in 1923, shortly before he became simultaneously the party's first Prime Minister and Foreign Secretary the following January, except as a repository for British foreign direct investments.[21] MacDonald was more concerned about opposing the factors which he felt had prompted a war he opposed breaking out in 1914, and spent his first ten months in government concentrating on promoting better relations across Europe and in Russia, rather than giving much thought to either the Commonwealth or the empire.[22] There was, nonetheless, reference in the 1924 election manifesto to MacDonald's administration's alleged success in strengthening 'the ties of sentiment with the Dominions upon which, rather than upon either force or any Imperialism, the very existence of the British Commonwealth of Nations depends'.[23] As a sign of this, the first conference of Commonwealth Labour parties was held the following year, though only India was represented alongside the 'White' Dominions.[24] Followed by similar conferences in 1928 and 1930, this marked Labour starting to think systematically about empire. By the time of the statement of party policy, *Labour and the Nation* in 1927, co-operation across the 'Dominions and Dependencies ... .to take common action for the promotion of a higher standard of social and economic life for the working population of the respective countries' had become one of the aims of the party.[25]

The Communist Party, following Lenin's adaptation of Hobson's ideas, may have in contrast seen empire as economic exploitation and therefore as a constant threat to peace.[26] In the 1920s, however, the efforts of Chamberlain's acolyte, Leo Amery, as Dominions Secretary in the Tory government of 1924–1929 to promote economic co-operation and colonial development across the empire was probably a more important context for the development of Labour thinking on imperial matters. It was against this backdrop that the backbench MP, Leslie Haden-Guest, established a Commonwealth Labour Group of MPs. About 20–30 MPs seem to have regularly attended its weekly meetings. Its core, however, was a small group of figures like James Thomas – who had served as Labour's first Colonial Secretary in 1924 – now moving away from free trade towards Chamberlainite ideas of imperial preference and common external tariffs. For them such devices, and the tied loans Thomas also advocated, were a way of tackling domestic unemployment. This line of thinking culminated in the proposal for 'schemes of development with Crown Colonies involving considerable expenditure on equipment manufactured…..in Britain' put forward in the report resulting from the trades union talks with industry initiated after the 1926 General Strike and issued in March 1929.[27] Such ideas also featured in Labour's 1929 manifesto and led to the passage of the colonial development legislation largely developed by Amery under MacDonald's incoming second government.

This growing focus on imperial economic development was marked in other ways as well in the 1920s. One example was the endorsement of bulk purchase agreements for colonial products at the 1925 party conference. This could be seen as beneficially offering guaranteed markets for these products. That such arrangements might lock colonies into economic subservience and discourage diversification, while the prime beneficiary would be a metropolitan power dependent on imports for some 60 per cent of its foodstuffs, does not seem to have been noticed, even by the left-winger George Lansbury (who succeeded Haden-Guest as head of the Labour Commonwealth Group in 1927), for whom they were merely the first step towards international co-operation.[28]

Another scheme for the economic development of the empire emerged at the 1927 party conference. This was the idea of the surveying the vast land resources of the empire 'with a view to subordinating the private use of land to the general interest of a scientific redistribution of the population'.[29] Imperial emigration was also to be encouraged, despite the lack of enthusiasm of Dominion labour parties.[30] As *Labour and the Nation* (1927) made clear, even the primacy of native welfare invoked therein was structured around protecting them from policies that would be injurious to them but also, by preventing wage competition, to the working classes of Europe.[31]

Labour thinking on the military dimension of empire did not really develop in the 1920s, beyond considering the Committee of Imperial Defence too powerful.[32] To this there was later in 1935 also added a concern raised by the left-wing backbencher, Aneurin Bevan, about how far the Dominions were represented on this important body, and whether they had been consulted on the recent rearmament White Paper.[33] On the constitution of the empire there was meanwhile some movement through the application of the concept of trusteeship developed under the League of Nations to the empire in general. The revised edition of *Labour and the Nation* in 1928 thus spoke of extending the oversight of the League's Mandates Commission to the dependent empire and therein extending political rights already granted to Europeans as part of the preparations for self-government.[34] The important developments in imperial constitutional practice presaged by the 1926 Balfour Declaration, however, went unmentioned in these documents.

The ensuing Labour government of 1929–1931 and its immediate aftermath seems to have marked a transition point in a number of ways. It began with the Colonial Development Act 1929, into S.1(2) of which safeguards for fair wages and conditions, proscription on forced labour and the participation of the colonial territory in any increases in value resulting from the investment were all written in. Such concerns had not hitherto been conspicuous in party pronouncements on empire, but they were to become increasingly noticeable in the 1930s. Secondly, the Labour government was faced with taking forward the long-voiced commitment to Dominion status for India following the Irwin Declaration of October 1929,[35] a process complicated by the Viceroy imprisoning Gandhi the following May. Thirdly, while progress towards self-government in India stalled, the formal co-equal independence of the Dominions was recognised by the December 1931 Statute of Westminster. This welcome development from the Balfour Declaration fulfilled a long-standing Labour goal, but by then the government had fallen from power and been reduced to a parliamentary rump by the National Government landslide of October 1931. Fourthly, that National Government in 1932 negotiated a system of imperial preference commonly known as the Ottawa tariffs. During the 1930s they were also to preside over the consolidation of the empire financially through the development of the Sterling Area.

Labour thinking on empire and Commonwealth thus did not operate in a vacuum but necessarily reflected the actions of their political opponents. Another important contextual factor was Labour's interpretation of the circumstances of the fall of their government and subsequent heavy defeat in 1931. The idea that this was the result of a 'Bankers' Ramp' gave substance to the hitherto shadowy idea of some kind of international plutocracy. This resulted in a more critical appraisal of capitalist exploitation across the empire, as well as in Britain. With Lansbury as party leader from 1932–1935, there was accordingly a shift away from the liberal parliamentarianism which had characterised party thinking in the 1920s. Lansbury's *Labour's Way with the Commonwealth* in 1935 instead voiced for the first time a recognition of informal power structures, including constitutional facades of sham democracy in Southern Rhodesia and the West Indies, and the informal empire exercised by the British through their Portuguese satellite.[36]

An economic critique of empire, which had hitherto only been vaguely expressed, also began to emerge. Lansbury thus pointed to the way in which monopolistic trading companies exploited West African colonies, while in East Africa land seizures had been combined with the iniquitous hut tax to supply European settlers with a cheap supply of landless African labourers.[37] Similarly, a language of economic development was mere empty piety with the high land rents, cartelized labour markets and weak trade unions, and the enormous fiscal burden of 62.5% of taxes going on defence in India. Lansbury also, almost uniquely among the literature consulted for this paper, also drew attention to (some of) the particular disabilities experienced by women in India.[38] None of this would be resolved, he argued, by the Government of India Act 1935, which dropped the aspiration to Dominion status and, by preserving the sclerotic system of dyarchy, militated against responsible government.[39]

Such iniquities were intrinsically related to the 'colour bar'. 'With the possible exception of the Maoris', Lansbury complained, no 'native race has been admitted to full equality with the white inhabitants'.[40] The complicity of Dominion labour movements in this failing and the possible consequences for British Labour was bitterly acknowledged, particularly when 'South Africa may be laying the foundation of a racial war in which we shall be involved'.[41] Across the empire as a whole, the result of this 'colour bar' was the forcing of indigenous peoples into the global market 'under terribly low standards, to compete white people out of the markets'.[42] In the final chapter of the book, by Charles Roden Buxton with the somewhat unfortunate title 'Policy in Backward Colonies', there was therefore emphasis on the need to apply the ILO's 1930 Forced Labour Convention. Ultimately the hope was that the ILO would 'draw up a general code of regulations applicable to all tropical colonies'. This, the development of trade unions and more widespread education, were all seen as necessary to protect against exploitation both by settlers and by native elites. This need to protect against 'irresponsible buccaneers' thus became an additional rationale for the continuance of British trusteeship.[43]

It was not, however, grounds for the economic integration of the empire through the Ottawa system. Indeed, that system was seen as enforcing the existing racial divisions of labour within the empire and of hardening imbalances of trade and debt. Lansbury did not envisage some prototype of Schumacher and Keynes' Bancor scheme as a way of addressing this.[44] His critique did, however, lead him to emphasise the ideals of Commonwealth reciprocity 'as a means for leading the world along the way to an international federation'.[45]

This overarching internationalism was to be even more apparent in the writings of Lansbury's successor as party leader, Clement Attlee. Attlee had been general editor of the series in which Lansbury book appeared, and two years later he followed it up with his own statement on imperial and Commonwealth matters. Not least, he took further Lansbury's earlier critique of the economic and racial nature of the empire. For instance, he emphasised that the Commonwealth was 'essentially a money-lenders' empire' and that British Labour were the beneficiaries of an exploitative race. This meant that the simple nostrums offered by the party earlier of moves towards self-government had to be resisted when demands for this came from settler minorities.[46] This, however, might also apply when these same demands came from unaccountable native elites:

> There is no particular gain in handing over the peasants and workers of India to be exploited by their own capitalists and landlords. Nationalism is a creed that may be sustained with great self-sacrifice and idealism, but may also shelter class domination, and intolerance of minorities as well as economic exploitation.[47]

The challenge for Attlee was how to apply Socialism to the actual existence of the Commonwealth and empire. 'Simple surrender of all ill-gotten gains was undesirable and unpractical [sic].' Instead, Attlee saw the way forward through advancing economic co-operation. An earlier support for Guild Socialism can be detected in his enthusiasm for the experiments of New Zealand's first Labour government with nationalisation of imports and exports, cutting out wasteful and exploitative middle-men and thereby maximising returns to producers and minimising costs to consumers.[48] This was also a development of the import boards proposed by his fellow former Guild Socialist, G. D. H. Cole, during the 1931 crash.[49] Such egalitarian efficiencies, by ending self-interested distortions of markets would, Attlee assumed, prove a better mechanism for economic co-operation than the Ottawa system. By promoting this co-operation across those Dominions 'of European stock' Labour might 'show an example of how such a relationship can be extended to cover all those countries which are ready to share in collective security and the pooling of economic resources'. For Attlee, as for Lansbury, the British Commonwealth was thus simply a stepping point towards a world Commonwealth of nations.[50]

Attlee's book was re-issued twelve years later, by which time he was Prime Minister, having served as Dominions Secretary in Churchill's wartime coalition from 1942–1943. In his preface to this new edition the journalist Francis Williams, who served Attlee as his press advisor from 1945–1947, claimed that the 1937 text had been faithfully carried out by its author in government after Labour's landslide victory in 1945. Although Labour were arguably even more conscious of the military and economic significance of empire in light of wartime experience, Williams thus represents imperial developments following 1945 as matters of degree rather than paradigm shifts. In particular, he emphasised the rapid decolonisation in India, Burma and Ceylon.[51] Yet none of these developments had been explicitly foreshadowed in what Attlee wrote in 1937.

In *The Labour Party in Perspective* Attlee had flagged up his concern about bankrupt Newfoundland, but this had not exactly prefigured the only imperial experience from his wartime service as Dominions Secretary Attlee actually mentions in his memoirs: his visit there in 1942 and subsequent support for its inclusion in Canada in 1949.[52] He passed over in silence the Colonial Development and Welfare Act 1940, introduced to deal with wartime financial disruption in the dependent empire. This breach in the principle that the colonies should be self-supporting was the first significant foray into fiscal transfers from the metropole to the colonies. It was to be greatly extended by Attlee in 1945, leading to the creation of the Colonial Development Corporation [CDC], though this again had not been foreshadowed in his 1937 book. Indeed, he explicitly pointed therein to the difficulties of coming up with a formula to address the problems of advancement towards self-government over such varied territories at differing stages of political and economic development. This was, understandably, not so much a template for how to deal with events such as the Accra riots in 1948 as an indication of the direction of travel. It was also flexible to the international exigencies of postwar Britain's strategic or economic needs, as indicated by the 1946 Kenya White Paper.[53]

The only points on which Attlee was specific were on development of education, safeguarding of native land and reduction of onerous taxes, nationalised marketing of native products and the internationalisation of these products under the League of Nations.[54] These last objectives were not exactly mutually compatible. In practice Attlee's government, faced with the massive British dollar shortage of the postwar years and the important role colonial raw materials played in a reviving world economy for precious dollar earnings, focused on investment in and marketing of these products, not least through the Overseas Food Corporation (1948). Attlee had been impressed with the relative wealth of West Africa in 1937, but the attempt to recreate those circumstances in East Africa through the groundnuts scheme was foredoomed to failure.[55]

It has been argued that the Fabian Colonial Research Bureau founded in 1940 was more influential on Labour's postwar policies than any pre-war thinking.[56] One of its moving spirits was Arthur Creech Jones, who was also chair of the party's advisory committee on imperial issues. Creech Jones went on to serve Attlee as Colonial Secretary 1946–1950. In his introduction to *Fabian Colonial Essays* in 1945 he argued that wartime changes for the colonies had been vast. Yet there are echoes of Labour thinking in the 1920s in his observation that

> Their development is necessary for the larger security of the world; their products and resources are wanted in the outside world; their low standards depress our higher

levels; their disease threatens our health; their poverty, prejudices our prosperity – in short, these distressed areas must be developed and integrated as progressing regions into the commonwealth of free nations.[57]

One way of doing this was through raising the economic return to the colonies, though the technique for this remained the bulk purchase agreements first envisaged in the 1920s.[58] *Fabian Colonial Essays* also, however, developed Labour thinking by for the first time sketching out ideas of how to industrialise the colonies using loan capital at fixed interest rates, an innovation which the veteran Socialist journalist H. N. Brailsford argued would also help to create markets for British manufacturing exports.[59]

Attlee himself in retrospect focused more on political developments under his government. In his memoirs he contrasted the alleged timeliness of grants of self-government in India and Burma with the consequences of delay in the Dutch East Indies and French Indo-China.[60] Subsequently he was to celebrate the unique success of the British in voluntarily surrendering hegemony over subject peoples.[61] Although this was certainly an overstatement his government, in particular by incorporating India, had undoubtedly changed the Commonwealth into something like a multiracial association of free nations. This was a considerable and by no means certain achievement given the commitment Jawaharlal Nehru and the Congress had to establishing an Indian republic, thereby undermining the central position in the Commonwealth occupied by the Crown.[62] The future Labour Prime Minister, Harold Wilson, who was tangentially involved in these events as President of the Board of Trade, may have later described Nehru as 'in every sense a good Commonwealth man', but it was the willingness of the Attlee government to depart from monarchical arrangements that enabled this eventuality.[63]

This outcome of India remaining in the Commonwealth after it became the first republic to do so in 1950 was aided by the decision in 1948, at Attlee's prompting, that the term 'Dominion' and the prefix 'British' should be dropped, given the concerns Nehru had expressed about such terms since at least 1936.[64] This could thus be seen as fulfilment of the aspirations to use the Commonwealth as a stepping stone to internationalisation first sketched out by Lansbury. This would certainly appeal to Attlee, who shared Lansbury's views in this respect and went on to be a leading light of the Parliamentary group for World Government after his retirement from the party leadership in 1955.[65] These aspirations were also evoked in Labour's first statement of foreign policy after losing office in 1951, which emphasised:

> The Commonwealth in its present form is the supreme example of an international organisation which positively helps towards the development of a world society, since it imposes no limitations on co-operation between its members and other states outside … .The Labour Party, therefore, believes that Britain must put the Commonwealth before all other regional groupings.

The Attlee government, it proclaimed, had transformed the Commonwealth into 'a bridge between the peoples of European stock and the peoples of Asia and Africa'. As such, it had indicated how the party might finally accomplish its long-held ambition to achieve 'as rapidly as possible this peaceful transition from Empire to Commonwealth'. *Labour's Foreign Policy* also claimed that the lead given by the Attlee government had 'resulted in the great experiment of the Colombo Plan' of 1950.[66] The latter emerged from the Commonwealth Conference of Foreign Ministers held in Colombo in January 1950 with the twin aims of promoting economic co-operation and development in South-East Asia and thereby discouraging the spread of Communism.

This 1952 statement thus set out two aims for Labour's imperial policy: to further the transition to the Commonwealth and to promote what was starting to be called overseas aid. On the first of these the early 1950s were marked by interest in the idea of federations of colonies as a means to achieve the transition to independence. The party supported this in the West Indies in the 1954 draft policy document 'From Colonies to Commonwealth'. On economic grounds they had also helped to initiate such a scheme in Central Africa in the late 1940s, though they emphasised the need for African consent in a situation complicated by a large settler presence. It was therefore felt that Britain needed to retain sovereignty there and in East Africa for as long as was necessary 'to prevent domination by a racial minority, in order to ensure the achievement of democracy'.[67]

These were not the only areas where the transfer of power remained problematic. Creech Jones, in a critical letter to the party's recently appointed Commonwealth officer, John Hatch, complained both that there was an insufficient emphasis on Socialism in 'From Colonies to Commonwealth' and that the transfer of power should only happen to democratic governments.[68] It is not clear what Creech Jones had in mind, but the next iteration of the policy draft in March 1955 made clear party disapproval of what were seen as Communist attempts 'to use their constitution for the destruction of democracy' in British Guiana.[69]

Meanwhile, the aid agenda emerging in Colombo had already been amplified in *Labour and the New Society* in 1950. This marked an advancement from the inter-war language of trusteeship to the inculcation of development. Insofar as there had been thinking on this subject in the 1930s it had been around land and settlement and addressed through the prism of the high unemployment Britain suffered in that decade. The interests of the metropole in terms of global defence and preventing the spread of Communism to the less-developed world as a new sphere of the burgeoning Cold War remained apparent in the 1950 publication. This is perhaps unsurprising in the year that Attlee's Foreign Secretary, Ernest Bevin, called for Commonwealth co-operation with the Americans against Communism, of which the most tangible result was the British Commonwealth Forces Korea deployment from 1951 to 1957. This was thus the fullest example of Labour finally taking on the military aspects of the Commonwealth, albeit in a form which very much reflected the old rather than the new Commonwealth as BCFK was dominated by British, Canadian and Australian contributions.[70]

Meanwhile, *Labour and the New Society* largely concentrated on how to promote sustainable development. In pointing to the conflict between subsistence agriculture and export crops it foreshadowed the subsequent paper on 'Aid to Under-Developed Countries' by the St Lucian economist W. Arthur Lewis in May 1952. Pointing out that most of Britain's capital movement to the less developed world of around £500m per year then went to South America and the Middle East, Lewis noted that under-developed countries could only absorb more capital if education and training were expanded. This would facilitate the switching of labour from subsidence to marketised sectors of the economy that he was to develop two years later in his seminal Nobel Prize-winning paper.[71]

After going through various internal drafts, these two policy agendas came together in the published version of 'From Colonies to Commonwealth'. More prosaically entitled *Labour's Colonial Policy*, this appeared in three volumes in 1956. The first of these, *The Plural Society*, was Labour's most thorough attempt yet to think through how to achieve sustained self-government in the often deeply racially mixed societies of the colonies. It emphasised that Labour's aim 'is to encourage the peoples concerned, in their political life, to forget race and colour, and to think and act as human beings'. Otherwise how could Creech Jones' aspiration that handover occurred to democratic governments be attained? In societies where access to political power had long been structured around race this was, however, easier said than done. Indeed, the fear was expressed that attempts to remove racial considerations could prove so disruptive to existing social and political norms as to exacerbate racial tensions. Accordingly, it warned that it might 'be necessary to invest Governors with reserve powers for a period to protect legitimate minority interests against excessive nationalist ardour'. In contrast to the constitution-making of the previous decade, it also advised that 'for the protection of minorities ….the principles of the [UN] Declaration of Human Rights' might be included in these constitutions.[72] This could be seen as either cautious or prescient: at this stage, for instance, the Labour-supporting constitutional scholar, Sir Ivor Jennings, had not yet come to regret his optimistic omission of such provisions from the 1948 constitution of Ceylon.[73]

The Plural Society also stressed the need for safeguards for labour, including fair wages clauses which, in an earlier iteration, had been seen as essential preconditions for colonial investment.[74] Most of the discussion of economic policy towards the colonies, however, came in the aptly named second volume on *Economic Aid*, drawn up by a working party chaired by Barbara Castle. A restoration of the bulk purchase agreements run down by the Tories since 1951 was promised. It also welcomed the increase in funds available to the CDC to £20–30m a year in 1955, while arguing for increased pump-priming grants and direct grants to cover social investment. After all, these would thereby compensate for the net imports of capital from the colonies to the UK through the operation of the Sterling Area: 'While we have been lending money long-term to the colonies to build dams, railways, roads and factories, they have been lending money short-term to us through the accumulation of sterling balances'. Labour would therefore now sign up, having – as Lewis pointed out – rejected it when they were in government, for the UN's proposed Special Fund for Economic Development and commit to grants of 1% of GNP per annum towards it.[75] This would not only reverse the negative investment flows but address the lack of finance available for infrastructure development identified in earlier policy documents.[76]

The final volume of *Labour's Colonial Policy* addressed those *Smaller Territories* deemed unready for independence. Gone was the view, still being reiterated by Brailsford in 1945, that sudden independence 'would be to betray the peoples and our trust ... .[to] the penetration of the predatory and callous influences which socialists deplore'.[77] Now only those colonies which 'are too small or possess insufficient resources of wealth or manpower to become full sovereign nations of the Commonwealth' were excluded. It was still a developmental test, but it had been subtly rephrased. The door was also left open for circumstances to 'so alter as to enable them to attain such a status'. One way this might happen was through the federation route. More novel was the idea, following the proposals of Malta's Labour Prime Minister, Dom Mintoff in 1955, for which Hatch was a great enthusiast, that 'we should be prepared in suitable cases ... .to consider representation at Westminster'.[78] Lack of enthusiasm for the perceived welfare costs from the Conservative government helped to ensure that this scheme to nothing.[79] Other proposals, such as that Cyprus – a territory deemed too small for independence that was then wracked with guerrilla warfare – might be resolved through *enosis* with Greece were arguably just naive.[80]

As a statement of *Labour's Colonial Policy* these documents did not prove enduring. With decolonisation gathering pace under the Macmillan government it was decided as early as 1960 not to reprint them as they were already out of date.[81] George Cunningham, who became the party's Commonwealth officer in 1963, subsequently commented: 'Clearly the standards thought necessary for complete independence have been lowered over the years'.[82]

Labour's thinking about the transition to independence had been rapidly overtaken by external developments. This was not the only problem with these policy documents. Pointing out the contradictions between the aim of rapid self-determination for most territories and the commitment to end racial discrimination first, Richard Crossman commented: 'If we have to wait until all forms of racial discrimination have been outlawed, we shall run the colonies for the next 200 years'.[83] So far only left-wingers like Fenner Brockway had, however, raised the irony that Britain itself had yet to pass any legislation on the subject of racial discrimination;[84] James Griffiths concluding just after succeeding Creech Jones as Colonial Secretary in 1950 that 'there is no reason to believe that either legislation or administrative action can profitably be undertaken' to correct what was claimed to be a rare issue.[85]

This had certainly not been seen as a major problem before 1939. Buxton indeed blithely stated in 1935 that 'it is generally agreed that no class is so free from race or colour prejudice as the working class'.[86] With postwar immigration resulting in far more Commonwealth citizens in Britain, this issue however became increasingly a matter of concern for the party. The racial hierarchies of empire were no longer external, but now had to be confronted at home. A draft statement by the party's governing National Executive Committee [NEC] in 1958 estimated that between a quarter and a third of the British population were racially prejudiced – on what basis is unclear – with resulting tensions of the kind Labour had warned of in the colonial setting. Initially, however, Griffiths' view in 1950 that prejudice cannot be abolished by legislation was reiterated.[87] Nonetheless, by the time the final draft of this policy emerged in September 1958 it had been decided that it should still be severely discouraged by the passage of legislation to make racial discrimination a criminal offence.[88] With such decisions, Labour finally incorporated the metropole into its thinking about the plural society that the Commonwealth, not least through its own efforts, had become.

For some, not least with the revival of what were now multi-racial conferences of the various Labour parties across the Commonwealth in 1957 and 1962, this transformation sparked – if anything – a deepening of their attachment to the Commonwealth. Hugh Gaitskell, who had succeeded Attlee as party leader in 1955, accordingly celebrated the great multi-racial bridge of the Commonwealth linking rich and poor countries that 'owes its creation fundamentally to those vital historical decisions of the Labour Government' of 1945–1951. He did so in his 1962 party conference speech in which he made clear his dislike of the attempts Macmillan's Tory government had launched the previous year to join the European Economic Community.[89] Almost all the reasons Gaitskell cited for this dislike related to the Commonwealth. This was also true of the more balanced NEC statement on the subject. 'Unlike the Six', it proclaimed, 'Britain is the centre and founder member of a much larger and still more important group, the Commonwealth worldwide multi-racial association of 700 million'. If 'our membership were to weaken the Commonwealth and the trade of the underdeveloped nations, lessen the chances of East-West agreement and reduce the influence that Britain could exert in world affairs, then the case against entry would be decisive'.[90] It was the multi-racial Commonwealth that was praised, but Gaitskell's reasons for doing so harked back to Amery and beyond. Labour had not usually highlighted the Commonwealth's economic or geopolitical significance, but that was very much what Gaitskell was doing here in order to turn round the similarly framed arguments being deployed by his deputy leader, George Brown, and others in favour of European entry.

Gaitskell was, however, adding these traditionally Tory ways of thinking about the Commonwealth to the Labour lexicon just at the point where they were losing their potency. He may have done so armed with the critical views heard from Commonwealth Labour leaders at their recent conference, which ended with a communiqué stating that 'if Britain were to enter the Common Market on the basis of what has so far been agreed great damage would inevitably be done to many countries in the Commonwealth'.[91] New Commonwealth states like Nigeria were particularly critical of what was termed the neo-colonialism of Associated Overseas Territory [AOT] status, with Kwame Nkrumah of Ghana comparing the 1957 Treaty of Rome to the 1884 Treaty of Berlin that divided up Africa.[92] In a paper to the Shadow Cabinet in April 1962 Denis Healey acknowledged that AOT status was felt to involve competition with the privileged position of former French colonies, discrimination against tropical foodstuffs and subordination to Europe. Only the West Indies were prepared to accept it.[93] Yet Ghana was already trading more with the Six than Britain. The amendments to AOT status under the Yaoundé Convention signed in July 1963, meanwhile, did much to mollify the Nigerians. That year Nigeria opened negotiations for AOT status.[94]

Harold Wilson, who was to succeed Gaitskell as leader after the latter's sudden death in January 1963 and in many ways shared the latter's position on Europe, had already pointed out in 1960 that many in the Commonwealth were supportive of consolidation of European markets, hoping that it would facilitate access for their goods.[95] Indeed, a Fabian pamphlet in 1962 pointed out that this was already happening.[96] The party's leading pro-European, Roy Jenkins, may have been exaggerating when in June 1961 he argued that most of the Commonwealth objections to European entry came from New Zealand,[97] but Gaitskell was certainly also exaggerating the objections from elsewhere.

Inter-Commonwealth trade was just not as important either for Britain or the other territories as it had been even under the Attlee government. Nonetheless Attlee's former President of the Board of Trade, Harold Wilson, still clearly hankered over the old bulk purchase agreement arrangements. These formed the centrepiece of his ten point plan for Commonwealth development of May 1963 in the aftermath of the failure of Macmillan's European negotiations.[98] It did not seem to occur to him that countries that objected to AOT status would be no more willing to sign up for this form of neo-colonialism either. They indeed still featured among many more references to the Commonwealth than ever before in a Labour manifesto during the 1964 election.

This enthusiasm was despite a number of changes which had undermined the traditional military and economic functions of the Commonwealth. For instance, in a paper shortly before that election Cunningham complained that in the thirteen years of Tory rule British trade with the Commonwealth had declined from 44 to 30 per cent of the total.[99] Yet this was hardly surprising since most British colonies had removed their preferences in favour of British goods by 1952.[100] Even in Australia and New Zealand James Callaghan, the shadow colonial secretary, was struck by the diminishing importance of imperial preference. Following his 1958 Commonwealth tour he reported that these two Old Commonwealth states were 'almost resigned to Britain entering' the Common Market. New Zealand, he also noted, were already negotiating directly with European countries over trade deals.

Callaghan was no more sanguine about the military dimension of the Commonwealth.[101] Gaitskell may have played this up in 1962. Four years earlier Callaghan was instead reporting his doubts about the utility of the Singapore base, if not yet of the East of Suez role. A year earlier he had also suggested reorganising the machinery of government handling Commonwealth and colonial affairs at the 1957 Commonwealth Labour conference.[102] The idea of amalgamating the Commonwealth Relations Office and the Colonial Office was subsequently considered by Hatch in 1960, only to be rejected on the grounds that Commonwealth countries would object.[103] With the Tories having combined the two offices under one minister from July 1962 onwards, however, such objections increasingly had less weight. Indeed, a paper from the former diplomat, Geoffrey McDermott, in 1963 advocated going further through creating a Foreign and Commonwealth Office. McDermott's rationale was that with Labour already committed to ministries of overseas aid and of disarmament then some consolidation was required.[104]

In responding to McDermott's paper, Cunningham reflected that the Commonwealth's 'physical institutions are few and growing fewer and weaker'. Hatch in 1960 had suggested replacing British ministries with a Commonwealth Secretariat as a means of tackling this deficiency. Cunningham in 1964 was more pessimistic: 'I believe the Commonwealth relationship is bound to weaken and eventually disappear between Britain and the Asian-African countries, leaving only its hard rock foundation, Canada, Australia and New Zealand'.[105] Yet it was the old Commonwealth, and its old functions, that were most conspicuously disappearing. Internal racial tensions removed South Africa and Southern Rhodesia in 1961 and 1965 respectively. Trade ties were weaker. The questioning of the East of Suez role, which was steadily growing on the backbenches in the run-up to Labour's return to power in the 1964 election,[106] was also to undermine the military dimension of the Commonwealth.

Ironically it was arguably Callaghan, who had spotted these developments relatively early, who was among those most fiercely resisting their consequences as the incoming Chancellor of the Exchequer in 1964. Yet his rationale for doing so reflected the ways in which the Commonwealth had changed. Callaghan, for instance, proved very reluctant to devalue sterling despite enormous pressures to do so in large measure because of a sense of obligation to maintain the value of former colonies' sterling balances and protect them from the resulting impact on their dollar trade.[107] It was the new Commonwealth that had emerged during the Attlee government that he was thus defending, and not the old Commonwealth of economic and military ties for which Gaitskell had belatedly become the most committed of Labour standard-bearers.

Part of Gaitskell's rationale for doing so was, of course, political. The Tories' European turn gave Labour an opportunity to seize the imperial, patriotic card. This opportunism clearly informed the accusations thrown at the Conservatives in Labour's 1964 manifesto that Macmillan's entry terms 'would have forced us to treat "the Commonwealth as third class nations"'.[108] The Commonwealth was commandeered as a trope to serve a Labour patriotic cause. This was also apparent in Labour's attempts to revive the Commonwealth as a geopolitical entity in a new setting. As George Thomson later put it: 'We appointed a minister to the United Nations, and we were going to form a great Commonwealth group at the United Nations, and we were all going to be a force in world affairs'. This was for Thomson 'a deeply disillusioning experience',[109] but it was also one which built on a tradition of Labour thinking about the Commonwealth. This was not simply the British-led military arrangement that the Commonwealth had been in two world wars, but an attempt to use it as an example of multi-racial global partnership. This included the 1964 idea of a Commonwealth consultative assembly which had echoes of the thinking in *Labour and the New Social Order*.

The manifesto proudly affirmed Labour's role in the transition of empire into Commonwealth, claiming 'No nobler transformation is recorded in the story of the human race'. The incorporation of Britain into that transformed, multi-racial entity was hinted at in the promise to legislate against racial discrimination, though tempered by the commitment to control immigration.[110] This suggests that, beneath the fine words, there remained a certain instrumentality. Nonetheless, a substantial, and lasting, change in the conception of the Commonwealth had been effected. In 1964 Cunningham argued that 'The Commonwealth is all in the mind'.[111] It certainly developed as a concept over time in the minds of Labour figures. However, it was the multi-racial Commonwealth of free (and varied) nations that Labour thinkers from Lansbury onwards had spoken of, rather than the backward-looking White core which Cunningham himself evoked, that increasingly sprang to mind.

Notes

1. Hobson, *Imperialism*; Friedburg, *The Weary Titan*; Judd, *Radical Joe*, chaps. 10 and 11.
2. Delisle Burns, "The British Commonwealth of Nations," 70–2.
3. Cole, *Labour in the Commonwealth*, chap. 1.
4. Morgan, *Labour in Power 1945–1951*, 188.
5. Henderson, *The Aims of Labour*.

6. Lansbury, *Labour's Way with the Commonwealth*, 51.
7. http://labourmanifesto.com/1900/1900-labour-manifesto.shtml [accessed 12 May 2018].
8. *House of Commons Debates*, 5th series, vol.60, c.1270, 1 April 1914.
9. *House of Commons Debates*, 5th series, vol.60, c.1277, 1 April 1914.
10. *House of Commons Debates*, 5th series, vol.60, cc.1303-7, 1 April 1914.
11. *Labour and the New Social Order*, 21–2.
12. Burns, "The British Commonwealth of Nations," 75.
13. *Labour and the New Social Order*, 21–2.
14. *Labour's Call to the People*, http://labourmanifesto.com/1918/1918-labour-manifesto.shtml [accessed 12 May 2018].
15. Sidney and Beatrice Webb, *New Statesman*, 2 August 1913; see also Ramsay MacDonald, *Labour and the Empire*, 50.
16. In contrast, empire and imperial preference was the prime issue in the 1924 statement of Conservative policy: Baldwin, *Looking Ahead*, 1–5.
17. Howe, *Anticolonialism in British Politics*, 29.
18. Burns, "The British Commonwealth of Nations," 71.
19. Burns, "The British Commonwealth of Nations," 79.
20. Gupta, *Imperialism and the British Labour Movement 1914–1964*, 129.
21. Ramsay MacDonald, *The Foreign Policy of the Labour Party*, 37.
22. Marquand, *Ramsay MacDonald*, chaps. 15 and 16.
23. http://labourmanifesto.com/1924/1924-labour-manifesto.shtml [accessed 12 May 2018].
24. Gupta, *Imperialism and the British Labour Movement 1914–1964*, 118.
25. *Labour and the Nation*, 4.
26. Howe, *Anticolonialism in British Politics*, chaps. 1 and 2.
27. Gupta, *Imperialism and the British Labour Movement 1914–1964*, 63–4, 83.
28. Gupta, *Imperialism and the British Labour Movement 1914–1964*, 66–7; *Labour and the Nation*, 44.
29. *Labour and the Nation*, 43.
30. Gupta, *Imperialism and the British Labour Movement 1914–1964*, 85; *Labour and the Nation*, 43.
31. *Labour and the Nation*, 44.
32. The National Archives, Kew [TNA]: CAB 21/469, Trades Unions Congress/Labour Party 'Note on the Committee of Imperial Defence' (February 1926).
33. *House of Commons Debates* 5th ser., vol.299, cc.554-5, 14 March 1935.
34. Burns, "The British Commonwealth of Nations," 84; *Labour and the Nation*. Revised ed. , 49.
35. For instance, MacDonald in April 1924 emphasised 'Dominion status for India is the idea and the ideal of the Labour government': cited in Lansbury, 61.
36. Lansbury, *Labour's Way with the Commonwealth*, 18, 29, 32.
37. Lansbury, *Labour's Way with the Commonwealth*, 34–5, 99–101.
38. Lansbury, *Labour's Way with the Commonwealth*, 40–7, 72.
39. Lansbury, *Labour's Way with the Commonwealth*, 59–60, 68–9, 73–6.
40. Lansbury, *Labour's Way with the Commonwealth*, 19.
41. Lansbury, *Labour's Way with the Commonwealth*, 9, 26–8.
42. Lansbury, *Labour's Way with the Commonwealth*, 85.
43. Buxton, "Policy in the Backward Colonies," 97, 102–16.
44. See Schumacher, "Multilateral Clearing," 150–65.
45. Lansbury, 10–14, 91.

46. Attlee, *The Labour Party in Perspective*, 228, 232, 241.
47. Attlee, *The Labour Party in Perspective*, 246.
48. Attlee, *The Labour Party in Perspective*, 229, 236; Attlee, "Guild v. Municipal Socialism."
49. Riddell, *Labour in Crisis*, 194.
50. Attlee, *The Labour Party in Perspective*, 234, 244. After retirement as party leader he was a prominent member of the 160 strong Parliamentary Group on World Government in the early 1960s.
51. Williams, "Preface,"9–12; Morgan, *Labour in Power 1945–1951*, 190–2.
52. Attlee, *Twelve Years Later*, 169; Attlee, *As It Happened*, 126–7.
53. Morgan, *Labour in Power 1945–1951*, 203.
54. Attlee, *Twelve Years Later*, 172–3.
55. Hogendorn and Scott, "The East African Groundnuts Scheme".
56. Morgan, *Labour in Power 1945–1951*, 189–90.
57. Creech Jones, "Introduction," 10–11.
58. See *Labour Believes in Britain*, National Executive Committee for the 1949 Conference, April 1949, 29.
59. Creech Jones, "Introduction," 16; Brailsford, "Socialists and the Empire," 29–30.
60. Attlee, *As It Happened*, 189–91.
61. Attlee, *Empire into Commonwealth*, 1.
62. Kumarasingham, "A New Monarchy."
63. Moore, *The Making of the New Commonwealth*; Wilson, "Nehru and the New Commonwealth."
64. TNA: CAB 129/30, CP(48)244, C. R. Attlee, "The Commonwealth Partnership" (26 October 1948); Kumarasingham, "The 'Tropical Dominions,'" 228.
65. Pippa Catterall, "Foreign and Commonwealth Policy in Opposition."
66. *Labour's Foreign Policy*, 2–3.
67. People's History Museum, Manchester: Labour Party Archives [LPA]: Labour International Committee minutes and papers [LIC], Statement of Policy on Colonial Affairs 'From Colonies to Commonwealth' (July 1954), 2, 5; Catterall, "Foreign and Commonwealth Policy," 91.
68. LPA: Labour Commonwealth minutes and papers [LCC], Creech Jones to Hatch, 11 September 1954.
69. LPA: LCC, Draft 'Colonies to Commonwealth', 3 March 1955, 8.
70. *Labour and the New Society* (London: Labour Party, 1950); Bullock, *Ernest Bevin*; Barclay, *The First Commonwealth Division*.
71. LPA: LCC, W. Arthur Lewis, "Aid to Under-Developed Countries" (May 1952); Arthur Lewis, "Economic Development with Unlimited Supplies of Labour."
72. *Labour's Colonial Policy: I the Plural Society* (London: Labour Party, 1956), 20–38.
73. Kumarasingham, *Constitution-Maker*, 259.
74. LPA: LCC, "From Colonies to Commonwealth" (July 1954), 3; *The Plural Society*, 43.
75. Lewis, "Aid," 20; *Labour's Colonial Policy II*, 13–21.
76. See, for instance, *Towards World Plenty* (London: Labour Party, 1952).
77. Brailsford, "Socialists and the Empire," 13.
78. *Labour's Colonial Policy III: Smaller Territories* (London: Labour Party, 1957), 18–21.
79. LPA: LCC, Secretary's Report (June 1956), 3; Secretary's Report (April 1957), 2.
80. *Smaller Territories*, 24.
81. LPA: LCC minutes, 10 May 1960.

82. LPA: LCC, George Cunningham, "The Smaller Colonial Territories" (4 September 1964). Of the territories he still felt were too small to realistically be candidates for independence only St Helena remains a dependency.
83. LPA: LCC, comments by Richard Crossman on *The Plural Society* (May 1956), 3.
84. For instance, TNA: CAB 134/994, Legislation Committee minutes, 22 April 1952.
85. TNA: CAB 21/1734, "Coloured People from British Colonial Territories" (29 March 1950), 4.
86. Buxton, "Policy in the Backward Colonies," 96. In contrast, Chuka Umunna decided not to run for the party leadership in 2015 having been advised by PLP colleagues that 'we don't think our white working class constituents would ever vote for a black man', *The New European* 19 July 2018, 13.
87. LPA: LCC, resolution by NEC working party on racial discrimination (July 1958), 4–7.
88. LPA: LCC, resolution by NEC working party on racial discrimination (September 1958), 3.
89. *Britain and the Common Market* (London: Labour Party, 1962), 3–32.
90. *Britain and the Common Market* (London: Labour Party, 1962), 33.
91. LPA: Labour Parliamentary Committee minutes and papers [LPC], 25 September 1962; LCC, Commonwealth Labour Conference in London (6-7 September 1962).
92. LPA: LCC, "Commonwealth Reactions to the Common Market" c.1961, 6.
93. LPA: LPC, Denis Healey, "The Common Market and the Coloured Commonwealth" (April 1962).
94. Alexander, "From Imperial Power to Regional Power," 195–6; Broad, *Labour's European Dilemmas*, 39.
95. LPA: LPC, Harold Wilson, "Britain's Relations with Europe" (15 June 1960).
96. Broad, *Labour's European Dilemmas*, 39.
97. LPA: LIC, Roy Jenkins and Robert Nield, "Dissenting Note" (June 1961).
98. LPA: LCC, Harold Wilson, "10 Point Plan for Commonwealth Development" (May 1963).
99. LPA: LCC, George Cunningham, "The Commonwealth" (16 September 1964), 4.
100. Schenk, "Shifting Sands," 20.
101. LPA: LCC, James Callaghan, "Report on Visit to New Zealand, Australia, Singapore, Indonesia, Burma and India" c.1959, 1–5.
102. LPA: LCC, James Callaghan, "Problems of Transfer of Power," 1.
103. LPA: LCC, John Hatch, "Commonwealth Relations Office and Colonial Office" (June 1960).
104. LPA: LCC, Geoffrey McDermott, "The Foreign Office, the Commonwealth Relations Office and the Colonial Office" (23 October 1963).
105. LPA: LCC, George Cunningham, "The Future of the Common Relations Office" (28 January 1964), 5.
106. Author's interview with Jeremy Bray, 30 October 1996.
107. Author's interview with Lord Callaghan of Cardiff, 13 November 1996; Gupta, *Imperialism and the British Labour Movement 1914–1964*, 377.
108. *Let's Go with Labour for the New Britain* (London: Labour Party, 1964), 19.
109. Catterall, "The East of Suez Decision," 625.
110. *Let's Go with Labour*, 18–9.
111. Cunningham, "The Future," 4.

Disclosure statement

No potential conflict of interest was reported by the author.

References

Alexander, P. "From Imperial Power to Regional Power: Commonwealth Crises and the Second Application." In *Harold Wilson and European Integration: Britain's Second Application to Join the European Economic Community*, edited by Oliver Daddow, 188–210. London: Cass, 2003.

Arthur Lewis, W. "Economic Development with Unlimited Supplies of Labour." *Manchester School of Economic and Social Studies* 22 (1954): 139–191.

Attlee, C. R. *As It Happened*. London: Heinemann, 1954.

Attlee, C. R. *Empire into Commonwealth*. Oxford: Oxford University Press, 1961.

Attlee, C. R. "Guild v. Municipal Socialism." *Socialist Review* 21 (1923): 213–118.

Attlee, C. R. *The Labour Party in Perspective*. London: Gollancz, 1937.

Attlee, C. R. *The Labour Party in Perspective - And Twelve Years Later*. London: Gollancz, 1949.

Baldwin, S. *Looking Ahead: A restatement of Unionist Principles and Aims*. London: National Unionist Association, 1924.

Barclay, C. N. *The First Commonwealth Division: The Story of the British Commonwealth Land Forces in Korea 1950–1953*. Solihull: Helion, 2010.

Brailsford, H. N. "Socialists and the Empire." In *Fabian Colonial Essays*, edited by Rita Hinden, 19–35. London: Allen & Unwin, 1945.

Broad, R. *Labour's European Dilemmas: From Bevin to Blair*. London: Palgrave, 2001.

Bullock, A. *Ernest Bevin: Foreign Secretary 1945–1951*. London: Heinemann, 1983.

Buxton, C. R. "Policy in the Backward Colonies." In *Labour's Way with the Commonwealth*, edited by George Lansbury, 92–119. London: Methuen, 1935.

Catterall, P. (ed.). "The East of Suez Decision." *Contemporary British History* 7/3 (1993): 612–653.

Catterall, P. "Foreign and Commonwealth Policy in Opposition: The Labour Party." In *British Foreign Policy 1955–1964: Contracting Options*, edited by Wolfram Kaiser, and Gillian Staerck, 89–109. Basingstoke: Palgrave, 2000.

Cole, G. D. H. *Labour in the Commonwealth: A Book for the Younger Generation*. London: Headley, 1918.

Creech Jones, A. "Introduction." In *Fabian Colonial Essays*, edited by Rita Hinden, 9–18. London: Allen & Unwin, 1945.

Delisle Burns, C. "The British Commonwealth of Nations." In *The Book of the Labour Party: Its History, Growth, Policy and Leaders vol. 3*, edited by Herbert Tracey, 69–86. London: Caxton, 1925.

Friedburg, A. L. *The Weary Titan: Britain and the Experience of Relative Decline 1895–1905*. London: Princeton University Press, 1988.

Gupta, P. S. *Imperialism and the British Labour Movement 1914–1964*. New Delhi: Sage, [1975] 2002.

Henderson, A. *The Aims of Labour*. London: Headley, 1917.

Hobson, J. A. *Imperialism: A Study*. London: Nisbet, 1902.

Hogendorn, J. S., and K. M. Scott. "The East African Groundnuts Scheme: Lessons of a Large-Scale Agricultural Failure." *African Economic History* 10 (1981): 81–115.

Howe, S. *Anticolonialism in British Politics: The Left and the End of Empire 1918–1964*. Oxford: Clarendon, 1993.

Judd, D. *Radical Joe: A LIfe of Joseph Chamberlain*. London: Hamilton, 1977.

Kumarasingham, H. (ed.). "The 'Tropical Dominions': The Appeal of Dominion Status in the Decolonisation of India, Pakistan and Ceylon." *Transactions of the Royal Historical Society* 23 (2013): 223–245.

Kumarasingham, H. *Constitution-Maker: Selected Writings of Sir Ivor Jennings.* Cambridge: Cambridge University Press, 2014.

Kumarasingham, H. "A New Monarchy for a New Commonwealth? Monarchy and the Consequences of Republican India." In *Crowns and Colonies: European Monarchies and Overseas Empires,* edited by Robert Aldrich and Cindy McCreery, 283–308. Manchester: Manchester University Press, 2016.

Labour and the Nation. London: Labour Party, 1927.

Labour and the Nation. Revised ed. London: Labour Party, 1928.

Labour and the New Social Order. London: Labour Party, 1918.

Labour's Call to the People. London: Labour Party, 1918.

Labour's Colonial Policy II: Economic Aid. London: Labour Party, 1957.

Labour's Foreign Policy. London: Labour Party, 1952.

Lansbury, G. *Labour's Way with the Commonwealth.* London: Methuen, 1935.

Marquand, D. *Ramsay MacDonald.* London: Cape, 1977.

Moore, R. J. *The Making of the New Commonwealth.* Oxford: Oxford University Press, 1987.

Morgan, K. O. *Labour in Power 1945–1951.* Oxford: Oxford University Press, 1984.

Ramsay MacDonald, J. *Labour and the Empire.* London: Allen, 1907.

Ramsay MacDonald, J. *The Foreign Policy of the Labour Party.* London: Cecil Palmer, 1923.

Riddell, N. *Labour in Crisis: The Second Labour Government 1929–1931.* Manchester: Manchester University Press, 1999.

Schenk, C. "Shifting Sands: the International Economy and British Economic Policy." In *British Foreign Policy 1955–64: Contracting Options,* edited by Wolfram Kaiser, and Gillian Staerck, 19–32. Basingstoke: Palgrave, 2000.

Schumacher, E. F. "Multilateral Clearing." *Economica n.s.* 10/38 (1943): 150–165.

Williams, F. "Preface." In *The Labour Party in Perspective – And Twelve Years Later,* edited by C. R. Attlee, 9–24. London: Gollancz, 1949.

Wilson, H. Nehru and the New Commonwealth." 8th Nehru Memorial Lecture, 2 November 1978. Accessed June 24, 2018. https://www.cambridgetrust.org/assets/documents/Lecture_8.pdf.

Imperial Citizenship or Else: Liberal Ideals and the Indian Unmaking of Empire, 1890–1919

Mark R. Frost

ABSTRACT
This article examines three connected campaigns for Indian imperial citizenship which spanned the period 1890 to 1919, and their impact on the emergence of radical South Asian anticolonialism. It shifts our focus from individuals and ideologues who sought the status of British imperial citizens, to address the agitations which commenced to attain such a status within a reconstructed British Empire. Specific attention is paid to the conditions which encouraged South Asian patriots to imagine that the ideal of equal imperial citizenship within an imperial federation was a feasible political objective, to the illiberal official retreat from such an ideal, and to the political ramifications of this retreat. In conclusion, this article argues that the quest for Indian imperial citizenship, which spanned the Empire from South Africa to Canada, has been a much-neglected chapter in the evolution of anti-colonial nationalism in South Asia which deserves to be reinserted in the grand meta-narrative of the region's twentieth century history.

In November 1954, Henry Hopkins, the British Colonial Secretary, remarked during a House of Commons debate:

> In a world in which restrictions on personal movement and immigration have increased we can still take pride in the fact that a man can say *Civis Britannicus sum*, whatever his colour may be, and we take pride in the fact that he wants and can come to the mother country.[1]

Six years earlier, the new British Nationality Act of 1948 made explicit the rights of 'citizens of the United Kingdom and Colonies' and new 'Commonwealth Citizens' to enter and settle in their 'mother country'.[2] Such rights had theoretically long existed. As the Lord Chancellor reminded Parliament when it debated the 1948 Act, a British subject (when in Britain, at least) could already enter and depart the country at any time, qualify for the franchise, become a member of the Privy Council or of Parliament, join the Civil Service (except in wartime and certain other circumstances) and 'own a British ship'.[3] Yet, it was only with the same Act's introduction that subjecthood entered the statute book as officially signifying citizenship. As Britain withdrew from its former colonial possessions, the declaration of current and former subjects as British citizens made political and economic sense. Immigrants who could claim *Civis Britannicus sum*, it was thought, would solve Britain's post-war labour shortage while at the same time shoring up the unity of the nascent Commonwealth from which many would arrive.[4]

The story of what transpired has been well told. Racially-incited violence in 1959 contributed to the British government's imposition of the first checks on Commonwealth immigration in 1962. Further restrictions followed, overseen by both Labour and Conservative governments, under the Commonwealth Immigrants Acts of 1968 and the Immigration Act of 1971.[5] Eventually, the death of *Civis Britannicus* reached its painful historical postscript with the ignominious 'Windrush scandal' of 2018, during which Commonwealth citizens and their descendants who had settled in Britain were threatened by the Home Office with the removal of their social benefits and deportation. In part a consequence of a staggering case of administrative amnesia, the British government had stamped out the final embers of a long-held liberal imperial ideal.

But this was not the first time that the principle of *Civis Britannicus* had been trumpeted by politicians before being dismantled and abandoned as they struggled to manage the complex societal changes it engendered. This article explores the causes and consequences of a previous official retreat that occurred through the period 1893 to 1919 when Indians, through a series of globally influential and interconnected campaigns, claimed and sought to exercise their rights as *Civis Britannicus*, only to discover the gulf that lay between liberal imperial rhetoric and reality. Importantly, this quest for imperial citizenship became much more than the elitist aspiration of a moderate Western-educated Indian minority devoted to constitutional modes of agitation – a trivial sideshow when compared with the mass nationalist mobilizations in the decades which followed that sought to end British rule. Rather, as this article will show, the liberal ideal of equal imperial citizenship played a neglected role in the evolution of Indian anticolonial radicalism, becoming, because of its subversive potential, of some concern to colonial officialdom.

Campaigns for imperial citizenship by colonised peoples have not featured heavily in the study of British decolonisation. The scholarship that exists focuses either on the theorising of imperial citizenship by European ideologues or the invention and performance of imperial citizenship by Western-educated Indian elites.[6] While this work has recovered ideas once obscured by nationalist emplotments in history-writing, it mostly examines individuals and their aspirations rather than agitations and mobilizations, and thus reinforces an impression, as one reviewer has expressed it, that the ideal of imperial citizenship emerged as a fleeting political ambition which never made the transition from inspiring 'individual careers' to 'becoming a viable political program'.[7]

Beyond the British case, however, work by Frederick Cooper, the noted historian of colonial Africa, has begun to reshape the field. Cooper has taken aim at a nationalist historiography that privileges 'a politics of unremitting struggle against an impenetrable colonial edifice rather than forms of political action and claim-making that depended on overlapping idioms and interaction between colonizer and colonized'. For Cooper, both kinds of politics combined to bring down European empires. One form threatened the destruction of colonial regimes through unified (often violent) resistance; the other challenged these regimes 'with the possibility that political action would produce concrete gains for different categories of people' and that 'ideologies might be reconfigured', and that notions of the 'politically possible or excluded might shift'.[8]

Cooper's masterful study of decolonisation in French West Africa between 1945 and 1960 reveals that conceptions held by both French and African leaders of future imperial citizenship within a Franco-African federation produced tangible political results. The negotiations both sides engaged in to realise their common, yet differently conceived, federation hopes produced a 'succession of concessions and reconfigurations' from which 'France's African population got something quite important' – the 'rights of a French citizen: to free speech, free assembly and equal justice, and, by 1956, to universal suffrage; and to freedom of movement'.[9] The present article builds on Cooper's approach to examine the political struggles waged from at least five decades earlier for equal Indian citizenship within a British-Asian imperial federation. But this study also highlights the striking differences between both cases. By comparison with post-1945 French Africa, a 'succession of concessions' on the part of the British did not eventuate. Rather, Indian claims for imperial citizenship produced a series of illiberal reconfigurations designed to limit the rights of non-Europeans and jettison any assumptions they may have had as to how far they shared in such rights.

It is in addressing the political ramifications of this contest, characterised by a series of claims made and official retreats, that the present article seeks to break new ground. For, as political leaders from and within India publicly tested the limits of imperial citizenship, threatening to expose the illiberal reality of British imperialism in the process, their quest became itself a radicalising project conducted with the implicit understanding, which ultimately became an explicit threat, that failure would result in the complete unbinding of the Empire.

Subjects as Citizens: Rights of Belonging to the Late British Empire

How, and in what ways, did Indians by the start of the twentieth century come to imagine their imperial subjecthood constituted an equal imperial citizenship?

Since the seventeenth century, the definition of a British subject included all those who owed allegiance to the crown by dint of their birth within the sovereign's domains, a status which the British Nationality Act of 1914 eventually codified to include any person born within the formal British Empire, or who claimed descent from a British subject father, or who became naturalised in Britain or its colonial possessions. As the political scientist Randal Hansen has noted, 'a basic feature of the doctrine underpinning allegiance is indivisibility; all subjects enjoy precisely the same relationship with the monarch and no distinction can be made among them'.[10] The logical corollary of this, as the young lawyer Mohandas Gandhi was quick to realise, was that privileges enjoyed by some loyal subjects ought to be enjoyed equally by others – in particular, the right to move and settle across the British Empire which Europeans had enjoyed from its beginning. As Empire-born Indian lascars discovered, this principle of indivisibility was in practice not always observed. The British Parliament in 1915, to limit their entry into Britain, amended the Navigation Acts to effectively deprive them of their subject status.[11] Nevertheless, the possibility of equal rights of imperial mobility and settlement returned from the mid-nineteenth century as Britain adopted a more laissez faire attitude to immigration, as it did to trade.

In 1849, the classical liberal state in Britain repealed the Navigation Acts as the free movement of persons, along with their goods and their ideas, increasingly became a legitimising trope of mid-Victorian imperialism. The global steamship revolution which took hold from the 1840s resulted in the arrival of many more lascars in Britain and their settlement in port-cities such as Southampton and Liverpool.[12] Their movement to the imperial centre was one part of a series of migration waves (coerced and voluntary) that occurred within and across the Empire over the remainder of the century and the first four decades of the next. Labour-intensive plantation and mining enterprises, from Trinidad, Mauritius and Ceylon, to Burma, Malaya, Natal and eventually Fiji, drew overseas Chinese and Indian workers. In India, overseas population movements were supported by colonial officials who explicitly maintained the right of Indians to move and settle anywhere across the Empire. As a senior official remarked in 1914, 'the policy of the Government of India has been to contend for the principle that there should be complete freedom for all British subjects to transfer themselves from one part of the Empire to another'.[13]

Grand plans hatched in the imperial capital reinforced this notion of free imperial movement and settlement. At the end of the nineteenth century, former and serving colonial civil servants, supported by their allies in the metropolitan press, plotted to redistribute India's 'superfluous' population across parts of the Empire whose economic development, it was thought, would benefit. Indian subjects were deemed better suited for such work in the tropical climes of Africa than Europeans, and even on occasion spoken of as laying a similar claim to being 'civilizers'.[14] Meanwhile, the British government displayed its increasing willingness to intervene beyond its borders to protect its far-flung subjects. The most famous formulation of British subjecthood as British citizenship came in 1850, when Lord Palmerston, speaking in Parliament, invoked St Paul's defence in the Acts of the Apostles:

> As the Roman, in days of old, held himself free from indignity, when he could say, *civis Romanus sum*, so also a British subject, in whatever land he may be, shall feel confident that the watchful eye and the strong arm of England will protect him from injustice and wrong.[15]

Palmerston made this statement at the end of his lengthy justification of his decision to send British gunboats to Piraeus to seek redress from the Greek government on behalf of a Gibraltar-born Portuguese Jew called David Pacifico. Three years earlier, Pacifico, who had previously served as Portuguese consul to Greece, had seen his Athens home ransacked by an anti-Semitic Greek mob. Whether the 'Don Pacifico Affair' exerted much impact east of Aden or not, the protection the British Crown afforded its subjects became known of and sought after, especially by ocean-crossing traders. Legislation in 1852 that was renewed in 1867, enabled China-born merchants based in the Straits Settlements of Singapore, Melaka and Penang to apply for naturalisation as British subjects. Several did, as British subjecthood provided security for their ships, and an insurance against the vagaries of laws and taxes imposed by the Qing officials they dealt with back in China. At the start of the new century, Straits-born Chinese, all of whom were legally British subjects and some of whom had dealings in China, strove to remind British authorities of their status once it appeared that the Qing government might move to claim them as its own nationals under the principle of *jus sanguinis*.[16]

The notion of imperial citizenship was also encouraged by high-profile British commitments to the future political rights that subjecthood promised. Queen Victoria's 1858 Proclamation to the 'Princes, Chiefs and People of India', which was delivered following the suppression of the 1857 Indian Rebellion, held the crown 'bound to the natives of our Indian territories by the same obligations of duty which bind us to all our other subjects, and these obligations by the blessing of Almighty God, we shall faithfully and conscientiously fulfil.' To commemorate the fiftieth anniversary of this Proclamation, King Edward VII bestowed upon India one of his own. Commenting on the extension of representative institutions of government across the Subcontinent, he noted that 'the time has come when, in the judgement of my Viceroy and Governor General and others of my counsellors, that principle may be prudently extended.' His 1908 Proclamation continued:

> Important classes among you, representing ideas that have been fostered and encouraged by British rule, claim equality of citizenship and a greater share in the legislation and Government. The politic satisfaction of such a claim will strengthen not impair existing authority and power.[17]

By this time, official and non-official discussions in the imperial metropolis regularly conflated subjecthood and citizenship, without clearly defining or without clearly defining either. A prominent imperial commentator observed in 1911 'how loosely' these terms 'are used and interchanged even by the Empire's leading statesmen': 'Such phrases as the "rights of British citizenship," or the "rights of British subjects," or the "liberties" of one or other, are frequently used in protest against legislative or administrative action which the responsible parties uphold as perfectly legitimate.'[18] Of more importance to Indians who had access to these debates were their countrymen who journeyed to Britain to lay claim to their common rights as British subjects and successfully exercise them. In the 1880s and 1890s, the Liberal Party of Great Britain fielded three Indian candidates in General Elections. The two unsuccessful candidates were the Middle Temple-educated barristers Lalmohan Ghose and W. C. Bonnerjee. The successful candidate was the Parsi merchant, scholar and Indian National Congress leader Dadabhai Naoroji, who was elected MP for Central Finsbury in 1892 on a platform which included his support for Irish home rule. In 1895, the Conservative Party fielded the Bombay-born barrister Mancherjee Bhownagree as the candidate for the North-East Bethnal Green seat in London, which he won and held until 1906. In one of the perversities of this era, Bhownagree was elected on a Tory anti-immigration ticket directed at recent East European Jewish arrivals in East London.[19] For his efforts, *The Eastern Argus and Borough of Hackney Times* vaunted Bhownagree as 'a true British citizen – acquainted with all those varied conditions of administration which makes the name of Britain great throughout the world today'.[20]

Gandhi's Test of Imperial Citizenship: Rights-Claiming in South Africa

India's most famous agitator for equal imperial citizenship was Mohandas Gandhi, who took great heart from the electoral success of Dadabhai Naoroji. For his South African crusade from 1893 and 1914, to revoke anti-Indian discriminatory legislation that restricted their immigration, their freedom to move, live, trade and own property across South African territories, and their right (for those few who initially qualified) to vote, Gandhi has been labelled a 'collaborative nationalist'.[21] As a key element within and between these campaigns, Gandhi made public avowals of his Empire-allegiance, such as through his organisation of volunteer ambulance corps during the Second Anglo-Boer War of 1899-1902 and Zulu Rebellion of 1906. However, the extent to which Gandhi's loyalty formed a complementary strategy in his overall quest for equal imperial rights has been little discussed. Likewise, the extent to which his efforts drew support from the imperial metropole, where they were regarded as a test-case of imperial citizenship that would determine the liberal future of the British Empire, has received scant attention.[22]

From the outset, Gandhi built his case for Indian rights in South Africa around the principle of the indivisibility of subjecthood upheld through Queen Victoria's 1858 Proclamation. In his speeches, pamphlets, petitions and newspaper articles, he referred to the Proclamation as 'justly and rightly called the Magna Charta of the Indians' and the Indian's 'Charter of Liberty',[23] a document that guaranteed Indians 'the same rights and privileges as are enjoyed by Her Majesty's other subjects' under 'the same principle of political equality that enabled Mr Naoroji to enter the House of Commons'.[24] Victoria had given her royal promise that all her subjects would be treated 'on a footing of equality without distinction of race, colour or creed'.[25] On Gandhi's lecture tour of India in 1896, he announced: 'We belong to the Imperial family and are children, adopted it may be, of the same august mother, having the same rights and privileges guaranteed to us as to the European children. It was in that belief that we went to the Colony of Natal, and we trust that our belief was well founded'.[26]

The endorsement which Gandhi's views received in London underlines Nicholas Owen's depiction of the city during this era as the liberal 'soft heart' of the British Empire.[27] Gandhi's South African campaign was naturally taken up in Westminster by Naoroji and subsequently Bhownagree. It was also supported in *The Star*, a radical newspaper founded by an Irish nationalist which enjoyed a circulation in the 1890s of roughly 150,000.[28] In the late-1890s, Gandhi's principal ally was *The Times*, which gave extensive coverage to his agitation. An editorial from 1895 recognised the right of Indians to move to and settle in South Africa, as well as their fundamental importance to its economic development, and called upon the Colonial Office to 'enlighten' the 'ordinary colonist' to recognise 'a fellow-subject in the Hindu or the Parsee' and ensure 'fair treatment is extended to British subjects of whatever colour.'[29]

Gandhi's key supporter at *The Times* was Sir William Wilson Hunter, a former Indian civil servant and the author of the paper's weekly 'Indian Affairs' column. Hunter, while he noted that the Proclamation of 1858 was 'no *Declaration des droits de l'homme*', fully supported Gandhi's stance on the full rights of imperial citizenship it pledged Indians.[30] Hunter argued that since British officials had 'laid down the principle of the "equal rights" and equal privileges of all British subjects in regard to redress from foreign States', the matter was not now 'a question of argument but of race feeling'. The attempt of the Natal authorities to 'deny the rights of citizenship to British Indian subjects' was in addition wrong because 'by years of thrift and good work in the Colony' Indians had 'raised themselves to the actual status of citizens'. In other columns, Hunter expanded his views on the economic case for Indian imperial citizenship: 'It is a mockery to urge our Indian fellow-subjects to embark on external commerce if the moment they leave India they lose their rights as British subjects and can be treated by foreign governments as a degraded and an outcaste race.' He also drew attention to the sacrifices Indian soldiers had made to win their equal status: 'it would be violation of the

British sense of justice to use the blood and the valour of these races in war and yet to deny them the protection of the British name in the enterprise of peace.'[31]

Gandhi deployed this metropolitan sanction in a circulatory exchange of print through which the rights-claiming idiom he shared with his metropolitan allies merged. The London newspapers to which Gandhi sent his petitions and pamphlets published summaries of, and commentaries on, his works. Gandhi obtained copies of these through the weekly editions these organs sent out to South Africa and other parts of the Empire via the imperial post. He then quoted excerpts from these summaries and commentaries as testimonials in his ongoing campaign literature or repeated their language (often verbatim and sometimes unattributed) in his subsequent writings and speeches. Gandhi also circulated these testimonials back in India. In this way, he made the congruence of his campaign with the liberal idealism of the imperial metropole a key feature of his platform, one which revealed how out of step the self-governing Colonies of the Empire were with the more enlightened 'mother land'. In this way, too, Gandhi made his campaign a highly-visible example of fellow imperial citizenship in practice, through a political language that transcended racial divisions to reveal the bonds of sympathy between fellow British subjects.[32]

Gandhi and Hunter both understood the Indian agitation in South Africa to have global political ramifications. Fully cognisant of moves to exclude Indians from entering Australia, New Zealand and Canada, Gandhi spoke of the South African situation as an 'Indian question' which had a 'local as well as Imperial significance'.[33] Meanwhile, Hunter advised his readers that: 'it is in Southern Africa that this question of their [the Indians'] *status* must be determined. If they secure the position of British subjects in South Africa, it would be almost impossible to deny it to them elsewhere. If they fail to secure that position in South Africa, it will be extremely difficult for them to attain it elsewhere.'[34] Moreover, both men's demands for Indian imperial citizenship carried a warning and, in Gandhi's case, an implicit threat. In 1897, while Gandhi was delayed in his disembarkation at Durban by an angry white mob, he remarked to a journalist upon the ill 'effects' of South African discrimination: 'not only through the colony, but throughout the British Empire, more especially the Indian Empire ... it will give the Indians a sort of feeling that will not be got rid of easily'. For the Empire 'to remain in harmony', he argued, Indian rights had to be respected.[35] Subsequently, he warned that the 'exclusive policy' of the self-governing Colonies was 'making a deep impression on the minds of the Indian people, and it cannot but make the task of government in India more and more difficult.'[36]

The alarms sounded in *The Times* were, if anything, starker and more portentous. Hunter warned in 1896: 'We cannot afford a war of races among our own subjects'.[37] A decade later, an especially foreboding editorial in the same paper lamented the 'lapse of years, and perhaps of generation' that 'may be needed to create, if indeed it ever can be created, such a spirit of common Imperial citizenship as will greatly mitigate the combined force of race prejudice and of self-interest'. It went on to describe the 'the graver injury' that the present falsehood of imperial citizenship 'threatens to do us, amongst our Asiatic fellow-subjects, and chiefly among our fellow-subjects in India', when these subjects, through their humiliating experiences overseas, 'discover that the doctrines which they have heard from professorial and official lips are in fact unreal'. Of special concern were the poorer classes of Indians abroad, 'pedlars, small traders, shopkeepers and coolies', who would return home to spread amongst their villages accounts of their mistreatment 'at the hands of British colonists, without interference or protection from the British *raj*':

> A more dangerous body of missionaries of discontent can hardly be imagined ... This conflict of rights and of interests is naturally inflaming passions and prejudices in the colonies and in India, which sap and blast the Imperial patriotism that must bind the Empire together, if the Empire is to last.[38]

Ensuring a Segregated Empire: Illiberal Reconfigurations at the Centre

The imperial dilemma which Gandhi's agitation in South Africa posed Whitehall officials was captured in an internal Colonial Office minute of March 1897, which observed: 'The whole subject is perhaps the most difficult we have to deal with. The Colonies wish to exclude the Indians from spreading themselves all over the Empire. If we agree, we are liable to forfeit the loyalty of the Indians. If we do not agree we forfeit the loyalty of the Colonists'.[39] As Gandhi had committed his energies to his South African agitation in the mid-1890s, the British government had knocked back, or made clear it would veto, immigration bills in the self-governing Colonies which explicitly barred Asian immigration on racial grounds. In addition to Natal, Australia and New Zealand had pushed for the exclusion of Indian immigrants, in what has been called a 'prophylactic' measure (given the then lack of such immigration), one demanded by white-supremacist politicians eager to build unifying nationalist platforms based not only on fears of a present 'yellow peril' but a future 'brown' invasion.[40]

At the London Colonial Conference of 1897, Joseph Chamberlain, as Secretary of State for the Colonies, expressed his sympathy 'with the white inhabitants of these colonies which are in comparatively close proximity to millions and hundreds of millions of Asiatics'. Yet he reminded the assembled colonial premiers of the 'traditions of the Empire which make no distinction in favour of, or against, race or colour'. His blunt advice was that any exclusion of imperial subjects 'by reason of their colour or by reason of their race ... would be an act so offensive to those people that it would be most painful, I am certain, to Her Majesty to have to sanction it'. Nevertheless, Chamberlain indicated that restrictions based on education, along the lines of the Natal Act of 1897, which required immigrants to prove their knowledge of a European language before entry, would be 'absolutely satisfactory'.[41] Thereafter, Australia introduced similar legislation in 1901 which resulted in the country's infamous 'dictation test'. Canada, in 1906, as we shall shortly see, also introduced legislation to exclude the entry of Indian subjects without making race the explicit grounds for this.[42]

In this manner, Chamberlain oversaw a reconfiguration in official thinking regarding *Civis Britannicus* to accommodate race feelings in the Empire's settler colonies. However, the illiberal influence of these colonies did not end there. At the 1907 Colonial Conference, the Australian and New Zealand premiers, as if resentful of earlier Whitehall efforts to muzzle them, resorted to bullish reassertions of their white-only political visions. Alfred Deakin, the Prime Minister of Australia, announced that he was 'determined to have a white Australia', and 'keep it white': 'we will have a white Australia, cost us what it may. We are anxious to let everyone know it'. Joseph Ward, the New Zealand premier, proclaimed that 'New Zealand is a white man's country, and intends to remain a white man's country; we intend to keep our country for white men by every effort in our power'.[43] When the matter of *Civis Britannicus* was debated, these leaders, along with the representatives of South Africa's Transvaal and Cape Colony, pushed for what was, in effect, a two-tiered British subjecthood which accorded equal rights to white subjects but withheld them from non-Europeans.

The catalyst for this reconfiguration were anomalies in the imperial system of naturalisation which meant that, owing to differing criteria applied across the Empire, a naturalised British subject in the colony where they had been granted naturalisation did not enjoy it in other colonies. The draft bill intended to resolve this issue generated anxiety amongst colonial premiers because it potentially enabled 'coloured' immigrants naturalised in parts of the Empire, such as Britain and the Straits Settlements, where exclusion on racial grounds was not in force, to legally proceed to enter and settle in the self-governing Colonies. Prime Minister Louis de Botha of the Transvaal requested that naturalisation granted in one colony 'should have effect beyond the borders of such Colony only when granted to a person of European birth or descent.' Dr Thomas Smartt, the Cape Colony Commissioner of Lands and Public Works, summed up the overall opinion of the Conference when he stated that it supported the principle that naturalised British subjects should 'have all the rights and privileges of British citizenship' in 'any Colony' if the issue of 'the non-Europeans' could be settled. Smartt sought a modification to the government's draft bill so as not to allow non-Europeans '*ipso facto*, to claim the rights of British citizenship in British possessions.' The Home Secretary Herbert Gladstone replied that although such an amendment would 'simplify matters' it was 'a matter of very considerable difficulty'.[44]

The issue lay unresolved until the 1911 Imperial Conference, which Winston Churchill attended as Home Secretary. When the Dominion delegates returned to discuss Empire-wide naturalisation, Wilfred Laurier, the Canadian Prime Minister, affirmed his support for the principle of 'a British subject anywhere, a British subject everywhere ... In other words, *civis Britannicus* is *civis Britannicus* not only in the country of naturalisation, but everywhere'. But Laurier then subsequently admitted that 'the colour question' was 'really the true difficulty at the bottom of every mind here, that you may naturalise a class of subject generally undesirable.' Joseph Ward registered New Zealand's support for the ideal of common imperial citizenship as long as it did not impinge on her power to exclude Asian imperial subjects. F. S. Malan, the Minister of Education for South Africa, also gave his support, provided local legislation continued to prevent the full transfer of the rights of *Civis Britannicus* from the 'country of naturalisation' to 'every other part of the Empire'. Malan's reformulation of *Civis Britannicus* was a restatement of the two-tiered notion of imperial rights aired at the 1907 conference, delivered with an Orwellian twist: 'A British subject anywhere in the Empire is a British subject everywhere in the Empire, but you do not necessarily give him all the rights of a British subject in all parts of the Empire.'[45]

Churchill's solution to the 'colour question' was, like Chamberlain before him, to transform it into an ostensible matter of class. He likened the autonomy of the Dominion governments to differentiate between imperial subjects to that which the British government exercised when it distinguished 'between different classes of white British subjects. We do not, for instance, put peers on the register for voting; and there are many distinctions which you draw in the Colonies.' Happy with this formula, the Conference agreed to the resolution that 'the effectiveness of local law regulating immigration and the like or differentiating between different classes of British subjects' would be assured, a stipulation that was entered into the statute books as part of the British Nationality and Status of Alien Act of 1914.[46]

However, the Conference's deliberations did not pass without an intervention from a concerned India Office. Lord Crewe, the Secretary of State for India, pleaded with the assembled delegates for their governments to show a more 'accommodating and friendly spirit' toward Indian immigration. In recognising their 'undoubted liberty' to determine 'the rules of their own citizenship' and immigration policies, Crewe conceded that the 'natural right' of every British subject 'to travel or still more to settle in any part of the Empire' was no longer tenable. Yet he warned of the momentous political stakes in play surrounding 'this difficulty between the white races and the native races' that threatened 'not merely the well being, but the actual existence, of the Empire as an Empire'. Crewe maintained that the 'question' of 'Indian disability in any part of the British Empire' was in India one that united 'all classes and all creeds and political schools', both loyal and anti-imperial. It was a particular asset to the latter becaue it put in their hands 'a weapon which they are not slow to use in attacking us. If, they ask, Indians are to suffer from disabilities in various parts of the Empire, what good is the British connection at all?'[47]

Crewe addressed the Conference with Gandhi's ongoing South African agitation clearly in mind. Three years later, Gandhi concluded this campaign, having launched his final *satyagraha* to mobilise Indian indentured labourers as well as Indian women. While his experiments with non-violent mobilisation were certainly a success, his agitation achieved only a partial victory for Indian imperial rights. The South African Indian Relief Act of 1914, which officially recognised Indian marriages, abolished the poll tax on Indian settlers, eased certain restrictions on their internal movement, and permitted educated Indians to immigrate, may have been applauded by Gandhi as another 'Magna Carta' of Indian liberty.[48] Yet Indians in South Africa still remained restricted in their purchase and ownership of property, in where they could live and trade, and they were still denied the franchise.

Gurdit Singh and the *Komagata Maru* Saga: A Second Test of Imperial Citizenship

No sooner was Gandhi's quest for imperial citizenship in South Africa winding down than another campaign erupted, which in a similar vein threatened to expose the falseness of liberal imperial pretensions. In March 1914, the Singapore-based Gurdit Singh, a wealthy Sikh involved in the labour-contracting business, chartered the *Komagata Maru*, a Japanese-registered steamer, to bring 376 would-be Indian migrants, 24 of whom were Muslims, 12 Hindus and the remainder Sikhs, into Canada through Vancouver.[49] Canada had been slower to legislate to exclude Indian imperial subjects than Australia, New Zealand and South Africa. In 1906, however, as Indian immigration grew, the government enacted a continuous journey requirement that prohibited entry to immigrants who were not arriving directly on through tickets from their country of nationality or domicile. These restrictions, which also required that Indian immigrants had in their possession at least 600 rupees to qualify for entry, were imposed by the Canadian authorities in the full knowledge that no such direct passages existed between India and Canada. In 1909, one year after their implementation, Indian arrivals plummeted from the previous total of 623 in 1908 to 6.[50]

Gurdit Singh recalled that at a Sikh 'sabha' he had attended in Hong Kong, having arrived in the city in December 1913, he was challenged to help his Indian brethren. In response he hatched a plan to 'vindicate our right of entering Canada' by chartering a steamship 'to fulfil the provisions of the existing law' requiring continuous passage, and by raising 10,000 Canadian dollars 'to be deposited in a Canadian Bank for the sureties of every individual of our community intending to land there'.[51] Singh was seemingly encouraged by the fact that in November 1913 56 Indian passengers aboard the *Panama Maru* steamer had gained entry to Canada by successfully appealing their case against the legislation designed to exclude them,.[52] Yet their success merely led the Canadian authorities to re-write their immigration regulations more tightly. When, in late-May 1914, the *Komagata Maru* arrived in Vancouver waters, the Canadian authorities prevented it from docking. After a two-month ordeal which drew international attention, the ship and its passengers were escorted out of harbour by gunboats of the Royal Canadian Navy and forced to sail back to Calcutta.

Gurdit Singh clearly intended his voyage to be a test of imperial principles from the outset, one that would have, whichever way the result went, a significant political impact. In his personal account, he described his mission as 'a test of the sincerity of the Government in framing the rules. If we complied with all the provisions ... it was up to the Government to permit us to land and prove itself to be just and fair.'[53] In the Punjabi prospectus for the voyage issued in February 1914, he proclaimed himself a champion of Indian rights who would

> fight out this case in the Supreme Court in Canada for the decision in our favour forever. If the Canadian Government will persist, then I will ask the necessary questions from my British Government. I will not return back *until the real result will be out*.[54]

He spoke similarly in an interview with an American journalist conducted on the eve of the *Komagata Maru*'s departure. When his interviewer asked him what would follow if he failed to gain satisfaction from the government of India as well as the courts in Canada, he reportedly responded (with a broad smile, while his companions gathered around him and laughed): 'I cannot answer.'[55] Critically, from its inception, his voyage was understood by others in the same vein. Ahead of his Vancouver arrival, Canadian journalists, having received London cables which relayed German reports of his intentions, sarcastically referred to his voyage as Gurdit Singh's 'great experiment.'[56] The British Ambassador to Japan, where the *Komagata Maru* stopped en route, reported back to the Foreign Office 'of the departure of 300 British Indians for Canada, to test the Immigration Laws of British Columbia.'[57]

Indian responses to the plight of the *Komagata Maru*'s passengers on their arrival in Canadian waters emphasised the abrogation of their rights as imperial citizens (and so revealed that the illiberal reconfiguration of *Civis Britannicus* secured at the heart of the Empire had yet to filter through to, or be acknowledged in, the periphery). Lahore's Indian-owned *Tribune* newspaper, conscious of 'an opinion' in British Indian circles that the '400 Hindus' onboard 'have deliberately been courting trouble' asked: 'But what about the rights of Indians as British subjects?'.[58] The London All-India Moslem League, in a protest delivered directly to the Colonial Office, warned of the 'intense feeling of indignation' that was brewing against not only Canada but the Imperial

Government for the failure to protect 'the interests of His Majesty's Asiatic subjects who, by right of imperial citizenship, consider themselves as much entitled to travel and settle in different parts of the Empire as the King's British or Colonial subjects.'[59]

The official British response was indicative of the anxieties that had been brewing since the commencement of efforts to reconfigure *Civis Britannicus*. In early-June 1914, the India Office cabled the Government of India for information as to 'how Indian opinion views present incident and its significance, as compared with the South Africa question.'[60] Viceroy Hardinge was informed by a senior member of his Council that although the impact of Gandhi's South African agitation in India was 'certainly more acute [...] I doubt if it involved such dangerous issues'. Particularly concerning was 'with what damaging effect the exclusion from another part of the Empire of Sikhs – men of a martial race that has done so much in the military service of the Crown – can be turned against us.'[61] Hardinge, in his cabled reply to Whitehall, played down the potential for widespread agitation when compared with the 'South Africa question' while recognising the threat to British authority in Sikh-dominated parts of the Punjab.[62] Nonetheless, in a private letter he sent to Crewe at roughly the same time, he expressed his anxiety at the deteriorating imperial situation regarding Indian emigration which appeared 'to daily grow worse': 'Canada, the United States and New Zealand are all on the point of legislation against the admission of Indians. This will make our position here very difficult, unless we are able to find, and you to support, some system of reciprocity.'[63]

Through June and July, the situation at Vancouver produced the agitation in India that many British observers had expected. Protest telegrams, petitions and memorials were sent to the Government of India (in most cases, being personally addressed to the Viceroy); the bulk of these arose from meetings held in Punjabi towns and cities. Provincial colonial officials were dispatched to investigate and reported back on the attendance at these protest meetings (typically no more than 500), their 'constitution' (in terms of the social background of the leading agitators), and the associations and individuals who had given them their support. Greater official attention was given to protestors of 'social standing', who were understood to carry more local influence and the involvement of students was carefully monitored. In contrast, the participation of petty shopkeepers, traders and other less-educated classes was deemed of lesser concern. The owner of 'a small soda water factory' who convened a protest meeting in the temple town of Tarn Taran was adjudged 'of no social or political importance'; the organiser of a meeting in Chandigarh, a 'wood, grass and lime contractor' who held 'the State gardens at Pinjaur on contract', was dismissed as 'a man of no particular position, with a tendency to self-advertisement'.[64]

Yet the participation of these humbler classes is especially interesting for it hints at how far Gurdit's Singh's test of imperial citizenship stimulated, via provincial temple and social welfare associations, the spread of a unifying rights-claiming idiom. The resolution of the Sri Guru Sabha in the strategically important military town of Bannu requested the Government of India to intervene to secure 'the most elementary rights of all British subjects to have free access to all parts of the Empire'.[65] The Khalsa Diwan of Ambala City, another strategically important military town, reminded the Viceroy that 'Indians are citizens of the British Empire and as such ought to be allowed an unobstructed right to live in any part of the British Empire'.[66] As well as differences of class, the support for Singh's Canadian mission on occasion transcended religion. A self-proclaimed mixed 'mass meeting of Peshawar Citizens of all nationalities' telegrammed the Viceroy to register the common Muslim and Sikh distress at 'Indian brethren who are suffering hardships in claiming their legitimate rights of entry into Canada'.[67]

Official fears that Singh's test of imperial citizenship would radicalise various classes of Indian opinion were realised on the *Komagata Maru*'s return. Soon after the ship departed Canadian waters, prominent Indian businessmen and educators based on the Pacific Coast put their names to a pamphlet entitled *An Open letter to the British Public from the Hindustanis of North America*. In what the *Vancouver Province* newspaper labelled a 'veiled threat', these authors warned of Sikh desertions in Britain's Indian army and police force once those aboard the *Komagata Maru* shared their experiences with their brethren back home.[68] When the ship docked at Budge Budge, near Calcutta, on 29 September, and British officials tried to herd its passengers onto a train headed to the Punjab, violence erupted which saw 18 of the passengers shot dead.[69] As has been well studied, the revolutionary Indian Ghadar party capitalised on the voyage's dramatic failure to rally Indian opinion in both North America and north India behind its call for an Empire-wide rebellion during World War One.[70]

For its part, the Government of India dealt with Indian claims to equal imperial citizenship in a way that, especially once war had broken out, only exacerbated the Punjab's lurch towards radicalism. The official attitude to such claim-making was revealed by the Special Tribunal which investigated the Lahore Conspiracy (as the failed Ghadarite rebellion of 1915 became known). A significant aspect of its findings concerned its interpretation of a public meeting in Lahore in August 1913 which had protested Canada's immigration restrictions well before Gurdit Singh launched his ill-fated voyage. The tribunal did not find the meeting seditious, regarding there to be 'nothing illegal in representing grievances', but it noted that 'an atmosphere of intemperance was most certainly created' through the impassioned language and 'words of hyperbole' that some speakers employed, and which in hindsight encouraged 'more violent spirits in the career of deplorable crime which they embarked upon'.

The Tribunal's overall conclusion was that constitutional agitation 'may easily drift into intemperate agitation, intemperate agitation into sedition, and sedition into active revolutionary methods'[71]. Such a view informed the wartime deliberations of the government that resulted in the infamous Rowlatt Act of 1919.[72] Fearful of the 'drift' from legitimate claim-making into outright rebellion, Britain's imperial state elected to impinge on the rights of Indians further, rather than address what it previously recognised to be their legitimate grievances.

Federalist Visions of Imperial Citizenship: The Home Rule for India Campaign

Any examination of the South Asian quest for imperial citizenship would remain incomplete if it did not mention one further agitation, which during World War One became the furthest India had come towards nationwide political mobilisation. In May and June 1914, Annie Besant, the Irish-English President of the Theosophical Society in India, protested the *Komagata Maru* incident in London alongside Lala Lajpat Rai, the Indian nationalist who had previously been arrested for sedition.[73] Besant on the podium, through press interviews and through articles, demanded Indians enjoy their full rights as imperial citizens, as promised by the 1858 Proclamation; she denounced Australia's and Canada's exclusionary immigration policies, rejected the 'colour bar' in the imperial civil service, and bemoaned the exclusion of India from Imperial Federation discussions in the capital. In a veiled threat she shared with an Australian journalist, she claimed: 'A rude and sudden awakening must come if Great Britain and the Empire persist in ignoring India's just claims for freedom and equality. They are loyal at present, but existing conditions are straining their loyalty to breaking point.'[74]

Meanwhile, Lajpat Rai captured the 'dilemma' in which the *Komagata Maru* incident placed the British government. In a letter to the London press, he marvelled that the Empire was 'on the threshold of a great agitation' amongst a once loyal people, the 'descendants, compatriots and co-religionists' of those who had saved the Empire during the rebellion of 1857, simply on account of these people seeking to act 'in exercise of their rights of British citizenship': 'They [The British Government] want the Indians to believe that they are the equal subjects of the King, but when the former claim their rights as such, they behave as if they have neither the power nor the desire to secure the same for them.' Lajpat Rai wondered aloud whether the fault was not so much the Government of India's 'as of those statesmen who have to reconcile their professions and principles of Liberalism with their policy of subjection'. He nevertheless warned that there was 'no half-way house between democracy and despotism', especially since the 'desire, the ambition, and the necessity of claiming British citizenship is no longer confined to educated Indians, but is permeating through the uneducated classes and even the masses.'[75]

Evidence for his latter claim was eventually provided by Besant's campaign for Indian Home Rule, which she launched from her Madras base at the start of 1914. The campaign's objectives operated at both a high imperial level, in which India took its equal place amongst the self-governing Dominions, and at a grounded local level, in which Indians were educated to behave as a progressive political citizenry. On the one hand, Besant desired to achieve self-government for India along the lines Ireland had been promised by the 1914 Government of Ireland Act, which made provisions for an Irish Parliament. She set out her Home Rule plan through 1914 and 1915 as part of the overall 'reconstruction of the Empire' after the War into an 'Imperial' and then 'World Federation'. Her newspapers proclaimed that 'the term Empire has broadened to signify a unification of peoples under a single scheme of government which should allow its co-ordinated parts the widest possible freedom of autonomy'. They challenged the 'individual Britisher' to 'merge his narrow patriotism into a wide internationalism' and the British government to 'evolve a scheme of imperial rule sufficiently plastic to admit of an adequate amount of Self-Government'.[76]

On the other hand, within this plan, Besant sought to create an Indian citizenry 'in which each has a voice "with a share of the power of guidance over the things he (or she) understands"'. In effect, she advocated a gradated form of universal suffrage, which included, as befitted the ideals of a noted British suffragist, the extension of the franchise to Indian women. All Indians of 21 years and older would gain the vote, in the sense that they would elect village (rural) and ward (urban) *panchayats* [assemblies] vested with local judicial and public works responsibilities. But, 'as the area become more extensive, and the questions arising more complicated, the interests concerned larger and more interdependent ... the electorates shall diminish in number, greater age and higher education being demanded as qualifications.' Sub-district or Taluq Boards and small municipalities would be elected by Indians of 25 years and over who had completed education up to school leaving level. Provincial parliaments would be elected by district councillors and all men and women of 35 years and over who had been 'educated to the graduate level'. The 'United States of India' Beasant envisioned would have a national 'Federal Parliament' whose membership would be elected by the provincial parliaments. This assembly would in turn send elected representatives to the 'Parliament of Empire', the highest authority in the coming world federation.[77]

The inclusive scope of Besant's mobilisation, especially once she eventually launched her Home Rule campaign as an explicit protest movement in 1916, was similarly ambitious. Local branches of her Theosophical Society located across all three Indian presidencies and several provinces, not to mention the Society's considerable publishing and distribution network, enabled her to attain a geographically impressive all-India reach. Initially, the high membership fees of her Home Rule League meant its social composition remained elitist.

Besant and her lieutenants directed the League's 'programme' of activism at an educated, particularly Western-educated, audience. Leaguers were encouraged to discuss Indian self-government with their friends and persuade them to join movement, to collect political facts and opinions, to form debating circles, to organise public lectures, to print and circulate pamphlets, and to collect funds. They were instructed to establish libraries filled with the 'nationalist' writings by Besant herself, and by authors such as J. S. Mill and the Cambridge historian J. R. Seeley (who had vigorously debated imperial federation and whether India could form part of it).[78] Yet as the movement intensified it captured supporters from beyond this narrow circle. Copies of Besant's Home Rule newspapers were distributed free or for one anna at railway stations. Her *New India* newspaper, which she published from July 1914 with the slogan (adapted from the Fenians) 'England's need is India's opportunity', achieved a readership of 10,000 and above.[79] Colonial officials reported that the paper had 'a very wide circulation in rural areas generally and [...] is giving the Home Rule movement a marked impetus among English-knowing people of all classes' with 'a specially large circulation in the lower ranks of Government service.'[80] They became particularly concerned by the circulation of articles from Besant's papers that were published as separate political pamphlets. It was estimated that by September 1916 the Theosophical Publishing House had sold more than 300,000 copies of these pamphlets, with titles such as *Citizenship, Social Service, Self Government for India* and *Home Rule and Empire*. Many of these pamphlets were published in vernacular editions with simple explanations of the movement's objectives.[81]

Moreover, to an extent that has been frequently overlooked, Besant's agitation strove to influence the future village citizen who formed such a key part of her Home Rule vision. An official government report from the Madras Presidency noted in December 1916: 'there are indications of initiation of a special campaign for village work based mainly on the distribution of vernacular pamphlets and the itineration of Home Rule preachers. Hitherto the district reports have for the most part pictured the Home Rule movements as confined to younger vakils and students in central towns, but in the report from the Guntur district for the past fortnight the collector lays stress upon the activities of the League in the delta villages of the Tesali taluk.'[82] Such village work included the production of posters, illustrated postcards, religious songs adapted for political purposes, and even popular dramatic performances. It was this work which appears to have ultimately prompted the Madras authorities to arrest and intern Besant in June 1917 for sedition. Her arrest only served to further popularise her campaign.[83] Her interment was protested by public meetings, processions, prayer gatherings, and a Home Rule swadeshi campaign, which eventually combined with metropolitan pressure in Britain to secure her release. By the time Besant was elected President of the Indian National Congress in December 1917, membership of combined Home Rule Leagues across India (despite their high fees) had risen to around 60,000.[84] More importantly, Besant was able to reflect in her presidential address that Home Rule had become 'intertwined with religion by the prayers offered up in the great Southern Temples – sacred places of pilgrimage – and spreading from them to village temples, and also by its being preached, up and down the country, by Sadhus and Sannyasins ... And that is why I have said that the two words, "Home Rule", have become a Mantram'.[85]

The grassroots nature of Besant's citizenry-making ambitions is especially revealed through the work she and her lieutenants undertook to prepare Indian women for their role as equal imperial citizens. In southern India, women featured prominently in the agitation for her release, thanks largely to the efforts of the Women's Indian Association (WIA), which Besant and her female allies established a month before she was interned.[86] *Stri Dharma*, the WIA's multi-lingual English-Tamil-Malayalam (and occasionally Telugu) journal, produced a range of discussions which branch members were encouraged to debate at local meetings. These included female education, 'Citizenship, the duties of men and women to the community', 'Why Indian women should have votes' and 'Women's suffrage' – which discussed, amongst other things, the practical issue of how women in purdah could vote without having to visit polling stations.[87] A key concern of the WIA leadership was that a lack of political participation by Indian women, given the changes underway in Britain, might present the British Government with a justification for withholding Indian self-government. In part, Besant and her Home Rulers promoted women's suffrage to gain, so *Stri Dharma* put it, the 'help and sympathy' of 8,000,000 enfranchised English women, and 'a large number of English men also'.[88]

Two further aspects of Besant's campaign are worth highlighting. The first is the considerable support she received from illustrious one-time 'extremist' Indian patriots, some of whom who had less than a decade earlier derided the moderate nationalist dream of imperial federation as unfeasible.[89] As we have noted, Lala Lajpat Rai joined Besant's campaign in London in 1914. He then went on to establish the Indian Home Rule League of America in 1917. The equally famous former-'extermist' Bepin Chandra Pal likewise endorsed Besant's vision of *swaraj* in articles published in her Home Rule newspapers.[90] Her most important ally, however, was Bal Gangadar Tilak, who established his own Home Rule League in April 1916, pushing Besant to launch hers a few months later. Although the two leaders ran their leagues independently, focusing on different parts of the country, both spoke on the same platforms and joined one another's organisations, as did many of their supporters (including the young Jawaharlal Nehru).[91] As the language Tilak deployed in his Home Rule speeches underlines, he shared the same vision of equal imperial rights for Indians won through their wartime allegiance, and he similarly warned, through a Marathi newspaper, that if Indians did not receive these rights soon 'the Empire would be lost'.[92]

The other striking feature of this mobilisation was the continuing role that Indian faith in the liberal 'soft heart' of Empire played within it. That faith was kept alive by the friendships and alliances that Besant, the former British socialist, and her Home Rule allies forged with left wing and liberal metropolitan sympathisers. In London, Pal became a convert to the 'Empire-ideal' whilst a member of the social circle of the prominent newspaper man W. T. Stead, a proponent of imperial federation.[93] Lajpat Rai met the Labour Party leader Keir Hardy while in Britain, as well as the Liberal (then Labour) politician Josiah Wedgwood, and the Fabians Sidney Webb and George Bernard Shaw (with whom he attended a Fabian summer school).[94] The climactic moment in Tilak's Home Rule campaign came when in 1918 he joined Besant in London to present India's demand for self-government. In Britain, Tilak made donations to the Labour Party (which had announced its support in principle, for Indian self-government), attended trade union congresses and became friendly with the left-wing leader and imperial federationist George Lansbury, then editor of *The Herald*. Tilak's plan of action in Britain was for him to work 'among the higher classes of people' while Besant worked 'among the Labour Party and women'.[95]

Nicoletta Gullace, in her study of Britain's wartime campaigns for franchise reform, has described the First World War as a 'Great War for citizenship'. It was equally a Great War for imperial citizenship with the year 1918 proving to be the apex of Indian Home Rulers' hopes in the Empire's liberal centre.[96] The Representation of the People Act at that year's start, and the General Election at its end, were eagerly anticipated in terms of their Empire-wide repercussions, as the farewell speeches for a Madras Home Rule delegation sent to Britain ahead of Tilak and Besant reveal. Indian Home Rulers expected that the democratic surge transforming the Empire's heart would flow out to the subcontinent, and a victorious British Labour Party to usher in Indian self-government and equal imperial citizenship. The prominent Home Ruler C. P. Ramaswamier announced:

> there are two new factors in English politics which are absolutely unparalleled in the history of English politics. One is the rise of English woman as a power in the English world. Six millions' of English women have been enfranchised today, and in the next election the destinies of the Empire will be partly in their hands ... [The second new factor is] the great labour democracy, for remember the balance of power is shifting. It is no longer the peer who is cultivating his land through his tenantry that is the centre of gravity today, nor is the Cambridge or Oxford graduate. It is the man who works with his brain and hand that is grasping power in England; and he puts the question what are you doing out in India?[97]

Rights Gone Wrong: Imperial Citizenship as a Radicalising Agent

The agitations we have explored were each in their own ways idealistic failures. From late-1918 into the following year, the British Labour Party's poor electoral showing at the General Election, the repressive Rowlatt Act, the 'diarchy' imposed through the 1919 Government of India Act, the Paris Peace Conference negotiations, and the shocking, veil-lifting, violence unleashed at the Jallianwala Bagh in Amritsar on April 13th – all combined to dissolve dreams of equal Indian citizenship within a post-war imperial federation. Nonetheless, this study has posited that such dreams, and the energy and resources directed towards them, need to be reinserted in narratives of the Indian unmaking of the British Empire, not least because of the political consequences of their failure.

In James Scott's contestation of Gramscian notions of false consciousness, he summarises arguments presented by the political sociologist Barrington Moore, writing that Moore 'implicitly asks us to imagine a gradient of radicalism' in the interrogation of the dominant stratum's claim to power by subordinate groups. 'The least radical step is to criticise some members of this dominant stratum for having violated the norms by which they claim to rule; the next most radical step is to accuse this entire stratum of failing to observe the principles of its rule; and the most radical step is to repudiate the very principles by which the dominant stratum justifies its dominance'.[98] While this linear explanation of radicalism hardly applies universally, it does help illuminate the career of South Asia's most influential anti-colonialist. To an extent that many accounts have obscured, Gandhi's political campaigns between 1893 and 1919 followed Moore's evolutionary pattern. Whereas the tendency has been to emphasise the dark night of the patriotic soul from which Gandhi suddenly emerged in early-1919, into the new revelatory light of *purna swaraj* (complete political independence), his ideological transition from wartime Empire-loyalist to post-war passive-resistance hero (nervous breakdown notwithstanding) represented less a political volte face than a clear progression.[99] Gandhi held out hopes for Indian imperial citizenship as late as mid-1918. He exhorted his 'Sisters and brother of the Kheda district', immediately following his *satyagraha* there, to enlist in Britain's armies en masse so that Indians, through their sacrifice, would 'secure the rights we want': 'We want the rights of Englishmen, and we aspire to be as much partners in the Empire as the Dominions overseas'.[100] When, in February 1919, he announced his intention to launch a nationwide *satyagraha* against the Rowlatt Act, he did so still in pursuit of equal imperial subjecthood, describing the new legislation as 'destructive of the elementary rights of individuals' and 'subversive of the elementary rights of citizenship'.[101]

The fundamental yet brilliantly simple addition Scott makes to Moore's formulation, one that helps us better understand not only Gandhi but other Indian patriots who pursued imperial citizenship, comes when he argues that in the gradient of radicalism the 'collective insistence, through petitioning, on the "rights" to which subordinate groups feel entitled carries an understood "or else"'.[102] This understood 'or else' – the threat of more radical action if the principles espoused by the dominant stratum are not adhered to –became an essential element of the linked campaigns we have surveyed from their commencement. In late-1917, this element might be said to have reached its comic apotheosis. In November of that year, Edwin Montagu, the Secretary of State for India, toured the country to assess in person its readiness for 'responsible' self-government. Besant reportedly surprised Montagu in his tent while he was dressing, pressed him to take up the offer of a lift in her motorcar (they were both on their way to see the Viceroy), and used their time together to impress upon him that India must be granted full control over its own executive political bodies and finances. In doing so, she made clear that for the cause of Indian Home Rule she had been forced to mobilise students (which she had done so, especially in Madras, through her Young Men's Indian Association). Besant's 'boys' would continue to forsake anarchy and stick to constitutional reform if Home Rule were granted. If it were not... she left the rest to Montagu's imagination.[103]

Evidence such as this highlights the historiographical narrowness of certain respected scholars who have criticised research into colonised peoples' aspirations towards imperial citizenship and federation because they represent (in hindsight) allegedly fantastic and unrealistic alternatives to the independent nation-state. Samuel Moyn, albeit with reference to the West African context post-1945 rather than our own, has asserted that 'for the history of federalism to be more than trivia, it has to be shown that it was actually possible'.[104] Richard Drayton, likewise writing in response to Cooper's work, has contended that federalism (and the imperial citizenship contained in it) was, owing to the reality of imperial power-relations 'almost from its beginnings a lie', a product of the 'tightly constrained political space of colonialism' and the 'forced poetics' of a subjugated political imagination in which the only avenue available for the colonised was to 'do business in the ideological currency of the colonial power'.[105]

Such criticism fails to really address Cooper's original and critical point (reinforced in his response to these critics) that the politics of the rights-concerned claim-maker and the politics of the romantic anticolonial revolutionary frequently combined in the process of decolonisation, with the former achieving tangible political gains as the latter prepared, sometimes in the wilderness of exile, for the longed-for moment of liberation.[106] Our earlier South Asian context sheds further light on how these two forms of politics interacted with and complemented one another. It suggests that that the quest for equal Indian citizenship within a future imperial federation contained from the outset the possibility of radical action; that it was a project understood by both its proponents and colonial officials in terms of it subversive radicalising potential (should it fail); that some of its proponents mobilised new political groups with that future possibility in mind; and that others (notably the revolutionary Ghadarite party) may have considered it a futile yet necessary pursuit if the truth about the Empire was to be exposed. Imperial citizenship was certainly 'almost from its beginning a lie', but a lie that Indians would first have to comprehend and experience if they were to be liberated from their imperial false consciousness and set on the path of revolution.

In this regard, Drayton is on firmer ground when he suggests that some colonised leaders may have viewed imperial federation and citizenship more as 'tactical goals'. In the South Asian context, it is the exact nature of these tactical goals that needs clarification. British sedition laws undoubtedly made the ostensible Empire-loyalist tone of Besant and Gandhi's wartime rights-claiming an attractive proposition – a politics of the feasible, especially for former-'extremists' such as, Lajpat Rai, Pal and Tilak, who might not have fancied, in some cases further, incarceration.[107] Nevertheless, official British fears of the 'drift' from legitimate claim-making to anti-colonial rebellion meant even such avowedly loyal dissent did not insure against detention. As India's Department of Criminal Intelligence made clear, Besant was ultimately arrested for having spread a theory of agitation in which 'any attack on what was called bureaucracy was permissible so long as it was accompanied by a perfunctory expression of loyalty to the Crown and the British connection.'[108]

More importantly, the imperial rights-claimers we have focused on in the South Asian context did not seek out, nor accept, merely the partial fulfilment of their quest for *Civis Britannicus*. Up until the very end, they united in their demand for the full 'rights of Englishmen' in what became an increasingly all-or-nothing gamble.[109] Whether or not the reality of the independent nation-state was inevitable, South Asian campaigns for imperial citizenship and federation force us to appreciate and understand that these were not merely 'hesitations' upon the long road to full independence, but for extended periods the preferred political choice of notable Indian patriots.

Notes

1. Quoted in Hansen, *Citizenship and Immigration*, 251.
2. British Nationality Act 1948. Accessed July 18, 2018. http://www.legislation.gov.uk/ukpga/Geo6/11-12/56/enacted
3. Dummett and Nicol, *Subject, Citizens, Aliens and Others*, 138–39.
4. Hansen, *Citizenship and Immigration*, 55–56.
5. For an excellent account, see ibid.
6. On the former, see Gorman, *Imperial Citizenship*; on the latter see Banerjee, *Becoming Imperial Citizens*.
7. See Claude Markovits' review of Banerjee, *Becoming Imperial Citizens* for H-Asia. Accessed July 18, 2018. https://networks.h-net.org/node/22055/reviews/22198/markovits-banerjee-becoming-imperial-citizens-indians-late-victorian. Banerjee, however, pays closer attention to the political mobilization for imperial citizenship in her discussion of Gandhi in South Africa.
8. Cooper, *Colonialism in Question*, 231–32.
9. Cooper, *Citizenship Between Empire and Nation*, 432.
10. Hansen, *Citizenship and Immigration*, 38–39.

11. See Fisher, *Counterflows to Colonialism*, 169–71.
12. Visram, *Ayahs, Lascars and Princes*.
13. Cambridge University Library [hereafter CUL], Hardinge Papers 87, Gillen to DuBoulay, 11 June 1914, *Correspondence with Persons in India*, vol. 7, 412–14.
14. 'Indian Affairs', *The Times*, April 7, 1896. The claim that Indians might also be 'civilisers' was made by Sir Lepel Griffin while presiding over a meeting of the East India Association that discussed Indian emigration to Africa; see 'India and Africa', *The Times*, June 24, 1896.
15. Quoted in Gorman, *Imperial Citizenship*, 33, n. 69.
16. Frost, "Transcultural Diaspora,"; see also Frost, "Emporium in Imperio," 29–66.
17. See Appendix to *His Majesty King George's Speeches in India*, 2nd ed.. Madras: Natesan, 1911, xvi–xxvii.
18. 'Editor's Note' to Sargent, E. B. *British Citizenship, an Inquiry as to its Meaning*. London: Royal Colonial Institute, 1911.
19. Bishopsgate Institute, George Howell Archive, HOWELL/9/4 part 2, election handbill 1895.
20. Quoted in Mukherjee, "'Narrow-Majority' and 'Bow-and-agree,'" 1–20, 6.
21. Arnold, *Gandhi*, 52.
22. Arnold in ibid. and Bannerjee's *Becoming imperial citizens* do not explore these dimensions. Nor do Brown, *Gandhi's Rise to Power* or, more recently, Guha, *Gandhi Before India*.
23. 'Letter to the *Natal Advertiser*, September 29, 1893' and 'The Indian Franchise', *Collected Works of Mahatma Gandhi* [hereafter *CWMG*] (Electronic Book, New Delhi, 1998), 62–3, 283–307. Accessed July 18, 2018. http://gandhiserve.org/e/cwmg/cwmg.htm
24. 'Letter to the *Natal Mercury*, September 2, 1895,' ibid. 269–70.
25. 'Interview to the *Natal Advertiser*, January 13, 1897,' *CWMG* 2, 1–9.
26. 'Speech at meeting, Madras, October 26, 1896,' *CWMG* 1, 426–48, 437.
27. Owen, "The Soft Heart of the British Empire,"143–84.
28. 'The Indian Franchise'; see also Simms, "In memory of *The Star* (1888-1960)."
29. Editorial, *The Times*, August 30, 1895.
30. 'Indian Affairs', *The Times*, June 24, 1895.
31. See Hunter's 'Indian Affairs' columns in *The Times*, September 4, 1895, January 27, 1896, and June 24, 1895.
32. See, *inter alia*, Gandhi's, 'The Indian franchise'; also 'Memorial to Natal Legislative Assembly', 'Memorial to J. Chamberlain', and 'The Grievances of the British Indians in South Africa: An Appeal to the Indian public,' *CWMG* 1, 328–32, 337–55, 359–407.
33. 'Letter to the *Natal Mercury*, September 2, 1895.'
34. 'Indian Affairs', *The Times*, March 16, 1896, original italics.
35. 'Interview to the *Natal Advertiser*, January 13, 1897.'
36. 'India makes the empire', *Indian Opinion*, August 20, 1904, reprinted in *CWMG* 4, 52–53.
37. 'Indian Affairs', *The Times*, January 27, 1896.
38. Editorial, ibid., November 10, 1906. This editorial was prompted by the failure of Gandhi's deputation to Whitehall, in protest at the implementation of the Transvaal Act, to draw anything more than private apologies and official handwringing.
39. Quoted in Daniels, "The Growth of Restrictive Immigration," 40.
40. Atkinson, *The Burden of White Supremacy*, 19–48.

41. The National Archives CO 885/6/30, C8596, 'Proceedings of a Conference between the Secretary of State for the Colonies and the Premiers of the Self-Governing Colonies at the Colonial Office London, June and July 1897,' 13–14.
42. Dummett and Nicol, *Subjects, Citizens, Aliens and Others*, 120–21; Atkinson, *The Burden of White Supremacy*, 43–8.
43. *Minutes of Proceedings of the Colonial Conference, 1907.* Cd. 3523. London: HMSO, 1907, 175–6, 538–39.
44. Ibid., 178–82, 534–40.
45. *Minutes of the proceedings of the Imperial Conference, 1911.* Cd. 5745. London: HMSO, 1911, 249–56, 262.
46. Ibid., 257, 270.
47. Ibid., 394–99. Crewe's warning received short shrift from the Dominion leaders. Laurier claimed that the entry of cheap Indian labour to Canada was so potentially disruptive to local labour conditions that *it* was, in fact, the real threat to imperial unity. Lee Batchelor, the Australian Minister for External Affairs argued that 'the mixture of black and white races ... would tend to a disunited Empire rather than a united Empire.' F. R. Malan remarked that for South Africa, 'it is not so much a question of labour as a question of self-preservation,' by which he meant the demographic survival of a white population already outnumbered by non-Europeans, for whom Indian immigration would pose a further threat. See 399–410 of same *Minutes*.
48. Arnold, *Gandhi*, 60.
49. Johnston, *The Voyage of the Komagata Maru*, 33.
50. Dummett and Nicol, *Subjects, Citizens, Aliens and Others*, 120–21.
51. Singh, Gurdit. *Voyage of the Komagatamaru or India's Slavery Abroad*. Calcutta: Author, 1928, 15–16.
52. Johnston, *The Voyage*, 19–23; Schwinghamer "The Immigration Act a weapon".
53. Singh, *Voyage of the Komagatamaru*, 16.
54. British Library, India Office Records [hereafter IOR], L/PJ/6/1325, Judicial and Political Department, translation of notice for voyage, Despatch No. 101, June 26, 1914, 19–20. Italics added.
55. Quoted in Johnston, *The Voyage*, 30.
56. IOR L/PJ/6/1325, Judicial and Political Department, clippings from *The Province* for 16 and 17 April 1914, Despatch No. 101, June 26, 1914, 21–23.
57. IOR L/PJ/6/1325, Judicial and Political Department, Conygham Greene to Foreign Office, 13 May 1914, Despatch No. 141, August 7, 1914, 3–4.
58. 'Four Hundred Hindus', *The Tribune*, April 29, 1914, reprinted in Waraich and Sidhu (ed.) *Komagata Maru*, 83.
59. IOR L/PJ/1325, Judicial and Political Department, London All-India Moslem League to Colonial Office, June 18, 1914, Despatch No. 141, 11–12.
60. CUL, Crewe Papers I.17.12, draft telegram from Crewe to Hardinge, sent on 9 June 1914.
61. CUL, Hardinge Papers 87, Gillan to DuBoulay, 11 June 1914, Correspondence with Persons in India, vol. 7, 412–14.
62. CUL Crewe Papers I.17.12, copy of return telegram (written) from Hardinge, received on 12 June 1914.
63. CUL, Hardinge Papers 120, Hardinge to Crewe, 11 June 1914, Correspondence with the Secretary of State for India, vol. 4, 95–98.
64. IOR L/PJ/6 file 1324, Judicial and Political Department, "'Komagata Maru' Resolutions from Public Meetings in India." See especially: copy of telegram from Mr Nanak Chand, Chairman, Public Meeting of the Citizens of Lahore, 9 July 1914; copy of

paragraph 14 of the 'Confidential Weekly Diary' of the Superintendent of Police, Lahore, for week ending 13 June 1914; copy of telegram, dated Tarn Taran 13 June 1914; translated note of petition (in Urdu) from Baba Nihal Singh Vedi of Chandigarh (Ambala, Punjab), 2 June 1914; report of R. A. Mant (Financial Secretary to Government of Punjab), 18 August 1914; report of J. S. Donald, Chief Commissioner of North-West Frontier Province, 31 August 1914. See also, Grewal, J. S. *Master Tara Singh in Indian History: Colonialism, nationalism, and the Politics of Sikh Identity*. New Delhi: Oxford Univ Press, 2017, 73–74; Waraich and Sidhu (eds) *Komagata Maru*, 56–57.

65. "'Komagata Maru' Resolutions from Public Meetings in India": copy of resolution passed by the Sri Guru Singh Sabha, Bannu, 21 June 1914; report of J. S. Donald, Chief Commissioner of North-West Frontier Province, 31 August 1914.
66. Ibid., copy of letter from Sardar Jhanda Singh, Pleader Secretary of Khalsa Miandoab Diwan, 21 July 1914.
67. Ibid., copy of telegram from secretary of public meeting held at Peshawar, dated 27 July 1914. Colonial officials recorded an actual 'mixed audience' at this meeting of around 250 (see report of J. S. Donald, Chief Commissioner of North-West Frontier Province, 31 August 1914).
68. As quoted in a 'Veiled Threat is made by Hindus', *Vancouver Province*, 8 August 1914, reprinted in Wariach an Sidhu (eds), *Komagata Maru: Key documents*, 102–3.
69. Johnston, *The Voyage*, 92–103.
70. Ramnath, *Haj to Utopia*, 48–9; Waraich and Sidhu (eds), *Komagata Maru*, 235–41.
71. The Special Tribunal; Judgement in Second Supplementary Case dated 5th January 1917, reprinted in Waraich and Sidhu (eds), *Komagata Maru*, 230–41, 234–35.
72. See especially IOR/V/26/262/2, *Sedition Report 1918*. Calcutta: Superintendent Government Printing, 1918.
73. Both had travelled to London to resolve separate legal actions directed at themselves and their associates.
74. 'India and the Empire', *The Times*, May 29, 1914; and 'India and Australia – an interview with Mrs Annie Besant', *The British-Australasian*, May 28, 1914, reprinted in Annie Besant, *India and the Empire: A Lecture and Various Papers on Indian Grievances*. London: Theosophical Publishing House, 1914, pp. 25–29, 30–39.
75. Lala Lajpat Rai, "A Greater Measure of Self-Government." *Daily News and Leader*, June 10, 1914, reprinted in Besant, *India and the Empire*, 88–93.
76. 'The Commonweal of the World: International Association 1, *The Commonweal*, January 30, 1914; 'The Imperial Ideal', ibid., January 30, 1914; 'Invitation to Conference on the Formation of the League for Self-Government', ibid., December 17, 1915.
77. Besant, Annie. *India: A Nation – A Plea for Self Government*. 1st ed. London: T. C and E.C. Jack, 1916, 89–91.
78. Owen, "Towards Nationwide Agitation and Organization," 159–95.
79. Ransom, *A Short History of the Theosophical Society*, 409.
80. Fortnightly report from Madras, 18 December 1916, quoted in Brown, *Gandhi's Rise to Power*, 27–28.
81. Owen, "Towards Nation-Wide Agitation"; Mortimer, J. S. "Annie Besant and India, 1913-1917", *Journal of Contemporary History* 18, no. 1 (1983): 61–78. The holdings of the Adyar Oriental Library of the Theosophical Society in India include the *Home Rule Grantha Mala (Malayalam) Series*, published by the Malabar Provincial Home Rule League and the Mahajana Sabha in Calicut.
82. Fortnightly report from Madras, 18 December 1916.

83. Ibid., 27–29; Mortimer, "Annie Besant and India"; Owen, "Towards Nation-Wide Agitation." On the decision to release Besant see Robb, Peter. "The Government of India and Annie Besant." *Modern Asian Studies* 10, no. 1 (1976): 107–30.
84. Owen, "Towards Nation-Wide Agitation." This figure includes the membership of Tilak's Home Rule League, discussed below.
85. Besant, Annie. *The Case for India – Presidential Address to the Indian National Congress, 1917*. London: Home Rule for India League, 1917, 31–32 .
86. IOR Mss Eur F341/33, *Women's Indian Association: Golden Jubilee Celebration, 1917-1967*. Madras: WIA, 1967, 1–2.
87. Jinarajadasa, D. 'Suggestions for Conducting a Branch Meeting', *Stri Dharma*, January 1918, 7–8; and 'Women's Suffrage', ibid., January 1919, 63–64; Tata, Mithan A. 'Why Indian Women Should Have Votes,' ibid., May 1918, 37–39.
88. Jinarajadasa, 'Women's Suffrage.'
89. As Pal pointed out, in a 1907 speech to Madras students: 'if we have the rights of freedom of the Empire as Australia has, as Canada has, as England has herself today, if we, the 300 millions of people, have that freedom of the Empire, the Empire would cease to be British. It would be the Indian Empire and the alliance between England and India would be absolutely an unequal alliance'. Pal, Bipin Chandra. *Speeches of Sri. Bipin Chandra Pal (delivered at Madras)*. Madras: Ganesh, 1907, 43.
90. Pal, Bipin Chandra. 'Indian Nationalism and the British Empire: 1. Autonomy Versus Independence', *The Commonweal*, April 28, 1916.
91. Owen, "Towards Nation-Wide Agitation"; Nethercot, *The First Five Lives*, 250–51.
92. Bal Gangadhar Tilak, *Lokmanya Bal Gangadhar Tilak, His Writings and Speeches*. Madras: Ganesh, 1920. 228–49. On Tilak's veiled threat see Divekar, *Lokmanya Tilak in England*, 41.
93. Lake and Reynolds, *Drawing the Global Colour Line*, 250–51.
94. Chand, *Lajpat Rai, Life and Work*, 89, 259–61.
95. Divekar, *Lokmanya Tilak in England*, 193, 577. On Indian ties with the British Left more generally see Owen, *The British Left and India*, 78–105.
96. Gullace, "The Blood of Our Sons," 117–41.
97. 'The Home Rule League Deputation', *New India*, 8 Mar 1918
98. Scott, *Domination and the Arts of Resistance*, 91–92; see also, Moore, *Injustice*.
99. Erikson, *Gandhi's Truth*, 227–393; Arnold, *Gandhi*, 104–14. An exception is Brown, *Gandhi's Rise to Power*, 246–49.
100. 'Appeal for enlistment: leaflet No. 1, 22 June 1918' and 'Appeal for enlistment: leaflet No. 2, 22 July 1918,' *CWMG* 17, 83–87, 139–42.
101. The Satyagraha Pledge, *CWMG* 16, p. 297; Telegram to Viceroy, (after) 24 February 1919, *CWMG* 17, 299.
102. Scott, *Domination*, 95.
103. Nethercot, *First Five Lives*, 269–70.
104. Moyn, "Fantasies of Federalism."
105. Drayton, "Federal Utopias and the Realities of Imperial Power," 401–6.
106. Cooper, "Routes Out of Empire," 406–11.
107. The constraints which British official definitions of sedition placed on Indian political language are discussed in Darnton, *Censors at Work*, 114–42. However, the motivations of prominent wartime imperial federationists cannot merely be reduced to their desire to operate within colonial laws. For the cosmopolitan idealism which underpinned their dreams see Frost, "Beyond the Limits of Nation and Geography," 143–58.

108. Quoted in Popplewell, *Intelligence and Imperial Defence*, 190.
109. Besant and Tilak's Home Rule alliance ultimately fell apart by early 1919 over the former's eventual retreat from this stance following the release of the Montagu-Chelmsford Report.

Disclosure statement

No potential conflict of interest was reported by the author.

ORCID

Mark R. Frost http://orcid.org/0000-0002-0105-1358

References

Arnold, David. *Gandhi*. Harlow: Longman, 2001.

Atkinson, David C. *The Burden of White Supremacy: Containing Asian Migration in the British Empire and the United States*. Chapel Hill: University of North Carolina Press, 2016.

Banerjee, Sukanya. *Becoming Imperial Citizens: Indians in the Late-Victorian Empire*. Durham, NC: Duke University Press, 2010.

Brown, Judith. *Gandhi's Rise to Power: Indian Politics, 1915-1922*. Cambridge: Cambridge University Press, 1974.

Chand, Feroz. *Lajpat Rai, Life and Work*. New Delhi: Government of India, 1978.

Cooper, Frederick. *Colonialism in Question: Theory, Knowledge, History*. Berkeley: University of California Press, 2005.

Cooper, Frederick. *Citizenship Between Empire and Nation: Remaking France and French Africa, 1945-1960*. Princeton, NJ: Princeton University Press, 2014.

Cooper, Frederick. "Routes Out of Empire." *Comparative Studies in South Asia, Africa and the Middle East* 37, no. 2 (2017): 406–411.

Daniels, Roger. "The Growth of Restrictive Immigration Policies in the Colonies of Settlement." In The Cambridge Survey of World Migration, Edited by Robin Cohen. Cambridge: Cambridge University Press, 1995.

Darnton, Robert. *Censors at Work: How States Shape Literature*. London: The British Library, 2014.

Divekar, V. D., ed. *Lokmanya Tilak in England, 1918-1919: Diary and Documents*. Pune: Tilak Smarak Trust, 1997.

Drayton, Richard. "Federal Utopias and the Realities of Imperial Power." *Comparative Studies in South Asia, Africa and the Middle East* 37, no. 2 (2017): 401–406.

Dummett, Ann, and Andrew Nicol. *Subject, Citizens, Aliens and Others: Nationality and Immigration Law*. London: Weidenfeld and Nicholson, 1990.

Erikson, Erik H. *Gandhi's Truth: On the Origins Militant Nonviolence* [First Published 1970]. New York: W. W. Norton, 1993.

Fisher, Michael H. *Counterflows to Colonialism: Indian Travelers and Settlers in Britain, 1600-1857*. Delhi: Permanent Black, 2004.

Frost, Mark R. "Transcultural Diaspora: The Straits Chinese in Singapore, 1819-1918." Asia Research Working Paper No. 10. Accessed July 18, 2018. https://ari.nus.edu.sg/Assets/repository/files/publications/wps03_010.pdf.

Frost, Mark R. "*Emporium in Imperio:* Nanyang Networks and the Straits Chinese in Singapore 1819-1914." *Journal of Southeast Asian Studies* 36, no. 1 (2005): 29–66.

Frost, Mark R. "Beyond the Limits of Nation and Geography': Rabindranath Tagore and the Cosmopolitan Moment, 1916-1920." *Cultural Dynamics* 24, no. 2–3 (2012): 143–158.

Gorman, Daniel. *Imperial Citizenship: Empire and the Question of Belonging.* Manchester: Manchester University Press, 2006.

Guha, Ramachandra. *Gandhi Before India.* London: Penguin, 2014.

Gullace, Nicoletta F. *"The Blood of Our Sons": Men, Women and the Renegotiation of British Citizenship During the Great War.* New York: Palgrave Macmillan, 2002.

Hansen, Randal. *Citizenship and Immigration in Postwar Britain: The Institutional Origins of a Multicultural Nation.* Oxford: Oxford University Press, 2000.

Johnston, Hugh. *The Voyage of the Komagata Maru: The Sikh Challenge to Canada's Colour Bar.* Delhi: Oxford University Press, 1979.

Lake, Marilyn and Henry Reynolds. *Drawing the Global Colour Line: White Men's Countries and the Question of Racial Equality.* Cambridge: Cambridge University Press, 2008.

Moore, Barrington. *Injustice: The Social Bases of Obedience and Revolt* [First Published in 1978]. Abingdon: Routledge, 2016.

Moyn, Samuel. "Fantasies of Federalism." *Dissent*, Winter 2015. Accessed July 19, 2018. https://www.dissentmagazine.org/article/fantasies-of-federalism

Mukherjee, Sumita. "'Narrow-Majority' and 'Bow-and-Agree': Public Attitudes Towards the Elections of the First Asian MPs in Britain, Dadabhai Naoroji and Mancherjee Merwanjee Bhownaggree, 1885-1906." *Journal of the Oxford History Society*, 2 (Michaelmas 2004): 1–20.

Nethercot, A. H. *The First Five Lives of Annie Besant.* Chicago, IL: Chicago University Press, 1960.

Owen, H. F. "Towards Nationwide Agitation and Organization: The Home Rule Leagues, 1915-18." In *Soundings in Modern South Asian History*, edited by D. A. Low, 159–195. London: Weidenfeld and Nicholson, 1968.

Owen, Nicholas. "The Soft Heart of the British Empire: Indian Radicals in Edwardian London." *Past and Present* 220, no. 1 (2013):143–184.

Popplewell, Richard J. *Intelligence and Imperial Defence: British Intelligence and the Defence of the Indian Empire.* London: Frank Cass, 1995.

Ramnath, Maia. *Haj to Utopia: How the Ghadar Movement Charted Global Radicalism and Attempted to Overthrow the British Empire.* Berkeley: University of California Press, 2011.

Ransom, J. *A Short History of the Theosophical Society.* Madras: Theosophical Publishing House, 1938.

Schwinghamer, Steve. "'The Immigration Act a weapon': *Panama Maru* and the Exclusion of Immigrants, 1913." Canadian Museum of Immigration at Pier 21. Accessed July 18, 2018. https://pier21.ca/blog/steve-schwinghamer/panama-maru-and-the-exclusion-of-immigrants-1913

Scott, James. *Domination and the Arts of Resistance: Hidden Transcripts.* New Haven, CT: Yale University Press, 1990.

Simms, Richard. "In Memory of the Star (1888-1960)." An Index to the Fiction Published in *The Star* Website. Accessed July 18, 2018. http://thestarfictionindex.atwebpages.com/the.htm

Visram, Rozinha. *Ayahs, Lascars and Princes: The Story of Indians in Britain, 1700-1947.* Abingdon: Routledge, 2015.

Waraich, Malwinderjit Singh, and Gurdev Singh Sidhu. eds. *Komagata Maru – A Challenge to Colonialism: Key Documents.* Chandigarh: UNISTAR, 2005.

Written Differently: A Survey of Commonwealth Constitutional History in the Age of Decolonisation

H. Kumarasingham

ABSTRACT

This article provides a survey and definition of the field of Commonwealth constitutional history since 1918, especially during and after global decolonisation. It asks what is Commonwealth constitutional history and how it differs from its English and Imperial counterparts. The article puts forward a working definition of Commonwealth constitutional history and introduces key and diverse writers who illustrate the range and potential of this history. The article provides an historiography and survey of constitutional history in the Pre-Commonwealth and Post-war Commonwealth periods while also assessing the opportunities of Post-British Commonwealth constitutional history. The objective of this article is to show how Commonwealth constitutional history can contribute to the historical study of state power and to see its worth to other disciplines and fields of history. Commonwealth constitutional history is a necessity to examine the politics, power and consequences of the British empire during the long age of decolonisation.

Introduction

The perceptive Florentine scholar of democracy, Giovanni Sartori, wrote in 1962 that 'one must be very careful about importing the British constitutional textbooks. They have not been written for export'. Nonetheless, British texts and histories on constitutions, governments, and institutions of state were found across the globe and they disproportionately dominated the field. This being so despite the infamous and widely held judgement that Britain, unlike almost every other country, had no written constitution. For Sartori, however, it was not that the United Kingdom had an unwritten constitution, but instead that it was 'written differently'.[1] The same could be said, in fact more so, for the constitutional history the Commonwealth. Nothing of this history was, or could be, uniform. The span and diversity of the British Empire and the torrents and dribbles of decolonisation that followed ensured a need for such historical assessments. Constitutional and political history became in this guise less a rarefied academic speciality and more a much taught and studied tool to provide, however weak or inapt, precedents, warnings, tuition, and ideas for building new Jerusalems beyond England's green and peculiar land. Yet it has become more and more true that such history has been relegated to collect dust instead of citations. With the rectifying of this trend in mind this article has three main aims. Firstly, it seeks to introduce and define the field of Commonwealth constitutional history since World War I, especially the post-war period and to see how it connected to politics. Secondly, it will briefly describe the impact and range of eight selected scholars to the field of Commonwealth constitutional history (other key writers shall be found throughout these pages). Finally, it will survey three key stages in twentieth century and modern Commonwealth constitutional history and argue for the importance of the subject for the contemporary teaching and writing of histories of imperialism and decolonisation.

What is Commonwealth Constitutional History?

The twentieth century witnessed the British Empire at both its greatest extent as well as its awesome demission. The century rebounded with the impact of colonialism. The history surrounding decolonisation is full of flux, ambiguity, messiness, complex density, and lack of cohesion. Nonetheless decolonisation as an ever-moving world phenomena should not detract from the quest to demarcate what Commonwealth constitutional history is, and why we should care to employ it to study the end of empire and the post-colonial results. Yet the cudgels of constitutional history are usually left untouched despite the force they can deliver to critiquing the colonial state and the inheritors that followed. As John Darwin observed the situation is one lately where 'historians of empire have shown a surprising indifference to constitutional matters, as if the rules of the political game did not matter intensely to contemporaries. This is a bizarre misjudgement'.[2] Lazy characterisations of constitutional history as an enterprise given to elitist, legalist and obscurantist esoterica only comfortable with slates of statutes and remote judicial portentousness is far from the mark. Commonwealth constitutional history instead is intrinsic to understanding the process of decolonisation and the post-independence travails. Commonwealth constitutional history can be broadly defined as the study of the sources, legitimisations, and control of state power through the prism, shared experience and consequences of British rule both direct and indirect. This definition gives Commonwealth constitutional history a crucial role in studying the end of the British Empire and the dynamics of the colonial state and its successors. To evade this research area entirely or insufficiently historical writing on the British Empire and Commonwealth becomes devalued and incomplete. Whether national, regional, transnational or global Commonwealth constitutional history inherently draws on the vast influences and constitutional manifestations linked to British imperial authority. This does not imply an exclusivity centred on the direct impact of Britain, but rather allows a history fertilised with imperial and Commonwealth comparisons and disparities. Therefore, the objective of Commonwealth constitutional history is to chart machinations, political desires, local cultures, negotiating gambits and personalities just as readily as it is an examination of official documents, legislation, institutional structure, and law. To be clear this is not traditional legal history, which is primarily and tellingly in the United Kingdom and Commonwealth a conscious adjunct to Law Schools not History ones and thus not unnaturally concentrates on Law almost exclusively. Nor is this a survey and history of successive constitutions. Instead Commonwealth constitutional history as defined above openly embraces broader historical concerns of the political, social and cultural to interrogate the imperial, colonial and post-colonial state in order to derive the crucial constitutional dimension of decolonisation. In turn this means for historians the need to go beyond the discipline and exact from Law and Social Sciences the necessary analytical and scholarly information on the state to infuse their historical study. A situation described by A. F. Madden in the 1950s that saw the political scientist Sir Kenneth Wheare, Gladstone Professor of Government at Oxford, not only give lectures to historians but also be Chairman of the History board was evidence of a time where 'there was no divorce yet between history and social studies' is too rare today.[3] Unlike its imperial cousin Commonwealth constitutional history carries the need to bridge and traverse British involvement as well as the post-independence era. The colonial period could not be ignored any more than the post-colonial. While clearly within the family Commonwealth constitutional history is still written differently from its older English and imperial sisters.

For most English school children from the nineteenth century to the 1950s constitutional history was central to their curriculum. Not as a dense dispassionate examination of governments and laws, but, as Michael Bentley explains, in a pedagogical and patriotic influence tied to the national story since 'England's constitutional history functioned not as the accompaniment but as explanation of her glory' and 'instilled a distinctive temper in the English nation' that saw in the country's constitutional history the genius and liberty of England.[4] This same English constitutional history impressed itself upon the colonial empire. Drummed into children and students, fortunate enough to have formal education, were the near omniscient superiority of the English and the verities of their constitution and empire. William Stubbs argued that to do English constitutional history was not to assemble facts and views, but instead the engage in the 'piecing of the links of a perfect chain' from the Saxons to the present. As Amanda Behm explains for historians like Stubbs this method showcased English political development, stability and liberty, which was 'encoded in the canon of an unwritten constitution' and encouraged the notion of British settler colonialism as carrying this superior 'history'.[5] For the ruled constitutional history was on one hand the history of England, and on the other, the constitutional history of British rule. To C. L. R. James the Whig progression of constitutional development lionised of England and the aspiration and question of when greater autonomy would come to the Anglo-Caribbean was answered from London and Government House with '"Self-government when fit for it". That had always been the promise'. James sardonically commented, not unrelatedly, '"Patriotism," says Johnson, "is the last refuge of a scoundrel." It is the first resort of the colonial Englishman'.[6] There was from the nineteenth century, as Nicholas Mansergh wrote, a strong feeling in English political and academic culture that self-government was associated with 'people of British origin who alone, by reason of history and aptitude in the art of government, were thought qualified to exercise its responsibilities'.[7] This showed a very distinctive cultural annexe to English constitutional history.

Imperial and Commonwealth history is simultaneously and indelibly linked to England, and markedly separate from it. The teleological progress of constitutional history slowed, stuttered, and sometimes deviated from traditionally ordained paths when confronted with the colours of local demands, colonial urges, and, of course, realities. Serialisation of English constitutional history did not always translate or read well in Commonwealth and colonial contexts. The works of renowned English constitutional historians around the end of the nineteenth century and beginning of the twentieth century like F. W. Maitland or the Oxford constitutional scholar A. V. Dicey travelled far from the Port of Spain to Port Moresby[8]. Yet constitutional historians like Stubbs and Maitland and such ilk were not historians of the British Empire, and nor did they claim to be. How could English ideas and institutions of cabinet government, parliamentary sovereignty, responsible advice, collective responsibility, prerogative powers, heredity within parliament and state, Christian assumptions, selective suffrage, and of course an unwritten constitution find meaning and form away from London. Such hallowed principles of liberty and highlights of English constitutional history did not effortlessly flow to the empire.

Discussing the export of the British political model A. F. Madden argued that in any period of British imperialism

> the product finally delivered at the frontier is different from the blueprint devised in the department. Distance has blurred the exactness of the copy, had aided the normal erosion of convention upon law and has permitted variants unsuspected at the centre or unknown in the prototype.[9]

The same could be said for English constitutional history. Traditionally imperial and Commonwealth constitutional history instead sought to take England as a reference point and chart the establishment and development of colonial government and settlement in the territory through an almost invariably English perspective. The Whig constitutional historians may have had a predilection for Stubbs' 'perfect chain' of historical development of English liberty, but historians of empire also saw in their field the need for a certain narrative and pride too. If, as Ronald Hyam, has argued British imperial power relied on prestige and 'conveying an impression of unquestionable omniscience' even if the reality were different[10], the constitutional history of England and its empire profited from this impression also. No equivalent of the Germanic intellectual tradition of *Staatsrecht* cohesively draped the constitution at home or the empire across the seas. No school of law or history determined the Commonwealth's laws and philosophy unlike many European traditions. Indeed as R. T. E. Latham pointed out in the late 1930s strictly speaking the 'Statute of Westminster is all that there is of the Commonwealth in law, and it is not very much'.[11] History, expedience and crises filled these considerable gaps. The constitutional and political history of the British Empire and Commonwealth was an idiosyncratic enterprise that like its subject never failed to evade uniformity, generalisation, or, despite enduring impressions to the contrary, of functioning under one law.

It is interesting to note that all the major writers who contributed lasting works and scholarship on the constitutional history of the British Empire and Commonwealth during the twentieth century and beyond rarely, if ever, labelled themselves as constitutional historians and a good many were not even to be found in academia let alone in the History common room. Martin Wight, J. D. B. Miller, and Alfred Zimmern gave respectively invaluable histories on colonial legislatures and constitutions, surveys of Commonwealth affairs and historical foundations for constitutional cooperation are seen as key scholars and theorists of International Relations; Dennis Austin, Sir Kenneth C. Wheare and Geoffrey Marshall who wrote historical works on governments and concepts of the Commonwealth hailed from the field of Politics; Sir Ivor Jennings and S. A. de Smith left invaluable works on the constitutional history of the 'old' and 'new' Commonwealth and both held Maitland's old chair of Downing Professor in the Laws of England in Cambridge; Sir Charles Jeffries, Sir William Dale and Sir Kenneth Roberts-Wray left major constitutional studies unquestionably and openly informed from their mandarin vantage in Whitehall; B. R. Ambedkar, Leo Amery, Lord Bryce, Sir Zelman Cowen, H. V. Evatt, Eugene Forsey, Patrick Gordon Walker, Lord Hailey, Richard Hart, Hugh Hickling, Sir Fred Phyilips, Sir B. N. Rau, H. M. Seervai and Eric Williams all commbined a talent for Commonwealth constitutional history with state or political office; Alpheus Todd, a parliamentary librarian in Ottawa, wrote the huge and much used constitutional and parliamentary history of the colonies and Dominions; and perhaps the most impressive historian of them all in terms of depth, range and citation, A. B. Keith, who we shall hear of again, was a prolific Indologist.

An Ecumenical Octet of Commonwealth Constitutional Writers

Political Scientist Anthony King in his study of the British constitution has a chapter entitled 'The Canonical Sextet' to describe some of the 'classical writers on the constitution'.[12] For the sake of brevity and reticence post 1918

Commonwealth constitutional history an ecumenical octet of writers are offered here to give a varied sample of the field of Commonwealth constitutional history and to exemplify its range. W. David McIntyre in his *The Britannic Vision* provides a fascinating study and brief description of key Historians and the Commonwealth. So as not to replicate him the Octet consciously leaves out those covered so expertly by McIntyre with the exception of A. B. Keith who is in need of further attention due to his contributions. The importance of Nicholas Mansergh will be recognised in a further section towards the end of the article. Obvious names like Sir Reginald Coupland, Lionel Curtis, Sir Keith Hancock, Dame Margery Perham, Sir Kenneth Wheare and Alfred Zimmern, among others, are omitted from the list – though all their names feature across this article.[13] Instead the list below aims to complement McIntyre's and to bring forward other writers, now past, who have contributed in various important ways to constitutional history of the Commonwealth and critically whose work has resonance beyond one state. Almost none of the writers below, as above, would likely describe themselves as constitutional historians of the Commonwealth. Nonetheless they all conform to my definition of Commonwealth constitutional history stated in the previous section as they have all weaved the constitutional story within their powerful narratives and impressed upon their reader the centrality of constitutional history to the study of the state's power and the conceptions of ruling as well as the effects of being ruled. The eight writers selected give a taste to the field, but in no way, provide a definitive or exhaustive list. All of them wrote constitutional history covering more than one place and all of them had latent interest in the constitutional affairs of other colonial and Commonwealth states. Below follows in order of birth a very abbreviated coverage of each.

Arthur Berriedale Keith (1879–1944)

Few constitutional histories of the late British Empire can avoid the writings of the Scot A. B. Keith – mainly because he wrote much of it. Keith was author of such books as *Responsible Government in the Dominions* (Oxford: 1928), *The Governments of the British Empire* (London: 1935), *Constitutional History of India, 1600–1935* (London: 1936), *The King and the Imperial Crown: The Powers and Duties of His Majesty* (London: 1936) and *Speeches and Documents on the British Dominions, 1918–1931: From Self-Government to National Sovereignty* (London: 1948). Educated at Edinburgh and Oxford universities in, among other subjects, Sanskrit, Pali, Greek, Latin and Logic Keith served in the Colonial Office from 1901 covering a wide array of areas including legal and political issues involving Natal, Nigeria, North America, the Caribbean, and Home Rule for Ireland. On his return to academia in 1914 till his death in 1944 he held the Regius Chair in Sanskrit and Comparative Philology at the University of Edinburgh and later acquired the additional position in the Law School of 'Lecturer on the Constitution of the

British Empire'. For Keith the interwar years were critical in the development of government, constitutional status and institutions across the empire and the end of World War I ushered in a great demand for his knowledge and words. He helped develop and promote the critical idea that political autonomy was not inimical to the Commonwealth. Keith was a rare scholar who could combine deep understanding of 'oriental' culture and history with an equal command of the United Kingdom, settler cases and much of the colonial world too. Dominion leaders like the William Mackenzie King would consult this constitutional polymath of empire and the veteran Canadian prime minister would on occasion visit Keith in Edinburgh after the imperial conferences in London. His writings would remain cited in constitutional and political events across the Empire-Commonwealth for decades after his death and his detailed studies remain the commanding source.[14]

B. Shiva Rao (1891–1975)

B. Shiva Rao was a well-regarded journalist who wrote for *The Hindu* and the *Manchester Guardian* and was well known to the major Indian political leaders. He had cut his political teeth helping Annie Besant's Home Rule for India movement. Shiva Rao also sat in the Constituent Assembly, a body tasked to frame a new constitution for India, and would later serve in both houses of the Indian parliament. He collated constitutional histories of countries across the world including Mexico, the U. S. S. R. and the Kingdom of the Serbs, Croats, and Slovenes as well as entries on the Statute of Westminster, the Irish Free State, Canada and Australia. *Select Constitutions of the World* originally was produced 'by order of the Irish Provisional Government in 1922'. Shiva Rao updated it with Irish approval while in London and published it in Madras in 1934 for those 'actively interested in the constitutional changes which are taking place in India'.[15] In terms of constitutional history of the Commonwealth he made two related contributions that continue to resonate. The lesser known service, and one that surreptitiously adds another name to the list, was to edit a collection entitled *India's Constitution in the Making* (Calcutta: 1960) of the notes, reports and memoranda of the incredibly erudite and influential Indian Constituent Assembly's Adviser, Sir B. N. Rau (1887–1953), who happened to be his elder brother. Herein detailed references to constitutional histories of the Dominions and elsewhere were used to argue in a measured manner how their example might be adapted for the republic's new constitution. Rau was adept at absorbing a massive amount of historical and legal texts and his service to independent India's constitutional framework rivals B. R. Ambedkar's. Aside from international influences Rau was also adept at drawing on India's own rich historical traditions and ancient texts such as the Code of Manu concerning government to situate the new state's constitutional pedigree for democracy. Yet in the end he favoured English and Commonwealth constitutional traditions, but not whole. Rau was active helping Burma with its first constitution and was instrumental in finding the formula in keeping republican India in the Commonwealth, which had hitherto been the preserve of realms. Shiva Rao's second service was to edit the multi volume *The Framing of India's Constitution – Select Documents* (New Delhi: 1966–1968), which remains the indispensable source of the debates and decisions of the Constituent Assembly. A separate volume contains from Shiva Rao a majestic section on the 'Historical Background' of the constitution, which not only draws on colonial India, but brings in the struggles, ideas and constitutional history from across India and the British Empire. Crucially it brings important Indian narratives and their engagement, frustrations and constitutional stratagems that were fundamental to Indian freedom. The works serve as an imperfect but necessary reminder of the historical foundations of the empire's greatest possession and the Commonwealth's most critical member. It remains in print with a mine of information showing how Westminster, colonial India, and the Commonwealth, with precious Indian innovations contributed to the constitution of the remarkable Indian republic.

C. L. R. James (1901–1989)

C. L. R. James in an example of a writer who sought with no little success to articulate the need for self-government and champion anti-colonialism. Several other writers did similar things fitfully fighting with their pen under the canopy of colonialism, but James had resonance. The Trinidadian James worked as a school teacher and among those he taught was Eric Williams, who openly imbibed the lessons of his mentor James during his time as a doctoral student in history under Vincent Harlow and Reginald Coupland in Oxford and later himself an articulator and representative of responsible government as independent Trinidad and Tobago's first prime minister. James was highly influential in the Caribbean and also in Africa impressing figures from Nkrumah to E. P. Thompson, with his tireless efforts to eradicate colonialism and racism. His works on slavery through colonialism remain powerful. While in later life he took on Marxist positions his earlier work appreciated the forms of government available in the empire, but attacked it not being offered to the Caribbean. He cuttingly critiqued colonial government and the political and personal prejudice it upheld in the West Indies and uses clear arguments for autonomy within the British Empire. His *The Life of Captain Cipriani: An Account of British Government in the West Indies* (Nelson: 1932) and its abridged focus on the Caribbean Crown Colony experience in *The Case for West Indian Self-Government* (London: 1933)[16] were written in the wake of the autonomy recognising Statute of Westminster Act 1931 tailored for the white settler Dominions. James cogently ridicules the colonial government and its impeding of racial equality and democracy despite British rule proclaiming the opposite. His powerful appraisal of Crown Colony government and his search for constitutional arrangements that suited in his mind the distinct polities of the West Indies having a population of many cultures were sincerely made. Like many anti-colonialists under the British Empire James knew his constitutional history and was keenly aware of constitutional developments beyond his own country, but within the imperial world. In the *Case for West Indian Self-Government*, for example, he sees options from Ceylon and Malta and views parallel experiences in Ireland and Quebec as pertinent. He saw no need to lazily and, as he put it, 'plastically' copy the English model. The anti-colonial writings of James underscore how constitutional history and the English idiom can be used to articulate a case for independence and highlight inequality and the hypocritical strains of English liberal-imperial constitutionalism. James shows the symbiotic relationship of social history and political history and their collective impact upon constitutional history. No one reading his classic history of cricket *Beyond a Boundary* can fail to see the politics of empire and race as well as the need for 'fair play' in society and state.

Sir Ivor Jennings (1903–1965)

The Bristol born Master of Trinity Hall, Cambridge and law professor Ivor Jennings engrossed himself in reading British and Imperial political history from the very beginning of his education. At a young age at the LSE he had already written key constitutional texts. Indeed, his name and works are still regularly cited by legal scholars due to his lasting works on the British constitution such as multiple editions of *The Law and the Constitution* (London: 1933), *Cabinet Government* (Cambridge: 1936) and *Parliament* (Cambridge: 1939) as well as on the complexities of that very Commonwealth constitutional expedient: conventions. What is less well known in British academia is that almost half of his career was spent outside Britain, especially in the 'New Commonwealth'. Jennings was a major 'constitution-maker' working as a constitutional adviser and constitutional commission member from Singapore to Sudan. In these critical assignments across the globe Jennings drew upon imperial and Commonwealth constitutional history with incredible dexterity. For Ceylon, where he was at his the most influential and served as vice-chancellor, for example, he recommended and incorporated in the constitutional documents lessons from seemingly unlikely locations such as Newfoundland and Ireland. Critically for Commonwealth constitutional history his accounts still provide first hand assessments of the cases he wrote on and his prolific books remain, however dated, often the most durable constitutional account of critical stages in state-building as well as capturing the constitutional mood and thinking during the heyday of decolonisation. Numerous editions of *The Constitution of Ceylon* (Oxford: 1949), *Constitutional Laws of the Commonwealth* (Oxford:

1952), *Some Characteristics of the Indian Constitution* (Madras: 1953) *The Approach to Self-Government* (Cambridge: 1956), *Constitutional Problems in Pakistan* (Cambridge: 1957) and *Democracy in Africa* (Cambridge: 1963) display his wide interests and, less openly, his involvements. Jennings' Commonwealth scholarly works and constitutional memoranda are always full of politics, personalities and history that seldom allowed legal doctrine or academic boundaries to trouble his ambitions or style.[17]

A. F. Madden (1917–2011)

Between 1985 and 2000 eight volumes of over 6000 pages and approximately 30 years of work *Select Documents on the Constitutional History of the British Empire* emerged with the imprimatur of Oxford historian Frederick Madden with the collaboration, at times, of D. K. Fieldhouse and later John Darwin, both of whom were immensely receptive to the virtues of constitutional history, which is very evident in their own substantial work. Madden's immense scholarship was in evidence as he completed the enormous publishing feat of covering over 800 years of constitutional history. However, they have never become even marginally read let alone cited or positioned anywhere near a History reading list. Part of this is due to the laborious type setting of the American publisher, but the subject and its coverage were mired by what Peter Burroughs described as 'changing fashions', which reduced constitutional history, once in vogue and central to imperial history, to be labelled 'antediluvian and blinkered'. Madden himself described it as an 'idiosyncratic project' when conceived in Sir Kenneth Wheare's study in All Souls in 1953. Yet like Wheare, Madden, did not see 'constitution' in narrow terms instead viewing constitutional history as crucial to understand governance, politics, institutions and cultures. Important since, as Burroughs assesses 'imperial history is – and will always be – utterly unintelligible without an intimate understanding of political institutions and public law in both Britain and its colonies'.[18] While Michael Brock wryly praised the 'unfashionable independence'[19] of a book project like Madden's few took up the intellectual message of Burroughs in seeing the value of constitutional history for their own fields of imperial and Commonwealth history. With Kenneth Robinson he presented a collection of important essays in *Imperial Government* (Oxford: 1963) for Margery Perham, with W. H. Morris-Jones *Australia and Britain – Studies in a Changing Relationship* (London, 1980), and with D. K. Fieldhouse another valuable edition entitled *Oxford and the Idea of the Commonwealth* (London: 1982). Madden was equally at home with the constitutional history of the Angevins as he was on the settlers of Australia, the planters of Antigua or the traders of Aden. It is hard to find an historian of imperial and Commonwealth government in the post war era with such remarkable breadth, command of detail and indefatigable dedication to Commonwealth history and government.

S. A. de Smith (1922–1974)

Stanley Alexander de Smith was a lucid LSE and Cambridge law professor who actively engaged professionally and academically with all parts of the Commonwealth, and his services were actively in demand. Like Jennings, despite his faculty home, he would not allow himself or his constitutional writings to be limited by what he called 'lawyers' law'. While famous for his works on Administrative Law it is his forays into the constitutional life of the 'New Commonwealth' that attract the attention of the Commonwealth constitutional historian. De Smith's *The New Commonwealth and its Constitutions* (London: 1964) remains a classic of its kind and skilfully brings in the constitutional history of South Asia and the newly independent states from South East Asia and Africa, describing the reception of the Westminster model in these lands and how British constitutional concepts developed or wilted there. De Smith also probed the terms and words inherent to the British constitution and their application in the Commonwealth, realising that the vocabulary of the constitution might be the same, but not necessarily the meaning. He was also very interested in thorny constitutional cases like Rhodesia, Nigeria, Malaya, Pakistan, and the neglected microstates of the Pacific. He spent time too on constitutional missions and commissions, including being secretary at Keith Hancock's request to the Buganda Commission in the mid 1950s and was Constitutional Commissioner to Mauritius. Unlike some British law scholars De Smith had the ability to write accessibly, not just about British constitutional affairs for a Commonwealth audience, but more importantly about constitutional issues affecting the Commonwealth itself.

D. A. Low (1927–2015)

After reading African history in Margery Perham's Oxford, Indian born and Haileybury educated Anthony Low took his first academic position as a Lecturer at the new Makerere University College in Kampala in 1951, wanting to understand colonial Africa first hand. He also became the East Africa correspondent for the *Times*. While in Buganda he met Hancock who helped him with his career in Britain and Australia and whom would be the subject of a biography by Low. African political history would be a continuing passion and arm of Low's - his first and last book over a period of some fifty years (and in-between) were on British East Africa. Increasingly Low, now moving between Canberra and England, became engrossed with the endgame of empire in the Indian subcontinent and produced elegant and powerful books examining the fissures of colonial power and investigating Indian and British motivations, collaborations and political manoeuvres. *Congress and the Raj – Facets of the Indian Struggle* (London: 1977) and *Britain and Indian Nationalism – The Imprint of Ambiguity* (Cambridge, 1996) continue to illuminate a complex and critical stage in Indian history. Later holding the Smuts chair in Cambridge, he scanned together, as few could, different parts of the Empire-Commonwealth to interrogate the politics and power relations at not just the end of empire, but also during the growth of national consciousness in the emergent post-independence states. This was amply in view in his collections *Lion Rampant – Essays in the Study of British Imperialism* (London: 1973) and *Eclipse of Empire* (Cambridge: 1991). Britain and the 'old' Dominions were not left out. He edited two superb volumes (one with David Butler) on constitutional crises involving heads of state in the post-war Commonwealth and covered Buckingham Palace and the emblematical constitutional crisis that dramatically befell Australia in November 1975 when the Governor-General sacked the prime minister, Gough Whitlam, while Low was close by as Australia National University vice-chancellor.[20] His last book *Fabrication of Empire – The British and the Uganda Kingdoms 1890–1902* (Cambridge: 2009) evidenced a Commonwealth scholar writing in his 80s upholding his consistent passion to understand the history of colonial and local government and the exercise of power by all. Above all he expressed, for all its faults, the connectedness Commonwealth history afforded.

C. A. Bayly (1945–2015)

World historian Sir Christopher Alan Bayly is a generation younger than the previous writer in the list, D. A. Low. Bayly, gained his doctorate on nineteenth century local politics in Allahabad under Jack Gallagher at Oxford in 1970, and was captivated by Indian history, despite being taught almost exclusively European history beforehand. For him and his cohort constitutional history of empire was prone to be viewed as dull repetition of endless disappointing commissions and hollow exhortations of Britain's civilising constitutionalism. Imperial history had been taught and written in outlets like the *Cambridge History of the British Empire* (the series began in 1929) with, as Bayly described, an 'unwritten purpose ... to demonstrate how the English values of "justice", "benevolence" and "humanity" were transformed into a universal ethos of free nations through the operation of the rule of law and democratic government'.[21] Crucially for historians like Bayly's, working on colonial India, the voice of the ruled in these histories had hitherto been absent. While primarily known for his original, expansive, and meticulously composed histories of eighteenth and nineteenth century imperial and South Asian history Bayly, later in his career, added the twentieth century to his unequalled historical repertoire. His powerful and inquisitive mind proceeded to disentangle Britain's imperial mission and to uncover its imperfections. With Tim Harper, their books *Forgotten Armies – The Fall of British Asia 1941–1945* (London: 2004) and *Forgotten Wars – The End of Britain's Asian Empire* (London: 2007) dramatically and skilfully displayed the constitutional and political schemes of the British and local leaders in a climactic context as well as the impact on the ruled. Bayly's *Recovering Liberties – Indian*

Thought in the Age of Liberalism and Empire (Cambridge: 2012) singed with captivating intellectual history of liberalism both in British and South Asian hands and emphasised how liberalism related to power and the state. With unparalleled and expanding reach his world history analysis became ever ready to originally draw constitutional and political connections across the 'modern world'. The British Empire and Commonwealth and its constitutional history were only a part of his intellectual domain, but became a progressively significant one in his majestic surveys of power, ideas and society.[22]

Pre-Commonwealth Constitutional History

Perhaps it is no surprise that one of the most important authorities on constitutional history across the British Empire in the early twentieth century held a position as ostensibly removed as Regius Chair of Sanskrit and Comparative Philology at the University of Edinburgh. Verses of the *Upanishads* might have helped Arthur Berriedale Keith decipher the myths and complexities of the British Empire's constitutional and political evolution. Before the modern Commonwealth came about in 1949 with the admission of India on its own republican terms the key constitutional moment in the interwar period was the imperial conference in 1926 held in the aftermath of the so-called King-Byng affair, which questioned the Crown's imperial powers in Canada to intervene in local affairs. The Balfour Declaration from the conference of Dominion leaders of 1926 famously described Britain and the Dominions as 'autonomous communities within the British Empire, equal in status, in no way subordinate one to another in any aspect of their domestic affairs or external affairs ... ', which gained legislative form in the 1931 Statute of Westminster. Keith wryly commented that the 'definition may be admired for its intention rather than for its accuracy', reminding his readers the often forgotten qualification in the declaration that followed: 'the principles of equality and similarity in status do not universally extend to function', as well as such incongruities as the 'rather stupid' ignoring of Northern Ireland.[23] For constitutional historians like Keith, events like the seminal 1926 Imperial Conference of British and Dominion leaders (with nominal representation from India) were not mere abstractions, but principles and policies for a new world order that gave flesh to Whig historical ambitions of transforming the empire. Did this apply beyond the "kith and kin"? Some had in mind the words of Lord Macaulay in 1833.

> It may be that the public mind of India may expand under our system till it has outgrown the system, that by good government we may educate our subjects into a capacity for better government, that having become instructed in European knowledge they may in some future age demand European institutions. Whether such a day will ever come I know not. But never will I attempt to avert or retard it. Whenever it comes, it will be the proudest day in English history.

History and politics were not so simple. Such statements as the above were crafted as 'alibis' of liberal imperialism and constitutional absolutism.[24] J. R. Seeley famously asked in 1883 how could England reconcile 'opposite extremes' in being 'despotic in Asia and democratic in Australia'.[25] The empire relied on those ruled believing that 'the proudest day' could be theirs. The first President of the Ceylon National Congress, Sir Ponnambalam Arunachalam, for example, quoted the above passage of Macaulay's in 1917 in his presidential address to the party faithful. Constitutional history of the empire travelled far. He stressed that 'England', 'in her dealings with dependent peoples, her staunch faith in the healing and ennobling power of popular institutions and has found in them the only sure remedy for the ills of the body-politic'. Yet, as Arunachalam recognised a problem was that the history that he and others received was that it was only the *genius* of English constitutional and political history and as such wilfully ignored local constitutional and political history. A constitutional, classical and historical scholar taught by the same Seeley at Cambridge, he pleaded with the Westminster and the Colonial Government for a university on the island and for schools to teach Sinhalese, Tamil and local history so that the Ceylonese could learn their own 'worthy' constitutional and political history. As he reminded Colonel Wedgwood the island had 'twenty centuries of autonomous rule before Westerners arrived here'.[26] Arunachalam and others like him across the colonial world, particularly in Asia, Africa, the Pacific and Caribbean, found that their political liberalisms that acknowledged a place within the empire was still frustrated and stunted. They were confounded at the settler and British denial of their country's and people's entry into the hallowed community of 'autonomous' Dominion states within the empire. For they knew, as A. V. Dicey, admitted to Keith, that 'Dominion' was shorthand for 'colonial independence', but as yet restricted to the white communities of Canada, Australia, New Zealand, Newfoundland, South Africa and the Irish Free State.[27] Indeed much could be taken from the cultural and geopolitical underpinnings of the revered Dominion constitutional status since, as few appreciated, other than allegiance to the Crown it mandated few other constitutional requirements. Reginald Coupland argued that Dominion status did not even mean having to function domestically under a parliamentary government.[28] In such circumstances admission criteria to the Dominion club was wilfully murky.

Keith, as a devout Indianist recorded his disappointment that there was still a strong instinct to keep pushing away 'such a day' and judged that India at the 1926 conference had 'fared badly in the constitutional discussion' and 'remained excluded from the constitutional discussions of the Expert committees'.[29] Keith had witnessed at first hand the gap between rhetoric and practice. Having been a civil servant at the Colonial Office and serving as secretary to several imperial conferences before taking his academic post in Edinburgh in 1914, he knew the realities. Indeed, in almost all his books, of which there are many, he inserted after his name and academic positions 'Formerly Assistant Secretary to the

Imperial Conference'. Another towering imperial and constitutional historian from the period was Coupland himself, the second holder of the Beit Chair in Colonial History at the University of Oxford. Like Keith, he was 'involved'. Serving on commissions in Palestine and India as well as authoring reports on contemporary issues affecting governance and reform across the Empire-Commonwealth, Coupland saw himself as using history to inform constitutional reform and spread the virtue of the Commonwealth outside his academic work with a range of connections and networks from the Cabinet to the Colonies well facilitated from the imperial cloisters of All Souls. Not all were convinced. The future first prime minister of Trinidad and Tobago, Eric Williams, would write in his 1944 seminal book *Capitalism and Slavery* that Coupland's presentation of British liberal imperial progress witnessed by the moral need to end slavery was 'merely poetic sentimentality translated into modern history'.[30] In his inaugural lecture as chair in 1921 Coupland also concentrated on the issue of race, nationality and the extension of the British Commonwealth to all peoples within the empire. Indeed, he went so far as to argue just years after the Treaty of Versailles and devastation of war that the British Commonwealth that he variously described as a 'miscellany of nations', 'motley company' and a 'unique experiment in international relations' could become an example to the world and become a 'British League of Nations'. If the British Commonwealth and Empire, however, were in this 'experiment' to fall apart and embrace narrowness and 'less generous ideals' it would then 'split into a chaos of alien sovereignties' and 'the hope of the world will be dimmed'. Interestingly reversing the judgement on Britain's constitution Coupland believed that in the British Commonwealth it is the constitutions that are written unlike their histories.[31]

As W. David McIntyre assesses, historians of this period which saw rapid constitutional change found themselves 'both as participants and interpreters'. This meant that for figures like Lionel Curtis, who believed in a great union or federation of Britain and the Commonwealth that history was a 'teleological progression of civilisations and constitutions to be manipulated for the cause'.[32] The Commonwealth for the dynamic Curtis was a rebuke to imperialism and empire since it ideally could bring shared government by uniting 'an Australian native, a London free-thinker, a Ugandan gentlemen, a Rand negro, an Egyptian merchant and a Singapore Chinamen' who lived under 'one rule and one peace'. For such historians, as Wm. Roger Louis argues, imperial history was inseparable 'from the perspective of British constitutions and administration'.[33]

The Australian Sir Keith Hancock was another who gravitated and shaped such thinking of the British Commonwealth as a model for world government. While based at All Souls in Oxford he was invited by Arnold Toynbee at Chatham House in the early 1930s to write what would become one of his lasting historical legacies the first *Survey of British Commonwealth Affairs*.[34] As Hancock wrote in a letter to Toynbee when drafting the final sections of the first volume, 'I am anxious in this last chapter to make the reader feel that the fate of the British Commonwealth is interwoven with the fate of world order'.[35] Commonwealth constitutional history became a way of collectivising a British race mantra that benevolently *guided* the world in its image and interest. The ambiguities of imperial and Commonwealth government meant its virtues could be proclaimed loudly without clarifying the constitutional necessities for attaining independence. Hancock himself, like other historians and civil servants of the period, preferred the word 'self-government' over that of 'independence', and even then this was dampened down with the proviso that self-government should be practiced 'wherever it can be followed'.[36] As Roger Louis notes, for Hancock a favourite phrase was 'sovereign equality' and seeing the Commonwealth as early as 1930 as 'a cooperative confederacy'.[37] Yet for Hancock this was always to be under the leadership of Britain and the settler Dominions, however multiracial the Commonwealth would become since Britishness and race counted more in this conception than country.[38] The problem of promoting the empire's constitutional 'procession' to self-government, as Alfred Zimmern called it, was that for too many communities in the interwar years it was not a procession, but a frustrating ordeal of fits and starts.[39] As Hancock himself recognised during the 1930s in Malta, for example, 'for a hundred years Malta's march had been like Sisyphus purposefully pushing his stone up the hill'.[40] As S. Gopal notes, All Souls during the inter-war years had an astonishing influence on British and colonial policy and constitutional ideas since it included aside from Hancock important figures like Leo Amery, Coupland, Curtis, Lord Halifax, Geoffrey Dawson, Penderel Moon, Sir John Simon, and Sir Maurice Gwyer and even included a fellow, L. Rushbrook Williams, who acted from Oxford as the foreign minister of the Indian princely state of Patiala despite it not having any foreign relations.[41] Whatever else high table at All Souls and other comparable bastions proved fertile ground for constitutional idealism. The ideas of world government bubbled in such places with Commonwealth thinking with its premise that this potential force in international affairs would march, naturally, in the interest of Britain and the white dominions. Such scholars and politicians saw themselves as divine custodians of the 'highest civilisation'.[42] Hancock's biographical subject, Jan Smuts, was another who knew how to smoothly pass the port at such tables and enthusiastically promoted his own Commonwealth vision of liberal world government, again under the leadership of the white dominions without brooking any interference or admitting contradiction in the domestic racial policies of South Africa. This was borne, as Mark Mazower argues, from an anxiety of the 'restless peoples of Asia and Africa' which led Smuts and others to imagine the British Commonwealth as a constitutional solution of government to bring together the 'civilised peoples' in a parliamentary harmony to administer the backward world and preserve their own.[43]

Hancock, whose historical scholarship ranged wide and deep over the empire, never, at his own admission, mastered India. Yet he recognised that after the second world war India would replace Canada as the 'pacemaker of constitutional and political change' in the Commonwealth and Empire.[44] If Hancock and Lord Linlithgow are to be believed Gandhi admitted in 1941 that he had never read the Government of India Act 1935, perhaps the most complex constitutional document ever to emanate from the British parliament, it was also the longest piece of legislation ever produced from Westminster. Supposedly Gandhi 'discovered to his surprise that it gave to a united India all the essentials of self-government'. Had he known earlier, according to the famously hardnosed Viceroy Linlithgow, who was no friend of the Mahatma, the option would have been taken and conflict with the British might have been avoided. A story well repeated by Hancock to other sympathetic ears.[45] This reveals a very warped and erroneous view of Indian history, but whatever else the reading of constitutional history, in its short or longue durée coverage, held ramifications for imperial and Commonwealth affairs and the post-war world.

Post-War and Professional Commonwealth Constitutional History

C.A. Bayly commented on how even after the second world war History departments, if they had Asianists, were often educated by those who had direct experience of the colonial empire and imparted their 'assumptions' to a new generation. While those that studied the Dominions were regaled in the Seeley tradition of the expansion of English civilisation. In this 'Commonwealth history was the history of progressive British settlement and constitutional benevolence' while Asian history was largely 'a narrative which had served to make European dominance appear the natural consequence of the weakness of oriental government' and the collapse of once notable civilisations owing to fatal flaws of the oriental.[46] Arguably the most dramatic charge in post-war constitutional history was to provide guidance in the creation of the Indian republic's constitution. India's freedom movement and her prominence in the empire meant that all eyes were on Delhi as not only the most important, but also the first non-white territory to emerge from the British Empire to take its independence. Constitution-making was critical and constitutional history essential to this unique task. India's Constituent Assembly started its work in 1946 and history – colonial and constitutional – was everywhere. The complexity of India's constitutional history befitted a continent that was the most populous colonial possession in history. Scores of scholars, charlatans and politicians wrote histories of British India and almost inevitably the power and the state was the core of their story. If the British colonial power in India produced a jumble of constitutional arrangements that mystified all but the most dedicated the task of crafting a new constitution for what was to be the world's largest democracy would be no easy task. Constitutional history was required and needed to be carefully sifted and pragmatically used to shape the newly independent state. Scholar-Civil Servants in early independent India like Sir Alladi Krishnaswami

Aiyer, Sir Girja Bajpai, Sir C. P. Ramaswami Iyer, V. P. Menon, Sir B. N. Rau, H. M. Seervai and M. C. Setalvad openly drew upon historical political and constitutional precedents from imperial and Commonwealth history to abet their preferences towards constitutional forms and reforms they perceived not only India's due, but also best suited for a New India. This erudite brood was active and agile in the deployment of historical analogy and a wide reading of common law to craft a constitutional order, both in the colonial and post-colonial periods. India by drawing on imperial, colonial, Westminster and Commonwealth precedents as well as making key deviations of its own became an *Eastminster*, as did many other states in the region.[47] The 1950 Indian constitution that the Assembly produced was soon lauded by the world, but especially by its citizenry. India would soon find itself, like the nineteenth-century English historians mentioned earlier, with scholars congratulating the country on its constitutional history, with the story patriotically spun into the nationalist fabric of India.[48] Nationalist history made the constitution the inevitable result of an anti-colonial struggle and the exclusive due of Indian autochthony – to use a word popularised by Wheare in constitutional studies[49] - without recognising the soils used from other cultures and influences including, obviously less popularly, the colonial period that clearly contributed to the Indian constitution.

The history of India's constitution-making period in the Assembly and its debates was even perceived as popular enough to produce in 2014 a well-received ten-part miniseries *Samvidhaan: The Making of the Constitution of India* in Hindi and launched in parliament by President Pranab Mukherjee. However, Commonwealth constitutional history is yet to catch on as a popular film genre. The drama of the transfer of power did place Commonwealth scholars at the fore of the scene through the need for historical accounts to understand the end of empire and the beginning of new and restored original states to use the distinction of C. H. Alexandrowicz.[50] Independent states needed constitutions and constitutional history from the Commonwealth was never more in vogue. In 1960 the Ghanaian Constituent Assembly, for example, glowing quotes from Ivor Jennings' *Approach to Self-Government* found their way into *Hansard* thanks to the Leader of the Opposition and a Parliamentary Secretary to the Government.[51] Even for the Dominions where there was no identifiable flag lowering ceremony a rummage in constitutional history periodically was carried out to see if anything useful could be found for the purposes of the national story and identity. Michael King in his popular 2003 history of New Zealand argued that November 25 be treated like an independence day due it being the date the country ratified the Statute of Westminster in 1947 – an opinion shared by then deputy prime minister Sir Michael Cullen in the 2000s.[52] There was an active need for constitutional history in the post-war era for those many territories in Africa still under colonial rule. Margery Perham prepared an annotated reading list on 'Colonial Government' and stated in her 1950 introduction that 'It is, of course, impossible to understand the government of the colonies to-day without considerable historical knowledge of the conditions, purposes, and principles which determined their earlier development'.[53]

In this context the early to mid-twentieth century constitutional history writers became constitution-makers, sometimes in reverse order. Commonwealth scholars like Wheare, Hancock, Keith, De Smith, Forsey, Jennings, Perham, Rau, David J. Murray, Vincent Harlow, Ronald Robinson and others were actively called upon to provide their constitutional and historical expertise to countries and commissions across the Commonwealth world. A felicity in history helped. In fact, the constitutional history of the British Empire and Commonwealth could be used as a vast arsenal from which deadly political and legal blows would be inflicted upon opponents. History wars by other means. In Pakistan, for example, in 1954 Ghulam Muhammad, the Governor-General, dissolved, without advice, a legislature that dared put a bill for assent that would limit his powers. The president of the Constituent Assembly challenged the decision in the courts and eventually Sir Ivor Jennings arrived offering precedents not only from other Commonwealth jurisdictions, but even from English rulers Oliver Cromwell, Charles II, William, Mary, and James II to justify the use of autocratic Crown power against parliament in a predominantly Muslim South Asian state in the twentieth century. Three centuries of desuetude of such power and the near consensus of this in the historical literature was no barrier for the Federal Court siding with autocracy over democracy.[54] Supposedly ceremonial heads of state based on the British model saw in their constitutional history and local traditions great power, which they often felt the need to exercise and protect. This often led to political conflict such as in Malaysia with the Sultans and Prime Minister Mahathir Mohamad[55] and the propensity of Governors-General in the Pacific islands to act in extraordinary ways during not infrequent constitutional crises that have beset the region.[56] Constitutional history arrayed for such improbable political manoeuvres not only stretched the use of history, but also laid a powerful legacy how history of this kind can be manipulated with very real consequences. From post-war Guyana to Sierra Leone, from Australia to Fiji constitutional history was employed for successful skirmishes against elected governments.[57]

Despite Colonial Officials arrogantly assuming that few understood the tenets of the British constitutionalism, what could compel the Nkrumah supporting Ghana Representative Assembly of around 3000 people to pass the following resolution in 1950?:

> That the people of the Gold Coast be granted immediate self-government by the British Government, that is full Dominion status within the British Commonwealth of Nations based on the Statute of Westminster. That the assembly respectfully demand immediate grant and sanction of full self-government for the chiefs and people of the Gold Coast.[58]

Nkrumah, and leaders like him, across the colonial world not only were highly aware of constitutional developments across the Empire and Commonwealth, but also keenly appropriated and absorbed constitutional history, which enabled a political vocabulary to parley with the Colonial Power. Using terms like 'Dominion status' or 'Self-government', and alluding to critical milestones like the Statute of Westminster, showed a shrewd understanding that displaying historical knowledge of advances in the British Empire provided cogent arguments and precedents that intensified the case for freedom. Cascades of constitutional dicta fell eloquently from the mouths of freedom fighters, whether in legislatures, market squares, Governor's residences or on release from prison. History, of course, did also show that the exposition of constitutional history to argue a point did not translate into its acceptance.

The post-war Commonwealth evidenced many remarkable transnational evocations of constitutional history. In the mid to late 1940s arguments made by G. G. Ponnambalam in the Ceylon State Council and to the Colonial Secretary advocated statutory representation for the Tamil minority listing historical precedents from asymmetric compromises for French Canadians in 1867, the Maori Representation Act of the same year in New Zealand or the position of Muslims from Cyprus to Mauritius as reasons for such protection. The Commission instructed to propose constitutional reforms for the island instead believed British constitutional history showed the opposite. His Majesty's Government agreed and the scheme was held to be derogatory to the history of self-government by subjecting it to parochialism unworthy of modern democracy.[59] Kamisese Mara looked to imperial and Commonwealth constitutional history to show what could happen if indigenous Fijians were not careful concerning land. In a speech to his followers and allies he stated 'We do not have to look for the answers' of what happens if native people were not protected since the sad historical examples of the Maori, Aborigines, Dyaks, Nagas, Zulus, and 'Kaffirs' in their native lands was more than enough.[60] As Donal Lowry has argued in a further case of transnational constitutional history the Northern Irish and Southern Rhodesians kept detailed notes of each other's history and relations with Britain seeing mutually beneficial lessons on how to deal with perfidious Albion.[61] Julius Nyerere, as Ellen Feingold argues, sought to place on the early bench of independent Tanzania black judges from West Africa and the West Indies including having a Canadian educated Dominican, Telford Georges, serving in Trinidad and Tobago to come to Dar-es-Salaam and become the first non-white Chief Justice of the territory. An awareness of the comparable constitutional and imperial history of these parts of the Commonwealth and Colonial Empire helped foster such appointments since they simultaneously gave symbolic importance and crucial expertise that made such transnational movements plausible.[62] Indeed the constitutional history of Britain was by no means the sole reference for the empire and Commonwealth. The Singaporean Chief Minister, David Marshall, like others, saw the constitutional and political history of India as critical for the non-settler possessions in their path to independence. Marshall told reporters in Bombay in 1955

> 'To us who live far away, India has been a midwife of the rebirth of Asia and the vanguard of Asian freedom. I want to sit at Mr Nehru's feet to learn as much as I can and absorb all I can'

He wanted to get self-government 'at a quicker pace' and like many saw in the recent constitutional and political history of India key lessons for his land.[63] Sir John Kerr in February 1975, was able, at their request, to discuss the position of the Governor-General of Australia to the Indian Law Institute and converse freely about the constitutional conundrum in Canberra with the Malaysian Prime Minister, Tun Abdul Razak, later that year in October where Prime Minister Gough Whitlam joked about whether the prime minister or governor-general would get to the phone first to the Queen to sack the other.[64] A shared understanding of Commonwealth constitutional history enabled Kerr to talk about such matters affecting the Australian Crown and Executive to an audience in the Indian Republic and to the prime minister of an indigenous Islamic monarchy in South East Asia knowing that for his interlocutors the crisis of what might seem of obscure and esoteric domestic detail would in fact be understood through history, education, experience but also a reading of shared imperial constitutional history that made an understanding of Australia's dramatic 1975 situation much more than just politely comprehensible. Constitutional framing and constitutional crises were often the periods that generated the most interest in, and need for, Commonwealth constitutional history.

Post 'British' Commonwealth Constitutional History

Over 70 years ago the name 'British Commonwealth of Nations' became officially retired with the recent inclusion of the new South Asian states of India, Pakistan and Ceylon as independent members. The name 'Commonwealth' eventually emerged. The dropping of 'British' was a deliberate ploy to promote the idea that the Commonwealth was an international organisation with a reach beyond London that embraced the wider world. Nicholas Mansergh believed that the 'the ideal of the Commonwealth remains the government of men by themselves'. As such he did not mourn at the dropping of 'British', but did regret the loss 'of Nations'.[65] Commonwealth constitutional history is indelibly linked to British and imperial constitutional history, but it is also more than that. Too often attention is drawn to the imperial and Commonwealth metropolis to the cost of understanding, comparing and using what might be described as trans-Commonwealth history, the Commonwealth world or just Commonwealth history since its span should be implicit. As D. A. Low put it in towards the end of his inaugural lecture in 1984 as Smuts Professor of the History of the British Commonwealth (renamed too on his retirement in October 1994 to the Smuts Professorship of Commonwealth History, a move Low lobbied for), the 'difficulty seems to lie in perceiving with the necessary clarity that the Commonwealth is no longer a British institution'.[66] Commonwealth history is the same and its constitutional branch no different. Global history needs to uncover the vast material available from Commonwealth constitutional history. Linda Colley's plea for the place of constitutions in global history is especially germane for the unparalleled constitutional dimension during the age of global decolonisation and in turn map its indelible mark across the post-colonial world.

> Constitutions illumine the extent of transnational and transcontinental political transfer over time and in different locations, and do so with rich empirical and individual detail. No less significantly, they help reveal the limits and tensions of transnational and trans-continental influences and borrowings, and how layering operates between the local and the universal ... Global historians have often neglected political history in favour of economic history, because the former subject has traditionally been organized around nation states. But tracing the spread of constitutions shows how the political, too, has been interwoven with transnational influences, aspirations, and pressures.[67]

'Constitutional Decolonisation', a term used by Trevor Munroe describing British withdrawal from Jamaica[68], was a crucial process in the lives of most states including the former Dominions. An unearthing of all these states' constitutional history will of course show British roots, but they also can shed light on other influential traces. To use an example of Dennis Austin's, the introduction of quasi-cabinet government to the Gold Coast in 1950 openly drew on the innovative 1931 executive council reforms in Ceylon[69], which in turn, as Colonial Service Officer John Smith recounts[70], was a popular idea in the Pacific territories in the 1970s and yet direct constitutional and historical comparisons between Ghana, Sri Lanka and the Pacific are near non-existent in contemporary imperial or Commonwealth history. A key and glaring need is to get better historical understanding of the impact of constitutional ideas and institutions on everyday people as well and in addition a greater sense of the public's impact on constitutional government and colonial authority. The question Carl Bridge and H. V. Brasted pose on how much did the subalterns and the bazaar alter the constitutional dynamic of the Raj through the force they heaped on the Indian National Congress, Muslim League and the British, remains largely unanswered as it does for the rest of the British Empire in the course of decolonisation.[71] This perspective is sorely required. A welcome exception is the growing recognition of the importance of indigenous history, which cannot be properly understood without the constitutional element. Indigenous history, for example, in, and covering, Australia, Canada, and New Zealand has seen a flourishing interest in recent years. No longer a backwater or the preserve of older patronising accounts of settler colonialism the serious historians that approach this subject and its enmeshment with colonialism utilise imperial and Commonwealth constitutional history to not only aid the comparative history element of their work, but also to uncover the mechanisms and heart of the relationship between indigenous people and colonialism. Without constitutional history, the land, the rights, the violence, the political relationships and the injustice of indigenous history would be incomplete and less powerful. It also has an explicit purpose in trying achieve redress for societies too long unsung or taken seriously in the citadels of power.[72] Indigenous history also serves to remind of the constitutional importance of treaties, delegations, petitioning and political culture as well as the that most Commonwealth of institutions the Crown, which as J. R. Miller argues of the First Nations of Canada still pervades the lineage, protections and protests of the indigenous polity – patriated or not.[73] No longer called Dominion history the comparative study of constitutions and cultures of Australia, Canada and New Zealand fizz with new objectives and concerns. It is hoped, however, that unlike their predecessors, the new wave of historians covering what was once termed the Britannic realms or settler states, will look to other parts of the Commonwealth to give further grist to their scholarly mills since they will find comparable experiences that resonate in places such as Burma, Malaysia, Southern Arabia, Nigeria, Guyana, South Africa, North-eastern India or the case John Lonsdale highlights in the 'Ornamental Constitutionalism' of the Gikuyu people in their search for protection of 'Victoria the Good' and her successors against the settlers in Kenya.[74]

Rich constitutional sources abound for the purposes of investigating current historical concerns such as citizenship, federalism, accommodation or exclusion of minorities, individual and collective rights, separatism, representation, transnational political schemes, power-sharing, and the style and substance of democracy. So much of this can be found from the academic labours of one person. Nicholas Mansergh is a Commonwealth scholar who should be more visible in the research of these topics. An argument could certainly be made to retrospectively place him, an Anglo-Irishman born in 1910 near Tipperary, as the first Head of the Commonwealth Historians. Perhaps it was being Irish born that propelled him to take an interest in constitutional history. Ireland during his lifetime, spanning as it did most of the twentieth century, was at the forefront of constitutional debates that affected the lives and passions for both islands touching the Irish Sea and beyond. Before he was thirty he had written three key books on Ireland (North and South) that traced its government and history expertly yet gilded with wit and humour.[75] After Oxford and serving during the war at the Dominions Office where his constitutional history interest could run with the needs of reality he became in 1947 the first Abe Bailey Research Chair in British Commonwealth Relations at the Royal Institute of International Affairs. The same year he attended in July the inter Asian conference in New Delhi and was transfixed with the possibilities of the Commonwealth and unlike many of his colleagues welcomed the entrance of India and the non-white Commonwealth world. Elected in 1953 as the first Smuts Chair in the History of the British Commonwealth at Cambridge, he published key constitutional and historical works on the High Politics covering the transformation of empire to Commonwealth including the two volume *Survey of British Commonwealth Affairs* supported by a two volume documentary collection covering from the 1930s to the 1950s.[76] Clearly undeterred by difficult historical and political cases he produced books and papers covering racial policies in South Africa, partitions in India and Ireland, and the British experiment of responsible government. Mansergh, who would become Master of St John's, Cambridge, wrote *The Commonwealth Experience* which most likely remains the most popular Commonwealth history written.[77] His most monumental service to Commonwealth constitutional history, however, was to be Editor-in-Chief of the extraordinary and weighty (in every sense) twelve volume *Transfer of Power* series that documented the end of British rule in India from 1942 to the end in August 1947.[78] For Commonwealth constitutional historians, these remain the pinnacle of the documentary genre and continue to be indispensable to South Asian scholars covering the unique and bewilderingly complex end of the British Raj. Till the end of his long life in 1991 he was a welcome visitor in the seminar halls of New Delhi. Mansergh's example led to Hugh Tinker's excellent documentary volumes on Burma in the early 1980s.[79] A decade or so later D. A. Low and S. R. Ashton, who worked for both the India and Burma sets, consciously evoked these collections when beginning the *British Documents on the End of Empire* project and series, which contains general volumes on British government policies regarding empire from 1925 to the 1970s as well as individual country volumes expertly introduced and edited by specialists and all teeming with invaluable detail and range of striking importance.[80] Fortunately, collections and sources are steadily emerging that rectify the blind spot of the above collections and give an equivalent view of local sources. As Saul Dubow recently argued with the illustration of South Africa for Commonwealth history, much can be gained from inverting the examination and looking at the Commonwealth 'from the outside in' and comparing nation based perspectives.[81] The dwindling Britishness acutely observed by James Curran and Stuart Ward must be replaced, as they do in the case of Australia, with a greater historical awareness of local experiences of empire and Commonwealth.[82] The constitutional experience is no small part of this. India has produced the *Towards Freedom* series which unearths Indian voices and perspectives hitherto woefully absent.[83] Canada and Australia's state supported documentary collections covering their constitutional and diplomatic relations with the world are another example.[84] Mark Hickford recently argued that constitutional history is essential to understand territorial and constitutional design in New Zealand and refreshingly seeks the local and indigenous history to do so over the usual preference for canonical texts from the English afar.[85] Countries while not formally members of the Commonwealth like Burma, Ireland, territories in the Near and Middle East along with the many 'indirect' lands affected by British imperial power need to be drawn back into the Commonwealth story and vice-versa, especially since their complicated constitutional histories and links with the British Empire and Commonwealth states need telling.[86] Indeed it is easy to forget how often Commonwealth constitutional practice lingered despite outward rejections – almost wholly for practical historical reasons. As the Irish assistant secretary of External Affairs, Frederick Boland, noted in a 1944 memorandum on the Taoiseach's right to advise a dissolution at a time when Ireland was a quasi-republic under De Valera and conspicuously neutral during the second world war:

> The parliamentary law of this State derives, like that of most democratically-ruled States, from the practice of the British "Mother of Parliaments". In our case, owing to our close association for so long with Great Britain and, latterly, with the British Dominions, we automatically turn to British and Dominion precedents in many of the constitutional problems with which we find ourselves from time to time faced.[87]

More scholarship is needed, especially, to understand local involvements and influence on empire and after, but the pressing importance is to convince historians of empire to use all these carefully collated and accessible editions of skilfully annotated primary sources and produce challenging new histories of empire and decolonisation sure of the constitutional dimension. Some contemporary legal scholars have been quicker than modern historians to appreciate the potential value of the vast reservoir of transnational constitutional ideas and thinking that the Commonwealth can provide with arguably greater significance than the hitherto focus Lawyers (and others) give to Europe and the USA as a source of thinking.[88] While the absence of constitutional historians concerned with the British Empire and Commonwealth remain formally few there are a select band of Law scholars who openly search and incorporate Commonwealth history when arguing legal issues before them.[89] The courtesy is rarely reciprocated by historians using law.[90] Constitutions and their history are too important to be left to lawyers alone.

Conclusion

Writing in 1979, A. F. Madden reflected from Oxford 'I have little doubt that I will be the last Reader in Commonwealth Government'. His Friday morning teaching seminar on imperial and Commonwealth constitutional sources was suspended that year with only a solitary New Zealander turning up.[91] Forty years on there are no posts in Commonwealth Government, and hardly any in Commonwealth History in Britain or abroad. Things have changed. As late as the 1970s as Ronald Hyam confided that 'Even if one's colleagues did not necessarily expect a personal commitment to the imperial idea, everyone else invariably assumed an imperial historian must be a true-blue flag-waving "Land of Hope and Glory" polemicist'.[92] Most imperial and Commonwealth scholars had been servants in some way of the British Empire perhaps in the armed forces or Colonial Service and there were also a few in the field who fought against British colonial rule creating a very real and formative connection with their subject. This is no longer the situation in the twenty-first century. Flag waving is not advisable and neither is incinerating them. Perhaps this creates an opportunity to interrogate the constitutional history of the Commonwealth more dispassionately, though ever alive to its contemporary influence.

A. G. Hopkins has stated that earlier historical delineations 'to define imperial history solely by the legal status of the countries formally connected to Britain' is today rightly unthinkable.[93] Commonwealth constitutional history is broader than that. Defined at the beginning of this article as being concerned with the study of the sources, legitimisations and control of state power through the prism, shared experience and consequences of British rule both direct and indirect it does have its proponents in the discipline. Indeed, to confine the focus to active Commonwealth scholars of Africa such as Saul Dubow, Philip Murphy, Sue Onslow and Sarah Stockwell covering thorny issues respectively as South Africa's apartheid and racial policies, the complexities and complications of the short-lived Central African Federation, the emergence of Zimbabwe, or commercial and business influence in the Gold Coast the incorporation of Commonwealth constitutional history is axiomatic and vital to their impressive accounts.[94] While it is far from true to say 'the Commonwealth strikes back', there are, nonetheless reasons to see its significance and ability to inform historical and political themes in ways it has not done so for decades. The constitutional factor in the study of imperialism and post-colonialism over the twentieth century especially and its bearings on the state's power need, however, to return to the historian's toolkit after being suitably reconditioned for modern purposes. Giovanni Sartori observed that English constitutional scholars unlike their European and American counterparts 'appear more inclined to address themselves to an MP by saying "you could" rather than "you cannot".'[95] There is even more that you can say with post 1918 Commonwealth constitutional history. It just needs to be written.

Notes

1. Sartori, "Constitutionalism: A Preliminary Discussion,"857.
2. Darwin, "Britain's Empires," 20.
3. Madden, "Commonwealth Government at Oxford," 39.
4. Bentley, *Modernizing England's Past,* 19–20.
5. Behm, *Imperial History and the Global Politics of Exclusion,* 14–16.
6. James, *The Life of Captain Cipriani,* 170–193.
7. Mansergh, *The Commonwealth Experience,* 55.
8. For example, Vincent Harlow, Beit Professor in his report to a constitution commission in Sudan in the early 1950s pressed a Dicey inspired framework on rights being applied to the vast North African territory. See Parkinson, *Bills of Rights and Decolonization,* 61–63.

9. Madden, "Some Origins and Purposes in the Formation of British Colonial Government," 2.
10. Hyam, *Understanding the British Empire*, 19 and passim.
11. Latham, *The Law and the Commonwealth*, 513.
12. King, *The British Constitution*, 15–38.
13. McIntyre, *The Britannic Vision*, 19–62.
14. For more detail on Keith's life see Shinn Jr, *Arthur Berriedale Keith 1879-1944*.
15. I gratefully thank Dr Donal Coffey for bringing this collection to my attention. Rao, ed., *Select Constitutions of the World*.
16. Virginia and Leonard Woolf published it in their Hogarth Press.
17. For an introduction to his Commonwealth constitutional writings see Kumarasingham, "Introduction."
18. Burroughs, "The Imperial Gospel According to Frederick Madden,"110–134.
19. Brock, "Introduction: Freddie Madden," 3.
20. Low, ed., *Constitutional Heads and Political Crises*; and Butler and Low, eds., *Sovereigns and Surrogates*.
21. A quote and point also made by Richard Drayton about Bayly. Drayton, "Where does the World Historian Write From? Objectivity, Moral Conscience and the Past and Present of Imperialism," 671–685.
22. His untimely death in April 2015 robbed us of his planned keynote for the workshop on Political Liberalism in and beyond Empire in Colombo in December 2015 from which the articles of this special issue arise. Chris' paper was to examine the ideas of political liberalism and their impact on Nehru, Jinnah and Senanayake in South Asia and compare with those of Kenyatta, Nyreree and Kaunda in Africa. We bubbled with excitement, but it was not to be.
23. Keith, *Responsible Government in the Dominions*, 1224–1225.
24. See Mantena, *Alibis of Empire*.
25. Seeley, *The Expansion of England*, 176–177.
26. Arunachalam, *Our Political Needs*, 26–27.
27. A.V. Dicey to A. B. Keith, 24 June 1912 cited in McIntyre, "Clio and Britannia's Lost Dream," 517 and fn. 4
28. Reginald Coupland, *The Times*, 20 February 1935 quoted in Robinson, "Autochthony and the Transfer of Power," 257.
29. Keith, *Responsible Government in the Dominions*, 1231.
30. Williams, *Slavery and Capitalism*, 45.
31. Coupland, *The Study of the British Commonwealth*, 9–26 Lionel Curtis writing in 1919 quoted in Lavin, *From Empire to International Commonwealth*, 159.
32. McIntyre, "Clio and Britannia's Lost Dream," 518, 519.
33. Louis, "Introduction," 27.
34. Hancock, *Survey of British Commonwealth Affairs – Volume I* and *Survey of British Commonwealth Affairs – Volume II*, part I 1940 and part II 1942.
35. Cotton, *The Australian School of International Relations*, 130.
36. Davidson, *The Three-Cornered Life*, 270.
37. Louis, "Sir Keith Hancock and the British Empire, 939, 946–947.
38. Hopkins, "Rethinking Decolonization," 217–18.
39. Miller, "The Commonwealth and the World Order: The Zimmern Vision and After,"159–60.
40. Ibid., 160.
41. Gopal, "All Souls and India, 1921–47," 86–106; and more generally see Symonds, *Oxford and Empire*.

42. Ibid., 86.
43. Mazower, *Governing the World*, 131–33.
44. Hancock, "Nicholas Mansergh," 8.
45. See Louis, "Sir Keith Hancock and the British Empire," 955, fn 84
46. Bayly, "The Orient: British Historical Writing about Asia since 1890," 89–90.
47. Kumarasingham, "Eastminster,"1–35.
48. Arvind Elangovan has observed this tendency and laments its cost on the study Indian constitutional history. See Arvind Elangovan, "The Making of the Indian Constitution: A Case for a Non-Nationalist Approach," 1–10.
49. Wheare, *The Constitutional Structure of the Commonwealth*, 89–113.
50. Alexandrowicz, "New and Original States," 390–403.
51. Robinson, "Constitutional Autochthony in Ghana,"46; and fn 25. The quote was Jennings' famous 'every country must have a Constitution to suit itself, a Constitution made to measure, not bought off the rack'.
52. King, *The Penguin History of New Zealand*, 420.
53. Perham, *Colonial Government*, xi–xii.
54. Kumarasingham, "A Transnational Actor on a Dramatic Stage, 33–56.
55. See for example Stockwell, "Princes and Politicians," 182–97. Further episodes have occurred with Mahathir's resumption of the premiership in May 2018.
56. Fraenkel, "Governors-general during Pacific Island Constitutional Crises and the Role of the Crown,"1–22.
57. See D. A. Low fn 19 above
58. "Draft report on disturbances in the Gold Coast, 1950", CO 53715812, no 1 in Rathbone, ed., *Ghana – Part I, 1941–1952, British Documents on the End of Empire*, 396–97.
59. 'Letter from Mr G. G. Ponnambalam to Mr Hall, 3 November 1945 in De Silva, ed., *Sri Lanka – Part II, 1945–48*, 143–46.
60. "Fiji Special Branch report of a meeting on 16 January. Annex: Translation of presidential address by Ratu Mara", 18 January 1965 in Lal, ed., *Fiji, British Documents on the End of Empire*, 200–206.
61. Lowry, "Ulster resistance and loyalist rebellion in the Empire."
62. See Feingold, *Colonial Justice and Decolonization in the High Court of Tanzania, 1920–1971*.
63. *Times of India*, 6 December 1955 in Tan, *Marshall of Singapore*, 332.
64. See Kelly, *November 1975 – The Inside Story of Australia's Greatest Political Crisis*; and Kerr, *Matters of Judgement*.
65. Harkness, "Philip Nicholas Seton Mansergh," 415–30.
66. Low, *Eclipse of Empire*, 21.
67. Colley, "Writing Constitutions and Writing World History," 175–76.
68. Munroe, *The Politics of Constitutional Decolonization*.
69. Austin, "The Transfer of Power," 4.
70. Smith, *An Island in the Autumn*, 182.
71. Brasted and Bridge, "The Transfer of Power in South Asia: An Historiographical Review," 114.
72. See an important recent intervention by McKenna, "Moment of Truth – History and Australia's Future." Other key accounts and proponent include Ford, *Settler Sovereignty*; Johnson, *The Land is Our History – Indigeneity, Law, and the Settler State*; Hickford, *Lords of the Land: Indigenous Property Rights and the Jurisprudence of Empire*.
73. Miller, "Petitioning the Great White Mother." Also see Miller, "The Aboriginal Peoples and the Crown"; and Arnot, "The Honour of the First Nations."

74. Lonsdale, "Ornamental Constitutionalism in Africa," 87–103.
75. This Irish context is highlighted by Harkness, "Nicholas Mansergh (1910–1991)," 87–95.
76. Mansergh, *Survey of British Commonwealth Affairs: Volume I* and *Volume II: Problems of Wartime Co-operation and Post-War Change 1939–1952* [1958] and *Documents and Speeches on Commonwealth Affairs 1931–1952* [1953] in two volumes all London: Oxford University Press
77. Mansergh, *The Commonwealth Experience*. Later revised and enlarged to two volumes in 1982 with Macmillan
78. Mansergh, Editor-in-Chief, *Constitutional Relations between Britain and India*.
79. Tinker, *Constitutional Relations between Britain and Burma*.
80. These treasure filled volumes are now (almost) all available online at www.bdeep.org thanks to Institute of Commonwealth Studies, University of London. The volume editors are an array of excellent Commonwealth scholars who take constitutional history seriously: S. R. Ashton, Sarah Stockwell, Ronald Hyam, David Goldsworthy, Wm. Roger Louis, Richard Rathbone, K. M. de Silva, A. J. Stockwell, John Kent, Douglas H. Johnson, David Killingray, Martin Lynn, Philip Murphy, Brij V. Lal, Simon C. Smith and Anne Thurston.
81. Dubow, "The Commonwealth and South Africa," 305.
82. Curran and Ward, *The Unknown Nation*.
83. *Towards Freedom - Documents on the movement for Independence in India*. Several volumes already published covering a single year edited by various Indian scholars and brought out by the Indian Council of Historical Research and Oxford University Press sine 1999.
84. *Documents on Canadian External Relations* have several volumes and varied topics published by the Canadian Government since 1967 and similarly *Documents on Australian Foreign Policy* published by the Department of Foreign Affairs and Trade since 2001.
85. Hickford, "Designing Constitutions in Britain's Mid-Nineteenth Century Empire."
86. In Ireland's case, recent work by Donal Coffey and Thomas Mohr complement work done before by Stephen Howe and Donal Lowry.
87. Lowry, "New Ireland, Old Empire and the Outside World, 1922–49," 190.
88. See for instance Lino, "Albert Venn Dicey and the Constitutional Theory of Empire," 751–80; De "'A Peripatetic World Court' Cosmopolitan Courts, Nationalist Judges and the Indian Appeal to the Privy Council," 821–51; and Harding, "The 'Westminster Model' Constitution Overseas," 143–66.
89. Examples of Law academics with open interest Commonwealth constitutional history include John Allison, Peter Cane, Rohit De, Shaunnagh Dorset, Charles Fombad, Andrew Harding, Mark Hickford, Coel Kirkby, Dylan Lino, Paul McHugh, Derek O'Brien, Mitra Sharafi, Asanga Welikala, Kevin Tan, Arun Kumar Thiruvengadam and Anne Twomey.
90. It would hard to find today an historian who could use the words "Public Law" in their article title like Robinson, *Public Law of Overseas France since the War*. Rare examples of imperial and Commonwealth historians doing law, however, include Drayton, "Whose Constitution? Law, Justice and History in the Caribbean: 6th Distinguished Jurist Lecture. (Distinguished Jurist Lecture series)." and covering an earlier period Cavanaugh, "Infidels in English Legal Thought." There is though a high level of South Asian legal historians scholars working on colonial and post-colonial laws. See Sharafi, "South Asian Legal History,"309–36.
91. Madden, "The Commonwealth, Commonwealth History, and Oxford, 1905–1971,"25.

92. Hyam, "Preface to the Third Edition," xi.
93. Hopkins, "Rethinking Decolonization," 215.
94. See for example Dubow, *Apartheid 1948–1994*; Murphy, "'Government by Blackmail',"53–76; Onslow, "The Man on the Spot," 68–100; and Stockwell, *The Business of Decolonization*.
95. Sartori, "Constitutionalism: A Preliminary Discussion," 857.

Acknowledgments

I would like to record my gratitude to Carl Bridge, Peter Cane, Donal Coffey, Jesus Chairez-Garza, Derek O'Brien, Asanga Welikala and especially Donal Lowry for their astute advice and assistance with the article. They are, however, absolved from any criticisms the contents may generate.

Disclosure Statement

No potential conflict of interest was reported by the author.

ORCID

H. Kumarasingham http://orcid.org/0000-0001-7424-6626

References

Alexandrowicz, C. H. "New and Original States." In *The Law of Nations in Global History*, edited by D. Armitage, and J. Pitts, 390–410. Oxford: Oxford University Press, 2017.
Arnot, D. "The Honour of the First Nations – the Honour of the Crown: The Unique Relationship of First Nations and the Crown." In *The Evolving Canadian Crown*, edited by Smith Jennifer, and D. Michael Jackson, 150–166. Montreal and Kingston: McGill-Queen's University Press, 2012.
Arunachalam, P. *Our Political Needs – An Address Delivered Before the Ceylon National Association*. Colombo: Colombo Apothecaries Printers, 1917.
Austin, D. "The Transfer of Power: Why and How." In *Decolonisation and After – The British and French Experience*, edited by W. H. Morris-Jones, and G. Fischer, 3–34. London: Frank Cass, 1980.
Bayly, C. A. *Forgotten Armies – The Fall of British Asia 1941–1945*. London: Allen Lane, 2004.
Bayly, C. A. *Recovering Liberties – Indian Thought in the Age of Liberalism and Empire*. Cambridge: Cambridge University Press, 2012.
Bayly, C. A. "The Orient: British Historical Writing About Asia Since 1890." In *History and Historians in the Twentieth Century*, edited by Peter Burke, 88–119. Oxford: Oxford University Press, 2002.
Bayly, C. A., and T. Harper. *Forgotten Wars – The End of Britain's Asian Empire*. London: Allen Lane, 2007.
Behm, A. *Imperial History and the Global Politics of Exclusion – Britain, 1880–1940*. London: Palgrave Macmillan, 2018.
Bentley, M. *Modernizing England's Past – English Historiography in the Age of Modernism 1870–1970*. Cambridge: Cambridge University Press, 2005.

Brasted, H. V., and C. Bridge. "The Transfer of Power in South Asia: An Historiographical Review." *South Asia – Journal of South Asian Studies* xvii, no. 1 (1994): 93–114.

Brock, M. "Introduction: Freddie Madden." In *Perspectives on Imperialism and Decolonization – Essays in Honour of A. F. Madden*, edited by R. F. Holland, and G. Rizvi, 1–8. London: Frank Cass, 1984.

Burroughs, P. "The Imperial Gospel According to Frederick Madden." *The Journal of Imperial and Commonwealth History* 30, no. 3 (2002): 110–134.

Butler, D., and D. A. Low, eds. *Sovereigns and Surrogates – Constitutional Heads of State in the Commonwealth*. London: St Martin's Press, 1991.

Cavanaugh, E. "Infidels in English Legal Thought: Conquest, Commerce and Slavery in the Common Law From Coke to Mansfield, 1603–1793." *Modern Intellectual History* published online 69 (2018): 1–35. doi:10.1017/S1479244317000580.

Colley, L., "Writing Constitutions and Writing World History." In *The Prospect of Global History*, edited by James Belich, 160–177. Oxford: Oxford University Press, 2016.

Cotton, J. *The Australian School of International Relations*. Houndmills: Palgrave Macmillan, 2013.

Coupland, R. *The Study of the British Commonwealth – An Inaugural Lecture*. Oxford: Oxford University Press, 1921.

Curran, J., and S. Ward. *The Unknown Nation – Australia After Empire*. Melbourne: Melbourne University Press, 2010.

Darwin, J. "Britain's Empires." In *The British Empire – Themes and Perspectives*, edited by S. Stockwell, 1–20. Oxford: Blackwell, 2008.

Davidson, J. *The Three-Cornered Life – The Historian W. K. Hancock*. Sydney: UNSW Press, 2010.

De, R. "'A Peripatetic World Court' Cosmopolitan Courts, Nationalist Judges and the Indian Appeal to the Privy Council." *Law and History Review* 32, no. 4 (2014): 821–851.

De Silva, K. M., ed. *Sri Lanka – Part II, 1945–48, British Documents on the End of Empire*. Series B. London: HMSO, 1997.

De Smith, S. A. *The New Commonwealth and its Constitutions*. London: Stevens and Sons, 1964.

Drayton, R. *Whose Constitution? Law, Justice and History in the Caribbean: 6th Distinguished Jurist Lecture. (Distinguished Jurist Lecture Series)*. Port of Spain, Trinidad and Tobago: Judicial Education Institute of Trinidad and Tobago, 2016.

Drayton, R. "Where Does the World Historian Write From? Objectivity, Moral Conscience and the Past and Present of Imperialism." *Journal of Contemporary History* 46, no. 3 (2011): 671–685.

Dubow, S. *Apartheid 1948–1994*. Oxford: Oxford University Press, 2014.

Dubow, S. "The Commonwealth and South Africa: From Smuts to Mandela." *Journal of Imperial and Commonwealth History* 45, no. 2 (2017): 284–314.

Elangovan, A. "The Making of the Indian Constitution: A Case for a Non-Nationalist Approach." *History Compass* 12, no. 1 (2014): 1–10.

Feingold, E. R. *Colonial Justice and Decolonization in the High Court of Tanzania, 1920–1971*. Houndsmills, Basingstoke: Palgrave Macmillan, 2018.

Ford, L. *Settler Sovereignty: Jurisdiction and Indigenous People in America and Australia, 1788–1836*. Cambridge, MA: Harvard University Press, 2010.

Fraenkel, J. "Governors-General During Pacific Island Constitutional Crises and the Role of the Crown." *Commonwealth & Comparative Politics* 54, no. 1 (2016): 1–22.

Gopal, S. "All Souls and India, 1921–47." In *The Statecraft of British Imperialism – Essays in Honour of Wm. Roger Louis*, edited by R. D. King, and R. W. Kilson, 86–106. London: Frank Cass, 1999.

Hancock, W. K. "Nicholas Mansergh: Some Recollections and Reflections." In *The First British Commonwealth – Essays in Honour of Nicholas Mansergh*, edited by N. Hillmer, and P. Wigley, 3–9. London: Frank Cass, 1980.

Hancock, W. K. *Survey of British Commonwealth Affairs, Volume I, Problems of Nationality 1918–1936*. Oxford: Oxford University Press, 1937.

Hancock, W. K. *Survey of British Commonwealth Affairs – Volume II, Problems of Economic Policy, 1918–1939*. London: Oxford University Press, part I 1940 and part II. 1942.

Harding, A. "The 'Westminster Model' Constitution Overseas: Transplantation, Adaption and Development in Commonwealth States." *Oxford University Commonwealth Law Journal* 4 (2004 Winter): 143–166.

Harkness, D. "Nicholas Mansergh (1910–1991): Historian of Modern Ireland." *Études irlandaises*, Hors-Série L'Irlande Aujourd'hui / *Ireland Today*, 1994, pp 87–95.

Harkness, D. "Philip Nicholas Seton Mansergh – 1910–1991." *Proceedings of the British Academy* 82 (1993): 415–430.

Hickford, M. "Designing Constitutions in Britain's Mid-Nineteenth Century Empire – Indigenous Territorial Government in New Zealand and Retrieving Constitutional Histories." *Journal of Imperial and Commonwealth History* 46, no. 4 (2018): 676–706.

Hickford, M. *Lords of the Land: Indigenous Property Rights and the Jurisprudence of Empire*. Oxford: Oxford University Press, 2011.

Holland, R. F., and G. Rizvi, eds. *Perspectives on Imperialism and Decolonization – Essays in Honour of A. F. Madden*. London: Frank Cass, 1984.

Hopkins, A. G. "Rethinking Decolonization." *Past and Present*, no. 200 (2008): 211–247.

Hyam, R. *Understanding the British Empire*. Cambridge: Cambridge University Press, 2010.

Hyam, R. "Preface to the Third Edition." In *Britain's Imperial Century – A Study of Empire and Expansion*. 3rd ed, xi–xiii. Houndsmills, Basingstoke: Palgrave Macmillan, 2002.

James, C. L. R. *Beyond a Boundary*. London: Hutchinson, 1963.

James, C. L. R. In *The Life of Captain Cipriani – An Account of British Government in the West Indies and the Pamphlet The Case for West Indian Self-Government*, edited by Bridget Brebreton. London and Durham: Duke University Press, 2014.

Jennings, I., and H. Kumarasingham, eds. *Constitution-Maker – Selected Writings of the Sir Ivor Jennings*. Cambridge: Cambridge University Press, 2015.

Jennings, I. *Constitutional Laws of the Commonwealth, Volume 1: the Monarchies*. Oxford: Oxford University Press, 1957.

Jennings, I. *Constitutional Problems in Pakistan*. Cambridge: Cambridge University Press, 1957.

Jennings, I. *Cabinet Government*. Cambridge: Cambridge University Press, 1936.

Jennings, I. *Parliament*. Cambridge: Cambridge University Press, 1939.

Jennings, I. *Parliament*. Cambridge: Cambridge University Press, 1939.

Jennings, I. *Some Characteristics of the Indian Constitution – Being Lectures Given in the University of Madras During March 1952 Under the Sir Alladi Krishnaswami Aiyer Shashtiabdapoorthi Endowment*. Madras: Cambridge University Press, 1953.

Jennings, I. *The Constitution of Ceylon*. 3rd ed. Bombay: Oxford University Press, 1953.

Jennings, I. *The Law and the Constitution*. London: University of London Press, 1933.

Jennings, Ivor. *Democracy in Africa*. Cambridge: Cambridge University Press, 1963.

Jennings, Ivor. *The Approach to Self-Government*. Cambridge: Cambridge University Press, 1958.

Johnson, M. *The Land is Our History – Indigeneity, Law, and the Settler State*. New York: Oxford University Press, 2016.

Keith, A. B. *Constitutional History of India, 1600–1935*. London: Methuen, 1936.

Keith, A. B. *Responsible Government in the Dominions*. 2 vol. Oxford: Oxford University Press, 1928.
Keith, A. B. *Speeches and Documents on the British Dominions, 1918-1931: From Self-Government to National Sovereignty*. London: Oxford University Press, 1948.
Keith, A. B. *The King and the Imperial Crown: The Powers and Duties of His Majesty*. London: Oxford University Press, 1936.
Keith, A. B. *The Governments of the British Empire*. London: Macmillan, 1935.
Kelly, P. *November 1975 – The Inside Story of Australia's Greatest Political Crisis*. Sydney: Allen & Unwin, 1995.
Kerr, J. *Matters of Judgement – An Autobiography*. Melbourne: Macmillan.
King, A. *The British Constitution*. Oxford: Oxford University Press, 2007.
King, M. *The Penguin History of New Zealand*. Auckland: Penguin, 2003.
Kumarasingham, H. "A Transnational Actor on a Dramatic Stage – Sir Ivor Jennings and the Manipulation of Westminster Style Democracy: The Case of Pakistan." *UC Irvine Journal of International, Transnational, and Comparative Law* 2 (2017): 33–56.
Kumarasingham, H. "Eastminster – Decolonisation and State-Building in British Asia." In *Constitution-Making in Asia – Decolonisation and State-Building in the Aftermath of the British Empire*, edited by H. Kumarasingham, 1–35. London: Routledge, 2016.
Kumarasingham, H. "Introduction." In *Constitution-Maker – Selected Writings of the Sir Ivor Jennings*, 1–18. Cambridge: Cambridge University Press, 2015.
Lal, Brij V., ed. *Fiji, British Documents on the End of Empire*. Series B, vol. 10. London: HMSO, 2006.
Latham, R. T. E. *The Law and the Commonwealth*. reprinted from W. K. Hancock, *Survey of British Commonwealth Affairs, Volume I, Problems of Nationality 1918-1936* [1937]. Oxford: Oxford University Press, 1949.
Lavin, D. *From Empire to International Commonwealth – A Biography of Lionel Curtis*. Oxford: Oxford University Press, 1995.
Lino, D. "Albert Venn Dicey and the Constitutional Theory of Empire." *Oxford Journal of Legal Studies* 36, no. 4 (2016): 751–780.
Lonsdale, J. "Ornamental Constitutionalism in Africa: Kenyatta and the Two Queens." *The Journal of Imperial and Commonwealth History* 34, no. 1 (2006): 87–103.
Louis, Wm. R. "Sir Keith Hancock and the British Empire: The Pax Britannica and the Pax Americana." *English Historical Review* CXX, no. 488 (2005): 937–962.
Louis, Wm. R. "Introduction." In *Historiography – The Oxford History of the British Empire - Volume V*, edited by R. W. Winks, 1–42. Oxford: Oxford University Press, 1999.
Low, D. A. *Fabrication of Empire – The British and the Uganda Kingdoms 1890–1902*. Cambridge: Cambridge University Press, 2009.
Low, D. A. *Eclipse of Empire*. Cambridge: Cambridge University Press, 1999.
Low, D. A. *Britain and Indian Nationalism – The Imprint of Ambiguity*. Cambridge: Cambridge University Press, 1996.
Low, D. A., ed. *Constitutional Heads and Political Crises – Commonwealth Episodes, 1945–85*. London: Macmillan, 1988.
Low, D. A. *Congress and the Raj – Facets of the Indian Struggle*. London: Heinemann, 1977.
Low, D. A. *Lion Rampant – Essays in the Study of British Imperialism*. London: Frank Cass, 1973.
Lowry, D. "New Ireland, Old Empire and the Outside World, 1922–49: The Strange Evolution of a Dictionary Republic." In *Ireland: The Politics of Independence, 1922–49*, edited by M. Cronin, and J. Regan, 164–216. Basingstoke: Macmillan, 2000.
Lowry, D. "Ulster Resistance and Loyalist Rebellion in the Empire." In *An Irish Empire?": Aspects of Ireland and the British Empire*, edited by Keith Jeffery, 191–214. Manchester: Manchester University Press, 1996.

Lynn, M., ed. *The British Empire in 1950s – Retreat or Revival*. Houndsmills, Basingstoke: Palgrave Macmillan, 2006.

McIntyre, W. D. *The Britannic Vision – Historians and the Making of the British Commonwealth of Nations, 1907–1948*. Basingstoke: Palgrave Macmillan, 2009.

McIntyre, W. D. "Clio and Britannia's Lost Dream: Historians and the British Commonwealth of Nations in the First Half of the 20th Century." *The Round Table* 93, no. 376 (2004): 517–532.

McKenna, M. "Moment of Truth – History and Australia's Future." *Quarterly Essay*, no. 69 (March 2018): 1–86.

Madden, F., ed. *Select Documents on the Constitutional History of the British Empire and Commonwealth*. 8 vol. Westport, CT: Greenwood Press, 1985–2000.

Madden, F. "Commonwealth Government at Oxford – Some Personal Reflections." *Journal of Commonwealth & Comparative Politics* 31, no. 1 (1993): 36–44.

Madden. F., and D. K. Fieldhouse, eds. *Oxford and the Idea of Commonwealth – Essays Presented to Sir Edgar Williams*. London: Croom Helm, 1982

Madden, F. "The Commonwealth, Commonwealth History, and Oxford, 1905–1971." In *Oxford and the Idea of Commonwealth – Essays Presented to Sir Edgar Williams*, edited by Frederick Madden, and D. K. Fieldhouse, 7–29. London: Croom Helm, 1982.

Madden, A. F., and W. H. Morris-Jones. *Australia and Britain – Studies in a Changing Relationship*. London: Frank Cass, 1980.

Madden, F. "Some Origins and Purposes in the Formation of British Colonial Government." In *Essays in Imperial Government*, edited by K. Robinson, and F. Madden, 1–22. Oxford: Basil Blackwell, 1963.

Mansergh, P. N. S. Editor-in-Chief, *Constitutional Relations Between Britain and India: The Transfer of Power 1942–47*, XII volumes, co-editor, vols. i-iv with E. W. R. Lumby and vols. v-xii with Penderel Moon. London: HMSO, 1970–83.

Mansergh, P. N. S. *The Commonwealth Experience*. 2 vol. London: Macmillan, 1982.

Mansergh, P. N. S., ed. *Documents and Speeches on Commonwealth Affairs 1931–1952* [1953] in two volumes all London: Oxford University Press.

Mansergh, P. N. S. *Survey of British Commonwealth Affairs: Volume I: Problems of External Policy 1931–1939*. London: Oxford University Press, 1952.

Mansergh, P. N. S. *Survey of British Commonwealth Affairs: Volume II: Problems of Wartime Co-Operation and Post-War Change 1939–1952*. London: Oxford University Press, 1958.

Mantena, K. *Alibis of Empire – Henry Maine and the Ends of Liberal Imperialism*. Princeton, New Jersey: Princeton University Press, 2010.

Mazower, M. *Governing the World – The History of an Idea*. London: Allen Lane, 2012.

Miller, J. D. B. "The Commonwealth and the World Order: the Zimmern Vision and After." In *The First British Commonwealth – Essays in Honour of Nicholas Mansergh*, edited by N. Hillmer, and P. Wigley, 159–174. London: Frank Cass, 1980.

Miller, J. R. "The Aboriginal Peoples and the Crown." In *Canada and the Crown: Essays on Constitutional Monarchy*, edited by D. Michael Jackson, and Philippe Lagasse. Montreal and Kingston: McGill-Queen's University Press, 2013.

Miller, J. R. "Petitioning the Great White Mother: First Nations' Organizations and Lobbying in London." In *Canada and the End of Empire*, edited by Phillip Buckner, 299–318. Toronto: UBC Press, 2005.

Munroe, T. *The Politics of Constitutional Decolonization: Jamaica 1944–1962*. Mona: University of the West Indies, 1972.

Murphy, P. "'Government by Blackmail': The Origins of the Central African Federation Reconsidered." In *The British Empire in 1950s – Retreat or Revival*, edited by Martin Lynn, 53–76. Houndsmills, Basingstoke: Palgrave Macmillan, 2006.

Onslow, S. "The Man on the Spot: Christopher Soames and Decolonisation of Zimbabwe/Rhodesia." *Britain in the World: Historical Journal of The British Scholar Society* 6, no. 1 (2013): 68–100.

Parkinson, C. O. H. *Bills of Rights and Decolonization – The Emergence of Domestic Human Rights Instruments in Britain's Overseas Territories.* Oxford: Oxford University Press, 2007.

Perham, M. *Colonial Government – Annotated Reading List on British Colonial Government with Some General and Comparative Material upon Foreign Empires, etc.* Oxford: (Nuffield College) Oxford University Press, 1950.

Rao, B. S. *The Framing of India's Constitution – Select Documents.* 5 vol. New Delhi: Indian Institute of Public Administration, 1966–1968.

Rao, B. S., ed. *Select Constitutions of the World.* Madras: Madras Law Journal Press, 1934.

Rau, B. N. In *India's Constitution in the Making*, edited by B. S. Rao. Calcutta: Orient Longmans, 1960.

Rathbone, R., ed. *Ghana – Part I, 1941–1952, British Documents on the End of Empire.* Series B, 1 vol. London: HMSO, 1992.

Robinson, K., and F. Madden, eds. *Essays in Imperial Government.* Oxford: Basil Blackwell, 1963.

Robinson, K. "Autochthony and the Transfer of Power." In *Essays in Imperial Government*, edited by K. Robinson, and F. Madden, 249–288. Oxford: Basil Blackwell, 1963.

Robinson, K. "Constitutional Autochthony in Ghana." *Journal of Commonwealth & Comparative Politics* 1, no. 1 (1961): 101–111.

Robinson, K. *Public Law of Overseas France Since the War.* Oxford: Institute of Colonial Studies, 1954.

Sartori, G. "Constitutionalism: A Preliminary Discussion." *American Political Science Review* 56, no. 4 (December 1962): 853–864.

Seeley, J. R. *The Expansion of England – Two Courses of Lectures.* London: Macmillan, 1883.

Sharafi, M. "South Asian Legal History." *Annual Review of Law and Social Sciences* 11 (2015): 309–336.

Shinn Jr, F. R. *Arthur Berriedale Keith 1879–1944 – The Chief Ornament of Scottish Learning.* Aberdeen: Aberdeen University Press, 1990.

Smith, J. *An Island in the Autumn.* Kinloss: Librario, 2011.

Stockwell, A. J. "Princes and Politicians: The Constitutional Crisis in Malaysia, 1983–84." In *Constitutional Heads and Political Crises – Commonwealth Episodes, 1945–85*, edited by D. A. Low, 182–197. London: Macmillan, 1988.

Stockwell, S. *The Business of Decolonization : British Business Strategies in the Gold Coast.* Oxford: Oxford University Press, 2000.

Symonds, R. *Oxford and Empire: The Last Lost Cause?* Oxford: Clarendon Press, 1986.

Tan, K. Y. L. *Marshall of Singapore – A Biography.* Singapore: Institute of Southeast Asian Studies, 2008.

Tinker, H. *Constitutional Relations Between Britain and Burma: The Struggle for Independence 1944–1948*, 2 vol. London: HMSO, 1983–84.

Wheare, K. C. *The Constitutional Structure of the Commonwealth.* Oxford: Oxford University Press, 1960.

Williams, E. *Slavery and Capitalism.* Chapel Hill: University of North Carolina Press, 1944.

Winks, R. W., ed. *Historiography – The Oxford History of the British Empire - Volume V.* Oxford: Oxford University Press, 1999.

An Acutely Embarrassing Affair: Whitehall and the Indian-South African Dispute at the United Nations (1946)

Lorna Lloyd

ABSTRACT
Before the Second World War it was a cardinal Commonwealth principle that intra-imperial disputes must be kept away from international fora. Yet in 1946 the not-yet-independent India complained to the United Nations about South African legislation discriminating against people of Indian origin. It did so without seeking Britain's approval, and went on to level fierce criticism at Britain's opposition to the UN General Assembly's discussion of the matter.

This article explains the circumstances which led to these events; uncovers the divergent responses of the relevant British government departments – the India Office, the Dominions Office, and the Foreign Office – and shows how they were resolved; depicts the way in which Britain's delegation to the General Assembly handled the matter; and discusses the significance and consequences of the dispute for South Africa and for Anglo-Indian relations.

Background

From the initial emergence of an Indian community in South Africa, European settlers sought to limit its size and encourage the idea of returning to India. The first Indians had arrived as a result of an 1860 agreement between the governments of India and the then colony of Natal for indentured Indian labourers to work on Natal sugar plantations. From 1874 they were no longer required to return to India after completing their contract, and in 1875 Lord Salisbury, the Secretary of State for India, assured Delhi that, after serving their indentures, the Indians would be 'in all respects free men, with privileges no whit inferior to those of any other class of Her Majesty's subjects resident in the Colonies'.[1]

But European settlers had no intention of allowing this to happen. They wanted to get rid of or at least severely restrict the rapidly rising Indian presence[2] – Indian traders and professionals having followed in the wake of the labourers. The Europeans therefore began introducing anti-Indian measures such as imposing a £3 annual 'licence' payment on Indian settlers (1895), denying them the vote (1896), requiring immigrants to pass a European language test, and placing restrictions on trade (1897). The stage was set for troubled Indian-South African relations and intermittent, but increasingly severe, crises as the Government of India felt an ongoing responsibility towards the descendants of people who had emigrated under an intergovernmental agreement.

In 1911, a year after the formation of the Union of South Africa, the Government of India terminated the indentured labour system after failing to receive satisfactory assurances regarding the treatment of Indians. Two years later the introduction of South African legislation preventing Indian immigration gave rise to Mohandas (Mahatma) Gandhi's spectacular *satyagraha* (non-violent) campaign. In 1914 Gandhi and the then South African defence minister (and future prime minister) General Jan Christiaan Smuts settled the dispute in a spirit of compromise, and in the process formed a deep, lifelong friendship that was unaffected by their considerable political differences. Gandhi described Smuts as 'a man of God'[3] and gave him a pair of sandals he had made. Smuts wore them for 'many a summer' though he felt unworthy of standing 'in the shoes of so great a man'.[4]

Anti-Indian feeling re-emerged after the First World War and there was a major crisis in 1925 following the introduction of a Class Areas bill, making it unlawful for Indians to acquire town property for trading or residence except in designated areas. It was resolved at a round table conference between representatives of India and South Africa. The resultant Cape Town Agreement (1927) said that Indians who were willing to conform to 'western standards of life' could stay in the country; the Union Government would help them to attain such standards; and an Indian agent would be appointed to ensure effective communication between India and South Africa.[5]

In 1938 there was a third major crisis when the Class Areas bill was revived and an 'Interim' Act banned the sale or hire of property and the issue of new trade licences to Indians in the province of Transvaal (where there was a small Indian community). Smuts settled it when he became Prime Minister in 1939. But anti-Indian feeling in Natal was reaching new levels, and allegations of Indian 'penetration' in its largest city, Durban, led in April 1943 to legislation extending the life of the Interim Act and preventing further property transfers in the province. There was uproar in India, and Dr N B Khare (an Indian member of the Council which assisted the Viceroy – the governor – in the administration of India) was spoiling for a fight.

Smuts swiftly reached agreement with the Natal Indians about licensing their occupation of buildings (the Pretoria Agreement). Unfortunately, during the passage of the requisite legislation the Natal Provincial Council attempted to restrict the *acquisition* as well as the *occupation* of property. Indian fury reached new heights. The Viceroy, Field Marshal A P Wavell, was sympathetic, but because of wartime considerations London turned a blind eye to Indian distress.

Smuts again broke the tension by blocking the Natal ordinance and setting up a commission to enquire into the lives of South African Indians. But by the time the commission reported the atmosphere in Natal had become too poisonous for reason to prevail, and Smuts' United Party was losing ground to Dr D F Malan's *Herenigde Nasionale* Party (HNP – the Reunited National Party – which embraced *apartheid*). The consequence was that in January 1946 Smuts told Wavell that he would introduce legislation restricting Indian rights to acquire and transfer property. Incensed, Dr Khare determined to draw international attention to the so-called 'Ghetto Act' (as it was known in India) by complaining to the newly-established United Nations (UN).

London was aghast but powerless to intervene directly. This was, because, first, although India had not yet achieved sovereign statehood, it was a full UN member and, as such, enjoyed the same rights and duties as every other member. It could therefore take disputes to the organisation. Second, Britain was treating India 'as much like a Dominion Government as possible'[6] as it hurtled towards independence. This meant India was increasingly asserting its own, independent line, particularly where its interests diverged from those of Britain or other Commonwealth members. Third, Britain had not intervened directly with South Africa on India's behalf since 1923, and after India appointed an agent to South Africa in 1927 the latter had corresponded directly with the Union government on all matters. Any attempt to intervene now would cause grave difficulties with South Africa, especially if Britain gave the impression of favouring India.

Attempts to avert open confrontation

Britain therefore resorted to diplomatic channels. The first move came from the Viceroy, who enjoyed a close relationship with Smuts (now a Field-Marshal). On learning of the proposed segregatory legislation Wavell privately asked him to desist, and suggested a conference. Smuts did not reply.

Wavell persevered, asking the minister in charge of Britain's India Office (IO), Lord Pethick-Lawrence, to get the Dominions Office (DO) to urge Smuts to reconsider. Pethick-Lawrence was personally sympathetic to the Indians, but thought it unwise to press South Africa. However, he did as asked, and Britain's high commissioner in South Africa, Sir Evelyn Baring, was contacted. Baring reported that Smuts was determined that the legislation should go through, but had privately indicated a willingness to administer it liberally.

London now tried to discourage India from pursuing the UN route. In early April it sent Delhi a telegram setting out four arguments against internationalising the dispute. The first was that as the Indians in South Africa were almost wholly South African nationals, their treatment was unquestionably a domestic matter, and it would do India no good if its complaint was dismissed by the UN. (Article 2.7 of the Charter forbade UN intervention in matters which were 'essentially within the domestic jurisdiction' of member states.)[7] India was unmoved. For the point was not that India expected to win (it did not); rather, it wanted the publicity that could be gained by formally submitting the matter.

Britain's second argument was that India's complaint would neither stop the bill becoming law nor encourage Smuts to negotiate, and UN discussions would limit Smuts' ability to administer the law in a liberal way. This, too, cut no ice. India's patience had been strained beyond endurance. It had no faith in South African goodwill, and had to consider the extent to which South Africa's actions had outraged the Indian public.

The third argument was that UN discussion might backfire on India, given its caste system and political problems with minorities. If it succeeded in overcoming the domestic jurisdiction hurdle, local minorities might also complain to the UN. However, India had already dismissed this as a remote possibility which should not stop it from going ahead. Fourth, Britain argued that internationalising the dispute would conflict with the imperial doctrine of *inter se* whereby intra-Commonwealth relations were not regarded as international, and disputes between members were kept away from international bodies. This carried even less weight. The South African issue was allegedly the chief reason many Indians wanted to leave the Commonwealth. Manifestly, the Commonwealth connection had not made Britain noticeably sympathetic to Indians overseas, and there was also anti-Indian prejudice in some of its members.[8]

Having thus dismissed Britain's arguments and learned in mid-May that he would soon have to relinquish his post, Khare moved swiftly. On 3 June the offensive 'Ghetto Act' became law. On 17 June the Viceroy's Council decided to lodge a complaint with the UN, and this was done on 22 June. Khare rejoiced that India had acted 'like a fully independent Government' and struck 'a radical blow on the very conception of the Empire'.[9] He left office a few days later.

India's complaint[10]

India gave four reasons for going to the UN. First, it had a moral responsibility for the descendants of indentured labourers who had gone to Natal at the latter's request and under mutually agreed conditions. One of these was that former indentured labourers could settle as free men, with all the rights and privileges of citizenship. It was its duty to ensure the promise was fulfilled.

Second, the 1927 Cape Town Agreement was binding in international law and entitled India to be involved in the matter. South Africa's failure to confer over the Ghetto Act violated the Agreement. And, although the Agreement had not been registered as a treaty with the League of Nations, the treatment of Indians in South Africa had nonetheless been transferred from the domestic to the international sphere through South Africa's acceptance of limits on its freedom of action.

Third, denying human rights on racial grounds violated both Article 1.3 of the UN Charter (which said one of the UN's purposes was to promote and encourage 'respect for human rights and for fundamental freedoms for all without distinction as to race') and Article 55 (which spoke of promoting 'universal respect for, and observance of, human rights and fundamental freedoms').

Finally, the treatment of Indians in South Africa was not just damaging Indian-South African relations. It raised a wider political question: the Union's undemocratic nature was 'contrary to the democratic basis of the UN' and was strikingly similar to 'the Nazi principle and practice of race superiority'.

Britain's initial response

It was abundantly clear to Britain that any public discussion at the UN would be acutely embarrassing. As South Africa might, at best, only win by a small majority,[11] London had to think the unthinkable: the possibility of an unfavourable outcome. There was also an immediate complication at the bureaucratic level, in that three Whitehall departments were directly involved: the IO, the DO, and the Foreign Office (FO). They were all trying to navigate along the same hazardous channel and the courses they took were nuanced by their different professional remits.

The India Office

The IO oversaw the administration of India, which was conducted on the spot by the Viceroy. When there was a conflict between Indian and UK interests, the Viceroy's officials tended to take 'the view which [they] thought was right for India'[12] and, in any case, British supervision had been hugely relaxed. India was more a client than a ward, and the IO was more than ever a representative of its interests in London. But at the same time the IO was part of the machinery of British government. Its officials had therefore to keep both these slippery balls in the air at the same time. Thus, although they were very much on India's side, they recognised that from the imperial perspective India's action was 'deplorable'.[13]

There was clearly no future in repeating the dissuasive arguments that had been put to India in April. Moreover, the Viceroy sympathised with the Indians and was committed to supporting India (although he and Pethick-Lawrence privately agreed that India's complaint was a 'rather empty gesture').[14] The advent in India (on 4 July) of a caretaker government of officials did not affect its determination to forge ahead. Going to the UN was 'one of the few issues on which Hindus, Muslims, Anglo-Indians and Europeans and other communities [were] united'.[15] The dispute would have to run its UN course.

The best the IO could hope for was to ensure that India's case was fairly stated and treated in inter-departmental discussions, and represented as much as possible in the instructions given to Britain's delegation to the UN General Assembly. And as regards the line to be taken at the UN, the IO urged strict neutrality. However, in the inevitable bargaining about the instructions, the IO's prospects were dim. Its competent and talented officials did their best to fight India's corner, but they were in a 'rather ... delicate'[16] position in Whitehall and felt disadvantaged in pressing India's viewpoint. Moreover, as regards this particular dispute, the IO had less clout than the DO and the FO, and it could not rely on the support of the Colonial Office (CO), with whom it was often at variance over the treatment of Indians in various colonies. It was in a weak ministerial position, too. Pethick-Lawrence had excellent standing in India, but lacked a strong personality and close ministerial associations. He was hardly a match for more influential and abrasive colleagues.[17] And his junior minister, Arthur Henderson, was, according to his then private secretary, not only 'useless' but also 'the most contemptible individual I have ever known'.[18]

The Dominions Office

The DO was established in 1925, with responsibility for Britain's relations with the self-governing dominions: Canada, Australia, South Africa, New Zealand, Newfoundland (whose dominion status was suspended in 1933), and Ireland. By 1946 the dominions were firmly established on the international stage and for the most part had cut the British apron strings. However, there remained much that was special about intra-Commonwealth diplomacy, and the DO continued to have an instinctive concern for the dominions' happiness and well-being. In this context the DO was horrified at the prospect of Commonwealth linen being washed in public, as that would result in its members having to take sides. But it had no constructive suggestions about how to prevent that happening.

More specifically, given Malan's growing electoral strength, it was vital to avoid conveying the 'impression that it is the Union Govt. who are at fault & that it is for them to make some concession'.[19] The Ghetto Act was 'the minimum' legislation 'necessary to ensure ... [Smuts] position in the Union'.[20] And Smuts was not just a much-admired and widely-respected world statesman, he was also the key to maintaining South Africa's Commonwealth connection. As Sir Hartley Shawcross, Britain's Attorney-General (the government's chief legal adviser), later put it: 'We regarded him as a very loyal friend of this country and were fearful ... of anything which damaged his standing in South Africa'.[21] UN discussion of India's complaint could do just that. It might also endanger the Union's internal peace.

For these, essentially political, reasons the DO was desperate to avoid UN involvement. If India would not withdraw, the domestic jurisdiction route went in the most promising direction. It was also the South African line, and might be endorsed by the many UN members with 'racial Achilles heels'.[22] But if there was a discussion, the DO was at one with the IO in wanting the

British delegation to avoid expressing any opinion on the merits of the case, and (as will shortly be seen) it shared the IO's unhappiness about using the Cape Town Agreement to buttress the legal argument.

However, in the wheeling and dealing which would occur over the instructions, the DO, like the IO, was not in a noticeably strong position. It was a relatively small, stuffy department, whose officers were generally not good enough to get into the FO and who were encumbered with pettifogging bureaucratic procedures. The position of Secretary of State for the Dominions was not highly-regarded, and the Department's Permanent Under-Secretary (PUS – the senior official) Sir Eric Machtig, was too shy and reclusive to be an efficient Whitehall operator. Nor did the FO take the DO or the dominions very seriously, its attitude varying 'from patronizing tolerance to mild derision'.[23] Furthermore, the CO condescendingly regarded the DO as 'only a post-office'.[24] (And significantly for his standing in Whitehall – 'where status and salary so often go together'[25] – Machtig was paid less than other departmental heads.) In many quarters the DO's remit would probably have made it more popular than the IO, and possibly the FO. But in the bureaucratic hierarchy it lagged well behind the latter. Fortunately for the DO, the FO also favoured the domestic jurisdiction line.

The Foreign Office

The FO, which was the lead department as regards Britain's UN policy, was one of the great offices of state, towering above the IO and DO. The foreign secretaryship was a plum cabinet position and its holder, Ernest Bevin, was a combative political heavyweight who was close to Prime Minister Clement Attlee. His staff were first class, and devoted to him. And the FO legal adviser, Sir Eric Beckett, who made the running in determining Britain's line in New York, was an unusually gifted and astute lawyer who seldom put a foot wrong.[26] It was a very strong team, which took a hard-headed approach to British interests as an imperial power and one of the wartime 'big three'.

To the extent which it concerned itself with South Africa and India, the sympathies of its UN (Reconstruction) Department probably veered in the South African direction. And as far as instructions to the UN delegation were concerned, the FO initially consulted only the DO. An early memorandum uncritically cited a South African government paper (commended by the DO) which was breathtakingly offensive in its references to South African Indians. *Inter alia*, the genesis of the problem was alleged to lie in 'coolies or untouchables' refusing to go home because there was no caste system in South Africa; and Natal Europeans were 'in danger of being swamped' by fecund Indians with frugal lifestyles.[27] White civilisation in South Africa was at risk.

In this regard, therefore, the two departments were unlikely to fall out. But the FO's view about the instructions to the British delegation to the Assembly had a different emphasis from that of the DO. Beckett was wholeheartedly behind the domestic jurisdiction argument on purely legal grounds. As an imperial power and a permanent member of the Security Council Britain could not remain silent, and at this early moment in the UN's life it was vitally important that there should be a correct interpretation of the Charter provisions relating to the crucial issue of how far the organisation was entitled to intervene in its members' domestic affairs. That is to say, it should be interpreted restrictively. In strictly legal terms, it was a powerful case.

Resurrecting the idea of a conference

Of course, the ideal outcome for all three departments would be the withdrawal of the dispute from the Assembly's agenda, and in early August Baring reported that this was the thinking of moderate Indian leaders in South Africa. Conditions were deteriorating in Natal, where Indians were being denied loans, losing jobs, and suffering from a partial trade boycott. The leaders feared outbreaks of violence, and UN discussions would exacerbate the problem. Accordingly, they wanted the complaint withdrawn in favour of a conference.

Britain could not intervene to suggest this. Smuts, who was very confident about his prospects at the UN, would not make an overture. But in view of Baring's message and DO reports that Indian nerves might crack, and despite the IO thinking it futile, Pethick-Lawrence telegraphed Wavell saying, 'it was felt an effort should be made to avoid discussion in UNO'.[28] However, the initiative would have to come from India, which would probably have to suspend the trade boycott as a condition of talks.

Wavell reminded London in some detail that they had already been down this track, and India had taken full account of the possibility of economic reprisals against Natal Indians. The Interim Government under Jawaharlal Nehru (which had taken office on 2 September) was 'convinced that they have scored a good deal by the reference to U.N.O.' and delegates to the General Assembly were probably 'looking forward to making emotional speeches'.[29] Nehru said Smuts had to make the first move and the Ghetto Act must be suspended. There was no hope of either.

The door to negotiations was clearly closed. Yet there were lingering hopes of finding a way to get the hot potato dropped. US reports suggested that India would like to withdraw its complaint, but Britain could not act on them because of its inability to intervene directly. This consideration also led the DO to reject suggestions that Attlee might offer to mediate, or that the subject might be broached over dinner when Smuts was on an about-to-occur visit to London. By October Machtig had accepted that it was doubtful India 'would *in any circumstances* agree to cancel their request to U.N.O.'[30] As far as Whitehall was concerned, that was that.

Drafting the brief for the British delegation[31]

Departmental representatives met regularly over the summer of 1946 to thrash out a cabinet paper. By 2 October, when it had finally been agreed and printed, the now lengthy document identified six factors to be taken into account in determining the instructions for the British delegation to the UN General Assembly.

First, it was 'a new, and regrettable, departure' for a dispute between two Commonwealth members to be taken to an international body. Second, India's future as a Commonwealth member was uncertain and might be affected by Britain's attitude. The Soviet bloc would support India and the discussions would 'provide an opportunity for malicious or ill-informed attacks against administration in part of the British Colonial Empire'. If the dispute was not ruled out under Article 2.7 of the Charter, there could be future complaints about the treatment of Indians elsewhere.

Third, the Ghetto Act was 'the work of the liberal elements headed by Field Marshal Smuts'. His defeat at the UN would benefit the Nationalists, who were 'far less considerate of Indian welfare'. Fourth, the Nationalists were making political hay by suggesting that Britain must have approved India's action.

Fifth, the memorandum discussed the legal considerations: whether the dispute was a matter of domestic jurisdiction, and whether it involved interpreting the provisions of the Charter relating to human rights and fundamental freedoms. And, sixth, Beckett maintained that those provisions did not constitute binding obligations.

The memorandum then identified four policy options. Policy I was to take no part in the discussions. This was hardly sustainable. It would not be consonant with Britain's leading Commonwealth role. Nor, as a great power and one of the leading framers of the Charter, could Britain remain silent in discussions about its 'vital parts'. Britain's interests as a colonial power were also affected, since accusations were 'all too likely to extend beyond the immediate sphere ... to the treatment of native communities and minority groups in British territories generally'.

Policy II, which had alternative sub-sections, involved announcing that Britain would not express a view on the merits of South Africa's action or India's complaint, while reserving the right to comment on the interpretation of the Charter, and possibly also (briefly) on the status of the 1927 Cape Town Agreement.

Policy II(a) entailed accepting the admissibility of the dispute and then refraining from participating any further in the debate. In so doing, Britain would help 'destroy the corner-stone of the South African defence' and win India's support. It would also

> constitute a rebuff to the liberal elements in the Union ... open the way for further cases to be brought before the Assembly in connexion with racial minorities in

other parts of the world (including the British Colonial Empire), and ... it might act to the disadvantage of those countries, including the United Kingdom, where human rights are not specifically embodied in a Written Constitution.

Under Policy II(b) Britain would argue that the dispute was excluded under Article 2.7 of the Charter because almost all those discriminated against were Union nationals. If necessary, the delegation might express an inclination to share doubts about whether the Cape Town Agreement was an international obligation. And if India took its stand on the application of the human rights provisions of the Charter, Britain could point out that it had consistently maintained that there had to be an agreed bill of human rights before human rights questions could be taken to the UN. The disadvantage of Policy II(b) was that Britain's delegates would 'in effect, be working to destroy part of the Indian case'.

Policy III was to support India. But this

> could only be justified by a decision that the United Kingdom must do everything to favour the future of the Indian relationship with this country, even to the extent of alienating South African friendship, prejudicing the development of a liberal policy towards the coloured populations in South Africa, opening the way for attacks on our administration in other parts of the world, and introducing a rigid interpretation of the human rights provisions of the Charter.

Policy IV, wholeheartedly supporting South Africa, would 'go furthest toward alienating Indian sympathy and creating a bond' between independent India and the Soviet bloc. However, it offered maximum support for Smuts as the leader of a friendly government that was 'relatively liberal in its racial policy'.

The memorandum concluded that Britain should adopt Policy II(b). It should be possible to oppose India without giving offence and it was in Britain's interests to do so. More particularly, Britain should seize the opportunity to put on record its view that until the Charter's human rights provisions were closely defined

> no one can state what precisely is meant by the terms 'human rights' and 'fundamental freedoms'. This consideration is particularly important when it is remembered that, possessing a humane and tolerant practice but no written constitutional guarantees, we in the United Kingdom must be specially on our guard against high-sounding formal texts which may not be seriously enforced even in those countries which are loudest in their support.

This was unsatisfactory from the IO point of view but the FO, and in particular its legal adviser, was in charge and the IO could hardly question Beckett's judgment as a lawyer. On the other hand, it had made sure that India's views were fully explained in an annex to the draft brief, as well as making clear its vehement opposition to Policy II(b), which would go down very badly in India. If, as Beckett insisted, Britain's delegate had to speak on the legal aspects of the case, the IO wanted him to do so only if South Africa's claim of domestic jurisdiction was unlikely to succeed.

On one aspect of the brief the IO had joined the DO in opposing the FO. This concerned the claim that British policy was bolstered by the failure to register the 1927 Cape Town Agreement as a treaty with the League of Nations. The DO did not think there was the 'remotest chance' South Africa would raise it, and it would be 'a little dangerous' for Britain to do so.[32] For although South Africa had not registered intra-Commonwealth agreements with the League, it regarded relations between Commonwealth members as the same as those with foreign states. If Britain now appeared to reject this claim, there was 'a possibility of controversy with the Union as to its international status and even of a general discussion as to the status of the members of the Commonwealth'.[33] If at all possible this must not happen.

The IO had three reasons for wanting to avoid using the non-registration argument. First, the Cape Town Agreement was unquestionably an international agreement in the 'accepted sense'.[34] Second, Britain could hardly argue that the Agreement was not a valid international agreement just because the Government of India had not registered it, for it was the UK that registered agreements on India's behalf. Moreover 'a large number of instruments *which we sh^d wish to regard as international agreements* were not so registered'.[35] Third, the Cape Town Agreement showed that South Africa had admitted India's special concern.

For Beckett, however, the details of the Agreement and the merits of the case were beside the point. The UN's competence to discuss the dispute was a straightforward legal question. Non-registration of the Cape Town agreement demonstrated that it was a domestic matter. Intra-Commonwealth agreements,

> even when they *were agreements* and indeed agreements of the greatest importance, were not in general registered at Geneva ... because the members of the Commonwealth did not ... regard them as international agreements .... The Governments of the Commonwealth regarded them as domestic or constitutional arrangements.[36]

Beckett was a lawyers' lawyer.

Failing to reach agreement

The Cabinet Office asked that the memorandum be shortened and this was done by Paul Gore-Booth, the official who headed the FO's UN department and was joint secretary to relevant cabinet committee. His resultant two-page summary recommended arguing that the dispute should be ruled out under Article 2.7 of the Charter because most South African Indians were Union nationals – the earlier Policy II(b). More generally, Britain should as far as possible keep out of the debate. This conclusion was firmly endorsed by the Dominions Secretary. But Pethick-Lawrence dissented, saying India's view must be heard and Britain must avoid giving the impression that it was taking sides. That meant not participating in UN discussions. Even intervening to speak on the interpretation of the Charter risked an adverse reaction which might affect India's attitude to Commonwealth membership, and push it into welcoming Soviet arms. Accordingly, Pethick-Lawrence favoured the earlier Policy I. If the Cabinet nonetheless decided otherwise, they should express the hope that in the future, as in the past, India and South Africa would confer and, in so doing, affirm India's right to concern itself with the conditions of South African Indians. But on all occasions British delegates must maintain absolute neutrality on the dispute's merits.

The Cabinet decision

On 25 October, as expected, the Cabinet approved Gore-Booth's revised memorandum on the grounds that 'it would be impossible for the United Kingdom Government, as one of the leading members of the United Nations to dissociate themselves entirely from all discussion of this matter'. However, 'every effort should be made to prevent the Assembly from discussing the merits of the complaint',[37] and British delegates should avoid doing so both in public and in private contacts. It was as much as the IO could have hoped for.

The General Assembly

By then the General Assembly was under way, having opened on 23 October. On 24 October, Philip Noel-Baker (the Secretary of State for Air, who in effect led the British delegation)[38] hosted a 'harmonious and almost hilarious lunch party'[39] for the Indians. He then travelled to the Assembly with Mrs Vijaya Lakshmi Pandit (who headed the Indian delegation). Both made hugely successful plenary speeches, and Noel-Baker delighted Pandit by being 'the first to come up and congratulate me even though my statement had been liberally sprinkled with ... anti-imperialist jargon'.[40]

24 October: the General Committee

India's complaint, like all the items on the draft agenda, was first considered by the General Committee (also called the Special Committee), which comprised the Assembly president, the seven vice-presidents, and the chairs of the six standing committees. This was the body responsible for the conduct of Assembly business. It therefore considered which items should be discussed and by which of the Assembly's committees, and reported its decisions to the full Assembly. (The one alternative was for a matter to be sent direct to a plenary meeting.) Once the latter had ruled on the report, substantive consideration of each approved item could begin in the relevant committee, which would submit a resolution for consideration at a plenary meeting of the Assembly.

The General Committee reached India's complaint on the evening of 24 October (before the UK Cabinet had approved the delegation's instructions). The British hoped to avoid any discussion of the dispute, and advised Smuts to keep his powder dry for the substantive committee stage. But just as the item was on the point of being nodded through, Smuts objected that the reference to 'Indian nationals in the Union' was wrong. The Secretary-General said the wording would be changed, but Smuts demanded that the dispute be deleted from the agenda as it concerned a matter that was within the Union's domestic jurisdiction.

This prompted a two-and-a-half hour debate of precisely the kind that the British wanted to avoid. It 'quickly showed signs of getting out of hand'[41] as the Soviets strongly supported India's contention that the dispute was an important political question involving the breach of an international agreement, which had led to virtual economic warfare. It looked as though they would win the day and the dispute would be sent to the First (Political) Committee, as every delegate supported India and no-one spoke up for South Africa. Feeling obliged to intervene, Shawcross suggested asking the Sixth (Legal) Committee whether the dispute was *ultra vires*. After a hard fight, he succeeded in ensuring the adoption of an American proposal that it be considered jointly by both the First (Political) and Sixth (Legal) Committees. The Indians were jubilant: the merits of their complaint would be discussed and Assembly opinion seemed to favour them.

29 October: the British delegates' misgivings

In view of this the British delegation realised that, politically speaking, their instructions to take no view on the merits would place them in an awkward and exposed position. Shawcross believed the legal argument he was propounding was unsound, given the inclusion of the word 'essentially' in Article 2.7 and the reference, in Article 55, to 'fundamental freedom for all without distinction as to race'.[42] Most of the 'leading members' of the Sixth (Legal) Committee shared his view. The delegation therefore warned London that it must expect defeat 'and that this might create an unfortunate impression'. Not only that, there would probably be 'very powerful' pressure to treat the dispute as a test case of the reality of the Charter's human rights provisions.[43]

One partial escape route from this looming dilemma would be for the Assembly to ask the International Court of Justice (ICJ) for an advisory opinion on the applicability of Article 2.7. This would not head off debate on the substance of the complaint, as a proposal to go to the ICJ would attract wide-ranging political arguments. Nonetheless, if carried, it would remove the dispute from the UN's political spotlight at least for a while; and if the Court's decision went against South Africa it could contribute to an eventual solution inasmuch as it might increase the pressure on the Union to settle and climb down gracefully. A telegram was duly despatched to London on 29 October, reporting developments and the delegation's latest thoughts, and asking for further instructions.

Meanwhile, the Assembly's consideration of the General Committee's report was imminent. Smuts had originally intended at this stage to ask the Assembly to reject its recommendation and dismiss the Indian complaint. This would have prompted a long and acrimonious debate. The British persuaded Smuts and Pandit that it would be better to have the matter first discussed in committee and the President accordingly announced that the parties had agreed that the dispute should be discussed in joint sessions of the First (Political) and Sixth (Legal) Committees (subsequently referred to as the Joint Committee).

Nonetheless, by now the British delegation was getting 'very worried'.[44] Bob Curson (the IO delegate) was warning London that trouble was brewing: the Indians were determined to air their grievances thoroughly and obtain 'a prestige victory'.[45] They felt entitled to Britain's support, but expected neutrality, and would 'certainly be very bitter indeed' if Britain seemed to be supporting South Africa.[46] The British turned to the friendly Canadians and wondered if they could persuade the disputants to enter into direct discussions. However, Ottawa would not put Canada's head above the parapet for fear of drawing attention to British Columbia's discrimination against Asians.[47]

4 November: the Cabinet reconsiders the delegation's instructions

Sir Stafford Cripps, the influential President of the Board of Trade, was 'very disturbed'[48] by the reports from New York and called for British policy to be reconsidered. The FO disagreed, telling Attlee that it had always recognised that India might press its case. The Dominions Secretary, Lord Addison, supported the FO.

When the Cabinet considered the matter on 4 November. Pethick-Lawrence emphasised the strength of feeling in India and the 'serious repercussions' if Britain's delegates were not neutral on both the admissibility and the merits of the dispute. They should take no part in UN discussions. Addison retorted that it was important for the Commonwealth to have India's complaint dismissed or referred to the ICJ. Other ministers agreed. As the Cabinet minutes put it, 'The point at issue was not the merits of the Indian case ... but the expediency of its being discussed'. The delegation 'should be made aware of the probable repercussions' of setting an unfortunate precedent for UN intervention in domestic matters:

> Once such intervention began, it would be difficult to set limits to it. Other Governments would see the weight of this argument.... the United States Government would hardly welcome discussion by the United Nations of the rights of negroes in the United States. And in India itself there were questions of differential treatment between different communities which the Government of India would not wish to have discussed by the General Assembly.

The Cabinet accordingly reaffirmed its earlier decision that British delegates 'should express no opinion on the merits of the question, but should support the view that this was a matter of domestic jurisdiction'. If this was not accepted, they should support a reference to the ICJ.[49]

Naturally, the delegation was unhappy with this response, and on 14 November it again asked the Cabinet to reconsider the matter. Shawcross fundamentally disagreed with Beckett's contention that the human rights provisions of the Charter could not be invoked until they had been clearly defined. It was, he said,

> 'really beyond argument and is expressly conceded by Smuts that there are certain fundamental human rights which are universally recognised and in regard to which a right of humanitarian intervention has been claimed to exist in international law apart from the charter'.[50]

In response, Beckett reiterated his disagreement with Shawcross:

> no doubt the Delegation are right in saying that certain forms of treatment even of nationals constitute a breach of an international obligation and ... the extermination of a section of the population falls into this category ... where you have something of this kind there is nothing in the Charter to prevent such an issue being raised and the domestic jurisdiction clause would not exclude it. For the moment, however, there is only really international authority for something in the nature of crimes against humanity and unless and until we know the meaning of human rights and fundamental freedoms in the Charter there is nothing to bring any form of discrimination as between nationals outside the domestic jurisdiction clause.[51]

The outcome of the Cabinet discussion on 18 November was predictable. After summarising its 4 November decision, the minutes say the Cabinet took note of the delegation's report that a majority of delegations would probably support a request for an ICJ ruling on the admissibility of the dispute, that Smuts might not ask for more, and that the delegation proposed to support such a proposal. After the meeting, the FO told the delegation that it had to obtain Smuts' approval for such a course, and it was not itself to take any initiative in that direction. But by then it was beginning to look as if Britain was whistling into the wind: further soundings had revealed the absence of the anticipated support for an advisory opinion, and that the proposal might even fail.

The Joint Committee 21–30 November

India's complaint was discussed at six Joint Committee meetings between 21 and 30 November. Mrs. Pandit opened by moving a strongly-worded resolution criticising South Africa. Smuts congratulated her on her speech, rejected India's complaint, and asked for an advisory opinion on the admissibility of the dispute. He was supported by Heaton Nicholls, his high commissioner in London, who offended many with a badly-argued and poorly-delivered speech. Mrs. Pandit, on the other hand, was cheered, and speaker after speaker supported her during what became a long and bitter debate on human rights.

Because the Indians performed so well, and the South Africans handled their case so badly, Shawcross had to play a larger than anticipated role in the debate and the British lobbied hard for votes. By 27 November Shawcross felt it would be safe to propose amending the Indian draft resolution so that the General Assembly decision would be postponed until after the ICJ had determined what, if any, international obligation had been broken by South Africa. The Indians were hurt and angry by Shawcross' action and the Indian delegation's report on the Assembly described him as having 'perfervidely' supported the Union.[52]

As the Committee reached the end of its work, it was clear that the vote would be close. South Africa withdrew its resolution in favour of a British-US-Swedish one asking the ICJ for an advisory opinion as to whether India's complaint touched on something that was essentially within the Union's domestic jurisdiction. India, meanwhile, sought to attract more votes by withdrawing its resolution in favour of a more conciliatory French-Mexican one.

In the event the British-US-Swedish resolution was never voted on. After a heated and confused discussion the French-Mexican resolution was put to the vote and obtained a small majority.[53] The Ukrainian Foreign Minister, who was in the chair, then ruled that it was unnecessary to vote on any other resolutions. Pandit shook hands with Smuts and condemned the British for betraying India.

The plenary vote, 8 December[54]

The Indians were 'in high fettle'[55] as the relevant plenary meeting approached, and the IO was not discomforted with the way things were working out. But although the DO and FO disliked the French-Mexican resolution, the delegation decided not to table an amendment or a separate resolution. Nor would the Americans or anyone else take a lead, so it was left to Smuts to table an amendment seeking an advisory opinion from the ICJ. (Bevin had persuaded Smuts to stay in New York for the plenary in order to increase the chances of success.)

Meanwhile, everyone was lobbying furiously. The Americans agreed to speak second in favour of Smuts' amendment and, together with the British and South Africans persuaded the Netherlands, Belgium, New Zealand, and Argentina to support a reference to the Court. And, *inter alia*, the Indians won over France, China, the Communist bloc, Mexico, the Philippines, and the Arab states.

The plenary debate on the joint committee's recommendation took place over 11 hours on 7 and 8 December. It started off in '[c]onditions [that] were just about as favourable for the South Africans as they could have hoped', and the Belgian chairman was 'helpfulness itself'.[56] Smuts tabled his amendment. The

US and El Salvador supported him. Then it was Pandit's turn. In a loudly applauded speech,

> She 'spurned legal arguments' and demanded a verdict on a proven violation of the Charter. Over the years India had 'appealed, complained, protested, sought compromises and agreements, and finally has been forced into retaliation and to bring this matter before the bar of world opinion'. It was now too late to argue about domestic jurisdiction. Unless allegiance to the Charter was a mockery they must decide this 'test case' and respond to the '[m]illions of voiceless people who, because of their creed or color,]sic.] have been relegated to positions of inferiority, [who] are looking to us for justice … . [who] have been moved to intense indignation at all forms of racial discrimination which stands focused on the problem of South Africa'.

> During her speech Pandit had appealed for British support, but so had Smuts, and Shawcross felt impelled to respond to the latter's request. This was because the mood of the Assembly was 'overwhelmingly in favour of India' and at first it looked as if every speaker would oppose Smuts' amendment. Shawcross' speech was brief, eloquent and warmly-applauded, but he antagonised Pandit by referring to 'Indian politicians, so unhappily divided by communal strife and discrimination in their own country' and by warning against 'appeals to the emotions by practised orators'.

However, Mrs. Pandit held the Assembly in the palm of her hand and there was 'hectic applause from the galleries and subdued clapping from the floor' when she accused Shawcross

> of bad taste in referring 'with evident and unconcerned glee' to differences in India which the British were responsible for fomenting. '[N]either aggressive nor humble,' but wiping a fortuitous tear from her eye … she made a final plea to the emotions and conscience of those 'who held the political fate of Asia and indeed the world in their grasp'.

By the end of the 'long and sometimes emotional debate'[57] it was clear India would win a majority vote, but it was doubtful whether there would be the necessary two-thirds majority if the Assembly determined (by a simple majority vote) that the treatment of Indians in South Africa was an 'important question' (Article 18.2 and 18.3 of the Charter). Voting at South Africa's request, the Assembly did so decide. It then voted on, and rejected, South Africa's amendment seeking an advisory opinion. It was midnight and the atmosphere was tense when the Assembly voted on the French-Mexican resolution. It was done openly and on an alphabetical basis, the first state to vote being chosen randomly. In calculating the requisite two-thirds figure abstentions were not counted – so that only at the end of the voting procedure would the result be known. India won by the barest majority: 32–15 with 7 abstentions. Pandemonium broke out.

As regards individual votes, Australia's is worth noting. Australia had been primarily responsible for inserting Article 2.7 into the Charter and there was an 'audible gasp'[58] when, it abstained early on in response to a 'strong' Indian request.[59] The British thought this had encouraged others to follow suit, and the South Africans thought it had conclusively determined the outcome. However, Canada and New Zealand, voted with Britain (the leader of New Zealand's delegation expressing horror at the way in which India had whipped up emotions: 'It was a "disgraceful exhibition of hamacting [*sic.*]" and an especially painful one coming from India which hardly had a perfect human rights record').[60]

Impact

The dispute had indeed been an emotional issue, especially for India. It believed it had right on its side and that its 'dignity and prestige'[61] were at stake. It was therefore very cross that Britain had – as India saw it – taken sides against it. Several additional factors exacerbated the tension. Britain was 'one of the main stumbling blocks'[62] on two other issues that mattered a lot to India (South-West Africa and trusteeship). The Indians (unjustifiably) felt in some way let down by Britain when they were soundly beaten in elections to the Security Council. And Indian worries about the deteriorating situation at home made them suspicious of British intentions regarding the transfer of power. There had also been personality clashes. Shawcross was arrogant, brilliant, 'tended to shoot, rhetorically speaking, from the hip'[63] and went all-out to win his cases. Pandit was hot-tempered, dramatic, 'highly temperamental',[64] and deployed her theatrical skills to great effect, not least in her attacks on Shawcross.

Meanwhile Krishna Menon, the London-based Secretary of the India League (which campaigned for Indian independence) was a generally baleful influence. He had some saving graces, being idealistic and 'very cordial ... when it suited his own ends'.[65] But he was also 'congenitally' dishonest; 'unscrupulous, egotistical and unreliable'; and 'an infernal nuisance'.[66] Even India's British friends, Noel-Baker and Curson, described him as 'pathological' and 'an evil influence, consumed with an overwhelming bitterness'.[67]

Unsurprisingly, the irritation arising from all these factors rubbed off on some British delegates, especially those from the DO – the junior minister Arthur Bottomley and two officials, Ben Cockram and Geoffrey Shannon. Their reactions also reflected the DO's support for Smuts; its antipathy to Krishna Menon; irritation with the Indians (who were 'very tiresome on occasion');[68] sheer weariness;[69] and lack of calibre (Bottomley, while likeable, was 'no great intellect').[70] Overall they appeared not to have tried to understand or establish good relations with the Indians – perhaps because it was generally assumed that independent India would quit the Commonwealth. Further, in their report on the Assembly the two officials made dubious assertions about the Indians being uncooperative and throwing 'taunts and jibes'.[71] (It is hardly surprising that the 1947 merger of the IO and DO into a new Commonwealth Relations Office was dismal, with 'no attempt at integration, very little at co-ordination and [with] differences ... resolved only at the ministerial level').[72]

But all this needs to be put in context. Relations between the Indian and UK delegates were on the whole 'very cordial', 'friendly' and 'co-operative'.[73] They were keen to get on, and did so. The Indians, who had had a very difficult journey to New York, appreciated British assistance with travel arrangements at a time of transport shortages. The British invited them to Commonwealth discussions, and helped them 'find their bearings'.[74] For their part, the Indians made it clear at the outset 'that they were out to function and co-operate to the fullest possible extent as one of the Commonwealth group'.[75] And although they sometimes demonstrated independent-mindedness by taking a different course from the UK, they were generally cooperative on issues where they did not clash with Britain.

Personal qualities were also important in keeping things on an even keel. Noel-Baker, Curson, and K P S Menon (a popular and distinguished Indian delegate) contributed to the maintenance of very good personal relations throughout. Noel-Baker, who understood Indians 'better than most'[76] and appreciated the political importance of the dispute for them, cultivated Pandit and, together with Curson, made sure at every stage that she knew in advance and in detail the reasons 'for our qualified support of General Smuts'.[77] And Curson was the perfect liaison person. He knew the dispute from every Whitehall angle; understood the UN; and got on so well with the Indians that they spoke extremely frankly in his presence.

However, the FO feared India might hold Britain's attitude against her in the future, a fear reinforced by a senior Indian official saying Britain's support for South Africa would cast a long shadow over Anglo-Indian relations. But the UN clashes made no 'deep or lasting impression in India',[78] and by June 1947 there was little interest there in the dispute. Nor did the Indians bear lingering personal grudges. Nehru felt no bitterness; Pandit spoke well of Shawcross in her memoirs; and the Indian delegate and jurist, M C Chagla, pointed out that 'wordy duels' and 'vituperative language' are part and parcel of courtroom debates and did not infringe on friendships. Though 'outwardly aggressive', Shawcross 'was a friendly soul', he said.[79] Moreover, Pandit's later high commissionership in London was her most enjoyable assignment, and even Krishna Menon formed a firm friendship with a South African high commissioner in London.[80]

Furthermore, the Indian and South African delegates managed 'to some extent'[81] to maintain good relations, and the Indians had excellent relations with Smuts. Nehru had reminded the delegation that they were the inheritors of Mahatma Gandhi's high ethical and moral traditions, and Gandhi had told Pandit that her 'mission would be a failure' if she lost Smuts' goodwill.[82] Gandhi would not sacrifice 'his friendship and respect for the sake of gaining a majority vote'. So she shook his hand after each debate, and after the final vote she asked him to forgive her if she had 'said anything which was not up to the high standard Gandhiji had imposed on me'.[83]

Liberalism?

However, the dispute proved unfortunate for Smuts in several ways. First, he had shown himself to be a poor tactician. He was responsible for South Africa's case being 'badly represented';[84] underestimated the Indians; did not listen to advice; and was 'completely out of his element' in the General Assembly.[85] He had witnessed but not heeded the humanitarian aspect of the 1945 San Francisco conference which established the UN, and dismissed the Assembly's bark as harmless, thinking his personal prestige and his country's international standing would protect the Union from serious criticism.[86] Not so. It was a sorry performance.

Second, in terms of domestic politics it was a considerable setback, as the outcome provided a good deal of ammunition for his political opponents. Smuts tried to counter this by making some very modest reforms to South Africa's racial laws. But this failed to have the desired effect and his United Party was deemed to have lost an important by-election 'mainly because of Smuts's alleged liberal attitude towards Indians'.[87] The 1948 general election ushered in a long period of Nationalist rule and, with it, the application of the system of racial *apartheid* and South Africa's growing international isolation.

Third, the UN defeat was in effect also a defeat for the Smuts version of liberal internationalism, with its emphasis on the values of western Christian civilisation and white supremacy. Evidently, this was no longer internationally acceptable. Smuts and his ideas had become 'an anachronism'.[88] And Britain, by putting too much faith in Smuts and effectively becoming South Africa's cheerleader, failed to uphold liberal values and ideals.

But although it was not then apparent, Britain had set in motion its helter-skelter withdrawal from empire. As Lord Beloff put it, 'Once the Indian Empire was given up there seemed little point in hanging on to the remainder. If there was threat of trouble, there was no point at all.'[89] The 'modern creed'[90] of liberal democracy was a powerful spur to the process, as was the CO's 'very liberal' attitude to independence and the arrival in the CO of a post-war generation of idealistic and slightly 'pink' officials who positively looked forward to dismantling the empire.[91]

Furthermore, the 1946 dispute contributed to a rather different kind of liberalism being introduced onto the international stage. For in effect the UN had spoken out in favour of a liberal interpretation of Article 2.7 and, more generally, put racial discrimination of a formal kind on the international agenda. This proved to be the thin end of a wedge into the walls of state exclusivity. For one of the characteristics of the second half of the twentieth century was the gradually widening attention the international community paid to how states treated their citizens – which was in marked contrast to the practice of the previous 50 years. Thus in 1948 the UN adopted the Universal Declaration of Human Rights. The Declaration had no legal force. And it was the product of the events of the Second World War, not the Indian-South African dispute. But the latter had contributed to its tone, helping to create an environment in which matters which had earlier been firmly beyond international concern could now be cautiously introduced. Moreover, the Declaration was followed in 1966 by two covenants on human rights: one on civil and political rights and the other on economic, social, and cultural rights. Both came into force ten years later, and by the end of the century had been ratified by most of the world's states.[92] They had no enforcement provisions, but alleged breaches could be highlighted and possibly cause embarrassment. Several regional instruments aiming at the protection of human rights were also established. The milieu of international discourse was slowly amended in a liberal direction. The same phenomenon had occurred within many states by the end of the century, and despite some faltering, it remains a powerful ideal.

Not too much must be made of all this. Paper announcements or even promises may not much influence the world's social fabric, but the atmosphere surrounding the treatment of human beings changed. This development cannot be attributed to the way in which the Indian-South African dispute was dealt with in 1946. But the UN's response to it was one of the tributaries which converged to add a liberal hue to international politics. In that sense the dispute is a historical landmark.

Notes

1. Quoted in Hancock, *Survey of British Commonwealth affairs*, 179.
2. In 1870, Natal's Indian population was 6,448; in 1884 it was 27,000, in 1891 it was 35,00; and in the 1890s the Indians outnumbered Europeans: see *ibid*. 178–9. The Transvaal also introduced tough anti-Indian legislation but most South African Indians lived in Natal where, in 1946, there were 233,000 Europeans and 228,000 Indians.
3. Pandit, *The Scope of Happiness*, 206.
4. Smuts quoted in Beinart, "The Day my Father Lost his Country". Dr FD Tothill alerted me to this.
5. Agreed communiqué announcing Cape Town Agreement, Annex V to FO draft memorandum for Cabinet Steering Committee on International Organisations, IOC (S)(46), 2 Oct. 1946, London: India Office Records (IOR), L/E/9/1403.
6. Cabinet Delegation and Wavell top secret telegram S/3 to Attlee, 4 May 1946, IOR, L/P&J/5/337.
7. The only exception is when the UN is taking enforcement action under Chapter VII of the Charter.
8. Indians had grievances in East Africa and Ceylon, Australia had a 'white' immigration policy, and the Canadian province of British Columbia discriminated against Asians.
9. Khare, *My Political Memoirs or Autobiography*, 183.
10. For the sources of quotations in this section, and a longer discussion of India's case, see Lloyd, "A Most Auspicious Beginning," 133–5. On the background to the dispute, see Lloyd, "A Family Quarrel," 703–25.

11. Paul Gore-Booth (Head of Reconstruction Department, FO) draft memorandum, 24 Jul. 1946, Kew, The National Archives (TNA), UN1691/432/78 FO371/59785.
12. Trevelyan, *The India we Left*, 246.
13. G H Baxter (senior official, IO) minute, 3 Jul.1946, IOR, L/E/9/1403.
14. Wavell to Pethick-Lawrence, 8 Jul., Pethick-Lawrence to Wavell, 25 Jul. 1946, IOR, L/PO/474.
15. R N Gilchrist (IO) minute for J.P. Gibson (Head of Political Department), 29 Jun. 1946, IOR, L/E/9/1403.
16. Gibson minute, 29 Jul. 1946, IOR L/E/9/1403.
17. Lord Shawcross interview, 1990.
18. East, *A Part of All that I Have Met*; private communications and conversations 1987, 1988.
19. Machtig minute, 1 Aug. 1946, TNA, DO121/107.
20. FO draft memorandum, 2 Oct. 1946.
21. Lord Shawcross to author, 19 Feb. 1990.
22. Gilchrist minute, 29 Jun.1946.
23. Garner, *The Commonwealth Office 1925–68*, 142. Brian Barder conversation (1999). Interviews: Arthur Menzies (1998), Bill Peters (1998), Basil Robinson (1998).
24. Parkinson, *The Colonial Office from Within*, 96.
25. Cross, "Whitehall and the Commonwealth," 201.
26. Fitzmaurice, "Sir Eric Beckett". Beckett was probably 'the most gifted person ever to have held the post'. See also Fitzmaurice and Vallat, "Sir (William) Eric Beckett," 267–326.
27. *South Africa's 'Indian problem'. Background to the new legislation*, Public Relations Officer, South Africa House London, 10 Apr. 1946.
28. Pethick-Lawrence telegram 15024 to Wavell.
29. Wavell telegram to Pethick-Lawrence, private & secret, 15 Oct. 1946 in Mansergh and Moon, *The Transfer of Power*, vol. 8, *1942–47*, document 469.
30. Machtig to Monteath (PUS, IO), secret & confidential, 2 Oct. 1946, TNA, DO35/1290.
31. Unless otherwise indicated, quotations in this section are from the FO draft memorandum, 2 Oct. 1946.
32. Charles Dixon (Constitutional Adviser, DO) minute, 1 Aug 1946, TNA, DO35/1122/G715/36.
33. Dixon to Berkeley (FO), 13 Sep. 1946, TNA, DO121/107.
34. Curson (IO) minute, 13 Sep. 1946, IOR, L/E/9/1403.
35. Gore-Booth minute, 9 Sep. 1946, TNA, UN2388/432/78 FO371/59787.
36. Beckett minute 10 Sep. 1946, IOR L/E/9/1403. On the doctrine of *inter-se*, whereby Britain insisted that intra-imperial relations were of a special, non-international nature and, accordingly, were not governed by international law, see Fawcett, *The British Commonwealth*, 144–207.
37. CM9(46), minute 3, http://filestore.nationalarchives.gov.uk/pdfs/large/cab-128-6.pdf.
38. See Jebb, *The Memoirs of Lord Gladwyn*, 194.
39. Noel-Baker to Arthur Bottomley (Parliamentary Under-Secretary, DO), 7 Mar. 1947, Noel-Baker papers, Churchill College Cambridge.
40. Pandit, *Scope*, 213.
41. Ben Cockram (DO official attached to British embassy Washington) to Sir John Stephenson (senior official, DO), 30 Oct. 1946, TNA, UN3736/432/78 FO371/59794.
42. UK delegation telegram 1395, 1 Nov. 1946, TNA, UN3325/432/78 FO371/59792. Curson said Shawcross never actually said that he or his government considered

India's complaint inadmissible under Article 2.7. See 'Summary of discussions', 27 Jun. 1947, IOR, L/E/9/1405.
43. UK delegation telegram 1332, 29 Oct. 1946, TNA, DO 121/107.
44. Hugh Keenleyside memorandum, "The India and South Africa Problem", enclosed in New York telegram 83, 1 Nov. 1946. Document 862 in Page, *Documents on Canadian External Relations*.
45. Shawcross during UK delegation meeting, 3 Nov. 1946, TNA, UN3640/434/78 FO371/59974.
46. Curson telegram 1395 to R M J Harris (Pethick-Lawrence's Private Secretary), private & personal, 3 Nov. 1946, IOR, L/E/9/1403.
47. On Canada's policy, see Henshaw, "Canada and the 'South African Disputes'," 9–12.
48. Cripps minute for Attlee, 31 Oct. 1946, TNA, DO35/1293/G715/46.
49. CM94(46) minute 1, http://filestore.nationalarchives.gov.uk/pdfs/large/cab-128-6.pdf.
50. UK delegation telegram 1668, 14 Nov. 1946, TNA, DO35/1293/G715/46. Looking back, Shawcross thought 'the British were right on a strict legal basis but, possibly correctly from a broader point of view, most of the delegates were concerned with the politics of the human rights moment': Lord Shawcross to author, 19 Feb.1990.
51. Beckett minute, 18 Nov. 1946, TNA, U3704/432/78, FO 371/9794.
52. Report of the Indian delegation to the second part of the first session of the General Assembly of the United Nations 1946, Lucknow, 27 Feb. 1947, New Delhi: Indian National Archives, 2(19)-UNOI/47 1947.
53. By 24 to 19 with 6 abstentions and 5 absent.
54. For the sources of unreferenced quotations in this section, see Lloyd, "Auspicious Beginning," 146–8.
55. Curson to Anderson, 2 Dec.1946, IOR L/E/9/1404.
56. Tothill, *South African-Australian Diplomatic Relations 1945–1961*, 408.
57. Australian delegation cablegram, 9 December 1946. Document 302, in Hudson and Way, *Documents on Australian Foreign Policy*.
58. Sole, *This Above All*, 102.
59. Tothill, *South African-Australlian*, 409.
60. Berendson to Fraser, 23 Dec. 1946, quoted in Battersby, "New Zealand, Domestic Jurisdiction, and Apartheid," 109.
61. Jha, *From Bandung to Tashkent*, 25.
62. Minute on Curson to Anderson, 28 Nov. 1946.
63. Shawcross obituary, *The Guardian*, 11 Jul. 2003, http://www.theguardian.com/news/2003/jul/11/guardianobituaries.obituaries.
64. Chagla, *Roses in December*, 231.
65. Garner minute, 9 Feb. 1954, TNA DO35/9014; Curson top secret report on Krishna Menon, 31 Dec. 1946, IOR L/E/9/1396; Curson note on the Indian Delegation, 27 Dec. 1946, IOR, L/E/9/IOR, L/E/9/1392.
66. Shawcross interview; P H Gore-Booth (High Commissioner, New Delhi) to Joe Garner (PUS Commonwealth Relations Office) 3 Feb. 1962, TNA, DO196/209; Garner minute, 9 Feb. 1954, Malcolm MacDonald (High Commissioner, New Delhi) to Lord Home, 18 Sep. 1957, TNA, DO35//9014.
67. Curson to Shannon (DO), 18 Jan. 1947, IOR, L/E/9/1392; Curson to Anderson, 28 Oct. 1946, IOR, L/E/9/1396.
68. Curson to Shannon, 18 Jan. 1947.
69. 'Lasting for at least three months, a regular session is a grinding task': Gore-Booth, *With Great Truth and Respect*, 159.
70. Interviews: Lord Shawcross, Sir William Dale (1998), Geoff Murray (1999).

71. Cockram and Shannon confidential note, 19 Dec.1946, IOR L/E/9/1392.
72. Garner, *Commonwealth Office*, 288.
73. Pethick-Lawrence to Wavell, private & secret, 22 Nov. 1946 in Mansergh and Moon, *The Transfer of Power*, vol. 9, *1942–47*, document 78; Curson note on Indian delegation, 27 Dec. 1946.
74. Pethick-Lawrence private & secret to Wavell, 8 Nov. 1946, in *Transfer of Power*, vol. 9, document 18.
75. Ibid.
76. Pandit, *Scope*, 213.
77. Noel-Baker to Bottomley, 7 Mar. 1947, Noel-Baker papers.
78. Curson to J D Peek (Cabinet Office), 7 Mar. 1947, C&0 1067/47, IOR, L/E/9/1405.
79. Chagla, *Roses*, 242, 243. Chagla became a distinguished judge, diplomat and member of the cabinet.
80. See Egeland, *Bridges of Understanding*, 202.
81. Curson note on Indian delegation, 27 Dec. 1946.
82. Pandit quoted in Cockram note enclosed in Cockram (Washington) to Shannon, 19 Aug. 1947, IOR, L/E/9/1405.
83. Pandit, *Scope*, 206, 211.
84. Curson during interdepartmental discussion, 24 Jun. 1946, TNA, DO35/3284.
85. 'He did not hear very well, especially when listening to interpretations … he knew nothing about rules of procedure and how they could be manipulated': Sole, *This above all*, 101–2.
86. See Tothill, "Evatt and Smuts," 187–8; See also Dubow, "Smuts," 66.
87. Lord Listowel (Pethick-Lawrence's successor at the IO) in Henshaw, "Britain and South Africa at the United Nations," 87–8. Tothill points out that in 1948 the Nationalists won office with 37.7% of the vote (401,834 votes) to the United Party's 49.2% (524,230 votes): Tothill email.
88. Tothill, "South African-Australian," 444.
89. Beloff, 'The British Empire', manuscript in author's possession.
90. Ibid.
91. Sir Brian Barder conversation, 1999. British Diplomatic Oral History Programme interviews: Denis Doble 29 Mar. 2004, Brian Barder 6 Mar. 1997; Rex Browning nd, https://www.chu.cam.ac.uk/archives/collections/bdohp/.
92. In May 2018 there were 170 parties to the covenant on civil and political rights and 167 parties to the covenant on economic, social and cultural rights.

Acknowledgements

When I first researched this topic, I was assisted by the Nuffield Foundation, the National Archives of India, the Nehru Memorial Library, the India Office Library and Records, the British National Archives and the libraries of Keele University, Central Manchester and the FCO. Individuals who helped me included Ambassadors CS Jha and Khub Chand; Professors Sarvepalli Gopal, Partha Sarathi Gupta, KP Saksena and Jack Spence; Drs TG Ramamurthy and Panigrahi; Mr BR Curson and Mr Kenneth East. This article additionally benefited from research in the South African National Archives, the UN Archives in New York and the US National Archives; online documents; and correspondence, conversations and interviews with, and material provided by, Lords Beloff and Shawcross, Drs FD Tothill and Peter Henshaw, Sir Brian Barder and Lady Barder, Sir William Dale, Mr Arthur Menzies, Mr Geoff Murray, Mr Bill Peters and Mr Basil Robinson. Dr Tothill also made valuable comments on earlier drafts. Professor Alan James remains my keenest and most constructive critic. I thank them all.

Disclosure statement

No potential conflict of interest was reported by the author.

References

Battersby, John. "New Zealand, Domestic Jurisdiction and Apartheid, 1945–47." *The Journal of Imperial and Commonwealth History* 24, no. 1 (1966): 101–117.
Beinart, Peter. "The Day my Father Lost his Country." *The Atlantic*, 16 Dec. 2016. http://tinyurl.com/he2kcjj.
Chagla, M. C. *Roses in December*. Bombay: Bharatiya Vidya, 1974.
Cross, J. A. "Whitehall and the Commonwealth." *Journal of Commonwealth Political Studies* 2, no. 3 (1964): 189–206.
Dubow, Saul. "Smuts, the United Nations and the Rhetoric of Race and Rights." *Journal of Contemporary History* 43, no. 1 (2008): 45–74.
East, Kenneth. *A Part of All that I Have Met*. unpublished memoir, 1988.
Egeland, Leif. *Bridges of Understanding. A Personal Record in Teaching, Law, Politics and Diplomacy*. Cape Town & Pretoria: Human & Rousseau, 1977.
Fawcett, J. E. S. *The British Commonwealth in International Law*. London: Stevens & Sons, 1963.
Fitzmaurice, Sir Gerald. "Sir Eric Beckett." *The Times*, 14 Sep. 1966.
Fitzmaurice, G. G., and F. A. Vallat. "Sir (William) Eric Beckett, KCMG, QC (1896–1966)." *The International and Comparative Law Quarterly* 17, no. 2 (1968): 267–326.
Garner, Joe. *The Commonwealth Office 1925–68*. London: Heinemann, 1978.
Gore-Booth, Paul. *With Great Truth and Respect*. London: Constable, 1974.
Hancock, W. K. *Survey of British Commonwealth Affairs*, vol. 1, *Problems of Nationality 1918–1936*. London: Oxford University Press, 1937.
Henshaw, Peter. "Britain and South Africa at the United Nations: 'South West Africa' 'Treatment of Indians' and 'Race Conflict', 1946–61." *South African Historical Journal* 31, no. 1 (1994): 80–102.
Henshaw, Peter. "Canada and the 'South African Disputes' at the United Nations, 1946–61." *Canadian Journal of African Studies* 33, no. 1 (1999): 80–102.
Hudson, W. J., and Wendy Way, eds. *Documents on Australian Foreign Policy*. vol. 10, *1946, July–December*. https://dfat.gov.au/about-us/publications/historical-documents/Pages/volume-10/1946-july-december-volume-10.aspx.
Jebb, Gladwyn. *The Memoirs of Lord Gladwyn*. London: Weidenfeld & Nicolson, 1972.
Jha, C. S. *From Bandung to Tashkent: Glimpses of India's Foreign Policy*. London: Sangam Books, 1983.
Khare, N. B. *My Political Memoirs or Autobiography*. Nagppur: Nakshatra Press, 1959.
Lloyd, Lorna. "'A Family Quarrel': The Development of the Dispute Over Indians in South Africa." *The Historical Journal* 34, no. 3 (1991): 703–725.
Lloyd, Lorna. "'A Most Auspicious Beginning': The 1946 United Nations General Assembly and the Question of the Treatment of Indians in South Africa." *Review of International Studies* 16, no. 2 (1990): 131–153.
Mansergh, Nicholas, and Penderel Moon, eds. *The Transfer of Power 1942–47*, vol. 8, *The Interim Government, 3 July-1 November, 1946*. London: HMSO, 1979.

Mansergh, Nicholas, and Penderel Moon, eds. *The Transfer of Power, 1942–47*, vol. 9, *The Fixing of a Time Limit, 4 November 1946–22 March 1947*. London: HMSO, 1980.

Page, Donald M., ed. *Documents on Canadian External Relations*. vol. 12, *1946*. http://gac.canadiana.ca/view/ooe.b1603413E_012/1?r=0&s=1.

Pandit, Vijaya Lakshmi. *The Scope of Happiness. A Personal Memoir*. London: Weidenfeld & Nicolson, 1979.

Parkinson, Sir Cosmo. *The Colonial Office from Within*. London: Faber & Faber, 1947.

Sole, Donald. *This Above All. Reminiscences of a South African Diplomat*. (unpublished undated memoirs).

Tothill, F. D. "South African-Australian Diplomatic Relations 1945–1961." *unpublished PhD thesis*, University of South Africa, 1995.

Tothill, F. D. "Evatt and Smuts in San Francisco." *The Round Table* 389, no. 96 (2007): 177–192.

Trevelyan, Humphrey. *The India we Left*. London: Macmillan, 1972.

A Liberal Ghost? The Left, Liberal Democracy and the Legacy of Harold Laski's Teaching

Brant Moscovitch

ABSTRACT
This article explores the ways in which British socialism may have supported and strengthened liberal ideas held by postcolonial leaders who were educated in Britain. It attempts to do so by examining the role of liberalism in Harold Laski's teaching at the London School of Economics and Political Science (1920–50), with particular attention to his Indian students. Laski, a self-declared Marxist, promoted socialism in his voluminous writings, frequent speeches, and in his lectures, which were attended by many future post-colonial leaders. Although often rigid in its adhesion to socialist dogma, Laski's thought nevertheless reflected the malleability of political ideologies, incorporating liberal and pluralist elements in its makeup, which were in turn conveyed to students. This article focuses on how two former pupils, G.L. Mehta and Renuka Ray, responded to Laski's thinking in the context of early Nehruvian India. Drawing on students' lecture notes, political writings and assessments of their former professor, I suggest that Laski, and British socialism more generally, served to both radicalise students' desire for economic planning while moderating their understanding of how to generate political change by reinforcing liberal norms, including a belief in constitutionalism and representative government.

Introduction

In his message to the second annual anniversary celebrations of the Harold Laski Institute of Political Science in Ahmedabad, Jawaharlal Nehru referred to the organisation's namesake as a great teacher whose students could be found all over the world. Laski 'taught not only economics and politics', Nehru affirmed, 'but also how to apply them to human welfare'.[1] The Institute was established in 1954, four years after Laski's passing, in part to commemorate his legacy of teaching Indian students at the London School of Economics and Political Sciences (LSE). Laski lectured at LSE from 1920 to 1950, during which time he formed close and often enduring relationships with numerous students who later assumed significant roles in India's government and Foreign Service, including V.K. Krishna Menon (Defence Minister of India 1957–62), as well as G.L. Mehta (Ambassador to the United States, 1952–58), women's rights advocate Renuka Ray and K.R. Narayanan (President of India 1997–2002). So extensive was the list of students he taught that a rumour emerged after his death: a chair was reserved, so the story went, for the professor's ghost at every cabinet meeting in Delhi.[2] Beyond India, Laski mentored N.M. Perera, leading member of the Ceylonese Trotskyite Lanka Sama Samaja Party, as well as several high profile Canadians, including Prime Minister Pierre Trudeau (1968–79; 1980–84) and philosopher C.B. Macpherson. If Nehru's comments, vague as they may have been, contain some truth, the implications would have been widespread and significant in shaping the thinking that informed many intellectual and governing elites throughout the former British Empire.

As a great deal of work has shown, the period following World War I witnessed a rising number of foreign and colonial students attending British universities, long before the influx of Commonwealth migrants after the Second World War.[3] By 1925, there were 1329 students from the colonies and dominions studying in British universities, as well as 1071 from India alone.[4] In the 1927–28 academic year, there were 1102 Africans, (including South Africa, Egypt and Rhodesia) one hundred and eighty-four Canadians and 1339 Indians.[5] They came for multiple reasons, in particular to enhance their employment prospects in fields such as law and medicine; for Indians in particular, a trip to the UK was necessary for entrance into the Indian Civil Service. The traffic had lasting and often conflicting results, perpetuating the entrenchment of the English language, raising questions of race and identity through cross-cultural interactions and, ironically, promoting nationalism in students who frequently tasted freedom for the first time while in Britain and returned with a greater desire to terminate the empire that supressed it at home.

Far less scrutiny, however, has been devoted to the implications of this educational migration on political thought. This omission is noteworthy, perhaps particularly so regarding Laski, whose teaching, especially of foreign students, is widely acknowledged as his most lasting legacy.[6] To be sure, most existing commentary suggests Laski, and British education more generally, promoted a strong bias towards socialism in foreign students. The American politician Daniel Patrick Moynihan summed up this position most colourfully with his belief that British universities exerted a lasting influence over the ideological beliefs of leaders throughout the decolonising world. Laski in particular, Moynihan wrote, 'once molded the minds of so many future leaders of the "new majority"', by which he meant anti-capitalist countries hostile to the United States.[7]

Yet as Bayly's work on Indian liberalism convincingly argued, liberal ideas can be traced in the thinking of those traditionally considered socialist and sympathetic to the Soviet Union, including Jawaharlal Nehru, while liberals like G.K.

Gokhale could cite Laski to support their own positions.[8] Laski, though a self-declared Marxist, maintained liberal and pluralist elements in his thought into the 1930s, and arguably throughout his life, raising questions about the malleability of political ideologies, how his teachings were interpreted, their impact on the history of late colonial and early post-colonial Indian political thought, and how, more generally, ideas are exchanged, embraced and altered when moving transnationally. Echoing Glenda Sluga and Timothy Rowse, moreover, a further question arises: how far can an ideology like liberalism be stretched, geographically, temporally or ideologically, before it loses meaning?[9] If Laski can be described as retaining some fundamental liberal beliefs, in short, what were they, how did they relate to his Marxism, and how were they transmitted and finally digested by those facing historical and political challenges distinct from the context in which Laski developed and promoted his ideas?

This article asserts that, in addition to being present in Laski's socialism, core liberal concepts are evident in the responses he elicited from many of his students. I begin by discussing Laski's primary ideas, including his notion of economic democracy and revolution by consent, before proceeding to draw from student lecture notes to assess what Laski conveyed in his classes. I continue by examining in detail two Indian students, G.L. Mehta and Renuka Ray, who left extensive and representative reflections on Laski's thought, noting both their approval of Laski's socialism while drawing on his work and lectures to promote a respect for constitutional process and representative democracy. I conclude by suggesting that the presence of liberal ideas in Laski's socialism appealed to a global desire for a compromise between capitalism and communism during the early Cold War.

Laski's Lecture Theatre

Harold Joseph Laski was born in Manchester in 1893. His parents were Polish Jews who immigrated to England in the middle of the nineteenth century, part of the large wave of Jewish migrants fleeing the Pale of Settlement that included the family of Ralph Miliband, as well as future Israeli Prime Minister Moshe Sharett (1954–55), both future Laski students. Though Laski rejected religion, he claimed that the sense he gained of being treated differently for no tangible reason contributed to his eventual embrace of socialism.[10] Laski's father, Nathan, became a successful cotton merchant and embraced a belief in Gladstonian Liberalism that his son would reject from a young age. A gifted youth, Harold Laski attended Manchester Grammar School, where he claimed to have first developed a revulsion of what his future colleague at LSE, R.H. Tawney, termed the 'acquisitive society' around him.[11] He subsequently read history at New College, Oxford, where he developed an interest in Fabian socialism.[12] Rooted in the reformed liberalism of thinkers such as L.T. Hobhouse and J.A. Hobson, as well as Fabian socialism, Laski's emerging intellectual trajectory was shaped by a belief that the traditional liberalism to which his family subscribed overlooked a 'whole class of human beings' at home and abroad.[13]

By 1920, his growing reputation, earned teaching and writing in North America, including stints at McGill University, Harvard and Yale, helped him secure a position lecturing at LSE. He obtained a Professorship in 1926 and remained at the School until his death in 1950. [LSE] During his tenure, LSE emerged as a leading centre of higher education for Britons as well as for foreign elites. The School, founded in 1895 by the Fabian socialists Sidney and Beatrice Webb, along with George Bernard Shaw and Graham Wallas, witnessed a period of profound growth after World War I under the Directorship of William Beveridge (1919–1937). This included substantial new funding from the Rockefeller Foundation, a physical expansion in central London that some derided, in stark contrast to aesthetic beauty of Oxbridge, as a new empire of concrete, and the creation of new professorships that placed LSE at the forefront of the emerging social sciences.[14] In addition to Laski, Bronislaw Malinowski became Professor of Anthropology [1927–42] while Friedrich von Hayek and Lionel Robbins emerged as leading free-market advocates in Economics. Yet while many overseas students formed intellectual and personal relationships with LSE faculty members – Jomo Kenyatta, for instance, studied under Malinowski, and Indian liberal B.R. Shenoy was influenced by Hayek's work – no other teacher attracted the intense following and devotion that Laski did.

There were several reasons for this, beginning with Laski's charisma in a classroom. Depictions of his classes at LSE are consistent regardless of regional background or time. Gladstone Mills, a Jamaican student who attended the School during its wartime evacuation to Cambridge, singled him out as a 'particularly stimulating and witty teacher'.[15] Mills remembered that one of Laski's courses, 'Social and Political Theory', attracted students from Cambridge as well as American G.I.s who were stationed in a nearby camp. His class was often 'so crowded that if you did not arrive at least 20 minutes before the lecture, you had to resort to standing or sitting on the floor'.[16] Lee Kuan Yew, who briefly attended LSE before moving onto Cambridge, described Laski as magnetic and scintillating.[17] The future Indian politician and diplomat, B.K. Nehru, made sure to rouse himself out of bed for Laski's Wednesday morning lectures, despite electing to sleep in on most other days.[18] For her part, Renuka Ray fondly recalled Laski providing her and G.L. Mehta the opportunity to refute fellow student (and Laski's future colleague) Lionel Robbins' remarks on the responsibilities of the British Empire – according to Ray, Mehta's witty retort sent the class into fits of laughter.[19]

Laski's charisma and Socratic style of teaching both entertained and stimulated, while his commitment to politics, and particularly to Indian independence, further attracted students from the Subcontinent. He worked intimately, for instance, with V.K. Krishna Menon, a student of his who graduated with an MSc in Political Science in 1934 and remained in London until after independence, including a stint as India's first High Commissioner to the UK from 1947 to 1952. Laski collaborated with Menon through the latter's India League, a London-based anti-colonial organisation where Laski spoke frequently, denouncing British imperialism and the abuses of colonial authority, including the Amritsar Massacre and the Bengal Famine.[20] Relationships like this between colonial activists and metropolitan radicals enabled agitators like Menon to form contacts that furthered their ability to organise and protest.[21] Laski played an important role in this process as someone with a position commanding respect, while in turn using the India League to continue communicating his ideological message to students.

That message was powerful in its own right. His first books, *Studies in the Problem of Sovereignty* (1917) and *Authority in the Modern State* (1919), advanced a pluralist worldview that emphasised the importance of power centres other than the state, such as churches or civic organisations.[22] These early essays were grounded by preoccupations with authority, freedom and obligation to the state that would remain lifelong interests. Laski's evolving thought was shaped by the inequities and labour unrest he witnessed throughout the post-war Atlantic world. These included his involvement in the 1919 Boston Police Strike that led to his leaving a lectureship at Harvard, and a series of disputes in Britain, culminating in the 1926 General Strike, which resulted in severe productivity losses yet failed to ease labour tension. The governments' truculent responses to the demands of labour's supporters for improved conditions fuelled Laski's belief that what he described as 'abstract political democracy' was unresponsive to the needs of those without economic influence.[23] The Depression and 1931 political crisis, which lead to the creation of the Tory-dominated National Government, increased his scepticism of Fabian gradualism and further encouraged him to see Marxism as the necessary vehicle to advance 'economic democracy', which he believed was vitally needed to avert disaster.

For Laski, what this meant was to effectively engender practical economic liberty so that virtually everyone had the opportunity to maximise their potential. In his 1936 book, *The Rise of European Liberalism*, he followed Marxist thinking in arguing that the growth of liberty in seventeenth and eighteenth Europe was an exclusive type of liberty, enjoyed only by the emerging bourgeoisie. The attempts by English radical groups, such as the Levellers, to extend political rights to other groups in society failed in the early modern period, yet this was indeed the revolution that Laski now called for in the early twentieth.[24] In 'The Decline of Liberalism', an address delivered four years later during the Second World War, Laski reasserted that in the existing system of social organisation, man's capacity for growth was restricted.[25] Indeed, in order to enjoy the same opportunities, one needed economic democracy.

Moving far away from his earlier pluralism, Laski hence concluded that the change he desired would require a strong state to undertake radical transformations in the existing organisation of society. This would feature mass nationalisations, including the establishment of a public role in health, education and industry, and, more generally, a movement toward an increasingly planned society, underpinned by '... a new conception of property in which social ownership and control replace individual ownership and control'.[26] It would require the state to own and control the land, import-export trade, transport, fuel and power while also assuming control of capital and credit, including nationalising the Bank of England.[27] In order to carry out reforms, Laski envisioned a committee of experts advising the cabinet, who would then obtain the necessary approval of parliament.

Student testimonies and lecture notes affirm that there was significant overlap between his writing and his teaching, something further corroborated by the appearance of his books in his syllabi.[28] Robbins went so far as to question Laski's ability to convey 'truth' and be 'objective', calling his teaching 'systematically propagandist'.[29] Laski's courses at LSE focused primarily on the history of British and French politics, political theory and government. By the late 1920s, Krishna Menon's lecture notes not only reflected Laski's increasing disenchantment with reformed liberalism but also a shift in his thought to a greater acceptance of state power over the individual. Menon took his classes in 'Public Administration' and 'Political Ideas'. In his notes from a class entitled 'Political and Social Theory' in 1928, Laski presented students with his reading of the social fallout from the Industrial Revolution. As Menon recorded it, the enduring lesson was that '... private enterprise cannot be left unfettered', as it was contrary 'to the well-being of society'. Laski affirmed that the history of the nineteenth century 'proves it'.[30]

As Laski grew more radical in the 1930s into World War II, increasingly advocating mass nationalisations and expressing admiration for the economic achievements, if not the politics, of the Soviet Union, student notes again reflected the shift. The Canadian philosopher C.B. Macpherson, for instance, noted Laski's elusiveness on the matter of violent revolution. In one of his lectures on Marxism in 1934, with many on the left still bitterly disappointed about the formation of the National Government three years prior, Laski, he recorded,

> seems more inclined to the necessity for forceful revolution in the change to any socialism. Yet he was quite clear that we in England at any rate should aim first at constitutional procedure, the conditions not being ripe for revolution.[31]

Laski's aversion to violence made him highly sceptical of revolution. What was needed, rather, was a revolution by consent. As he described as early as 1933, in *Democracy in Crisis*, his ideal was for a socialist government to be elected and, crucially, for the political and economic establishment to accept its legitimacy.[32] This essentially called for one class to cede its power in favour of ensuring economic rights for the rest; economic democracy would be achieved, and political democracy preserved. Yet Laski viewed this as a long shot. One class, he affirmed, was highly unlikely to participate in its destruction at the hands of another, which was essentially what Laski's revolution called for. The rise of fascism in Europe, or the failure of the second Labour government in 1931 underscored this.

> The establishment of socialism in terms of democratic peace involves so profound a revolution in the psychology of the privileged class, so rapid an adjustment to new motives and new values, that a doubt whether it is practicable is at least a permissible speculation.[33]

In *The Road to Serfdom*, his colleague Friedrich Hayek emphasised Laski's equivocation, affirming that the question of whether a Labour government could risk its policies being overturned following the next general election was one that Laski left open.[34]

Tracing Laski in G.L. Mehta and Renuka Ray

Laski's progressive move away from pluralism, his increasing faith in the state and his scepticism of the possibility for democratic change highlighted an illiberal stream in his thought. There is debate amongst scholars of Laski as to the extent to which liberal ideas remained palpable in his thinking later in his life. One of Laski's early biographers understood his career as containing distinct phases, which by the early 1930s articulated a clear rejection of pluralism.[35] Michael Freeden, on the other hand, has argued that liberalism seeped into the development of British socialist thinking, a trend that he suggests Laski's writings demonstrated. Freeden posits that equality, for Laski, 'was an extension of self-government because its absence meant the rule of limited numbers and the wielding of undue influence; it was, *pro tanto*, essential to freedom'.[36] For the purposes of this article, it suffices to identify fluidity and ambiguity in his work; indeed, this paper is less concerned with scrutinising Laski's work in itself or locating ideological breaks and phases than in addressing the assessments of his students and those who drew inspiration from him.

In a highly polemical book, the classical liberal commentator Sanjeev Sabhlok recently took aim at Laski for instilling in Jawaharlal Nehru a reckless understanding of property rights, namely that they were relative and not to be accorded the sanctity traditionally accorded in classical liberalism.[37] What Sabhlok labels as India's poor performance since Independence – by which he means the disappointments of the so-called Nehruvian-inspired 'licence raj', plagued by overregulation and red tape – was a result of the first Prime Minister's socialism, which Laski played a crucial role in promoting. Sabhlok's argument is not new, and in fact traces back at least to John Kenneth Galbraith, the American Ambassador to New Delhi from 1961 to 1963, who asserted that 'the centre of Nehru's thinking was Laski'.[38]

There is at least some visual evidence of Nehru's attachment to Laski. Outside Prime Minister's former bedroom in Teen Murti, preserved in what is now the Nehru Memorial Museum and Library, rests a small selection of pictures, one of which is of the bespectacled LSE academic. How significant was Laski in shaping Nehru's ideology? The two met through Menon and his India League in the early 1930s. They stayed in touch for the rest of Laski's life, meeting during Nehru's trips to the UK. In their surviving correspondence, Laski seems to have offered some minor political advice to Nehru,[39] as well as council about Indira Nehru's (later Gandhi) education.[40] Yet the evidence linking Laski to Nehru contains more smoke than gun than Galbraith and Sabhlok acknowledge. It would be more accurate to say that the two were intellectual soul-mates who recognised their similar ideas that emerged from the same stew of Fabian socialism, reformed liberalism and sceptical admiration of the Soviet Union's economic achievements. Indeed, if Nehru drew inspiration from Laski, the professor saw Nehru as someone who shared his worldview. In 1945, Laski alluded to the future Prime Minister as a kindred spirit, saying that Nehru was distinct among Congress leaders as someone who appreciated the connection between politics and economics.[41] For Nehru, as for Laski, the central issue was poverty in India. Freedom must be attained in order to tackle this problem.[42] Laski accurately noted in 1939 that Nehru desired more than a political revolution, but that he wanted '... a social revolution, which would effect a complete change in India's economic system'.[43] British rule, he continued, was fundamentally opposed to that transformation, which could only be procured after independence.[44] Laski's stance against imperialism in South Asia, as we have seen, played a major part to endearing him to Indian nationalists. Yet his intellectual inspiration was equally compelling and perhaps more enduring, particularly for those, like Nehru, who were committed to constitutionalism and representative democracy but looking to supplement it with social, or economic democracy.

This is more clearly evident in two of Laski's students, G.L. Mehta and Renuka Ray, who present more empirical case studies in how Laski's thinking was interpreted by his Indian pupils. After attending Elphinstone college in Bombay, Mehta enrolled at LSE, where his courses included psychology, political ideas and government.[45] Following graduation in 1924, Mehta embarked on a job writing for the English language newspaper *Bombay Chronicle*. He was also active in business, briefly worked on the Planning Commission and eventually joined the Indian Foreign Service. Like Jawaharlal Nehru and other British-educated South Asians, Mehta maintained a strong cultural and intellectual affection for numerous British thinkers, including Shaw and Tawney. He also requested several works by British authors, while also ordering periodicals such as the *New Statesman* and *Punch* to be sent to his residence in Calcutta.[46] Notably, Mehta furthermore maintained as a profound, life-long admiration of Bertrand Russell. This led him to review the philosopher's books and retain copious clippings related to Russell's work in his personal papers. He later earned a Master's degree in Bombay in which he focused on Russell's philosophy.

Laski was no doubt one of a legion of writers that informed Mehta's thinking, but one whose impact remained palpable and also reflected and attested to Laski's extensive following in India. 'Hardly any British thinker or writer, with the possible exception of Bertrand Russell, is so well-known to the present generation in India as Prof. Harold J. Laski.'[47] He reviewed Laski's work for decades following his graduation, and the two maintained a correspondence. Laski thanked Mehta for reviewing his work and expressed gratitude for the general interest he and his father displayed for his recent writings. He wrote that there were few people whose goodwill he was more concerned with than India's freedom fighters.[48] Mehta continued to review his work during the Second World War as well.[49]

The influence of Fabian socialism, LSE and Laski specifically is evident in Mehta's writings on democracy in the early post-colonial state. Discussing LSE's founder, Mehta wrote that

> Sidney Webb's masters were Bentham and John Stuart Mill and he stressed from the earliest days that the democratic ideal of 'the greatest happiness for the greatest number' cannot be fulfilled merely by extending political democracy but that economic democracy was also essential for its full realisation.[50]

Mehta's reading of Laski further shaped his understanding of the concept of economic democracy. Writing on the fourth anniversary of Indian independence in 1951, he argued,

> We cannot expect men to devote their time to the pursuit of creative activities so long as most of the time of the majority of men is spent in the simple task of staving off starvation, and satisfying their elementary needs of food, clothing and shelter.[51]

This is precisely what Laski argued for, namely that citizens required established economic rights, without which the full development of the individual, and freedom, was impossible. For Laski in particular, political democracy was always desirable, but its contemporary manifestation contained demons within it because it maintained the power of the dominant class at the expense of everyone below. Remembering Laski in 1950, Mehta wrote in *The Times of India* that Laski maintained 'that the effective cure for the evils of political democracy lay not only in better education as well as civil training and discipline but also in a more equitable social order which ensures economic opportunity for all'.[52] Mehta came close to arguing for the state to guarantee specific economic rights.

Mehta declared this to honour Laski's passing, but the timing was also significant in another way. It was two months after the inauguration of the Indian Constitution, whose prime author, another LSE graduate, B.R. Ambedkar, had successfully embedded ideas of social democracy into Indian law in an attempt to offset historical inequalities. Ambedkar gave concrete expression to the idea of expanding political democracy, affirming 'a political democracy without an economic and social democracy is an invitation to trouble and danger'.[53] In the aftermath of independence, Indians grappled with the question of what principles their democracy should be founded upon. The search for ideological precepts which would provide a foundation to the new state motivated students to continue engaging with ideas about democracy that they grappled with during their time in London.

Mehta's intellectual appreciation of his former professor derived from his interpretation of Laski's effort to build the theoretical foundations for a more inclusive democracy. Renuka Ray had similar reflections. She later recalled that '… when I joined the London School of Economics, I came across some of the great thinkers and educationists of the period who perhaps exercised a great influence in moulding my future career in many ways'.[54] In particular, she argued that the emphasis on making democracy more inclusive was consistent with LSE's fundamental project, which was not to spread communism but to expand the meaning of democracy.

> Those years were the hey-day of the London School of Economics as the centre of progressive and socialist thought not only in England but throughout the world. There were students from all parts of Asia and Africa, apart from the European countries. In the twenties it was the only institution of its kind. The school vibrated with life and the search for a democratic political system wherein not only political liberty but economic and other freedoms would be possible. It opened many doors for me because it fostered every school of thought.[55]

Ray's paternal grandparents were members of the *Brahmo Samaj* reformist movement founded by Rammohan Roy in the 1820s.[56] Politically minded from a young age, the political environment at LSE suited her well, and she became the only woman on the Indian Students' Union executive committee.[57] Following graduation, she devoted her life to public service and women's rights. She would later become involved in the All-India Women's Conference, dedicated to the uplift of women and children, becoming President in 1932 and again in the 1950s. Ray worked on the Hindu law bills in the 1940s (eventually passed as the Hindu code bills, which sought to codify Hindu personal law, in the 1950s), was one of fifteen women on the Constituent Assembly and worked with refugees from East Pakistan following Partition, eventually being appointed Union Minister for Rehabilitation in West Bengal. She was also a member of the Lok Sabha from 1957 to 67. As Ray wrote in 1953, she encouraged women to become involved politically and economically, in planning and development.[58]

While not singling out Laski, Ray used language is in line with her erstwhile professor and the profound intellectual legacy she attributed to LSE. On the day of India's independence, Ray looked ahead to new challenges, such as banishing poverty and ill health, warning against forgetting 'that we have yet to achieve economic independence without which political freedom has little meaning'.[59] For Ray, this meant ensuring economic freedom, as well as the rights of women and minorities; ideas, again, that resonated in a country in the midst of constitutional debates that sought to address historical inequities.

For Indian students like Ray and Mehta, notions they engaged with as students in Britain became more compelling not only when they seemed to apply to problems facing India but also when they bore similarity to thought being produced by Indian nationalists. For students already familiar with the works of thinkers such as Dadabhai Naoroji, Laski's emphasis on the Marxist-Leninist idea of capitalism leading to a search and domination of foreign markets, control over raw materials and adjustment of tariffs to protect the home market must have seemed familiar.[60] Moreover, for both Mehta and Ray, Laski shared fundamental similarities with Mohandas K. Gandhi. As Asha Mehta has written, for Indian socialists, there was a parallel between the effort of some British socialists to link socialism and democracy and Gandhi's emphasis on non-violence and a decentralised economy; when they, in short, accepted '*Satyagarha* as a revolutionary weapon'.[61]

G.L. Mehta, for instance, wrote,

> No one, so far as I am aware, has argued better than he the vital thesis that there are moral limits to the authority and sovereignty of the State and that, in the ultimate analysis, the citizen has the right to disobedience because the final sanction in any civilized political society is the conscience of its citizens. Indeed, if any political basis were needed for Gandhiji's theory and practice of 'Satyagraha', Laski's treatises on sovereignty and some of his later books such as 'The Danger of Obedience' and 'Liberty in the Modern State' provide that basis.[62]

As he was familiar with Laski's writings after he graduated, Mehta could have emphasised Laski's increasing affinity for the role of the state. Yet he chose to stress Laski's early writings, in which he articulated scepticism of state authority and a belief that the individual had the right to resist an oppressive government they judged to be immoral.[63] Coupled with his enduring preference for non-violent political change, Mehta's admiration for both Gandhi and Laski prompted him to see a parallel.

Ray's writings, moreover, suggested that Laski's message on economic freedom may have owed some of its legitimacy in her eyes to its similarity to the Mahatma's thinking. Ray had travelled with Gandhi around India before going to London. She claimed that, despite reserving great accolades for LSE and her time in Britain, she never found another system 'comparable to the Gandhian one'.[64] In a piece entitled 'Gandhiji is most valuable contribution to Indian life and thought', it is evident she drew inspiration from Gandhi that could easily be attributed to Laski.[65] Ray affirmed that,

> To Gandhiji, economic and social freedom against a background of an incorruptible moral base was of paramount importance. According to him, swaraj could only be real when each individual could develop to be self-reliant and express himself to the fullest without interfering with the same rights of others. This was the basis of the Sarvodya Society in which he believed.[66]

In her memoirs, she later affirmed that for Gandhi, swaraj was not only political, but economic and social as well, and that he believed in right to for female self-expression.[67] Elsewhere, Ray compared Gandhi's concept of swaraj to Nehru's understanding of democracy, which, again, was not only political, but also affirmed 'economic and social freedom'.[68]

She might as well have been speaking of Laski. To his admiring colonial students, Laski's ideas overlapped with other sources of inspiration, from both India and Britain. Gandhi and Laski made especially peculiar intellectual bedfellows, given their emphatically distinct political and economic views. Gandhi's focus on the village unit, distaste for industry and scepticism of socialism was far removed from Laski's hope for a centralised industrial civilisation, which was much closer to Nehru's vision for India's future. For Ray and Mehta, their embrace of Laski's socialism did not transform them into Laskites, but Gandhian democratic socialists. Elements of British socialism, bearing Laski's distinct language and emphasis, were seen to be commensurate with more local thinking that diverged significantly from Laski's beliefs.

'The Case for Democracy'

In her memoirs, Ray criticised Nehru, suggesting he should have gone further in implementing many of the socialist reforms he believed in and that he was too considerate of the opposition.[69] She nevertheless still praised India's first Prime Minister for his commitment to democracy.[70] Depending on interpretation, the difference between communism and the practical steps required to engender a social revolution that would usher in a new economic system, in Britain or India, could be quite narrow. The primary difference, as both Nehru and Laski understood it, was deference to democratic practice, constitutionalism and an abhorrence for violent revolution. Students remembered their professor in two principal ways. As we have seen, Laski's writings and lectures advocated expanding the traditional notion of political liberty to include what he identified as economic democracy. The inevitable corollary to this question, which Laski wrestled with throughout his career, was how to generate and maintain a social revolution.

The most obvious contemporary example for enforcing economic freedom was the Soviet Union, which, as Nehru pointed out, was similar to India insofar as it was an agricultural country seeking to rapidly address mass illiteracy and poverty.[71] Laski admired Moscow's efforts in theory, if not always in practice. His LSE colleague, Hayek, had the opposite belief. For the Austrian economist, socialism paved the road to totalitarianism, the case study being the rise of National Socialism in Germany. Laski's biographer Herbert Deane furthermore argued that Laski's views on democracy shifted with the winds, often criticising the ideology for barely masking its subservience to capitalism, sometimes praising it, particularly when in juxtaposition to the Nazi alternative during World War II.[72] Yet the majority of his students recalled his affinity for democracy and demonstrated a deep belief in the idea themselves.

Laski's affirmation for the democratic path to change was most evident in the early to mid 1920s, when his writings were more influenced by pluralism. He conveyed this message to students outside the classroom as well as inside. In 1923, for instance, he participated in a debate against Shapurji Saklatvala about the desirability of reorganising society through parliamentary methods.[73] Saklatvala, a British Communist of Parsi origins, had strong sympathies for the USSR and the Communist International. According to a reviewer of the debate, Saklatvala's rhetoric was colourful and dramatic. He argued that the public was being prevented from hearing the facts about Russia. 'Scratch the Russian', he said, 'and you will find the civilizer of Europe'.[74] Minor reforms through parliamentary means were useless. 'Such small reforms as had been secured during the last century', he argued, 'were snatched from the hands of the exploiters of the poor'.[75]

Laski followed Saklatvala, according to the reviewer, with a 'brilliant speech'.[76]

> So far as the Russian Revolution was concerned, he thought that violence was inherent in it. He abhorred dictatorship of all sorts; he had no sympathy with either Lenin or Mussolini. He was one of those who believed in the truth of democracy. By constant harmonious discussion the truth was bound to emerge. Only such changes were worth while as were secured by the method of peaceful persuasion.[77]

'Democracy', Laski argued, 'was the greatest hope for the future ... ' Continuing with an example which he personally exemplified,

> ... Mr. Laski said that the very fact that in this country a Labour Government was looked upon as a possibility, proved the efficiency of Parliament. The emancipation of the Jewish race, and the rise into national prominence of the Labour and Socialist parties were real achievements.[78]

At this point, Laski had confidence in the prospects of revolutionary change being procured though democratic channels. 'In this way and in course of time', the writer continued, 'he had no doubt that all that reformers desired would be secured, and secured without any of the doubtful blessings of wanton destruction and terrorism'.[79]

On this occasion, the article describing the debate suggested that Laski could moderate radical arguments, arguing to students in favour of democracy by providing historical examples of its success and warning of the possibilities of violence inherent in revolutionary change. Indeed, Mehta, a student from this period, remembered his professor in an obituary affirming that Laski believed in the inevitability of social change, and the 'impossibility of maintaining unrequited privileges'.[80] The social order needed to change – according to Mehta, Laski felt this development was inevitable. Nevertheless, Mehta continued,

> in his incisive book 'Communism' published some years ago, he declined to accept the Communist argument of a violent upheaval and contended that once the foundations are shaken, there is no guarantee that the forces of the Right will not seize the initiative ... [81]

According to Mehta, Laski – an admiring critic of Burke – conjured his spirit of preferring reform to revolution.

Laski's writings contain an aversion to violence, yet they also convey a scepticism that any worthwhile change in social organisation could be procured without force. Given this ambiguity, can we reach a generalisation about what students took away from Laski's classes? Continuing from the passage quoted above, Mehta wrote that Laski ' ... also argued the case of evolutionary socialism while condemning playing with revolution' and 'mouthing revolutionary phrases'.[82] Defending the use of constitutional methods for social change in a political democracy, he recalled Laski's observation that 'this is less dramatic than the revolutionary way but it is at least as enduring' and that it has 'the supreme merit of avoiding the immense pain and bitterness the revolutionary way is bound to inflict'.[83] Inspired both by Gandhi's support for non-violence and Laski's thinking, Mehta chose to remember this rather than Laski's more ambiguous thoughts on violence.

Speaking again on Republic Day in 1952, Mehta remembered Laski while emphasising the importance of political democracy in India's five-year-old republic. Mehta underscored the significance of the path paved with persuasion and cooperation as opposed to coercion and violence.

> Heroic methods and shortcuts are likely to have results sometimes precisely the opposite of what are intended. When a democratic method is abandoned, there is no knowing what forces may be generated. It is easy to castigate democracy. But as Prof. Laski remarked, if you can destroy the case for democracy in 20 min, you can destroy the case for any other system of government in five.[84]

As Mehta understood it, Laski did not see democracy as an inherent good, but rather, reminiscent of Sir Winston Churchill's quip on the same topic, the least bad option.

Writing in her memoirs, Ray remembered Laski's lectures on classical liberalism and the *Communist Manifesto*, later published in books, and how his radical stances 'influenced the minds of the youth in my day'.[85] More particularly, he

> ... understood and conceded that there might be much to learn from Marxist theories and even the revolution that was taking place in post-war Russia under the new Soviet regime. Yet he was not enamoured of the totalitarian aspect of the latter. Harold Laski

was a man who inherently believed in freedom of thought for all races and for all peoples.[86]

Her later emphasis on the individual recalls Laski's thinking on economic rights.

> The main difference between Communism and Democracy, as I see it, is that the structure and the frame work of a Democratic state must be so fashioned as to encourage and foster the creative personality of the individual. He must be helped towards the fullest self expression in consonance with the common good of all.[87]

The support for democracy that students encountered even in the most radical of classrooms complemented the practice of political freedom through parliamentary democracy and freedom of expression that they witnessed around them. As Sumita Mukherjee and Shompa Lahiri have noted, the relatively free environment that Indian students found themselves in contrasted to the political oppression at home.[88] The deviation from India was impressive and striking, even for the future revolutionary S.C. Bose.[89] By highlighting its opposite, exposure to freedom helped to incite nationalist aspirations. Yet it also inculcated preferences for particular political ideas closely linked to nationalism and nation building. Lahiri notes that the Bengali writer and Civil Servant R.C. Dutt's positive impression at observing people enjoying the right to governing themselves first hand and concludes that seeing a 'democracy in action' sowed the seeds of Dutt's nationalism.[90] Mukherjee has moreover shown the positive impressions students had about British political life, pointing to a claim by Fazl-I-Hussain, a Punjabi politician, that he learnt what 'independent nations call liberty' and grasped the 'distinction between freedom and slavery' at Cambridge in 1900. The Indian journalist Frank Moreas admired democracy while a student at Oxford in the 1920s, while another writer, the author Mulk Raj Anand, was impressed by the challenge miners posed to the government during the General Strike in 1926 while a student at University College.[91]

Democracy could inspire nationalism, but many nationalists also desired democracy in its own right. Sunil Khilnani has written that democracy was given to the Indian people through the 'political choice of an intellectual elite'.[92] One of the great ironies of Britain's imperial legacy was the role overseas education, itself the product of centuries of authoritarian rule that created an English-speaking elite dependent on British education for career advancement, played in convincing that large elements of that intellectual elite of the merits of democracy. As Kumarasingham has detailed elsewhere regarding the first decade of independence in India, Pakistan, Ceylon, Malaysia and Singapore, nine of the twelve figures who became prime ministers were Oxbridge-trained. This connection to British education was to a degree that far surpassed even the settler colonies, and becomes even greater when we take into consideration the number of advisors, such as Menon, P.N. Haksar and B.K. Nehru, who attended LSE and other British institutions.[93] Their experiences in Britain, including the ideas they engaged with in their classes, played an important role both in advancing new criticisms of democracy in its contemporary form and, in a more general but no less important sense, promoting ideas of democracy, the rule of law and constitutionalism at a time when alternative political systems seemed viable. As Benjamin Zachariah has observed, totalitarian alternatives, from Italian fascism to Nazism, were often held up in India as other political models that could be used to initiate radical social and economic change.[94] Soviet communism in particular was admired for its associations with anti-colonialism and for being relatively less harmed by the Great Depression than the capitalist democracies.

Despite his firm stance against British rule in India, Mehta nevertheless admired the British system of government, visiting parliament during his time in England.[95] His trip to Westminster exposed him to the practical elements of liberal democracy. He later expressed his opinion in the importance of the British inheritance when it came to the rule of law, an independent judicial system, parliamentary government and its democratic procedures and the idea of democracy as inspired by thinkers like Mill.[96] Students were also impressed by the act of holding free elections. Jawaharlal Nehru recounted his interest in the 1906 General Election in his autobiography while at Harrow.[97] Renuka Ray supported the Labour Party in the 1922 General Election, visiting housewives in their homes, engaging in what she called 'street-by-street canvassing'.[98] She claimed to have convinced many people to vote, in part by offering to baby sit while they were out.[99]

Ray further spoke of the effects of Britain's post-war socialist reforms undertaken through democratic means, suggesting it exerted a significant influence on her.[100] She specifically emphasised the advancement of socialism in England and other western countries by evolution, not revolution, again evoking Laski's revolution by consent and signalling her approval of change by constitutional methods.[101] In a speech in 1951, Ray pontificated that while the state had a duty to advance economic and social equality of opportunity, it must be vigilant to maintain individual liberty and freedom of expression.[102] Her belief in the necessity for socialism to address inequality did not negate her embrace of liberal tenets, which like Mehta, and indeed Nehru, found inspiration in Laski. Commenting on his former teacher, Mehta observed that although Laski was 'an ardent advocate (or "proponent" to use his own favourite word) of radical transformation of the existing social and economic order', he 'was somewhat conservative and cautious so far as formal government' is concerned.[103] Mehta recalled that a 'partiality for the British political system was, to quote one of his favourite expressions, "an inarticulate major premise" of his political thought'.[104]

The Limits of Laski's Liberalism

The reflections of Ray and Mehta lend greater support to the argument that ideologies distinct from liberalism could act as vehicles for liberal ideas in the late imperial and early postcolonial state. This was particularly true when complemented by the lived, day to day political experience witnessed in a liberal democracy, which highlighted the efficacy of political structures inherent to that system of government, while also underlining the hypocrisy of British rhetoric on freedom and its incommensurability with empire. Conceptions of economic democracy, as promoted by Laski in and outside LSE, found further justification when more indigenous thinkers like Gandhi could be seen to be articulating compatible views. The extent to which liberal ideas continued to animate Laski's teaching does not, surely, mean that he encouraged a coherent set of political positions that could be characterised as liberalism, or still more that his students were liberals in a strict sense. It does, however, suggest that the early postcolonial, Cold War period continued to be shaped by men and women who had adapted ideologically malleable thinking they were exposed to during the pre-war, late imperial era, during which the teachings of even an avowed Marxist could be flexible, multifaceted and a source of inspiration for liberal precepts.

Mehta understood Laski as trying to bridge the gap between Marxism and individual liberty, and was in no way oblivious to the intellectual challenge this effort entailed. His desire to reconcile the two philosophies, Mehta wrote, was 'a source of much of Laski's basic inconsistencies and reveals a lack of intellectual integration'.[105] To be sure, Laski's more disparaging critics could be as ardent in their denunciations as his champions were in their praise. Another Laski student and future politician, M.R Masani, moved to the left while at LSE in the late 1920s, when he was active in student politics and had the opportunity to tour the Soviet Union. After graduating, he helped found the Congress Socialist Party (CSP), a short-lived organisation which encouraged the Congress to embrace socialist policies, and was a regular contributor to its periodical. His radicalism nevertheless waned in the late 1930s, in part due to Stalin's purges and the Molotov-Ribbentrop Pact. By the time of Independence, Masani was advocating for a mixed economic approach to India's development; with the expansion of the Nehruivian project in the 1950s, he moved further right, eventually adopting a classically liberal position.

If Laski represented a fount of moral wisdom for some students, Masani found his offerings to be poisonous. 'It is not unfair', he later wrote,

> to say that a whole generation of Indians, from Jawaharlal Nehru and Krishna Menon onwards, sat metaphorically at Laski's feet and swallowed neat the wisdom that flowed from his fluent lips and pen. Laski was articulate, but not profound. He was terribly confused about fundamentals, with the result that his attitude towards communism and the Soviet Union was ambivalent, and consequently, often self-contradictory.[106]

Far from Laski's hope to reconcile elements of liberalism with Marxism, Masani saw the two ideologies as strictly opposed. Unlike Mehta and Ray, he understood Laski's equivocation regarding the question of whether a Labour government could allow its work to be overturned due to the next general election as nothing more than Leninism-lite.[107]

If Masani's stance was, like Moynihan's, somewhat alarmist, it was not without its merits. Other students, from Mehta to the British thinker Ralph Miliband and Canadian Pierre Trudeau, all recognised tensions and conflicts in Laski's thought; that, however, was what they found most compelling about it. For Trudeau, Laski rejected Stalinism and the classical liberal state, and searched for the middle ground between the two.[108] Believing that angering everyone was a sign one was on to something, Trudeau admired the fact that Laski was disagreeable to purists on both sides of the Iron Curtain.[109] Reflecting the sentiments of Laski's Indian admirers, Trudeau held that what was particularly valuable was his effort to reenergise the free, liberal state with egalitarian ideas inspired by socialism while avoiding the construction of a Soviet-style state that was antithetical to democracy. For two generations of students, exposed to the promises of rapid development through communism without the burdens of consensual politics and the rule of law, Laski offered the source for a potential third way between the extremes, and in doing so helped propagate liberal ideas well after World War II and his passing.

Notes

1. J. Nehru, "Message from the Prime Minister of India, Pandit Jawaharlal Nehru to the Harold Laski Institute of Political Science, Ahmedabad," August 17, 1956, P.G. Mavalankar Papaers, Subject Files: Personal Files, Nehru Memorial Museum and Library (hereafter NMML).
2. Eastwood, *Laski*, 94.
3. Mukherjee, *Nationalism, Education and Migrant Identities*; Lahiri, *Indians in Britain*.
4. J. Wilkie (Board of Education) to Sir Maurice Hankey, September 21, 1926, ED 24/1994, The National Archives, UK.
5. "University of London: Students from Overseas in the Universities and University Colleges of Great Britain and Ireland 1927–1928," William Beveridge Papers, 5/29, LSE.
6. For a general biography of Laski's life and work, see Kramnick, *Harold Laski*. For more in depth accounts of Laski's ideas, see Lamb, *Problems of Democracy*; Lamb, "Laski's Ideological Metamorphosis," and Newman, *Harold Laski: A Political Biography*. A critical view of Laski can be found in Deane, *Political Ideas of Harold J. Laski*. For a personal but more hagiographic appraisal, see Martin, *Harold Laski, 1893–1950*. For a general account of Laski's relationship with his Indian students, see Moscovitch, "Harold Laski's Indian Students."
7. Moynihan, "The United States in Opposition," 44.
8. Bayly, "The Ends of Liberalism," 606, 621. See also, Bayly, *Recovering Liberties*.
9. Sluga, "Global Liberalisms Introduction," 526.
10. Laski, "Why I am a Marxist." *The Nation*, January 14, 1939, 76.
11. Ibid.
12. Ibid.
13. Ibid.
14. Dahrendorf, *LSE*.

15. Mills, *Grist for the Mills*, 82.
16. Ibid., 83.
17. Yew, *The Singapore Story*, 105.
18. B. K. Nehru, in Joan Abse, ed., *My LSE*, 26.
19. Ray, *My Reminiscences*, 35.
20. In a 1937 conference about civil liberty in India, for example, both Laski and Menon spoke, the latter about civil liberty in Bengal. For more, see *Manchester Guardian*, September 17, 1937, 20.
21. Owen, *The British Left and India*.
22. See, for example, Laski, *Studies in the Problems of Sovereignty*, 25.
23. Laski, "Why I am a Marxist," 78
24. Laski, *The Rise of European Liberalism*, 226.
25. Laski, *The Decline of Liberalism*, 13.
26. Ibid.
27. Laski, *Reflections on the Revolution of our Time*, 307–08. Laski believed that this would be run by many people, including businessmen. Something along the lines of Gosplan, the body responsible for central economic planning in the USSR, would be created, in which a committee of experts would advise the Cabinet, who would in turn bring proposals to Parliament for approval (309–10).
28. Ray, *Reminiscences*, 34–35. Ray wrote: 'His [Laski's] lectures on European liberal thought in the nineteenth century and his commentary on the *Communist Manifesto* of Mark and Engels, which were later published as books, give an indication of his radical views.' See, for instance, LSE Calendar, 1934–35; LSE Calendar, 1949–50, LSE.
29. Robbins, *Autobiography of an Economist*, 82.
30. "Political and Social Theory, Lecture notes from Laski, 4 March 1928," Krishna Menon Papers, box 3, file 3/10, NMML.
31. C. B. Macpherson, journal, February 14, 1934, C.B. Macpherson Papers, University of Toronto Archives.
32. Laski, *Democracy in Crisis*, 240–41.
33. Ibid., 241. See also, Laski, *Communism*, 82, 88–90.
34. Hayek, *The Road to Serfdom*, 62–63.
35. Deane, *The Political Ideas of Harold J. Laski*.
36. Freeden, *Liberalism Divided*, 306.
37. Sabhlok, *Breaking Free of Nehru*, 106.
38. Quoted from Kramnick, *Harold Laski*, 589.
39. H. Laski to J. Nehru, November 6, 1935, J. Nehru Papers (hereafter JNP), Correspondences, Part I Volume no. 42, NMML.
40. See H. Laski to J. Nehru, February 18, 1936 and J. Nehru to H. Laski, February 20, 1936, JNP. Correspondences, Part I Volume no. 42, NMML.
41. Intelligence assessment by Ronald Bedford, sent to India, concerning Laski speech, November 14, 1945, L1/1 1439.
42. Ibid.
43. H. Laski, "Pandit Nehru," *Daily Herald*, June 1934 (no further details), JNP, Part IV, Articles on Jawaharlal Nehru, NMML.
44. Ibid.
45. Basu, *G. L. Mehta*, 57.
46. Ibid., 113. Some of the books included H.N. Brailsford's *Subject India* and Cole's *Fabian Socialism*, as well as books by Robins (and Hayek), the complete works of Milton, Alexander Pope, Alfred Lloyd Tennyson and Joseph Addison.

47. G. L. Mehta, "Harold J. Laski," n.d., no. 81, G.L. Mehta Papers (hereafter GLMP), Speeches and writings, 3rd and 4th Instalment, NMML.
48. H. Laski to G. L. Mehta, January 7, 1931, GLMP, 3rd and 4th Instalment Part 1, Correspondences, NMML.
49. G. L. Mehta, "Revolutionary Cure for Hitlerism: Disorder Dreaming of the New Order." *Free Press Journal*, March 18, 1941, GLMP, 3rd and 4th Instalment Part 1, Speeches and Writings, File 15.8.1951 S. No. 27, NMML.
50. G. L. Mehta, "Sidney Webb." *Amrita Bazar Patrika*, October 17, 1947, GLMP, Speeches and writings, 3rd and 4th Instalment Part 1, NMML.
51. G. L. Mehta, "The Real Meaning of Progress," August 15, 1951, *Independence Supplement*, GLMP. 3rd and 4th Instalment Part 1, Speeches and writings, NMML.
52. G. L. Mehta, "Erudite Scholar and Creative Thinker." *Times of India*, March 27, 1950, GLMP, 1st Instalment, Subject Files, NMML.
53. H. S. Dwivedi and R. Sinha, "Dr. Ambedkar: The Pioneer of Social Democracy," 661–66.
54. R. Ray, Oral History Interview, p. 7, NMML
55. Ray, *Reminiscences*, 33–34.
56. Ibid., 4.
57. Ibid., 37.
58. See, R. Ray, "Women and the Five Year Plan," no. 22, January 19, 1953, Speeches and writings, Renuka Ray Papers (hereafter RRP), NMML; R. Ray, "Women as Citizens of Free India," no. 14, July 6, 1951, Speeches and writings, RRP Papers, NMML.
59. R. Ray, "Message on 15 August 1947," Speeches and writings, RRP, no. 6, NMML.
60. Laski, *Communism*, 113.
61. Gupta, "Fabianism and Indian Socialism."
62. G. L. Mehta, "Erudite Scholar and Creative Thinker." *Times of India*, March 27, 1950. GLMP, NMML.
63. See: *Studies in the Problem of Sovereignty*, 19.
64. Ray, *Reminiscences*, 32.
65. Ray, "Gandhiji is Most Valuable Contribution to Indian Life and Thought," RRP, Speeches and writings, no. 76, NMML.
66. Ibid.
67. Ray, *Reminiscences*, 23, 48.
68. Ray, "Nehru and parliamentary Democracy," 59.
69. Ray, *Reminiscences*, 214.
70. Ibid.
71. Nehru, *Nehru: The First Sixty Years*, 127–28.
72. Deane, *The Political Ideas of Harold J. Laski*, 225–28.
73. *The Indus*, 3, no. 1 (July 1923).
74. Ibid., 8.
75. Ibid., 3, no. 1 (July 1923), 9.
76. Ibid.
77. Ibid.
78. Ibid.
79. Ibid.
80. G. L. Mehta, "Erudite Scholar and Creative Thinker." *Times of India*, March 27, 1950, GLMP, 1st Instalment, Subject Files, NMML.
81. Ibid.

82. Ibid.
83. Ibid.
84. G. L. Mehta, "A.I.R. broadcast on 'Renewal of Faith'," January 26, 1952, GLMP, No. 32, Speeches and writings, 3rd and 4th Instalment Part 1, NMML.
85. Ray, *Reminiscences*, 34–35.
86. Ibid.
87. R. Ray, "What Are Democracy's Best Answers to Communism," radio talk, n.d. (between 1946 and 1949), Speeches and Writings, RRP, NMML.
88. Mukherjee, *The Experience of the England Returned*, 218.
89. See Lahiri, *Indians in Britain*, 155–57, including the views of R. C. Dutt, N. G. Ranga, S. C. Bose and Krishnabhabani Das.
90. Lahiri, *Indians in Britain*, 155.
91. Mukherjee, *The Experience of the England Returned*, 221–23.
92. Khilnani, *The Idea of India*, 34.
93. Kumarasingham, *Constitution-Making in Asia*, 13–14; Guha, "The LSE and India."
94. Zachariah, "British and Indian Ideas of 'Development': Decoding Political Conventions in the Late Colonial State," 169.
95. Basu, *G. L. Mehta*, 64–66.
96. G. L. Mehta, Oral Interview, Centre of South Asian studies, July 7, 1970, 22–23.
97. Nehru, *Autobiography*, 17.
98. Ray, *Reminiscences*, 38.
99. Ibid.
100. R. Ray, "Socialism," RRP, Speeches and Writings, No. 93, NMML.
101. Ibid.
102. R. Ray, "Some Aspects of Constructive Nation Building," January 26, 1951, RRP, speeches and writings, no. 13, NMML.
103. V. K. Krishna Menon. Quoted in G. N. Singh. "Laski – The Teacher and the Political Scientist." Ahmedabad: Harold Laski Institute of Political Science, 1957.
104. Ibid.
105. G. L. Mehta, "Laski Memorial Lecture," GLMP, 5th instalment, NMML.
106. M. Masani, *Bliss Was It In That Dawn*, 22–23.
107. M. Masani, "The Economics of Freedom," speech, Bombay (1965). Accessed May 1, 2016. http://indianliberals.in/liberals-detail/?id=1
108. P. E. Trudeau, "Blum et Laski," *Cité libre* 1, no 1 (June 1950): 38. (Author's translation from French original: "Socialistes, ils rejetaient néanmoins la primauté du stalinisme. Et démocrates, ils dénonçaient quand même l'État libéral"). For Miliband, see Miliband, "Harold Laski's Socialism"; Newman, "Class, State and Democracy."
109. Trudeau, "Blum et Laski."

Acknowledgments

The author would like to thank Maria Misra and Nicholas Owen for their comments on earlier drafts.

Disclosure statement

No potential conflict of interest was reported by the author.

Funding

This was supported by the Fonds de recherche Société et culture of Québec under file 168179 and by the Beit Fund under reference B/1/1.

References

Abse, Joan, ed. *My LSE*. London: Robson, 1977.
Basu, Aparna. *G.L. A Many Splendoured Man*. Delhi: Concept, 2001.
Bayly, C. A. "The Ends of Liberalism and the Political thought of Nehru's India." *Modern Intellectual History* 12, no. 3 (2015): 605–626.
Bayly, C. A. *Recovering Liberties: Indian thought in the Age of Liberalism and Empire*. Cambridge: Cambridge University Press, 2012.
Dahrendorf, Ralf. *LSE: A History of the London School of Economics and Political Science, 1895-1995*. New York: Oxford University Press, 1995.
Deane, Herbert. *The Political Ideas of Harold J. Laski*. New York: Columbia University Press, 1955.
Dwivedi, H. S., and Ratan Sinha. "Dr. Ambedkar: The Pioneer of Social Democracy." *The Indian Journal of Political Science* 66, no. 3 (July–September 2005): 661–666.
Eastwood, G. *Harold Laski*. London: Mowbrays, 1977.
Freeden, Michael. *Liberalism Divided: A Study of British Political Thought 1914-1939*. Oxford: Clarendon, 1986.
Guha, Ramchandra. "The LSE and India." *The Hindu*, November 23, 2003. http://www.hindu.com/thehindu/mag/2003/11/23/stories/2003112300120300.htm.
Gupta, Asha. "Fabianism and Indian Socialism." In *Essays on Fabian Socialism*, edited by M. M. Sankhdher and S. Mukherjee. New Delhi: Deep & Deep, 1991.
Hayek, Friedrich A. *The Road to Serfdom*. Chicago: University of Chicago Press, 1944.
Khilnani, Sunil. *The Idea of India*. London: Penguin, 2004.
Kramnick, Isaac, and Barry Sheerman. *Harold Laski: A Life on the Left*. London: H. Hamilton, 1993.
Kumarasingham, Harshan, ed. *Constitution-Making in Asia: Decolonisation and State-Building in the Aftermath of the British Empire*. London: Routledge, 2016.
Lahiri, Shompa. *Indians in Britain: Anglo-Indian Encounters, Race and Identity, 1880-1930*. London: Frank Cass, 2000.
Lamb, Peter. *Harold Laski: Problems of Democracy, the Sovereign State and International Society*. New York: Palgrave Macmillan, 2004.
Lamb, Peter. "Laski's Ideological Metamorphosis." *Journal of Political Ideologies* 4, no. 2 (1999): 239–260.
Laski, Harold. *Communism*. London: Thornton Butterworth ltd., 1927.
Laski, Harold. *The Decline of Liberalism*. London: Oxford University Press, 1940.
Laski, Harold. *Democracy in Crisis*. Chapel Hill: The University of North Carolina Press, 1933.
Laski, Harold. *Reflections on the Revolution of our Time*. London: George Allen & Unwin, 1943.
Laski, Harold. *The Rise of European Liberalism: An Essay in Interpretation*. London: Allen & Unwin, 1936; reprint, London: Allen & Unwin, 1962.
Laski, Harold. *Studies in the Problems of Sovereignty*. London: H. Milford, 1917.
Martin, Kingsley. *Harold Laski, 1893-1950: A Biographical Memoir*. London: J. Cape, 1969.
Miliband, Ralph. "Harold Laski's Socialism." In *Socialist Register*, edited by L. Panitch, 239–263. London: Merlin, 1995.

Mills, Gladstone. *Grist for the Mills: Reflections on a Life*. Kingston: Ian Randle Publishers, 1994.

Moscovitch, Brant. "Harold Laski's Indian Students and the Power of Education, 1920–1950." *Contemporary South Asia* 20, no. 1 (March 2012): 33–44.

Moynihan, D. P. "The United States in Opposition." *Commentary* 59, no. 3 (1975): 33–44.

Mukherjee, Sumita. *Nationalism, Education and Migrant Identities: The England-Returned*. London: Routledge, 2010.

Mukherjee, Sumita. "The Experience of the England-Returned: The Education of Indians in Britain in the Early Twentieth Century and its Long-Term Impact." *DPhil thesis*, University of Oxford, 2007.

Nehru, Jawaharlal. *An Autobiography*. London: John Lane the Bodley Head, 1936.

Nehru, Jawaharlal. *Nehru: The First Sixty Years*. Edited by Dorothy Norman. Vol. 1. New York: John Day, 1965.

Newman, Michael. "Class, State and Democracy: Laski, Miliband and the Search for a Synthesis." *Political Studies* 54 (2006): 328–348.

Newman, Michael. *Harold Laski: A Political Biography*. London: Merlin Press, 2009.

Owen, Nicholas. *The British Left and India: Metropolitan Anti-Imperialism, 1885–1947*. Oxford: Oxford University Press, 2007.

Ray, Renuka. *My Reminiscences: Social Developments During the Gandhian Era and After*. New Delhi: Allied, 1982.

Ray, Renuka. "Nehru and Parliamentary Democracy." In *Nehru and Parliament*, edited by Subhash C. Kashyap, 59–66. New Delhi, 1986.

Robbins, Lionel. *Autobiography of an Economist*. London: Macmillan, 1971.

Sabhlok, S. *Breaking Free of Nehru: Let's Unleash India!* New Delhi: Anthem Press, 2008.

Sluga, Glenga, and Timothy Rowse. "Forum: Global Liberalisms." *Modern Intellectual History* 12, no. 3 (2015): 523–528.

Yew, Lee Kuan. *The Singapore Story: Memoirs of Lee Kuan Yew*. Singapore: Prentice Hall, 1998.

Zachariah, Benjamin. "British and Indian Ideas of 'Development:' Decoding Political Conventions in the Late Colonial State." *Itinerario* 23, no. 3–4 (November 1999): 162–209.

The Post-Colonial Constitutional Order of the Commonwealth Caribbean: The Endurance of the Crown and the Judicial Committee of the Privy Council

Derek O'Brien

ABSTRACT

Amongst Britain's former colonies the independent countries of the Commonwealth Caribbean represent something of an anomaly in so far as the majority of them remain constitutional monarchies and continue to retain the Judicial Committee of the Privy Council (JCPC) as their final appellate court, even though the region has had its own final appellate court – the Caribbean Court of Justice – since 2006. This is in marked contrast to Britain's former colonies in Africa and South Asia, the majority of which switched to republicanism soon after independence and at the same time abolished rights of appeal to the JCPC. This paper seeks to uncover the reasons for this anomaly by examining how the path that led to independence was shaped by a particular conception of Dominion status and by the willingness of nationalist leaders to embrace a dual identity: equal parts West Indian nationalist and Empire loyalist. It will also examine the phenomenon of the 'postcolony'; being the persistence of the colonial order following the acquisition of constitutional independence. The paper has three aims. Firstly, to contribute to a better understanding of the impact of Dominion status and all that it symbolised in a region which is often overlooked in the scholarly literature on this topic. Secondly, better to understand the competing political forces that led three countries in the region to adopt republicanism, but inhibited its adoption elsewhere in the region. Thirdly, and finally, to enhance discussion of the complex nexus between republicanism and the abolition of rights of appeal to the JCPC where political and juridical considerations do not neatly align.

Introduction

In his recent monograph, *The Empire's New Clothes*, Philip Murphy, recounts a lecture given to the Institute of Commonwealth Studies by the Jamaican judge, Patrick Robinson, on the twin movements in his country to establish a republic and to end appeals to the Judicial Committee of the Privy Council (JCPC). At the end of this lecture, in which Robinson rehearsed the long history of British oppression in the West Indies, Murphy posed this question: 'That's all fine. But what kept you so long?' This question was presumably intended to highlight the disparity between Britain's African colonies which gained independence at around the same time as Jamaica and which rapidly made the transition from monarchical to republican status – Ghana (1960), Tanginikya (now Tanzania) (1961), Nigeria (1963), Kenya (1964), Malawi (1966) and the Gambia (1970). At the same time as they became republics, each of these former colonies also abolished the right of appeal to the JCPC. By contrast, of the 12 independent countries of the Commonwealth Caribbean,[1] only three have adopted republicanism – Guyana (1970), Trinidad and Tobago (1976), and Dominica (1978); while only four have abolished the right of appeal to the JCPC – Guyana (1970), Barbados (2006), Belize (2010) and Dominica (2015).

It is, of course, true that Britain's white settler Dominions have been equally slow to embrace republicanism: Canada, Australia and New Zealand all remain constitutional monarchies, and were also tardy in abolishing the right of appeal to the JCPC.[2] However, the comparison of Britain's Caribbean colonies with the 'white' settler Dominions is uneasy in at least three respects. Firstly, in marked contrast to the 'white' Dominions, Britain's settled colonies in the Caribbean endured almost two centuries of slavery followed by a further century of 'crown colony rule' before finally being granted independence and Dominion status in the 1960s and 1970s. Secondly, a number of Britain's Caribbean colonies do not trace their roots to English settlers, but were either ceded, as in the case of Grenada, or conquered as in the case of Trinidad and St Lucia. Thirdly, since 2006, the region has had its own final appellate court, the Caribbean Court of Justice (CCJ), which is paid for collectively by all of the independent countries in the region and which was established to hear appeals in civil, criminal and constitutional matters.

The loyalty of so many of Britain's former colonies in the Caribbean to the Crown and their continued willingness to vest ultimate legal sovereignty in the JCPC is, therefore, a striking anomaly, the reasons for which I seek to uncover in this paper. I will begin by examining how the path that led to independence was shaped by the pursuit of a particular conception of Dominion status, which corresponded with that of the older 'white' settler Dominions. I will then turn to examine the distinctive nature of Caribbean nationalism, which was characterised by the commitment of its leaders to the values and institutions of British political liberalism and by their willingness to embrace a dual identity: equal parts West Indian nationalist and Empire loyalist. Finally, I will turn to explore the reasons why so few of these 'postcolonies' have managed to excise these residual symbols of colonial rule from their constitutional systems.

The paper has three aims. Firstly, to contribute to a better understanding of the impact of Dominion status and all that it symbolised in a region which is often overlooked in the scholarly literature on this topic. Secondly, better to understand the competing political forces that led three countries in the region to adopt republicanism, but inhibited its adoption elsewhere in the region. Thirdly, and finally, to enhance discussion of the complex nexus between republicanism and the abolition of rights of appeal to the JCPC where political and juridical considerations do not neatly align.

Independence and the Pursuit of Dominion Status

The origins of Caribbean nationalism are commonly traced by scholars to the end of World War I with the return home of soldiers who had served in the British West Indies Regiment, such as Captain Arthur Cipriani and Uriah Butler, who were to become iconic figures as leaders of the nationalist movements in Trinidad and Tobago and Grenada respectively. As a result of the contribution which West Indians had made to the war effort, which they regarded as equal to that of the self-governing Dominions, there was an expectation that the values and institutions of British political liberalism, in particular, a democratically elected and representative legislature, would be extended to the Caribbean and that they would be rewarded with a greater voice in the government of their territories. For the previous half century, and longer in the case of Trinidad and St Lucia, Britain's West Indian colonies had been subject to 'crown colony' rule. This meant the autocratic rule of a Governor, appointed by the British Government, who presided over both the Executive and Legislative Council in each colony, and who had the final say on all matters affecting the colony, subject to instructions from London.[3]

Initially, at least, Caribbean nationalism was defined by its opposition to this system of crown colony rule, as Representative Government Associations sprang up across the region,[4] organising public meetings and presenting petitions to the British authorities calling for the addition of elected members to the region's Legislative Councils.[5] During the inter-war years this resulted in incremental reforms to the system of crown colony rule that marginally enhanced the representativeness of the regions' legislatures. In addition to introducing a small number of elected members into the Legislative Council, this included reducing the number of officials and nominated unofficials, widening the franchise, and relaxing the qualifications for candidates. However, the elected members in the Legislative Council were always in a minority, and the final say on matters affecting each territory ultimately resided in the Governor. In this way the essence of crown colony rule was preserved.

Various justifications were offered for the British Government's refusal to extend to its Caribbean territories the kind of responsible self-government enjoyed by white settlers colonies, such as Australia, Canada and New Zealand. According to a report by Major EFL Wood (later Lord Halifax), who had been sent to the West Indies in 1921 in response to the demands of nationalists for a greater voice in government, responsible government was inappropriate for these colonies for a variety of reasons. These included: the racial and religious heterogeneity of some of the islands[6]; the absence of a leisured class willing and able to take an active part in political life; the smallness and isolation of many of the islands; and the tiny proportion of qualified voters.[7] These justifications did not, however, dispel the suspicion amongst nationalists that the underlying reason for opposing responsible government was the fear that it would, in effect, mean rule by a black majority.[8] This sense of discrimination was heightened by the Balfour Declaration of 1926, which highlighted the contrast between the autocratic system of crown colony rule to which Britain's West Indian colonies were subject and the autonomy and equality of status enjoyed by Britain's 'white' Dominions.[9] As Arthur Cipriani[10] told Trinidad's Legislative Council in 1930:

> The people of this Colony have got the education, the ability, the civilization, and the necessary culture to administer their own affairs ... Crown Colony rule may be well for the jungle and the wilds of Africa, but it has outlived its usefulness in these colonies.[11]

West Indians, he argued, were as entitled to Dominion status as Canadians or Australians.

Aware, however, that no one territory was likely to be granted Dominion status in its own right, West Indian nationalists began to turn their attention towards the possibility of creating a federation, which would enable them to achieve Dominion status. In anticipation of a visit to the region by a Commission appointed by the British Government to examine the possibility of a closer union between Trinidad and Tobago, the Windward Islands and the Leeward Islands – The Closer Union Commission (CUC) – nationalist leaders gathered for a six-day conference in Roseau in Dominica at the end of October 1932, at the conclusion of which they agreed to press the British Government for a federation of all the islands and a draft federal constitution was prepared. The CUC was not, however, persuaded that there was sufficient support for federation more widely in the region, and instead recommended further modest constitutional reforms.

The prospect of Dominion status receded even further as a result of the the report of the Moyne Commission, which was dispatched to region in 1938 to investigate 'the social and economic causes' of the wave of strikes and civil disorder that engulfed the region in the 1930s. Though the Commission was aware of nationalist frustrations with the refusal of the British authorities to dismantle the system of crown colony rule which continued to deny them an effective voice in government, it concluded that the region's problems required social and economic solutions, rather than radical constitutional reform. As a result it recommended the establishment of a West Indian welfare fund, financed by an imperial grant of £1 million per annum for a period of 20 years.

The award of this grant provided the ostensible justification for rejecting nationalist demands for self-government, since this would be inconsistent with the British Government's need to retain overall control over distribution of the welfare fund.[12] However, in truth there was never any prospect of the British Government acceding to nationalist demands for self-government in the Caribbean or to its other dependent colonies, as was made clear in a statement by the Secretary of State for the Colonies, Oliver Stanley, in 1943:

> We are pledged to guide colonial people along the road to self-government within the framework of the British Empire ... [However], it is no part of our policy to confer political advances which are unjustified by the circumstances, or to grant self-government to those who are not yet trained in its use.[13]

A similar sentiment, was expressed, albeit more bluntly, in 1943, by Herbert Morrison, then Home secretary in Churchill's Wartime cabinet:

> ... to talk about grants of full self-government to many of the dependent territories for some time to come ... would be like giving a child of ten a latch key, a bank account and a shot-gun.[14]

While it was difficult for nationalist leaders to press their claims for responsible self-government in the shadow of World War II,[15] as the War approached its end they resumed their demands. This coincided with a discernible shift in the British Government's attitude towards its colonies in the region, which was in no small part due to increasing pressure from the Americans, whose interest in the region had increased as a result of the 'Destroyers for Bases Agreement' in 1940; a lend-lease deal under which the US provided Britain with 50 'mothballed' warships in exchange for 99 year leases of military bases throughout the Caribbean.[16] From the American viewpoint there was a distinct incongruity in helping Britain to win the war if the end result was the reinstatement of the old colonial system.[17]

The first sign of this shift in attitude was a new Constitution for Jamaica in 1944, which at the time was adjudged by the Colonial Office to be the most politically mature of Britain's colonies in the region. The 1944 Constitution provided for a bicameral legislature in which the dominant body was an entirely elected House of Representatives with all of the official and nominated members concentrated in a second chamber, the Legislative Council, which could only delay Bills passed by the House by one year. At the same time, provision was made for the introduction into the executive council of persons elected from and removable by the legislature. This was a watershed moment and over the course of the next two decades the region experienced a wave of constitutional reforms greater than any it had experienced in the previous half century as internal self-government, but not Dominion status, was gradually extended to the remaining colonies. While the rate of advance varied – with Jamaica, Trinidad and Tobago in the vanguard, along with British Guiana and

Barbados – and the detailed features were not the same everywhere, the general direction of travel was towards the British model of government: the so-called Westminster model.

In the meantime, nationalist hopes for Dominion status had been revived by an invitation to attend a Conference convened by the new Labour Colonial Secretary, Arthur Creech Jones, at Montego Bay in Jamaica in 1947, to discuss the "'Closer Association of the British West Indian Colonies." Having previously voiced their support for federation at the Roseau Conference in 1932, Caribbean political leaders attending the Montego Bay Conference enthusiastically agreed to the appointment of a Commission,' The Standing Closer Association Commission (SCAC) which was charged with consulting and reporting on the form of federal government 'most likely to give effect to the aspirations of the people of the British West Indies.'[18] When it became clear, however, following publication of the SCAC report, in 1950, that there would be no immediate grant of Dominion status to the proposed Federation, the more radical elements amongst nationalist leaders withdrew their support. In British Guiana, for example, Cheddi Jagan, leader of the Marxist-leaning PPP, argued that the proposed Federation was a complete betrayal of nationalist aspirations.[19] In Jagan's view, it was 'nothing more than a glorified Crown Colony, the amalgamation of several units which will carry us no further to self-government.'[20]

Jagan's fears were to an extent confirmed by the federal Constitution that was promulgated by the West Indies (Federation) Order in Council 1957.[21] This was a disappointment even to those more moderate nationalists who continued to support the principle of federation, such as Eric Williams, the leader of the People's National Movement (PNM) in Trinidad and Tobago, who described it as 'a disgraceful constitution, colonialist from top to bottom'. Its only saving grace appears to have been the provision for a major review within five years of its inception,[22] which Norman Manley, leader of the People's National Party (PNP) in Jamaica, relied on when seeking to persuade Williams, to keep faith with the Federation: 'I am absolutely certain that at the end of the first five years if we unitedly wish to we will get Dominion status for the asking.'[23]

Before then, however, the Federation had already begun to unravel. In October 1961, in a referendum forced upon Norman Manley by Alexander Bustamante, the leader of the Jamaica Labour Party (JLP), who had denounced the Federation, Jamaicans voted by a majority of 54 per cent to secede. Even though the British Government had by now indicated its willingness to concede to nationalist demands for the grant of immediate Dominion status to the Federation, it was apparent it could not survive Jamaica's withdrawal. As Eric Williams wryly observed, 'One from ten leaves nought, not nine'.[24] As far as Williams was concerned, once Jamaica withdrew 'everything mash up.'[25] Five weeks after the general elections in Trinidad and Tobago, in December 1961, which were won by Williams' People's National Movement (PNM), it was announced that Trinidad and Tobago would also be withdrawing from the Federation. Two months later, the Secretary of State for the Colonies announced to the House of Commons that, following meetings with the Premier of Barbados and the Chief Ministers of the Leeward and Windward islands, he was dissolving the Federation.

The dissolution of the Federation was in marked contrast to the progress towards self-government in the individual territories, in particular Jamaica and Trinidad and Tobago. Upon Jamaica's withdrawal from the Federation the case for its independence had, as the Colonial Office acknowledged, become virtually irresistible; especially given the precedent of Cyprus and Sierra Leone, two equally small territories which had already been granted independence.[26] At the Jamaican Independence Conference in London in February 1962, which took place only four months after the referendum that had ended Jamaica's membership of the Federation, it was further agreed that the British Government would sponsor Jamaica's application for membership of the Commonwealth so that it could embark upon independence as a Dominion.[27] At a meeting of the Cabinet Colonial Policy Committee, which was taking place at the same time as the Jamaican Independence Conference was in session, it was also conceded that it would be impossible to refuse independence to Trinidad and Tobago, 'which was already independent for all practical purposes.'[28] As the former Colonial Secretary, Iain McLeod, recalled in a 1967 interview:

> You see, when you are giving independence to a country the size of Gambia, to islands the size of Malta and Cyprus, it's a bit much to expect Jamaica or Trinidad and Tobago to link their sovereignty with a whole collection of islands, many of which they would have to help almost as pensioners.[29]

At the subsequent Trinidad and Tobago Independence Conference held in London in June 1962 it was further agreed that the British Government would similarly support Trinidad and Tobago's application for membership of the Commonwealth.[30] Trinidad and Tobago thus followed Jamaica in embarking upon independence as Dominions and in the ensuing two decades all of Britain's remaining colonies in the region attained independence and Dominion status on the same terms.[31]

It is arguable that to this extent Caribbean nationalism had achieved its ultimate goal even if it had taken much longer than many nationalists would have wanted and even if it was not as part of a larger West Indian state. Dominion status meant that Caribbean Prime Ministers could now take a seat alongside the leaders of the old Dominions, together with the Prime Ministers of the newer South Asian and African Dominions, at the annual meetings of the Commonwealth Heads of Government. Arguably, however, Caribbean prime Ministers had more in common with the former than the latter. Like them they continued to swear an oath of allegiance to the Crown and retained the JCPC as their final appellate court. By contrast many of the post-World War II Dominions had already or were about to embrace republicanism and abolish appeals to the JCPC. In order to understand Caribbean political leaders' identification with what was already a somewhat outdated version of Dominion status it is necessary to understand the very distinctive nature of Caribbean nationalism.

Caribbean Nationalism: 'Civic Britannicus Sum'

Throughout the struggle for independence Caribbean nationalists, with very few exceptions, demonstrated an unwavering commitment to achieving independence within the framework of the British Empire. The intense nationalism and anti-imperialism that characterised the struggle for independence in so many of Britain's African and Asian colonies did not make its presence felt to anything like the same extent in the Caribbean.[32] Caribbean nationalists may have been opposed to the form of colonial rule but they did not criticise the imperial connection. The distinguished Caribbean scholar, Gordon Lewis, has referred to this as the fatal ambiguity lying at the heart of West Indian nationalism: the attempt to 'be an Empire loyalist and a West Indian nationalist at the same time.'[33] For Caribbean nationalists there was no incompatibility between the demand for responsible self-government and participation in the British imperial mission.'[34] ERD Evans, a member of the Jamaican Labour Party (JLP), and one of the first five elected members to sit on Jamaica's Executive Council thus justified his support for self- government in these terms:

> In order that in verity Jamaica will in every respect be an integral portion of the Great British Commonwealth of Nations and Jamaicans be de facto citizens of Empire – justifying the designation Civic Brittanicus Sum.[35]

This same sense of a dual identity permeates a speech to the Legislative Council of Trinidad and Tobago made by Arthur Cipriani in 1937:

> I look forward ... to the day when the British Government will say to us, and I know they will say it ... yes, we agree you must hold and control the administration of your won country and we will give you what we have given to the other parts of the great Empire, a full measure of Dominion status. Until that time comes, we, like true, loyal, honest and devoted members of the Great commonwealth of nations, must fight on ... for the right to live in our own country and for the right to hold and control its own administration.[36]

Cipriani was very typical of his generation of nationalists. T E Marryshow, for example, a close ally of Cipriani, and owner of the West Indian newspaper, is cariacatured by Gordon Lewis as a 'Royalist-Loyalist'. Even supposed firebrands such as Uriah Butler, who had been expelled from the Trinidad Labour Party for his 'extremist tendencies', and Alexander Bustmante, both of whom had been imprisoned for their involvement in the strikes and disturbances of the 1930s, remained thoroughly loyal to the British Empire and all that it represented. According to Millette, Butler 'epitomized perfectly the ideological commitment of the West Indian peasant to the benevolent despotism of the British monarchy.'[37] Though ideology was no part of Bustmanate's political makeup he was no less enthusiastic about Empire. In 1946, for example, upon his release from custody, following a charge of manslaughter, he shouted to his supporters: 'Long live British justice. Long live the British Empire. And long live Me.'[38] While this may have been characteristically tongue-in-cheek, two years later when he went to London in 1948 to conduct negotiations on constitutional reform Bustamante was clearly being sincere in declaring his loyalty to the British Empire:

> No one knows the weakness and bad things about England as well as I do. But in spite of all these weaknesses and all the bad, the breaking up of the British Empire would mean the end of democracy, the end of everything good on this earth.[39]

Even an avowed 'socialist', such as Norman Manley, was, according to Louis Lindsay, a 'pronounced' Anglophile.[40] In a coruscating essay, critiquing the 'myth of independence' in Jamaica, Lindsay castigates Manley and his fellow PNP leaders for their veneration of 'things and ways British.'[41] By way of example, he recounts how at the closing of the inaugural Conference of the PNP its leaders led the audience in an enthusiastic rendition of God Save the King.[42] Alexander also recounts how, at the same conference, Stafford Cripps scandalised the PNP's leaders with his criticism of the British Empire.[43] In Lindsay's view, the PNP was 'completely dominated by Afro-Saxon men, deeply steeped in the values of British political liberalism.'[44] Though there was certainly within the PNP, a radical, Marxist, anti-imperialist element, represented by the '4 Hs' (Ken Hill, Frank Hill, Arthur Henry, and Richard Hart), whose aim was to convert Jamaicans 'to switch their allegiance from the traditional attachment to the British crown and towards the sickle and hammer emblem of soviet communism,'[45] this element was expelled in 1952.

Following hard on the heels of the disbandment, in 1949, of the Caribbean Labour Congress, an umbrella organisation which represented trade unions from across the region, and the expulsion of the more racial element of the PNP, the only remaining torchbearers for anti-imperialism in the region were Cheddi Jagan's PPP in British Guiana. The PPP were much less in thrall to the values of British political liberalism, but soon found itself isolated from the mainstream of Caribbean nationalism as Bustamante and Manley in Jamaica, and Grantley Adams, leader of the Barbados Labour Party, united in support of British intervention in British Guiana in 1953 and the suspension of the Constitution just 133 days after the PPP's victory in the general election. Jagan found himself even more isolated in 1955 when the PPP split and Forbes Burnham, regarded by the British as more moderate than Jagan, left the PPP and went on to form the People's National Congress (PNC) in 1958.

For political leaders, such as Adams, Manley, and Bustmante, who were joined by Eric Williams in the mid-1950s, self-government was incomprehensible other than in association with Great Britain.[46] For these nationalist leaders independence did not connote a new beginning or a rupture with the colonial past, but rather an opportunity to entrench political liberalism by adopting a parliamentary model of government as the blueprint for independence. As Manley explained in a speech delivered five months before independence, defending the embodiment of the Westminster model in the draft independence constitution for Jamaica:

> I make no apology for the fact that we did not embark upon any original or novel exercise in constitutional building ... Let us not make the mistake of describing as colonial, institutions which are part and parcel of the heritage of this country. If we have any confidence in our own individuality and our own personality, we would absorb these things and incorporate them into own use as part of the heritage we are not ashamed of. I am not ashamed of any institution which exists in this country merely because it derives from England.[47]

A similar view was expressed by Eric Williams in 1955, shortly before his PNM won the general election in Trinidad and Tobago in 1956:

> I suggest to you that the time has come when the British constitution, suitably modified, can be applied to Trinidad and Tobago. After all, if the British Constitution is good enough for Great Britain, it should be good enough for Trinidad and Tobago.[48]

This conservative strain amongst Caribbean nationalists and the tendency to look to Britain for a model of governance was no more than a reflection of Caribbean culture, or perhaps more specifically its absence. As John Darwin argues, the West Indies had no indigenous, pre-colonial past for nationalists to evoke: 'language, tradition, sport and new patterns of post-War migration drew them towards Britain.'[49] Anne Spry Rush too notes that 'from the late nineteenth century a variety of British campaigns (official and unofficial) promoted loyalty to the Empire and admiration of all things British was encouraged in the media, through schools, churches, and at public events.'[50] By the early twentieth century, she observes:

> 'Britishness' was an integral part of the culture of colonialism that had long pervaded daily life in the British Caribbean. In newspapers, periodicals and monographs, in classrooms and churches, on playing fields, at meetings of voluntary organizations, and in public ceremonies Caribbean peoples had for decades been encouraged to identify with the social structures and cultural values touted as intrinsically British.[51]

According to Gordon Lewis, the British had sought through education to convert West Indians into 'coloured English gentlemen,' resulting in culturally disinherited individuals, 'caught between the dying Anglophile world and the new world of Caribbean democracy and nationalism seeking to be born.'[52] Many of the leading Caribbean nationalists of the 1950s, including Manley, Adams and Williams, were products of this culture. After being steeped in British values as part of their secondary education in the Caribbean, these men went on to study at Oxford and exactly the same could have been said of them as was said by the Soulbury Commission about Ceylon's political leaders at the time of its 1946 Constitution:

> It must be borne in mind that a number of them have been educated in England and have absorbed British political ideas. When they demand responsible government, they mean government on the British parliamentary model and are apt to resent any deviation from it as derogatory to their status as fellow citizens of the British Commonwealth of Nations and as conceding something less than they consider as their due.[53]

For Caribbean political leaders the parliamentary model of government was, accordingly, cast in the monarchical form familiar in Britain.[54] As Darwin notes, 'far from being a symbol of alien domination, in the Caribbean the Crown was a popular institution.'[55] Though this can seem somewhat counter-intuitive in a region so ravaged by the experience of slavery, and where the majority of its citizens were direct descendants of those former slaves, devotion to the Crown was in fact linked to the era of slavery as a result of a mistaken belief that Queen Victoria had played a part in the slaves' emancipation.[56] As a consequence, the Queen came to be viewed as a symbol of liberation and the annual Emancipation Day celebrations were viewed as an opportunity by colonial administrators as a means of promoting loyalty to the Crown.[57] Even after Queen Victoria's death, local participation in special activities designed to memorialise and celebrate the British royal family, such as Empire Day, funerals, jubilees and coronations was encouraged as a way of reinforcing loyalty to the Crown.[58]

The strength of this loyalty was noted by Major Wood in his 1922 report in which he commented on the remarkable degree of attachment of 'black' West Indians to the Crown.[59] It is also remarked upon in the memoirs of former colonial Governors, such as Hugh Foot,[60] and Sir Kenneth Blackburne;[61] with the latter offering the following description of the celebration of the Queen's Coronation on the Antigua Recreation Ground which was 'more crowded than for any cricket match':

> The crowd participated in the actual Coronation ceremony when I announced over loud speakers the time honoured phrases – 'Sirs, I here present unto you Queen Elizabeth, your undoubted Queen; wherefore all of you who are come to do your homage and service, are you willing to do the same?' The cry came back from the vast crowd and echoed round the town – 'God Save Queen Elizabeth'.[62]

Aware of the continuing popularity of the Crown amongst many West Indians, and its usefulness both as a symbol of continuity and as a foundation for nation-building in the post-independence era,[63] nationalist politicians were at great pains to demonstrate their own personal loyalty to the Crown.[64] Perhaps never more so than in the warm welcome which the Queen received from Bustamante and Manley when she visited Jamaica in 1953, only a few weeks after the British had suspended the Constitution of British Guiana and ousted its democratically elected leader. Indeed, demonstrations of loyalty to the Crown permeated each stage of the decolonisation process: from the Montego Bay Conference in 1947, which concluded with a pledge of allegiance to George VI; to the opening of the federal Parliament in 1958 by Princess Margaret; and, finally, to the first session of the Jamaican Parliament, which opened with a speech by the Queen, read on her behalf by Princess Margaret. This included a fulsome declaration of praise for the former imperial power:

> [B]oth my Government in the United Kingdom and my Government in Jamaica wish to maintain the bonds of friendship which have existed for over three centuries and have made it possible for Jamaica to proceed to independence peacefully and happily.[65]

As Gordon Lewis, caustically observes: 'for Jamaicans, colonialism ended not in a bang but a whimper.'[66]

The Postcolonies

The historian, Richard Drayton, has written about the problem of the 'postcolony' in the Caribbean, by which he means 'the persistence of the colonial order even after the acquisition of constitutional sovereignty.'[67] In the sections that follow I will examine the steps that have been taken to excise two of the most enduring and most visible symbols of the colonial order – the Crown and the JCPC – from the region's political and legal orders.

Caribbean Republics

As we have seen, at the time that the first countries in the region attained their independence, at the beginning of the 1960s, the leading nationalist politicians, were in the main constitutional monarchists. There were however pockets of resistance to the retention of the Crown in the postcolonial order. As the widely respected Jamaican political scientist, Norman Girvan, recalls of this period:

> In early 1962, several of us attended the sessions held in Kingston to solicit the views of the public on the design of the Jamaican Independence Constitution. Our main concern at the time was the retention of the Monarchy. We argued that it was contrary to the psychological necessities of nation-building that the Queen of England should be the head of State of Independent Jamaica ... It had the effect of embedding the core symbol of colonial governance into the institutions and rituals of the independent state.[68]

Though this was very much a minority view at the time, within a decade Guyana had become the first republic in the region, in 1970, to be followed six years later by Trinidad and Tobago, in 1976. Two years later, in 1978, Dominica became the first country in the region to embark upon independence as a republic. In each case the political context out of which the demand for republicanism grew was quite different and each, therefore, merits separate attention.

Guyana

As noted above, British Guiana and its PPP-led government stood very much outside the mainstream of Caribbean nationalism. It is perhaps not surprising, therefore, that it should have been the first country in the region to embrace republicanism. According to Cheddi Jagan, the PPP first advocated republicanism at the Independence Conference for British Guiana in London in 1962, but it was opposed by the conservative United Front, led by Peter D'Aguiar, and by Forbes Burnham's PNC who 'ambiguously supported monarchical status for some time to be followed later by republican status.'[69] However, three years later, when the time came to negotiate the terms of British Guiana's independence, Jagan's PPP, having been defeated in the 1964 election by a coalition of the PNC and UF, boycotted the Independence Conference in protest at the imposition of a state of emergency and imprisonment of a number of the PPP's leading members. In the absence of the PPP a compromise was reached between the UF and the PNC on the question of whether independent Guyana should be a republic. This entailed the inclusion of a provision in the independence Constitution – Article 73 (5) – which allowed for Guyana to become a republic if the National Assembly should so resolve by a majority vote of all its elected members after 1 January 1969.[70] Though British officials had some reservations about this provision, it was deemed a price worth paying. This was in part because it was thought a period of monarchical rule would enhance Guyana's credit-worthiness and improve the morale of expatriate businessmen and investors.[71] More importantly, it ensured the survival of the coalition, the future of which might otherwise have been jeopardised, leading to fresh elections, which might conceivably have been won by the even more fiercely republican PPP.[72]

Having won an outright victory in the elections of 1968, the PNC wasted no time in implementing Article 73 (5), which they considered to be a crucial step in achieving meaningful decolonisation. As Guyana's Minister for Information at the time explained:

> The British Crown is the symbolic head of Great Britain and it is from that country that we have struggled so long for our independence. It may be that some, very few, among us still accord to the British Crown a position of high idealism. But I cannot recall the British Crown successfully raising its voice in a public forum against British colonialism imposed upon millions of us across the world who now struggle to make our way as independent peoples. The fact that the British Crown today does not control the decisions of the British Government hardly seems an argument in favour of our retaining allegiance, however symbolic that allegiance may be.[73]

Guyana simultaneously abolished the right of appeal to the JCPC (see further below) and thereafter ploughed a quite different political furrow to its neighbours; abandoning the British parliamentary model of government and moving towards an executive style Presidency with the adoption of its 1980 Socialist Cooperative Republican Constitution.

Trinidad and Tobago

By the late 1960s, a new kind of postcolonial nationalism was emerging in the region, inspired not by British political liberalism but by the Black Power Movement in the United States, and calling for a decisive break with the 'historically white and racist imperial past.'[74] Though it was not the first,[75] the fiercest confrontation between a government and a popular nationalist movement inspired by the Black Power Movement was the so-called 'February Revolution' in Trinidad and Tobago in 1970.[76]

Between February and April 1970, Trinidad and Tobago was overwhelmed by a series of mass public demonstrations and marches, involving thousands of protesters. The protests, which had started in the capital, quickly spread throughout the country. They were only finally quelled following a declaration of a state of emergency on 21 April 1970, and the arrest and incarceration of the leaders of the National Joint Action Committee, which had orchestrated the demonstrations. Though a small group of youthful revolutionaries, calling themselves the National Union of Freedom Fighters, sought to continue the revolution by waging guerilla warfare, they failed to garner popular support for their cause and their endeavours ultimately came to nought; 18 of the group being killed by the police. The February Revolution was followed by the boycotting of the 1971 elections by the main opposition parties, calling into question the legitimacy of the PNP's landslide victory in those elections.

It was against this background that the PNP, still at this time led by Eric Williams, established, in June 1971, the eponymous 'Wooding Commission', chaired by the Chief Justice, Sir Hugh Wooding, to review the country's 1962 independence Constitution and to make recommendations for its reform 'with a view to encouraging the maximum participation of citizens in the political process'.[77] As the Wooding Commission noted, the survival of constitutional, parliamentary politics in the country was being challenged as never before.[78] In dealing with the question of whether Trinidad and Tobago should become a republic the Commission noted that there had been almost unanimous agreement about this issue amongst those making submissions to the Commission. In the Commission's view:

> [This] is no more than an expression of the fact that independence must involve the creation of indigenous symbols of nationhood. Among young people in particular the British Sovereign has no symbolic meaning. The thrust since Independence has been towards the discovery of a new identity which involves leaving behind the colonial heritage of subjection, imitation and external dependence. The oath which the Governor-General now takes on assuming office brings the problem sharply into focus. He swears to be faithful and bear true allegiance to HM the Queen. To most ears this is anachronistic. His oath quite obviously should be faithfully to serve the people of Trinidad and Tobago and to defend and uphold its Constitution.[79]

Though the Wooding Commission, which published its report in January 1974, made a number of other recommendations for reform of Trinidad's independence Constitution, the proposal that Trinidad and Tobago should become a republic with a President as head of state was one of the very few of its recommendations to be accepted by the Prime Minister.[80] According to Murphy, this was mainly as a sop to radical nationalists who had focused attention on the Crown as a symbol of colonial oppression and who had ridiculed Williams, once a scourge of colonialists, 'as nothing more than a black puppet of white economic interests.'[81]

Accordingly, when Trinidad and Tobago adopted a new Constitution in 1976 it made provision for a presidential head of state, elected by an electoral college comprising all of the members of the House of Representatives and the Senate.

Dominica

Dominica differs from both Guyana and Trinidad and Tobago where, at the risk of generalisation, support for republicanism was associated with a more radical, anti-colonial brand of nationalism, whilst the more moderate nationalists tended to favour retention of a constitutional monarchy. In Dominica, the proposal to adopt a republican Constitution on independence was originally put forward by the leader of the opposition Freedom Party, the 'conservative' Eugenia Charles. However, her reason for proposing republicanism was not because she wished to excise the remaining vestiges of colonialism, but rather because she felt that an executive-style President was the best safeguard against the dominance of the executive that had characterised self-government in the ten years that Dominica had been an Associated State. At the independence conference in London in 1978, Charles argued that having a purely ceremonial head of State was an expensive luxury which Dominica could ill afford. Instead, she wanted to have a President with responsibility for defence, internal security and foreign affairs.[82] In addition, the President would have 'the right to delay for one month or to the next sitting of the National Assembly any Bill which in his opinion affects special interests which have not had the opportunity of making their views known'.[83] However, the Government delegation led by the 'socialist' Prime Minister, Patrick John, refused to accept this proposal, arguing that it was the wish of the majority of people of Dominica that the Queen should remain the Head of State.[84]

As it proved impracticable to resolve this difference of views, the British Government initially concluded that, taking account of the relevant representation of the opposing delegations in the Dominica House of Assembly, it should proceed on the basis of the Government's proposal. However, following the Conference, a senior official from the Foreign and Commonwealth Office, R N Posnett, was dispatched to Dominica in May 1978 to see if agreement could be reached between the governing and opposition parties on this and other issues. By this point both sides had modified their position on this issue. The governing Labour Party was now prepared to accept a republican system, but not with an executive-style President. Instead they were happy for the President to be given certain responsibilities, such as the appointment of Chairmen of certain Commissions, such as the Public services Commission.[85] The Leader of the Opposition had also withdrawn her demand for an executive-style President, having, apparently, recognised that 'divided executive responsibility might be unworkable.'[86] Instead she was content for the President's powers to be restricted to non-executive matters. Thus Dominica embarked upon independence with a ceremonial President similar to the Presidents of Guyana and Trinidad and Tobago.

Caribbean Realms

The question of whether to embrace republicanism has featured prominently in the deliberations of the numerous constitutional review commissions that have reported over the last two decades, all of which, with one exception, have recommended the replacement of the Queen with an elected President. The exception is Belize, but this is because of concerns about Belize's security in the face of its border dispute with Guatemala and the fear that replacing the British monarch as head of state might decrease Britain's willingness to come to the aid of Belize in the event of an invasion by Guatemala.[87] Over the last two decades a number of the region's political leaders have also declared their intention to appoint a ceremonial President as Head of State in place of the Queen.[88] And yet, Guyana and Trinidad and Tobago apart, no other country in the region has managed the transformation from constitutional monarchy to republicanism (Dominica having embarked upon independence as a republic.)

Though they do not exclude the possibility of there being others, two reasons for this failure to switch to republicanism immediately stand out. The first, which we considered, in Part I is the historic loyalty to the monarchy in the region which dates back till at least the mid-nineteenth century and which has managed to survive independence. Perhaps the most extreme example of this loyalty is Grenada where, even after they had staged a Marxist coup, in 1979, the New Jewel Movement (NJM) retained the Queen as head of state. As the leaders of the NJM subsequently explained, there was no popular demand for abolishing the monarchy and at such an early stage of the revolution they did not want 'to frighten the horses'.[89] As recently as 2011, a report of a poll in the *Jamaican Gleaner*, noting that 60 per cent of respondents agreed that Jamaica would have been better off if it had remained a colony, ran under the headline: 'Give us the Queen!'[90]

Philip Murphy suggests that this residual enthusiasm for the monarchy may be based on 'a sense of respect and even genuine affection for Queen Elizabeth II', which may not survive her demise.[91] However, there is a second reason for believing that these realms are not about to become republics, which has nothing to do with the personal popularity of Queen Elizabeth II. This concerns the requirement in a number of countries for such a constitutional amendment to be approved by the vote of a majority of citizens in a referendum. To date, no government in the Commonwealth Caribbean has secured majority approval in a referendum for any constitutional amendment; apart from the Government of Guyana, which secured majority approval for the amendment of its 1970 Constitution, but in that case the referendum was widely believed to have been rigged.[92]

In a number of countries in the region the task of amending their Constitution is made even harder by the requirement of a super-majority of two-thirds of voters in a referendum: Antigua,[93] St Vincent and the Grenadines,[94] and Grenada.[95] In the only referendum to be held in the region since independence in which the question of becoming a republic has been put directly to voters, in 2009, in St Vincent and the Grenadines, the proposal was rejected by 55 per cent of those who voted.[96] In Grenada, which held a referendum in 2016 on seven Constitution (Amendment) Bills, the question of replacing the Queen with a ceremonial President was not even included on the ballot papers, despite the fact that no less than two constitutional review commissions had recommended such a change.[97] Instead, voters in the referendum were asked merely to approve an amendment to the Constitution which would entitle public officials to swear allegiance to the State of Grenada rather than the Crown. However, even this relatively modest amendment failed to secure the support of a majority of voters in the referendum.

Even where the approval of a majority of citizens in a referendum is not expressly required by the constitution, as for example in Barbados, the government has been reluctant to effect such a fundamental constitutional reform without the mandate afforded by popular approval in a referendum. Thus, following the recommendation of the Forde Commission, in 1998, that Barbados should become a republic,[98] the Government decided, even though it could easily have attained the two thirds legislative majority required in both Houses of Parliament to amend the Constitution, it would proceed instead by way of a referendum. A Referendum Act was introduced in 2005 and a date was fixed for the referendum to coincide with the general election in 2008. In the event, however, the referendum was not held in 2008 and has been deferred by successive governments ever since.

The JCPC

As early as 1921, Arthur Berriedale Keith had declared the JCPC to be 'in the process of obsolescence.'[99] Five years later, the Balfour declaration of 1926 made it clear it was no part of the British Government's policy 'that questions affecting judicial appeals should be determined otherwise than in accordance with the wishes of the part of the Empire primarily affected.'[100] Of the original Dominions, Ireland abolished the right of appeal to the JCPC, in 1933, and South Africa followed suit in 1950. Amongst the new post-World War II Dominions,

India and Pakistan both abolished appeals to the JCPC very shortly after independence. For nationalist leaders in Africa, executive, legislative and juridical sovereignty were inextricably interconnected: delinking from the JCPC was, therefore, seen as a key step in their assertion of independence and sovereignty and by 1966 most of these ex-colonies had abolished all appeals to the JCPC.[101] It is true that in a number of other former colonies the JCPC survived for longer after independence – Sri Lanka only finally abolished appeals in 1971, Malaysia in 1985, and Singapore in 1994 – but the retention of appeals to the JCPC by the majority of Commonwealth Caribbean countries, over fifty years after the first countries in the region attained independence, is still a striking anomaly, made even more striking by the existence, since 2006, of the CCJ.

As noted above, only four countries have so far ratified the CCJ's appellate jurisdiction – Guyana, Barbados, Belize and, most recently, Dominica – and these do not include the region's most populous and, arguably, most politically influential countries – Jamaica and Trinidad and Tobago. That Trinidad and Tobago has not ratified the CCJ's appellate jurisdiction is made all the more curious by the fact that it has been a republic since 1976. As long ago as 1974, the Wooding Commission had expressly identified the link between republicanism and abolishing the right of appeal to the JCPC:

> Besides it seems incongruous that we should want to become a republic and yet look to a monarchical institution for justice form our courts. India, Pakistan, Nigeria, Ghana and Guyana are among other republics, which, while remaining in the Commonwealth, have disallowed any further appeals to the JCPC.[102]

Though Jamaica is not yet a republic, it is notable that the governing JLP, when announcing its intention to hold a referendum with a view to becoming a republic in the near future, did not link this issue with abolishing the right of appeal to the JCPC.[103]

All of this is not to say that the disjuncture between independence and retention of the right of appeal to the JCPC has passed unnoticed. As the former Chief justice of Barbados, Sir David Simmonds, one of the foremost supporters of the CCJ, has argued:

> The independence of the states of the region will not be complete, is not complete, when our constitutions entrench a foreign tribunal as our final court of appeal. It is inconsistent with independence: it is an affront to our sovereignty and the sovereignty of independent nations. You may say this is an emotional argument, but these psychological considerations are important and the symbolism is not to be discounted.[104]

This is linked to concerns at the juridical level about the JCPC's role as the final arbiter of the meaning of the region's constitutions. As Simeon McIntosh, has observed:

> [S]o long as we remain the 'subjects' of the British Crown with its Judicial Committee as the apex in the hierarchy of our legal system, it is to be expected that our

constitutional discourse would reflect a cluster of values, intellectual orientations and practices that carry a distinct British cast ... Our constitutional conversation is carried out in a 'foreign' voice. We are either silenced or are constrained to speak within the institutions and traditions of interpretation of the colonial constitutions that have been imposed on us.[105]

Constitutional interpretation involves the exercise of a powerful judicial discretion, which often requires judges to make decisions which are essentially policy decisions and which are not very different to the kind of decisions that are made by a democratically elected parliament. As the former Chief Justice of the CCJ, Michael de la Bastide has argued:

In making such decisions, [a judge] is not unearthing some universal verity but determining what is best for a particular society in the circumstances existing at a certain point in its history.

It was in his view, therefore, essential that those who make such decisions have an intimate and first hand knowledge of the society upon whose behalf the decision is made: not only because they will be better informed about the needs of that society, but also because residence in and membership of that society is the most salutary form of accountability.[106]

These are each very compelling arguments for abolishing the right of appeal to the JCPC, but they have not gained the political traction necessary to build the consensus that would be needed to effect such a constitutional amendment. This is in part because there are still those who advocate retention of the right of appeal to the JCPC on the grounds, firstly, that its appellate jurisdiction is available at no cost to the governments of those countries that still subscribe to its jurisdiction; and, secondly that it is composed of judges who are of the highest calibre and who are judicially independent, being free of the political influence and control that some of the region's governments have been accused of exerting over their national judges.[107] Though the latter are, undoubtedly, principled reasons for retaining rights of appeal to the JCPC, more often attempts to build the necessary consensus to abolish the right of appeal to the JCPC and replace it with a right of appeal to the CCJ have failed not for principled reasons but for reasons of partisan politics. In Jamaica and Trinidad and Tobago, for example, there have been spectacular U-turns on the issue of abolishing rights of appeal to the JCPC by, resepectively, Edward Seaga, the leader of the JLP, and Basdeo Panday, the leader of the United National Congress in Trinidad and Tobago, both of whom supported the establishment of the CCJ whilst in government, but then opposed it when no longer in power.[108] Indeed, in the case of Jamaica, Edward Seaga was one of the parties to proceedings before the JCPC, *Independent Jamaica Council for Human Rights (1998) v Attorney General Jamaica*,[109] in which the JCPC held that the PNP Government's attempt to abolish the right of appeal to the JCPC on the basis of a simple legislative majority was unconstitutional because it did not comply with the procedure for amending the entrenched provisions of the Constitution. The JLP has interpreted this decision to mean that that any amendment to the Constitution that involves the removal of the right of appeal to the JCPC must first be approved by a majority of voters in a referendum.

In the case of Trinidad and Tobago, it would be possible, in theory, to effect the necessary amendment to the Constitution without a referendum, and the PNM Government, which won the 2015 elections, has announced that it is committed to ratifying the CCJ's appellate jurisdiction.[110] However, it cannot secure the necessary two-thirds legislative majority required by the Constitution without the support of the opposition United National Congress, led by Kamla Persad-Bissessar, and she has previously made it clear when she was in office that she would not support any such move unless it had first been approved by a majority of voters in a referendum.[111]

This does not bode well for those campaigning to abolish the right of appeal to the JCPC. As noted above, the record across the region of attempts to reform the constitution by means of a referendum is, to say, the least very poor. Thus, even if the JLP in Jamaica and the PNM in Trinidad and Tobago were willing to put the issue to their citizens in a referendum the likelihood that voters would support such a reform is slim. It is even slimmer in countries such as Antigua, Grenada and St Vincent and the Grenadines, where a two thirds majority of voters in a referendum is required, so deeply entrenched are the provisions surrounding the right of appeal to the JCPC. It is, assuredly, no coincidence that in all four of the countries that have so far ratified the CCJ's appellate jurisdiction the amendment to their constitution has been effected by means of a legislative majority and without the need for a referendum to be held.

Conclusion

When Commonwealth Caribbean political leaders conceived of independence and Dominion status they adopted as their point of reference the 'white' settler Dominions of Canada, Australia and New Zealand, rather than the newer South Asian and African Dominions. Upon independence they would become constitutional monarchies and would retain the JCPC as their final appellate court. While all of these political leaders have since been replaced by a generation of politicians who have, at best, a vestigial memory of British colonial rule, its two most visible symbols – the Crown and the JCPC – endure.

Of the three countries that have adopted republicanism, each was affected by different political forces that marked them out from their neighbours. Guyana, as we have seen, had always stood outside the mainstream of Caribbean nationalism; Jagan and the PPP being much more fiercely anti-colonial and much less committed to the ideal of British political liberalism than, for example, the avowedly 'socialist' PNM in Jamaica. In Trinidad and Tobago republicanism was a response to a Black Power revolution, which rejected the tradition of British political imperialism inherited upon independence, and which made it impossible for the Prime Minister to retain political credibility so long as a 'white' British Monarch remained as Head of State. In Dominica, republicanism had nothing to do with anti-colonial sentiment. The government was in fact proudly pro-monarchical, but agreed to accept a ceremonial president as Head of State as a compromise to secure the opposition's agreement to the terms of the independence Constitution.

One feature, however, that these three countries had in common was that they were able to become republics without the need for a referendum. As we have seen, almost everywhere else in the region a referendum is required either expressly by the Constitution or, as in Barbados, by the perception that it would not be politically legitimate to effect such a constitutional amendment without a referendum. The exception is Belize but there are particular security concerns which explain Belizean exceptionalism. In combination with a residual loyalty to the Crown, the requirement for a referendum presents a formidable obstacle to republicanism. As we have seen, everywhere in the region that referendums on constitutional reform have been held they have, with one exception, been used as an opportunity for voters to give the government a bloody nose.

Even assuming, however, that the remaining realms were to overcome this obstacle and become republics there is no guarantee that they would at the same time abolish rights of appeal to the JCPC. In the Commonwealth Caribbean the adoption of republicanism and the abolition of the JCPC have not been seen as two sides of the same coin; with the exception of Guyana which abolished rights of appeal to the JCPC when it became a republic in 1970. Trinidad and Tobago had the opportunity to follow suit in 1976 when it adopted a republican Constitution, but Eric Williams chose not to accept the recommendation of the Wooding Commission in this regard. It is also notable that the only other republic in the region, Dominica, waited almost 40 years before finally abolishing rights of appeal to the JCPC. It could be argued that this was because Dominica did not possess at independence the resources necessary to establish its own second tier appellate court, but even following the inauguration of the CCJ in 2006, it was a further decade before Dominica signed up to its appellate jurisdiction.

Elsewhere the link between republicanism and the abolition of right of appeals to the JCPC has proved to be equally tenuous. Barbados, for example, has ratified the CCJ's appellate jurisdiction, but has fought shy of holding a referendum on whether to become a republic. Conversely, in Jamaica, where the JLP has declared that it wants Jamaica to become a republic within the lifetime of the current parliament, it has refused to give any indication of when, if ever, it will hold a referendum on abolishing rights of appeal to the JCPC.[112]

The constitutional identity of the majority of the region's countries thus remains fixed as it was at the time of their independence as they continue to define themselves as a political community in terms of their links to the

British Crown and to vest their ultimately legal sovereignty in that most imperial of courts, the JCPC.

Notes

1. Antigua and Barbuda, The Bahamas, Barbados, Belize, Dominica, Grenada, Guyana, Jamaica, St Kitts and Nevis, St Lucia, St Vincent and the Grenadines, and Trinidad and Tobago.
2. Canada abolished rights of appeal in 1949, Australia in 1986 (though the process actually began in 1968), and New Zealand in 2003.
3. See Wrong, *Government of the West Indies*.
4. See Wallace, *The British Caribbean*.
5. Proctor Jr, "British West Indian Society and Government in Transition 1920-60," 34.
6. Trinidad and Tobago and Guyana, in particular, being made up of separate communities of predominantly Christian Afro-Caribbean and Hindu Indo-Caribbeans.
7. Report by the Hon. EFL Wood on his Visit to the West Indies and British Guiana (December 1921-February 1922),' Great Britain, *Parliamentary Papers*, Cmd. 1679, 1922.
8. Wallace, *The British Caribbean*, 26.
9. Lewis, *The Growth of the Modern West Indies*, 108.
10. Cipriani was one of the first elected members of Trinidad's Legislative Council.
11. James, *The Life of Captain Cipriani*, 20-26.
12. Johnson, "The British Caribbean," 614.
13. Lee and Petter, *The Colonial Office*, 244.
14. Quoted by Millette, "Decolonization," 189.
15. In Jamaica the People's National party expressly instructed its supporters 'to abstain from agitation for constitutional reform.' See Lindsay, *The Myth of Independence*, 102.
16. Martin, "Eric Williams and the Anglo-American Caribbean Commission," 274-90.
17. Millette, "Decolonization," 188.
18. *Parliamentary Papers 1947-1948*, Cmd. 7291, Conference on the Closer Association of the British West Indian Colonies 7-11.
19. Jagan, *The Caribbean Revolution*, 25.
20. Jagan, op cit., 19.
21. Pursuant to British Caribbean Federation Act 1956.
22. s.118.
23. Jamaica National Archives, Manley papers, 4/60/2A/18.
24. Palmer, *Eric Williams*, 179.
25. *Sunday Guardian*, 5 November, 1961, quoted by Wallace 201.
26. TNA:PRO, CAB 128/35/2, 28 September 1961.
27. *Report of Jamaica Independence Conference*, 1962 Cmnd.1638, 6.
28. CAB 134/1561 2 February 1962.
29. Johnson, op cit., 620.
30. *Report of Jamaica Independence Conference*, 1962 Cmnd.1638, p2.
31. Barbados and Guyana (1966), the Bahamas (1973), Grenada (1974), Dominica (1978), St Lucia (1979), St Vincent and the Grenadines (1979), Antigua and Barbuda (1981), Belize (1981), and St Kitts and Nevis 1983.
32. Darwin, *Britain and Decolonisation*, 220.
33. Lewis, op cit., 207.
34. Putnam, 615-30.

35. Speech by ERD Evans, in Plain Talk, 14 January, 1939, p2. Quoted by Lindsay, op cit., 113.
36. Trinidad Hansard 1937 (Port of Spain: Government printing Office) 268–69.
37. Millette, "Decolonization," 204.
38. Girvan, "Assessing Westminster in the Caribbean," 97.
39. Mawby, *Ordering Independence*, 46.
40. Lindsay, "Slaying the Westmonster," 99.
41. Ibid., 101.
42. Ibid., 100.
43. Quoted in Alexander, *Presidents, Prime-Ministers and Governors of the English-Speaking Caribbean*, 17.
44. Lindsay, "Slaying the Westmonster," 101.
45. Ibid., 109.
46. Ibid., 114.
47. Jamaica Hansard, 1962, p719 and 751.
48. Sutton, *Forged from the Love of Liberty*, 129.
49. Darwin, *Britain and Decolonisation*, 220.
50. Rush, *Bonds of Empire*, 9.
51. Ibid., 2.
52. Lewis, op cit., 19.
53. *Ceylon: Report of the Commission on the Constitution* Cmd 6677 91945), 110. Quoted by Kumarasingham, *A Political Legacy of the British Empire*, 78.
54. Darwin, "A Third British Empire?," 76
55. Darwin, *Britain and Decolonisation*, 220.
56. Though Victoria did not ascend to the throne until 1837, four years after the Emancipation Act, freedom from the period of apprenticeship that was a condition of emancipation did not occur until the late 1830s, giving rise to a link in the minds of these former slaves between their freedom and Victoria's ascension to the throne. See Anne Spry Rush, op cit., 51.
57. Johnson, op cit., 597.
58. Ibid.
59. Wood, op cit.
60. Foot, *A Start in Freedom*, 124.
61. Blackburne, *Lasting Legacy*.
62. Blackburne, op cit., 152.
63. Lewis, op cit., 393.
64. Darwin, "A Third British Empire?," 85.
65. Quoted by Hart, *The End of Empire*, Chapter 28.
66. Lewis, op cit., 186
67. "Secondary Decolonisation: The Black Power Movement in Barbados, c.1970,"117.
68. Girvan, "Assessing Westminster," 96.
69. Jagan, op cit., 44.
70. Art 73(5) Constitution of Guyana.
71. Murphy, *Monarchy and the End of Empire*, 95.
72. Ibid., 95.
73. Quoted by Lutchman, "The Co-operative Republic of Guyana," 100.
74. Kate Quinn, op cit., 2.
75. This occurred in Jamaica in October 1968. See further Lewis, "Jamaican Black Power in the 1960s."
76. The following account is taken from Samaroo, "The February Revolution (1970) as a Catalyst for Change in Trinidad and Tobago," 97–116.

77. Report of the Constitution Commission 1974. Available at http://www.ttparliament.org/documents/1101.pdf
78. Ibid., Paragraph [20.]
79. Ibid., [138]
80. Ibid., [57].
81. Murphy, *Monarchy and End of Empire*, 157.
82. *Report of the Dominica Constitutional Conference*, 1977 Cmnd.6901, p19.
83. Ibid.
84. Ibid.
85. Dominica Termination of Association, 1978, Cmnd.7279. 5.
86. Ibid.
87. See further Grant, *The Making of Modern Belize*.
88. PJ Patterson in Jamaica in 2003, Portia Simpson-Miller in Jamaica 2012, Freundel Start in Barbados in 2015, and Andrew Holness in Jamaica in 2016. See Crilly, "Jamaica Unveils Plans to Ditch Queen as Head of State."
89. Answers to questions asked by Kate Quinn of former members of NJM at conference in Grenada. Note on file with author.
90. *Jamaica Gleaner*, 2011, June 28.
91. Murphy, *The Empire's New Clothes*, 91.
92. James and Lutchman, *Law and the Political Environment in Guyana*, 71.
93. s.47(5)(c).
94. s.38(30(b).
95. s.39(5)(c).
96. See further, Bishop, "Slaying the 'Westmonster' in the Caribbean?," 420–37.
97. In 1985 and 2006. Unpublished. On file with author.
98. Report of the Constitution Review Commission Barbados 1998. Unpublished. On file with author.
99. Quoted by Mohr, "A British Empire Court," 127.
100. Cmd. 2768, p19.
101. Ibhawoh, "Asserting Judicial Sovereignty," 31.
102. Report of Constitution Commission op cit., [354]
103. Crilly, "Jamaica Unveils Plans to Ditch Queen as Head of State."
104. Quoted by McIntosh, *Caribbean Constitutional Reform*, 266.
105. McIntosh, op cit., 294.
106. de la Bastide, "The Case for a Caribbean Court of Appeal," 402–3.
107. O'Brien, "The Caribbean Court of Justice and Its Appellate Jurisdiction," 356.
108. I am grateful to Kate Quinn of IALS, who commented on an early draft of this paper, for reminding me of this point.
109. [2005] UKPC 3.
110. Stabroek News, August 25, 2015. Available at https://www.stabroeknews.com/2015/opinion/letters/08/25/ccj-unlikely-to-replace-privy-council-in-trinidad-after-elections/
111. Ibid.
112. 'Holness Steers Clear of Giving CCJ Referendum Timeframe,' *Jamaica Gleaner*, July 7, 2016.

Disclosure statement

No potential conflict of interest was reported by the author.

References

Alexander, Robert, ed. *Presidents, Prime Ministers, and Governors of the English-Speaking Caribbean and Puerto Rico*. London, Westport, CT: Praeger, 1997.

Bishop, Matthew Louis. "Slaying the 'Westmonster' in the Caribbean? Constitutional Reform in St Vincent and the Grenadines." *British Journal of Politics and International Relations* 13 (2011): 420–437.

Blackburne, Sir Kenneth. *Lasting Legacy: A Story of British Colonialism*. London: Johnson Publications, 1976.

Crilly, Rob. "Jamaica Unveils Plans to Ditch Queen as Head of State." *Telegraph*, 16 April 2016.

Darwin, John. *Britain and Decolonisation: The Retreat from Empire in the Post-War World*. New York: St. Martin's, 1988.

Darwin, John. "A Third British Empire? The Dominion Idea in Imperial Politics." In *Oxford History of the British Empire: Volume IV: The Twentieth Century*, 64–87. Oxford: Oxford University Press, 1999.

de la Bastide, M. A. "The Case for a Caribbean Court of Appeal." *Caribbean Law Review* 5 (1995): 401–429.

Foot, Hugh. *A Start in Freedom*. London: Hodder and Stoughton, 1964.

Grant, Cedric Hilburn. *The Making of Modern Belize: Politics, Society and British Colonialism in Central America*. Cambridge: Cambridge University Press, 1976.

Girvan, Norman. "Assessing Westminster in the Caribbean: Then and Now." *Commonwealth & Comparative Politics* 53, no. 1 (2015): 95–107.

Ibhawoh, Bonny. "Asserting Judicial Sovereignty. The Debate Over the Abolition of Privy Council Jurisdiction in British Africa." In *Legal Histories of the British Empire: Laws, Engagements and Legacies*, edited by Shaunnagh Dorset, and John McLaren, 30–44. Oxon: Routledge, 2014.

Jagan, Cheddi. "Federation of the British Caribbean." In *The Caribbean Revolution*, 31–42. Oris Press Agency, 1979.

James, Cyril Lionel Robert. *The Life of Captain Cipriani, An account of British government in the West Indies, with the pamphlet 'The Case for Indian Self-Government'*. Durham, NC: Duke University Press, 2014.

James, R. W., and H. A. Lutchman. *Law and the Political Environment in Guyana*. Guyana: Institute of Development Studies, University of Guyana, 1984.

Johnson, Howard. "The British Caribbean from Demobilization to Constitutional Decolonization." In *The Oxford History of the British Empire Vol IV*, edited by Judith Brown, and Wm Roger Louis, 614. Oxford: Oxford University Press, 1979.

Kumarasingham, Harshan. *A Political Legacy of the British Empire: Power and the Parliamentary System in Post-colonial India and Sri Lanka*. London/New York: IB Tauris, 2012

Lee, J. M., and Martin Petter. *The Colonial Office, War and Development Policy Organisation and the Planning of the Metropolitan Initiative, 1939–1945*. Commonwealth Papers no. 22, published for the Institute of Commonwealth Studies by Maurice Temple Smith, London, 1982.

Lewis, G. K. *The Growth of the Modern West Indies*. Kingston, Jamaica: Ian Randle Publishers, 2004.

Lewis, Rupert. "Jamaican Black Power in the 1960s." In *Black Power in the Caribbean*, edited by Kate Quinn, 53–75. Gainesville, FL: University Press of Florida, 2014.

Lindsay, Louis. *The Myth of Independence: Middle Class Politics and Non-Mobilization in Jamaica*. Mona, Jamaica: Institute of Social and Economic Research, University of the West Indies, 1997.

Lutchman, Harold A. "The Co-operative Republic of Guyana." *Caribbean Studies* 10 (1970).

Martin, Tony. "Eric Williams and the Anglo-American Caribbean Commission: Trinidad's Future Nationalist Leader as Aspiring Imperial Bureaucrat, 1942–1944." *Journal of African American History* 88, no. 3 (2003): 274–290.

Mawby, Spencer. *Ordering Independence: The End of Empire in the Anglophone Caribbean, 1947–69*. Basingstoke, Hampshire: Palgrave Macmillan, 2012.

McIntosh, Simeon. *Caribbean Constitutional Reform: Rethinking the West Indian Polity*, 266. Kingston, Jamaica: Caribbean Law Publishing Company, 2002.

Millette, James. "Decolonization, Populist Movements and the Formation of New Nations 1945–1970." In *General History of the Caribbean Vol 5*, edited by Bridget Bretherton, 97–115. Paris: UNESCO, 2004.

Mohr, Thomas. "A British Empire Court – A Brief Appraisal of the History of the Judicial Committee of the Privy Council." In *Power in History: From Mediaeval to the Post-Modern World*, edited by Anthony McElligott et al., 125–142 Dublin: Irish Academic Press, 2011.

Murphy, Philip. *Monarchy and the End of Empire*. Oxford: Oxford University Press, 2015.

Murphy, Philip. *The Empire's New Clothes: The Myth of the Commonwealth*. London: Hurst and Company, 2018.

O'Brien, Derek. "The Caribbean Court of Justice and Its Appellate Jurisdiction: A Difficult Birth." *Public Law* (2006): 344.

Palmer, Colin. *Eric Williams and the Making of the Modern Caribbean*. Chapel Hill: University of North Carolina Press, 2006.

Proctor Jr, Jesse Harris. "British West Indian Society and Government in Transition 1920–60." In *The Aftermath of Sovereignty West Indian Perspectives*, edited by David Lowenthal, and Lambras Comitas, 31–65. New York: Anchor Books, 1973.

Putnam, Lara. "To Study the Fragments/Whole: Microhistory and the Atlantic World." *Journal of Social History* 39, no. 3 (2006): 615–630.

"Secondary Decolonisation: The Black Power Movement in Barbados, c.1970." In *Black Power in the Caribbean*, edited by Kate Quinn, 117–135. Gainesville, FL: University Press of Florida, 2014.

Rush, Anne Spry. *Bonds of Empire: West Indians and Britishness from Victoria to Decolonization*. Oxford: Oxford University Press, 2011.

Samaroo, Brinsley. "The February Revolution (1970) as a Catalyst for Change in Trinidad and Tobago." In *Black Power in the Caribbean*, edited by Kate Quinn, 97–116. Gainesville, FL: University Press of Florida, 2014.

Sutton, Paul, ed. *Forged from the Love of Liberty: Selected Speeches of Dr Eric Williams*. Port of Spain, Trinidad: Longman, Caribbean, 1981.

Wallace, Elisabeth. *The British Caribbean: From the Decline of Colonialism to the End of Federation*. Toronto: Unviersity of Toronto Press, 1977.

Wrong, Hume. *Government of the West Indies*. Oxford: Clarendon Press, 1923.

Primitive Liberals and Pirate Tribes: Black-Flag Radicalism and the Kibbo Kift

Hana Qugana and Simon Layton

ABSTRACT

The Age of Catastrophe (1914-1945) has long been considered a crisis of liberalism. As a political platform and moralistic worldview, the hollowness of liberalism's promise was exposed when total war struck at the heart of Europe, undermining its presumption of imperial hegemony over much of the world. What emerged in its wake, amid the swells of irremediable nationalisms, is the subject of this article. Blinded by the fog of war and bright lights of modernity, historians often fail to catch the glimpses of alternative aspirations, which escaped the age's ruptures so as to reinvent and redeem humanity from the depths of its bloody past. Against a backdrop of neglected case studies from Britain and elsewhere – from the Luddites to the Kindred of the Kibbo Kift – this article seeks to show how the spectre of death inspired new ideals of youth and civility that rejected the arrogance of imperial masculinity and industrialised oppression, turning instead to visions of global kinship that were socialist and anarchic, romantic and utopian, primitive and piratical.

To understand the new [...] we must first cast a glance at the old.[1]

I

H. G. Wells' *The Shape of Things to Come*, published in 1933, recounts a 'universal history' from the year 2106.[2] Understood as an 'imaginative forecasting of the future', the work speaks to the widespread fears and nascent realities of modernity's destructive potential, when total war undermined Europe's hegemony over much of the world.[3] Extending from the First World War to the outer reaches of the twentieth century, the story 'carr[ies] interpretation into prophecy', indulging liberals' preoccupations with technological, imperial, and ecological collapse in the early twentieth century.[4] But if Wells 'distorted' history, he did so less out of a fatalistic resignation to a failed world order, than as a prescription for social change 'in the universal interest of mankind'.[5] Evocations of calamity and holocaust aside, his history played host to a 'discussion of social and political forces and possibilities' for collective human endeavours in what C. A. Bayly describes as a 'century of unbridled imagination'.[6] In what Eric Hobsbawm preferred to call the 'Age of Catastrophe', Wells saw a viable opportunity to rehabilitate something primordial, yet identifiably modern: an 'intellectual commonweal' of all humankind that 'neither absorbed nor destroyed individuality', but promoted individual 'freedom and enterprise upon a higher level of life'.[7] It is this aspirational quality of the text that we foreground here, to explore the janus-faced nature of liberalism in the nineteenth and twentieth centuries. By taking appeals to primitivism seriously as political and moral discourse, this article traces different contours of a liberal search for a pre-imperial past, which attempted to salvage a post-imperial future from the wrecks of empires and nation-states.

Like other early works of science fiction, *The Shape of Things To Come* is a portrayal of mass annihilation, imbuing war with a cataclysmic capacity to cause 'ontological rupture on a huge scale'.[8] It tells of a series of world wars beginning in 1914, but abating when a mysterious pestilence annihilates half the world's population. These wars 'released the human mind to the potentialities and dangers of an imperfectly Europeanised world – a world which had unconsciously become one single interlocking system, while still obsessed by the Treaty of Westphalia and the idea of competing states'. The 'modern' free-market economy collapsed 'under the internal stresses of European nationalism'; newfangled chemical arsenals contaminated the earth and sapped the 'strength of the belligerent populations'. World war had primed humanity for this moment: 'the micro-organisms had taken a leaf out of the book of the Foreign Offices and found in mankind's confusion an opportunity for restoring the long-lost empire of germs'.[9]

In Wells' view, nothing short of omnipresent plague could compel the human race to 'abandon [...] the old administrative institutions'.[10] Could human societies, in turn, take a page from the book of ecology, and render the primitive political? As Dipesh Chakrabarty reminds us, a 'shared sense of a catastrophe' challenges humans to consider alternative – even pestilential – forms of collectivity, 'an us, pointing to a figure of the universal that escapes our capacity to experience the world'.[11] If an ensuing chain of catastrophes ever did reduce the imperial order to rubble, what would emerge in its place? For Wells' contemporary and fellow torch-bearer of the 'New Liberalism', L. T. Hobhouse, the 'world-state of the not impossible future' would arise from a gradual shift in human consciousness, towards individual autonomy and localised 'self-direction'. '[A]s Englishmen', he suggested, the nation would learn to transcend its petty partisanships and expensive international rivalries (epitomised by the naval race for dreadnoughts), and to transform its empire into an essential champion of self-governance.[12] The politics of the possible are similarly vindicated in Wells' 'future history' by the 'reorganization of human affairs as a World-State' premised on a new contract of social justice and equal opportunity. The text concludes at a point in the distant future, when 'the curtain of separatist dreams, racial fantasies and hate nightmares' had 'thinned out and passed away'. Spectres of catastrophe had transformed what it meant to be social; united in pursuit of self-interest, 'the whole race is now confluent', and (in venturing into outer space) 'is becoming as much a colonial organism as any branching coral or polyp'.[13]

In disavowing democracy as a means of realising the 'possibility of world order, universal sufficiency and ever increasing human vitality',[14] this liberal cosmopolitan ideology poses a challenge for a historiography that 'tends to reinforce a relatively straight-forward association between totalitarianism and extremism, and [...] imply the moral superiority of liberal democracy'.[15] For Hobsbawm, Bayly and others, it was not a Wellsian 'raid of germs',[16] but the parasitic agents of fascism that brought about an international 'crisis of liberalism' during the World Wars, in which the 'commitment to constitutional government' foundered, and 'the rule of law' succumbed to 'dictatorship and absolute rule'.[17] While Wells concurred that the 'intellectual content of fascism was limited, nationalist and romantic' (its will to power 'violent and dreadful'), in its fidelity to an ideal of 'public service' it was 'not an altogether bad thing'. As 'a counter movement to a chaotic labour communism', it was 'a bad good thing' that could in theory succeed in 'handling education and private property for the public benefit'.[18]

Subject to the deafening blasts of fascism and communism, historians have struggled to hear, let alone give voice to appeals for democracy's reinvention amid the dissolution of empire. Only the stark ideological dichotomies of Hobsbawm's 'age of extremes' appeared through the fog of war and blinding lights of modernity; the 'calls for an otherwise unidentified "civil society"' gave voice only to 'lost and drifting generations'[19] – Wells' 'lost and suffering generations, the "generations of the half-light"' – whose failure to fall in line evoked a time before politics itself.[20] Hobsbawm saw the bearers of these standards as bewilderingly 'inarticulate', 'primitive rebels' without a cause.[21] Although liberal mantras of 'progress' certainly indulged colonial notions of primitiveness in mutually constitutive ways,[22] the two concepts were not necessarily mutually exclusive; in important respects, liberal appeals to the primitive were essential to realising a postcolonial humanity.

Expanding on Leon Stover's interpretation of *The Shape of Things To Come* as a 'dialectical unity' of 'destruction and creation, darkness and light', Philip Coupland has argued that Wells 'was not forced to be either a liberal *or* an authoritarian, but could seek "liberal" ends by means which were anything but'.[23] This article seeks to illuminate neglected aspects of this political shadowland, in which the colourful banners of constitutional politics fluttered alongside those of a radically new, yet wilfully primitive politics of self-empowerment – a politics that was unashamedly 'savage' and undemocratic, yet which nevertheless pursued the collective goals of liberal modernity.

The subjects we identify in this article called 'for a global approach to politics' without indulging what Chakrabarty calls 'the myth of a global identity'. Their worldviews did not 'subsume particularities' in a Hegelian ideal of universalism; theirs was 'a "negative universal history"'[24] that frequently 'accommodat[ed] different cultures at different stages of economic and social development'.[25] Many of them not only disputed the Occident's exclusive claim to civilisation, but in the same breath accepted and appropriated Orientalist tropes of 'noble savagery' as their own. Not necessarily eschewing (sometimes promoting) violence, theirs was a productive impulse of a more global, pre-modern humanity, through which they raged against the proverbial machine.

The peculiar visions of kinship considered here reveal a diverse set of flags – 'pirate flags' that forswore traditional politics and championed social change 'in defiance of King Death'.[26] The emblem of the skull and crossbones in particular raised recurring spectres of mortality that captured and inspired radical ideals of selfhood and belonging throughout the nineteenth and early twentieth centuries. Rejecting the arrogance of imperial masculinity and mechanised oppression, such totems posited countervailing images of vitality through death, civility through savagery, and peace through violence. Those who flew the legendary skull and crossbones not only conveyed and perpetuated a historically symbolic act of defiance, but expressed themselves within modes of thought that were socialist and libertarian, romantic and utopian, primitive and piratical.

By bringing out a piratical discourse nestled deeply within radical political traditions, we seek to shed light on a possibility Wells raises, but does not explore. Piracy appears episodically in *The Shape of Things To Come* as an 'ancient practice' that readily appropriates and adapts the technologies of the modern world. But its threat remains peripheral and ultimately subsides, yielding to 'the sword of a new order'.[27] After considering a number of what we loosely identify as 'pirate tribes' from the nineteenth century to the onset of the First World War, we turn to a proto-survivalist movement inspired by them: the Kindred of the Kibbo Kift and its successors, the Green Shirts and the Social Credit Party of Great Britain (1920–1951). Beginning as Boy Scout separatists disillusioned by war and the jingoistic fantasies of Robert Baden-Powell, the Kibbo Kift instead espoused pacifism, co-education, and colonial self-determination under their charismatic leader (and Boy Scout renegade) John Gordon Hargrave. They championed the outlaws and bandits of English history, railing against the militarism that had savaged indigenous cultures around the world, and in turn brought savagery home to Europe. Finding in the woods and English countryside a utopian site of primordial awakening, they opposed the corruption of youth by attempting spiritual and social regeneration against the political, industrial, and martial violence that belied liberal-imperial claims to civilisation.

II

In his novel *Facing the Flag* (1897), Jules Verne's seminal 'mad genius', Thomas Roch, develops an explosive with the potential to destroy Earth itself – to 'burst our spheroid and scatter the fragments into space'.[28] Based partly on Eugène Turpin, whose experiments with picric acid proved deadly in the First World War,[29] Roach's efforts to sell his invention to the great powers of his day (first to his native France, then to Germany, Britain, and the United States) are met with condescension and disbelief. Failing to obtain recognition for a discovery offering 'superiority, invincibleness, omnipotence!' to any state willing to trust in his brilliance, Roach descends into paranoia and delusion: 'all notion of patriotism' becomes 'extinct in his soul'. His 'one thought, one ferocious desire' is 'to avenge himself [...] upon all mankind!' While institutionalised in a North Carolina asylum, he is abducted by pirates led by the notorious Ker Karraje, to share alike in the profits of their plunder within the hidden caves of a Bermudan island. There they live 'in a noble and superb independence, acknowledg[ing] the authority of no foreign power'. It is among them, a community 'not bound together by ties of race', 'the colonists of no state, either of the old or new world', that Roach rediscovers his latent genius.

Racially ambiguous and steadfastly apolitical, Verne's pirates are outcasts of empire – products of an exploited frontier of imperial expansion.[30] Karraje and his first mate (the engineer Serko) bond among the diggers, convicts, mutineers and deserters, all prospecting for gold in southeastern Australia. Their mateship is forged through piracy, as the motley crew steals a ship in Melbourne and proceeds to plunder ports in the western Pacific. Evoking the so-called 'golden age' of Caribbean piracy, they rise, hydra-like, as latter-day pirates of an imperial, global age.[31]

Yet Verne was a nationalist,[32] for whom the pirate could never be 'simply a rather primitive form of peasant rebel' who 'takes to outlawry through some brush with the State', finding a sense of belonging by fighting for something bigger than himself.[33] He imbued his pirates with a morality that was fundamentally irreconcilable with the civilised society that they parried and parodied simultaneously. Their impossible utopia is myopically 'modern', employing a revolutionary weapon, a pioneering submarine, and an electric power station; yet they seek nothing more from this technology than their own personal security and enrichment. The patriotic pursuit of technological and naval dominance was adapted for a 'tranquil existence' of perfect liberty and impunity. Despite his captivity, Roach is showered with riches and considers himself free; like the pirates themselves, he 'thinks nothing of the future' and 'lives but in the present'. When his weapon finally bears upon an armada of allied navies, the first-approaching British ship is annihilated; but the second flies France's tricolour. Roach's 'spark of patriotism' is rekindled, and turning on the pirates, he blows their island (and himself) into oblivion.[34]

Like the pirates who haunted early science fiction as dystopian byproducts of imperial modernity, their forebears in the 'golden age of piracy' were likewise the harbingers of catastrophe. Their 'banner of King Death' depicted skulls and crossbones, skeletons, wingless hourglasses, and plague-darts piercing the flesh of Saint Sebastian. The skull evoked the mortal remains of Adam, buried beneath the site of Crucifixion, where Christ's blood trickled down to anoint primitive man and redeem him from his fallen state.[35] Although designed to inspire terror and submission, such motifs denoted personal confrontations with mortality, and a rejection of states' attempts to claim death as the most potent symbol of sovereignty. Speaking to the specific calamities of their age, they declared themselves to be 'plagues' in an increasingly interconnected maritime world, where far-flung ports were drawn closer together by an imperial nexus of slavery and expropriation. Pirates and plagues became kindred evils – symptoms of a universal malady afflicting humankind in general.[36]

The 'pirate utopia', on the other hand, embodied the escapist fantasies of those who pined for 'lives of liberty' otherwise denied. It conveyed a psychologically unbridgeable, otherworldly realm – a 'protoanarchist pirate republic' that thrived on direct democracy and cosmopolitan belonging.[37] As Christopher Hill contended, the seventeenth-century spirit of the Levellers and Ranters lived on in the apocryphal colony of 'Libertalia', where pirates purportedly freed slaves, abolished private property, maintained common treasuries and redistributed wealth in ways that resonated specifically with the English radical tradition.[38]

III

The commonwealth of plunder that pirates forged among themselves stood in stark contrast to 'modern' society. Primitive and timeless, they defied laws of progress and appeared to renounce civilisation itself. But black flags and 'pirate' flags were overtly (if at times unrecognisably) political. Although they have typically eluded those historians who prefer to see the red banners foreshadowing the emergence of Marxist politics later in the nineteenth century, fragments of such flags exist, connecting the history of piracy and empire to more anarchic and libertarian strains of radicalism in ways that remain poorly understood.

The 'Luddites', for example, were not merely proto-revolutionary gestations of a nascent wage-slaving proletariat. As Lord Byron argued in his maiden speech to Parliament (against what became the Frame-Breaking Act of 1812), the 'irrational mob' of disemployed Nottinghamshire weavers being decried by his fellow peers could not be ignorant of their own oppression. 'You call these men a mob', he railed, 'desperate, dangerous, and ignorant'; but 'It is the mob that labour in your fields, and serve in your houses – man your navy, and recruit your army, – that have enabled you to defy the world'. Victory against Napoleon had caused the noble classes 'to enjoy our foreign triumphs in the midst of domestic calamity', and now an idle soldiery threatened lawful death upon a 'once honest and industrious body of the people'. The 'tender mercies of the bayonet and the gibbet', he warned, would 'restore Sherwood Forest as [...] an asylum for outlaws'. Such were the would-be Robin Hoods, who 'instead of rejoicing at these improvements in arts so beneficial to mankind, conceived themselves to be sacrificed to improvements in mechanism'.[39]

At the 'Peterloo Massacre' of 1819, hundreds of Manchester workers flew banners protesting a wide array of aristocratic privileges, demanding 'Annual Parliaments', 'Universal Suffrage', and a popular 'Vote By Ballot'. Several displayed variants of the revolutionary slogan 'Liberty or Death', and at least one (carried by one Joseph Healey) was black and white, emblazoned with a skull and crossbones. The constables were ordered to 'have at the flags' with sabres drawn. John Ashton was trampled to death beneath his black flag reading 'Unite and be Free! Equal Representation or Death!'[40] Healy and four other men were later found guilty of 'assembling with unlawful banners at an unlawful meeting for the purpose of exciting discontent'.

In subsequent medals, prints and illustrations, the Peterloo 'martyrs' were represented as skulls – rendered in death into totems of police brutality and state tyranny. The radical journalist William Hone, together with his illustrator George Cruikshank, satirised the Crown's soldiers in *The Man in the Moon* (1820), depicting police 'thrusting bayonets down the throats of a panic-stricken populace' beneath a black flag of a centred skull with eight bones arranged like the Union Jack.[41] The Kingston-born mulatto, William 'Black' Davidson, who 'ran away to sea instead of studying law', and was twice pressed into naval service, became active in radical circles in the wake of Peterloo; according to Peter Fryer, he was the custodian of a particular black flag belonging to the Marylebone Reading Society, which bore a skull and crossbones and read 'Let us die like men and not be sold as slaves'. Tasked with protecting the flag from police at an open-air meeting in Smithfield, London, in November 1819, he 'would have killed right and left' to defend it. He was hanged after the Cato Street Conspiracy the following year.[42]

The 1830 revolutions in Europe, long seen as an efflorescence of romantic nationalism and liberal constitutionalism, were similarly adorned with black flags. They accompanied the tricolour in Brussels and Antwerp during the Belgian Revolution; they flew from the Porte Saint-Denis in Paris, during the Canut revolt in Lyon, as well as in the First Carlist War in Spain.[43] In Britain, black flags were raised alongside the tricolour (at least 'in one or two cases', as Hobsbawm admits) during the 'Swing Riots' that swept Kent in the early 1830s.[44] Such flags heralded 'for the first time [...] a distinct influence of political radicalism' within England's peasant rebellions. They expressed a violent urge to burn crops and break machines that 'outraged' landowners in southern England; but they also expressed a 'formal refusal to recognise any leaders', painting their faces black through (as Hobsbawm equivocally suggests) 'either fear of public exposure or a primitive egalitarianism'.[45]

Black flags also preceded demonstrations against political opposition to the Reform Bill in 1831. In Scotland, they flew ahead of marches in Paisley and most notably in Glasgow, where agitators arranged 'a sort of telegraphic communication' whereby black would announce the Lords' rejection of the Bill, and marshall supporters 'in marching order to the tune of the Dead March in Saul'.[46] Some flags explicitly displayed the skull and crossbones, amid further calls for a revolutionary Liberty Tree to be planted on Glasgow Green.[47] As one paper put it, 'the argument of intimidation' that now characterised debates evoked the same 'unavowed influence of terror' that had marred the French Revolution: 'The black flag, already menaced, may be hoisted at Glasgow; and Manchester and Birmingham may pour forth their swarms of "the great unwashed." The doors of Parliament may be assailed, and their deliberations at once terminated'.[48] When the Reform Bill was initially defeated, black flags were hung in mourning in parishes, factories and workplaces across the country.

The function of black flags to express political dissent and to organise resistance in the nineteenth century was further demonstrated by the Chartists. In September 1843, on the fields of Kersal Moor, 'two hundred flags and banners fluttered in the soft breeze, with every variety of radical mottoes and devices'. While at least one 'splendid banner' referenced Peterloo with the words 'Murder demands justice!', another depicted 'a death's head and cross bones, and a hand grasping a dagger, with the interrogative inscription: "Oh tyrants! will you force us to this?"'[49] This was a different kind of reforming impulse than the one championed by the rising middle-class: the Anti-Corn-Law League should have been the Chartists' natural ally against the landed interest, but instead decried what it deemed to be a naïve 'misdirection of energy' – a spontaneous and counterproductive outburst, which (unless properly directed) could never succeed as a genuinely political movement.[50]

If black flags fluttered in what Hobsbawm called 'the high wind of social discontent which blew across Britain in successive gusts' in the early nineteenth century, the 'great social movements' from Luddism to Chartism nevertheless 'died away', along with the 'older methods of poor men's action' that had failed to articulate any coherent programme of political reform or revolution. Although the labouring poor formed a collective that was 'in its primitive way socialist', meaningful reforms occurred only when elites 'no longer regarded the British working class as revolutionary'.[51] Hobsbawm argued that it was only through effective organisation and heightened class-consciousness that the 'traditional', 'primitive' and 'archaic' forms of radicalism matured into movements that threatened genuine social change. Yet the black flags of primitive rebellion endured, as part of an emerging transnational politics that vied with Marxism for intellectual space within new dissident and revolutionary discourses.

Sitting uncomfortably between socialism and liberalism, anarchists at the turn of the twentieth century rejected 'statism' while advocating the autonomous association of free individuals. But their vision of the 'primitive' was more constructive than those who saw only a dialectical progress of history from the left, or championed a eugenicist social engineering from the right. In the English anarchist Edward Carpenter's eulogy for Peter Kropotkin, he looked forward to a 'day when the true human society will be realized on earth – that spontaneous, voluntary, non-governmental society whose germ was first planted ages ago among nearly all primitive peoples, but whose glorious flower and fulfillment awaits us'.[52]

On the eve of the First World War, on May Day 1914, Alexander Berkman addressed a rally against Standard Oil in New York's Union Square. Here, again, were banners and flags setting the agenda: one called for 'more liberty and more wages'; another simply cried 'Hunger'; but it was a skull and crossbones that ominously put the oil tycoons on notice. Reading simply '26 Broadway', the black flag singled out the Standard Oil headquarters in Manhattan as a target for anarchists' explosives. Two months later, members of the Anarchist Black Cross failed to contain a bomb intended for the Rockefeller family home, blowing-up themselves and much of their apartment on Lexington Avenue. Berkman himself had long been a proponent of 'propaganda by the deed', having attempted to assassinate the chairman of Carnegie Steel in 1892. From prison, he dreamed of a 'revolutionary Messiah' who, in a 'twinkling of an eye-lash', would rouse the 'workers against the handful of their despoilers', and see 'the banner of equality and brotherhood be planted upon the hills of a regenerated humanity'.[53] He was later deported to Russia, where the likeminded sailors of Kronstadt had flown their own skull-and-crossbones declaring 'Death to the Bourgeoisie!' When their fidelity to the freedoms of speech, assembly, and political expression was finally betrayed by the Bolsheviks in 1921, Berkman reported that 'The revolution is dead: its spirit cries in the wilderness'.[54]

IV

Two thousand kilometres away, a former serviceman stood at the fringes of his own political wilderness. Writings such as the scouting manual *Lonecraft* (1913), *The Scout* serial 'White Fox on the Warpath' (1914–1915), and a combat memoir *At Suvla Bay* (1916), had made John Hargrave a household name among the first generation of Boy Scouts and Girl Guides around the world.[55] In 1917, founding leader and Chief Scout Robert Baden-Powell appointed Hargrave 'Woodcraft Commissioner' of the Boy Scouts Association (BSA), making him the youngest member of the organisation's executive leadership in its history. Hargrave, or (as his young readership knew him) 'White Fox', campaigned for a sorely needed, dedicated space for training in outdoor scoutcraft. At the height of his popularity in 1919, the 24-year-old author and illustrator looked forward to assuming greater responsibility as Camp Chief of Gilwell Park, a 109-acre estate northeast of London, recently acquired by the BSA for expansion beyond its headquarters near Buckingham Palace. Hargrave was Baden-Powell's heir apparent, and yet his anointment never came. He was passed over in favour of Francis Gidney, a less-than-capable man four years his senior.[56] The incident would set him off on a trail that diverged from mainstream Scouting and into a world occupied by the movements, individuals, and histories to which this article has already made reference.

Hargrave's betrayal by the BSA came on the eve of a war meant to 'end war' – the last and great aberration in world history; 'the test or condemnation of constructive liberal thought in the world'. But in the intellectual maelstrom, war itself was only 'the mere smash of the thing. The reality is the uprooting, the incurable dislocation'.[57] Wells imagined a Europe remapped, where 'vanished' sovereigns left 'fresh frontiers' primed for new forms of politics. From this 'warring sea of men' would arise 'social reconstruction'; but the war itself was a 'mere preliminary phase in uniform'. The one to follow would be 'not of soldiers, but of whole peoples' – 'not of nations, but of mankind'.[58]

In the course of the war, Hargrave wore the uniform of a pacifist, serving as a stretcher-bearer in the Royal Army Medical Corps and 10th Irish division during the Dardanelles Campaign at Gallipoli and Salonika (1915–1916). Literally fetching 'men and pieces of men' from the battlefield, he witnessed the mechanised means of slaughter that Verne had foreshadowed and Wells now lamented. Confronted with this vision of violent modernity, he beheld his comrades' corpses, sinking into silver moonlit sand: 'the skeletons of the Xth sink deeper and deeper, to be rediscovered perhaps at some future geological period, and recognised as a type of primitive man'.[59] Although it was now up to the war's survivors to build new communities, and new histories, in Europe and throughout the world, Hargrave gleaned a future built upon 'primitive' bones, which (like those beneath Calvary) portended mankind's redemption. In 1913 and 1917, he wrote and revised a treatise for surviving in the wilderness, the frontispieces for which depicted a young Boy Scout in uniform, parading before the Union Jack. Before the war, Hargrave had defended the British Empire, its way of life and by extension, its history. But in the third and final edition of *Lonecraft*, published in 1921, a young clansman wearing a ragged jerkin now skipped ecstatically in the Boy Scout's stead, this time beneath a banner of 'no nations' picturing the planet Earth.[60]

As the BSA expanded its empire in an eastward, northerly arc towards Gilwell Park, Hargrave and a number of his followers convened due south of Headquarters at Denison House on Vauxhall Bridge Road in August 1920, establishing what would become the Kindred of the Kibbo Kift. Liberated from BSA bureaucracy, they revelled in 'no headquarters, no red tape, and no committee meetings', and championed a syndicate that would 'just get to work and DO IT'.[61] In the spirit of the invented meaning of 'kibbo kift' (an appropriation of Old Kentish, taken to mean 'proof of great strength'),[62] they drew up an ambitious 'Covenant' for a new 'Kin', outlining a basis for social reform on a global scale, along individualistic, self-deterministic and egalitarian lines.

Hargrave lamented how the Scouting movement's 'Backwoodsmanship' had precipitously declined under the BSA's wartime leadership. While the Ottoman soldiers he had encountered seemed to him to be '*born* scouts', in England 'the boy had been taken out into the woods by his Wicked Uncles, folded in the Union Jack and smothered'.[63] Hargrave increasingly sought 'to release conscious individualism' as a means of human survival.[64] Under a black and red 'banner of primitive man',[65] the Kibbo Kift recruited irrespective of nationality or gender; forging a 'community of Robinson Crusoes', each kinsman and kinswoman would contribute unique abilities to shape the 'federation' and serve the common interest as their own.[66]

The BSA's requital was swift and decisive. Perceiving a general threat to order and a personal challenge to his leadership, Baden-Powell found Hargrave guilty of 'treason' against the Chief Scout's flag, overseeing procedures that relieved him of his commission and saw him 'excommunicated' forthwith.[67] The smear campaign that ensued served not only to denigrate Hargrave, but to dissuade his admirers in Britain and abroad from following him off the well-trod paths of patriotism, towards 'a more deep-seated cultural decline'.[68] As the journalist, suffragist, and anti-slavery campaigner Henry Nevinson asserted, the 'general upheaval of all traditions and ideas since the Great War', coupled with the 'growing insistence of Indians themselves [...] following the widespread horror at the Amritsar massacre' (1919), provoked a discernible 'change in opinion' towards the British Empire especially.[69] Hargrave's condemnation in 1921 of 'the development in India of two [Scouting] movements – the official movement containing British boys (the sons of officials), and the native movement' – reflected a similar frustration. In light of the 'failure' of the BSA (and by extension Britain itself) to 'bring the two movements into one, by making the native movement conform to the *official* movement', he argued that the wishes of 'native' Scouts to dictate their own affairs should be respected, as should those of all Indians.[70] Despite the BSA's best efforts to dismiss his 'ultra views' as eccentric vanity,[71] the battle for young minds in the race for imperial reconstruction had begun.

Dubbed a 'rebel', 'revolutionary' and a 'Bolshie' by the BSA's official organs, Hargrave basked in his newfound notoriety. Shortly after the BSA acquired *The Trail* (an independent Scouting periodical, to which Hargrave regularly contributed), he led a party of 'like minds' into the paper's annual formal dinner, each dressed as variants of the 'Red Indian' and Robin Hood.[72] The Futurist aesthetics that became the hallmark of the movement emboldened its members to espouse a defiantly primitive and savage modernity.[73] Among the bemused Scouting elite sat an impressed guest of honour, H. G. Wells, who soon afterwards was welcomed onto the Kibbo Kift's Advisory Council. Also on the council were Nevinson, Norman Angell, Julian Huxley, Havelock Ellis, Emmeline Pethick Lawrence, Patrick Geddes, and Rabindranath Tagore.[74] These individuals, whose day-to-day lives often sat worlds apart from those of the middle-class Scouting mainstream, saw in Hargrave a kindred spirit who promised to pioneer a Morrisian 'now-here' of 'green cosmopolitanism'.[75] 'The Kibbo Kift are those who will stand faithful unto death for the truth', wrote Hargrave, 'for honour, for the upright life against greed, gain and sordid commercialism and industrial slavery' – for 'revolution by reconstruction' and the reinvention of 'the nation' itself.[76]

Baden-Powell had long derided the 'loose sweater with buckskin fringes and moccasins',[77] popularised by Hargrave and the BSA's American rival, the Woodcraft Indians.[78] Their frontier fantasies opposed the imperial urge to inculcate in Britain's boys the manly, patriotic and disciplined dictates of empire. In his foundational text *Scouting for Boys* (1908), Baden-Powell cast Native Americans as 'murderers' devoid of loyalty – to be tracked and hunted in revenge for 'raiding and murdering whites'.[79] 'Pirates' likewise drew his ire. Touring the Caribbean and North America in 1912, he lamented Panama's role as a 'great pirates' resort' where the 'great sea scout', Sir Francis Drake, met his ignominious end. In Jamaica he sought to counter the romance of Port Royal's 'daring and dangerous, open-handed and reckless' pirates with images of Kingston's 'dapper midshipmen, rolling jack tars, and puffy admirals, hospitable planters and beautiful Creoles'.[80] In the first edition of *Scouting for Boys*, he celebrated

> the pioneers of civilisation in Central Africa; the ranchmen, cowboys, and trappers of the West; the drovers and bushman of Australia; the explorers of the Arctic and Asiatic regions; the hunters and prospectors of South Africa; missionaries in all parts of the uncivilised world; and the constabularies of North-West Canada, South Africa, etc.

Such 'brave and loyal' men were 'accustomed to [...] taking their lives into their hands'.[81] Never mind that 'Captain John Smith' had once been a pirate; Baden-Powell lionised him as a man who 'would help any Christian [...] to fight against a heathen', whether 'against the Turks' or in colonial Virginia.[82] In his favourite play, J. M. Barrie's *Peter Pan* (1904), his sympathies lay neither with the 'Piccaninny tribe' nor the piratical crew of the 'cadaverous and blackavised' Captain Hook. He was interested solely in moulding 'boys' into 'MEN [...] of the best type'.[83]

Unlike the 'Drakes' and 'Smiths' of Baden-Powell's preferred history, the Kibbo Kift would not be reformed into servants of empire. They identified instead with the avowedly 'uncivilised' apostates of turbulent frontiers – the American Indian, the Australian Aborigine, the bandit, and the pirate –

weaving these cultures (as they understood them) into the pedagogical and organisational fabric of the movement. The pirate, Hargrave wrote, was 'bold and bad and brave': 'a keg of rum, /A sabre-cut, /A wooden leg or two, /A lot of talk of spars and sails – /Oh here's a fine to-do!'[84] As such, the 'bad boy' was not to be corrected, but encouraged:

> Just as savages delight in signs and 'blazes', the bad boy, being at heart no worse than a savage, hankers after these things. […] Anything 'black' appeals to the bad boy's mind. Darkness is full of mystery and adventure. He likes the Black Flag, the Black Hand, the Black Mask.[85]

'Sound moral and physical training' could be administered 'under this mask of the "Wild-Redskin-Gang-Idea"', or a 'Brotherhood of the Black Cross'. The boy 'who won't belong, for instance, to the Scouts' could thrive in a society that proudly flew 'The Black Flag' – for 'the "bad" boy', he wrote, 'is not so "black" as he likes to paint himself'.[86]

The Kibbo Kift's non-conformist syndicalism was reflected in the identities that each 'tribe' (not 'troop') within the movement created for themselves, through a diverse array of totems, sigils and banners. They adopted names like 'The Pirates of Penzance', 'The Hampstead Highwaymen', 'The Nottingham Outlaws', and 'The Birmingham Brigands'.[87] As a 'guide rather than a standard', the 'opening ceremony of a tribal moot' (in the Anglo-Saxon tradition) encouraged participants to 'compose their own rituals to suit their particular circumstances'.[88] Pirate-inspired clans (namely, the 'Beckenham Buccaneers' and the 'Freebooters' in Brockley) were particularly active on the southern periphery of the BSA's London empire, demarcated by the River Thames. Bill Tacey founded the Buccaneers shortly after witnessing Hargrave's mutiny at Denison House. Adopting the Robin Hood-inspired moniker 'Will Scarlet', he became part of Hargrave's inner circle tasked with implementing the Kibbo Kift's progressive scheme of camping, artistic pursuits, educational programmes and intellectual enrichment. Initially breaking trails into the London suburbs and surrounding countryside, their paths swiftly reached Scotland, the Low Countries, Germany, Hungary, and Russia.

V

According to Hobsbawm's dialectical understanding of 'primitive' and 'pre-political' societies, external forces 'disrupt the social balance of the kinship society, by turning some kins into "rich" families and others into "poor", or by disrupting the kin itself'.[89] For the Kibbo Kift, disruption resulted from the modernisation of imperial Britain's political economy that followed mass enfranchisement after the Great War.[90] Impelled by the Co-operative journal *Comradeship and Wheatsheaf*, the Buccaneers and other 'leftist' collectives within the movement tried to emulate Ernest Thompson-Seton's Woodcraft Indians, which 'functioned as small democratic, self-governing tribes based on a romantic view of Indian life'.[91]

For Hargrave, however, emulating 'pirates' or 'Red Indians' was never meant to be romantic. By ritualistically embracing colonial 'others' and societal 'outcasts' – those whose savage status exposed the hubris and hypocrisy of liberal imperialism and civilising discourse – his Kinsmen and Kinswomen were meant to empower themselves as individuals without patriotic allegiances or political representation. Hargrave sought to reconfigure England itself into 'a knowable unit of cultural and social relations'[92] by grafting the methods traditionally used by Europeans (to construct 'authentic' histories of colonised peoples) onto the histories the Kindred now told about themselves. Just as Robin Hood and his 'merrie men' of Sherwood Forest sought 'to establish or to re-establish justice [...] in a society of oppression',[93] Hargrave expected the Kibbo Kift to embody a collective of heroes, who took it upon themselves to redistribute material and cultural wealth in the common interest. 'The Spirit of Robin' channelled in the movement's official 1925 songbook would 'lead the crowd / To clearness and rebirth',[94] restoring a localised patriotism that was at once pre- and post-colonial – and radically communitarian.

Hargrave was ultimately unable to reconcile his own individualist libertarianism with the wider liberal-democratic sentiments within his movement. As the elected 'Headman', he exercised control from a personally appointed executive council of older, male acolytes, and was soon obliged to quell stirrings of dissent among some of his younger, now wavering supporters. Reflecting a wider rift in interwar Britain (and Europe) between anti-parliamentarians, and social and liberal democrats,[95] Hargrave's nepotism and alleged 'megalomania'[96] induced a faction of Kinsmen and Kinswomen to hold a vote of no confidence in 1925. He survived, and the rebels were expelled; but the Kindred itself soon splintered, losing members to the Labour movement, where they settled as the Woodcraft Folk. By 1931, Hargrave's loyalists had traded in their 'kinwear' for green paramilitary shirts. Joined by others drawn principally from the working classes and post-war legions of unemployed, they marched under a new flag, 'the Green Banner of LIFE', 'against the forces of Death – against needless Poverty and War'.[97]

With Robin Hood's investiture as the original 'Green Shirt', the revised movement signalled its opposition to a British mode of imperialism that had shifted from being (as the radical MP John Bright famously quipped) 'a gigantic system of outdoor relief for the aristocracy', to a frenzy of financial investment and resource extraction – in the mining districts of 'settler dominions' especially. Such regions became a critical outlet for the 'social imperialism' of emigrant surplus labour and overpopulated slums. Yet, as Norman Angell argued, empires' race for foreign territories misjudged 'certain economic facts' about how societies evolved. The 'primitive life of man' was far from 'idyllic'; but in shedding 'the primitive passions of other animals of prey', through rudimentary trade and 'industry, even of the more primitive kind, [...] the thing of prey becomes a partner and the attitude towards it changes'. By fetishising the savagery of 'the Congo cannibal, or the Red Indian, or the Bedouin', Europe's military powers sought to 'separate the moral from the social and economic development' of the peoples they dispossessed; and war was the inevitable result.[98]

Hargrave followed both Angell and J. A. Hobson[99] in perceiving the war as a global crisis of imperialism, which could only be defeated by attacking its capitalist roots at home:

> As an innovator The Kindred proclaims itself the guardian of a Britain that has lost itself in a meaningless and devastating commercial scramble. [...] It calls forth a new and vital patriotism which is not an appendage to war-manipulation, but on the contrary, by its practical operation in these islands, can, and will, eliminate the economic necessity for inter-national warfare.[100]

The new front in Hargrave's war against capitalism followed directly from the guild socialism espoused by Hobson, G. D. H. Cole, G. K. Chesterton and Bertrand Russell.[101] Identifying a select consortium of financiers who controlled the capital that fuelled imperial economies, and were thus the true instigators of the war, Hargrave turned to the theory of 'Social Credit' and its architect, C. H. Douglas.[102] Envisioned as a Morrisian 'craft' by which improved individuals embodied power through ideas and action,[103] Hargrave inflected Douglas' economic theorem with a social understanding that channelled the self-emancipatory spirit of the Luddites. To 'Ned Ludd', he wrote:

> I clasp your hand, you whom they call a half-witted man who went about breaking stocking-frames. You and your Luddite followers who led the forlorn attack against the Labour Saving Machine, and, at any rate, had clear enough sight to take a swipe at the thing that seemed to swallow your daily bread, were not quite such half-wits as they like to make out.[104]

In 1936, he completed his own history, linking the Green Shirts to 'King Lud and his army of Redressers', with the explicit intention of replicating the Luddites' 'winding sheet' of revolution.[105]

Waging war on international finance would not only pose a 'deterrent' to 'war making',[106] but to the enslavement of whole peoples held in thrall by imperial governments and the 'sinister interests' that, in turn, governed them.[107] Emulating the verse of Chartist poet William Cowper, Hargrave wrote that 'a man who must sell his labour in order to live is a slave, and a man who cannot sell his labour, but must take the "dole" or starve, is a slave further enslaved'. Quoting Cowper explicitly, he continued: 'Slaves cannot breathe in England; if their lungs / Receive our air, that moment they are free! / They touch our country, and their shackles fall'.[108] As 'the grand narratives of emancipation and enlightenment mobilized people in the colonial world to rise up and throw off imperial subjection',[109] the Green Shirts stood at 'the vanguard of a

Patriotic Revolutionary movement towards Economic Freedom': 'THE REVOLT OF THE BRITISH PEOPLE against the hidden power of Finance, against the dirty, crooked, hole-and-corner "wangles" of credit-mongers, banker-moneylenders, and their political sheepticks'.[110] The 'British People', he declared, 'are an enslaved people – enslaved to the Money Power'.[111]

Hargrave congratulated 'King Ludd' directly. Smashing machines that usurped people's labour was 'Good for you! – but not for us. We go about to take the Machine alive, to control its life's blood; a colourless blood, and invisible, but most potent'.[112] Wresting control from the financiers would require 'modern' technologies to unlock new ways of valuing and organising human activity. What both capitalists and socialists overlooked (by focusing on issues of ownership over the means of production), he argued, were the 'skills, knowledge and technology' that go into making 'what is actually sold', commodities that could be used not only to destroy, but improve the quality of human life. 'Built up over past' – and future – 'generations', knowledge capital was infinite;[113] its inheritance would be shared among all of humankind,[114] with limitless possibilities for developing mechanised technology without the need for labour.

The question of how this capital was to be monetised, managed and distributed formed Hargrave's key preoccupation, as his movement's post-schism agenda called for economic controls on purchasing power and a dividend to be paid out to every individual to compensate for wage discrepancies.[115] Medieval guilds (as he understood them) set an archaic precedent for rewarding work done not for a monetary wage, but for the betterment of society as a whole. 'With the further application of automatic mechanical processes to production, as advocated by the Kin', Hargrave contended, 'more and more people would find themselves out of work', 'receiving what has been aptly called "the wages of the machine," and with leisure on their hands'.[116] Thus his interpretation of Social Credit was neither reactionary, nor impulsive, presentist or merely topical. By looking back, it paradoxically foresaw 'a coming day' when work and leisure became indistinguishable, replaced by the creative urges of Cole's 'free communal service' and Morris' conception of craft.[117]

The Green Shirts were certainly anti-democratic; but by no means were they 'apolitical', as has been suggested.[118] Situated within Britain's 'substantial "middle opinion" in the 1930s [...] pursuing a "third way" between state socialism and unfettered market capitalism',[119] they operated a well-oiled propaganda machine, circulating periodicals, pamphlets, leaflets and other ephemera heralding the 'embod[iment]' of 'Social Credit as the only workable mechanism for implementing the "essentials" of the K.K'.[120] By January 1935, its in-house 'one-penny "rag"' entitled *Attack!* (formerly *Front Line*) reported a monthly circulation between 5,000 and 8,000 copies in and around London's working-class neighbourhoods.[121]

Born less out of opportunism or an 'irrational' turn of mind, Hargrave's ideology continued in a strain of liberal individualism conceived in response to the oppressive nature of imperial nation-states. But now he also contested the chimera of liberal democracy that sustained them in the hopes that something more organically liberal and free would take its place. Turning the weaponry of print capitalism against itself, the Green Shirts found 'a specific language in which to express their aspirations about the world'[122] – in the forms of direct action taken by an eclectic imagined community of England's 'radical' pre-imperial past. Hargrave praised 'the signing of the Great Charter at Runnymede' (the Magna Carta) and the monumental 'action of Oliver Cromwell and his Roundheads', as 'two of the greatest liberating movements which laid the foundations of our present constitutional system'. While neither an ardent constitutionalist nor a republican, he called for a new 'Economic Runnymede' in an attempt to 'range' his movement 'with the British people – and, indeed, with the people of the whole civilised world – in forcing the issue as yet only dimly sensed by the majority'.[123] Only when 'the Chartist movement became more and more powerful' did 'the House of Commons and the House of Lords, the system of General Elections, the party machinery, and the parliamentary procedure known to us, t[ake] shape'. If at least 'the People' in the mid-nineteenth century 'had some sort of democratic representative government in which the King was reduced to a figurehead',[124] Hargrave felt emboldened to demand more – 'to say openly what we all know in our secret hearts to be the truth: that our political machinery is out-of-date, is breaking down, and must be scrapped'.[125] A political cartoon from the 1920s depicted him trying to persuade Guido Fawkes to 'deliver the Goods!' not to parliament, but to the Kibbo Kift: 'you tried to blow it up – but we intend to make it fall into disuse'. Sitting alone and up high on a keg of 'Credit Pow(d)er', wearing the movement's green-hooded jerkin, Hargrave himself embodied the Robin Hood ideal of individual liberty, freedom from finance and from the proverbial Sheriff of Nottingham.[126]

Living somewhere between history, folklore and a utopian future, the English radicals to whom Hargrave turned formed a lynchpin of a dialectic that began with 'Propaganda', progressed to 'Agitational Demonstration', and ended in revolution.[127] Renamed again in September 1935, the Social Credit Party of Great Britain (SCP) boasted several thousand active members, maintaining a presence in most major cities in Britain.[128] Its Green Shirts became a regular fixture at demonstrations in and around London (especially at the Bank of England, singling out its Governor, Montagu Norman), where they engaged violently with the other 'Shirts' that coloured political tribes in the 1930s.

With the commencement of the Public Order Act (which outlawed paramilitary uniforms) in 1937, some Green Shirts felt compelled to take matters into their own hands. The years leading up to the Second World War saw a series of unsanctioned acts of defiance carried out largely by individuals identifying with the SCP – green shirts displayed on poles and bricks caked in green paint with its slogans in white, hurled through windows at Downing Street; a woman in a green crinoline accosting the Chancellor of the Exchequer, demanding Social Credit; young men and women being hauled out of the House of Commons weekly, calling for the 'National Dividend'; wheat sheafs burned outside a Wheat Commission meeting amid shouts of 'They burn the wheat we want to eat!' from the crowd; effigies bearing Norman's likeness burned and paraded on Threadneedle Street; the arrow of a lone green-clad archer shot into Downing Street (again). Hargrave had lost control of the behemoth he had created. It had arrived at the last stage of his dialectic: 'Final Conflict'.

VI

As Hobsbawm wrote in the *Age of Extremes*, the short twentieth century began as 'an era whose only claim to have benefitted humanity rested on the [...] triumphs of a material progress based on science and technology' – a progress rapidly undone by a 'return to what our nineteenth-century ancestors would have called the standards of barbarism'.[129] The subjects of this article faced the bearers of such 'standards', and made as many new ones in response to the respective crises of their times. Flying these flags, they confronted and challenged the violence of statism, patriotism, capitalism and colonialism, and posited for themselves new visions of both the past and future of human life on Earth. Like the pirates, bandits and outlaws of history, myth-history and literature, they stood at the crossroads of social change, not merely bearing witness to its upheavals and ruptures, but asserting their freedom and rejecting modernity's ceaseless wars upon the 'primitive'.

In search of new ways to adapt and effect their revolutions, they represented much more than a 'sort of pre-historic stage of social agitation'.[130] Hobsbawm's reluctance to credit certain movements with a politics of their own, casting them instead into varying states of primitiveness and archaism, sees them redeemed only by eventual, yet intangible manifestations of class-consciousness, 'solidarity' and common purpose. Yet for those who rallied to 'piratical' standards – however eclectic, amorphous or ambiguous – ephemerality and death were no barriers to their success. Far from being 'inevitable victims' who swam 'dead against the current of history',[131] primitive liberals and pirate tribes did not fail simply by being forgotten. They raised their flags in vexing winds, but the turbulence of the times was not of their making; the social, moral, and environmental death they acknowledged was universal. They conceived of humankind as a piratical organism, united in its microbial past and doomed inevitably to a cataclysmic future – the choice of destiny that the pirate tribe proffered would have us either reach into the stars or face shared annihilation.

Notes

1. L. T. Hobhouse, *Liberalism* (Oxford: Oxford University Press, 1940 [1911]), 7.
2. H. G. Wells, *The Shape of Things to Come* (London: Gollancz, 2017 [1933]), 15. Hereafter TSTC.
3. J. R. Hammond, "The Shape of Things to Come" in idem, *An H. G. Wells Companion*, 118–20.
4. TSTC, 11.
5. Adam de Hegedus, *The State of the World: Reflections on Peace and War in Our Time* (London: Jonathan Cape, 1946), 208.
6. Wells, *Things To Come: A Film Story Based on the Material Contained in his History of the Future 'The Shape of Things To Come'* (London: The Cresset Press, 1935), 9. Bayly, *Remaking the Modern World 1900-2015*, 332.
7. TSTC, 379, 422.
8. Bayly, *Remaking the Modern World*, 48.
9. TSTC, 21, 212, 211.
10. Ibid., 264.
11. Chakrabarty, "The Climate of History," 210.
12. Hobhouse, *Liberalism*, 238–41.
13. TSTC, 55, 422. See also Toye, "H.G. Wells and the New Liberalism." For Wells' engagement with twentieth-century Malthusian debates, see Bashford, *Global Population*. See also Hale, "Of Mice and Men"; Carey, *The Intellectuals and the Masses*.
14. TSTC, 29.
15. Fleming, "Political Extremes and Extremist Politics."
16. TSTC, 211.
17. Hobsbawm, *Age of Extremes*, 146. See also Mazower, *Dark Continent*.
18. TSTC, 126.
19. Hobsbawm, *Age of Extremes*, 11, 109–10.
20. TSTC, 30.
21. Hobsbawm, *Primitive Rebels*, 2. Hereafter PR.
22. See Chandra, "Liberalism and Its Other."
23. Philip Coupland, "H. G. Wells's 'Liberal Fascism'," 542.
24. Chakrabarty, "The Climate of History," 222.
25. Partington, "H. G. Wells and the World State."
26. Rediker, "Under the Banner of King Death."
27. TSTC, 148–9.
28. Jules Verne, *Facing the Flag* (New York: F. M. Lupton, 1897), Chapter XII.
29. Eugène Turpin unsuccessfully sued Verne for defamation in 1897, on the basis that he had in fact worked exclusively with the French government.
30. Gould, *Nineteenth-Century Theatre*, 26–7. See also Smyth (ed.), *Jules Verne*.
31. See Rediker and Linebaugh, *The Many-Headed Hydra*.
32. See Dine, "The French Colonial Empire."
33. PR, 3.
34. Verne, *Facing the Flag*, Chapter XVI.
35. Fricke, "A Liquid History," 63.
36. Rediker, *Villains of All Nations*, 11.
37. Idem, "Hydrarchy and Libertalia: The Utopian Dimensions of Atlantic Piracy in the Early Eighteenth Century" in Starkey, Moor and van Eyck van Heslinga (eds.), *Pirates and Privateers*, 29–46.

38. Christopher Hill, "Radical Pirates?" in idem, *The Collected Works of Christopher Hill*, Vol III, 161–87.
39. George Gordon Byron, "Speech of Lord Byron upon the 'Frame Work' Bill, delivered in the House of Lords, 27 February 1812," British Library, MS Egerton, 2030.
40. Francis Philips, *An Exposure of the Calumnies Circulated by the Enemies of Social Order: And Reiterated by Their Abettors, Against the Magistrates and the Yeomanry Cavalry of Manchester and Salford*. 2nd Edition (London: Longman et al., 1819), 30.
41. William Hone, *The Man in the Moon, A Speech from the Throne to the Senate of Lunataria, In the Moon* (London: William Hone, 1820); A. Stanley Walker, "Peterloo, Shelley and Reform," *PMLA* 40/1 (March 1925), 155.
42. Gilroy, *The Black Atlantic*, 13; Fryer, *Staying Power*, 216, 544 note 7. See also Rediker and Linebaugh, *The Many-Headed Hydra*, 322.
43. *Galignani's Messenger* 4798, 29–31 July 1830; *London Post*, 3 May 1834.
44. Hobsbawm and Rudé, *Captain Swing*, 102.
45. Ibid., 100–6.
46. James Edward Gordon, *Speech delivered by J. E. Gordon Esq. in the House of Commons, on Wednesday, the 13th of July, 1831, on the subject of a reform in Parliament* (London: R. Clay, 1831), 14.
47. Fraser, *Chartism in Scotland*, 14.
48. *The Cambridge Chronicle and Huntingdonshire Gazette*, 29 July 1831.
49. Robert G. Gammage, *History of the Chartist Movement, 1837-1854* (Newcastle-on-Tyne: Browne & Browne, 1894 [1854]), 60.
50. See Gibson, "The Chartists and the Constitution." We are grateful to the author for bringing two of the abovementioned flags to our attention.
51. Hobsbawm, *Industry and Empire*, 91, 121, 125–6.
52. Goodway, *Anarchist Seeds Beneath the Snow*, 52.
53. Alexander Berkman, *Prison Memoirs of an Anarchist* (New York: Mother Earth, 1912), 3–104, 226.
54. Idem, *The Bolshevik Myth* (New York: Boni and Liveright, 1925), 319.
55. *Lonecraft* was a modest financial success, prompting one of the founding fathers of the Scouting movement, Ernest Thompson-Seton, to accuse Hargrave of literary piracy and sue for compensation; British Library of Political and Economic Science, Papers of John Gordon Hargrave (BLPES/Hargrave), b.49.
56. Francis Gidney is credited with having nearly run Gilwell financially and managerially into the ground. He was forced to resign in 1923.
57. Wells, *The War That Will End War* (New York: Duffield & Company, 1914), 65–6, 60–1.
58. Ibid., 60, 14, 10, 12.
59. John Hargrave ('White Fox'), *At Suvla Bay* (London: Constable & Company, 1916), 139.
60. Idem, *Lonecraft*, 3rd Edition (London: Constable & Company, 1921).
61. Idem, quoted in Craven, "Redskins in Epping Forest."
62. Hargrave acknowledged the following as his source: James Orchard Halliwell, *A Dictionary of Archaic and Provincial Words, Obsolete Phrases, Proverbs, and Ancient Customs, from the Fourteenth Century* (London: John Russell Smith, 1852).
63. Hargrave, "The Origins and Development of the Kibbo Kift," *The Broadsheet* 2/13, August 1926, BLPES/Youth Movement Archive, Kibbo Kift (YMA/KK), b.168.
64. Idem, "Commonplace Book," 2 February 1925, BLPES/HAR, b.80.
65. Item 2012/463, Museum of London, Kibbo Kift Collection.
66. Hargrave, *The Confession of the Kibbo Kift: A Declaration and General Exposition of the Work of the Kindred* (London: Duckworth, 1927), 57.

67. Equating Hargrave's expulsion to religious excommunication is common in existing literature on the Kibbo Kift. See Elwell-Sutton, "A History of the Kibbo Kift."
68. For an account of one such incident involving the *Nederlandse Padvinders*, see Hargrave to Henry Rolf Gardiner, 9 March 1925, Cambridge University Library, Papers of H. Rolf Gardiner, C6/1/28. Stefan Collini, "Where did it all go wrong? Cultural critics and 'modernity' in inter-war Britain" in Green and Tanner (eds.), *The Strange Survival of Liberal England*, 247–74.
69. Henry W. Nevinson, "'India's coral strand', Saturday Review of Literature (New York), August 1924," in E. M. Forster et al., *E. M. Forster: the critical heritage*, Philip Gardner (ed.), 256–61 (London: Routledge, 1973).
70. Hargrave, "Deduction from 'Sign'," *The Plough* 1/ 2, July 1921: 35–8, 36; BLPES/HAR, b.88, f.5.
71. Robert Baden-Powell to Percy W. Everett, 25 July 1917, National Scout Archive, Baden-Powell House, London, United Kingdom, Papers and letters of Sir Percy W. Everett.
72. As recounted in Craven, "Redskins in Epping Forest," 137–8. See also a dinner menu and seating chart from the event, BLPES/HAR, b.88.
73. For two well-illustrated expositions of Kibbo Kift artwork (held at the Museum of London), see Ross and Bennett, *Designing Utopia*; Pollen, *The Kindred of the Kibbo Kift*.
74. For a discussion of the Kibbo Kift Advisory Council, its significance and politics, see Qugana, "The Cultural Politics of Englishness."
75. Holland, *William Morris's Utopianism*. See also Kent, "William Morris's Green Cosmopolitanism"; Gagnier "Morris's Ethics, Cosmopolitanism, and Globalisation."
76. Hargrave, *Tribal Training* (London: C. Arthur Pearson, 1919), 149.
77. Jeal, *Baden-Powell*, 502.
78. Thompson-Seton founded the Woodcraft Indians in the United States and the Woodcraft movement worldwide after being supplanted in Britain by the more establishment-friendly Baden-Powell. For a discussion of the nineteenth-century fascination in Native-American cultures, see Penny, *Kindred by Choice*.
79. Baden-Powell, *Scouting for Boys: a handbook for instruction in good citizenship*, Elleke Boehmer (ed.) (Oxford: Oxford University Press, 2010 [1908]), 77–8.
80. Idem, as quoted in "With Baden-Powell on His World Tour," *Boys' Life*, October 1912.
81. Idem, *Scouting for Boys*, First Edition, 340. This passage has been omitted from Boehmer's edition.
82. Ibid., 175.
83. J. M. Barrie, *The Annotated Peter Pan*, Maria Tatar (ed.) (London: W. W. Norton & Company, 2011 [1911]), 68; Baden-Powell, *Scouting for Boys*, First Edition, 340. For an introduction to racism in modern British education more widely, see Sherwood, "Race, Empire and Education."
84. Hargrave, untitled poem in an illustrated journal, 1 March 1912, BLPES/HAR, b.28.
85. Idem, "Making the Bad Boy Good," *Pearson's Magazine*, undated article clipping in BLPES/HAR, b.88. The periodical was also the first to publish Wells' novel *The War of the Worlds* (April-December 1897).
86. Ibid.
87. Idem, "White Fox Withdrawal," *The Plough*, April 1921, 18–20. Such names also appear in various issues of *The Mark* and *The Nomad* (1922-1925), BLPES/YMA/KK, b.165–6.
88. "Opening of a tribal mote," File of rituals, ceremonies and plays, 1928, BLPES/YMA/KK, b.7.
89. PR, 2.

90. See McCarthy, "Parties, Voluntary Associations, and Democratic Politics."
91. Rosenfield, "How We Tried to Be Good."
92. Esty, *A Shrinking Island*, 17.
93. Hobsbawm, *Bandits*, 46.
94. "Wabasso" [Tom C. Wycroft] and "Songan," "The Spirit of Robin Hood" in *Kibbo Kift Song Sheets Book One*, December 1925, BLPES/HAR, b.48.
95. Tom Villis, "The Forging of an Anti-Parliamentary Tradition" in idem, *Reaction and the Avant-Garde*, 72–106.
96. Baden-Powell's biographer has been a notable proponent of this characterisation; Jeal, *Baden-Powell*, 502.
97. Hargrave, "A Patriotic Revolution," *Attack!* 36, 1936, Beinecke Rare Book and Manuscript Library, Yale Collection of American Literature, Ezra Pound Papers (BRBML/YCAL/MSS 43), b.261.
98. Norman Angell, *The Great Illusion: A Study of the Relation of Military Power to National Advantage* (London: William Heinemann, 1912 [1909]), 401–2.
99. J. A. Hobson, *Imperialism: A Study* (New York: James Pott & Company, 1902). See also Wood, "J. A. Hobson and British Imperialism."
100. Hargrave, *The Confession*, 56.
101. Guild Socialism was, in turn, inspired by a pre-existing nineteenth-century tradition of social criticism whose proponents (such as John Stuart Mill, William Cobbett and William Morris) shed light on the 'evils' of industrialism; see Hutchinson and Burkitt, *The Political Economy of Social Credit*.
102. This is an interpretive alternative to an existing literature that tends to focus on the detail-oriented economic theorems of Social Credit's originator C. H. Douglas; see e.g. Finlay, *Social Credit*; Drakeford, *Social Movements and their Supporters*; Armstrong, "Social Credit Modernism"; Ross and Bennett, *Designing Utopia*, 107–35.
103. William Morris, "[Art: a Serious Thing]" in idem, *the Unpublished Lectures of William Morris*, Eugene D. Lemire (ed.), 36–53 (Detroit: Wayne State University Press, 1969), 45.
104. Hargrave, *The Confession*, 279.
105. Idem, notes and unpublished book titled *King Lud and his army of Redressers*, 1936, BLPES/HAR, b.14. Hargrave's history of the Luddites drew heavily on Frank Peel, *The Rising of the Luddites, Chartists and Plug-Drawers*, (London: Heckmondwike, 1880); see his annotated copy in BLPES/HAR, b.14.
106. Pound in idem, *Ezra Pound's Poetry and Prose: Contributions to Periodicals*, XI vols., Lea Baechler, A. Walton Litz and James Longerbach (eds.) (New York: Garland, 1991), 156.
107. Harrison, "Bertrand Russell," 9.
108. Hargrave, "PATRIOTISM belongs to Us!" in *Three Articles by John Hargrave*, c.1935, BLPES/HAR.
109. Said, *Culture and Imperialism*, xiii.
110. Hargrave, "A Patriotic Revolution."
111. Idem, "PATRIOTISM Belongs to Us!"
112. Idem, *The Confession*, 279.
113. For an introduction to the intellectual history of Social Credit, see Hutchinson and Burkitt, *The Political Economy of Social Credit*.
114. Armstrong, "Social Credit Modernism," 51.
115. Many Social Creditors feared that implementing socialism would merely switch which classes owned the nation's material wealth instead of changing the system to redistribute it on an equitable basis.

116. Hargrave, *The Confession*, 176. See also Thorstein Veblen, *The Theory of the Leisure Class: An Economic Study of Institutions* (New York: Macmillan, 1899); "List of Books, belonging to John Hargrave," BLPES/HAR, b.47.
117. Masquelier and Dawson, "Beyond Capitalism and Liberal Democracy."
118. E.g. Pollen, *The Kindred of the Kibbo Kift*; Craven, "Redskins in Epping Forest," esp. 12–13.
119. McCarthy, "Whose Democracy?", 228.
120. Hargrave, "From Kinsman to Green Shirt," pamphlet, 1935, BLPES/YMA/KK, b.70.
121. Hargrave to Pound, 4 January 1935, BRBML/YCAL/MSS 43. This figure was not insignificant compared with *The New Age*'s peak circulation of 3,000 copies per week; Martin, *The New Age under Orage*, 10.
122. PR, 2.
123. Hargrave, *The Confession*, 198–9. Also see idem, "There will be an economic Runnymede," *The Kibbo Kift Cartoons* 25, 8 July 1927.
124. Idem, "Political Impotence: A Diagnosis of the Present Situation," *K. K. Leaflet* 4, November 1925, BLPES/YMA/KK, b.70.
125. Idem, *The Confession*, 56.
126. Idem, "Remember, Remember – !," *The Kibbo Kift Cartoons* 42, 4 November 1927.
127. Idem, "From Kinsman to Green Shirt."
128. For a visual representation of the Kibbo Kift and SCP operations in Britain, see Ross and Bennett, *Designing Utopia*, 154–5.
129. Hobsbawm, *Age of Extremes*, 13.
130. PR, 10.
131. Hobsbawm, "Class Consciousness in History" in Mezaros (ed.), *Aspects of History and Class Consciousness*, 11–12.

Disclosure statement

No potential conflict of interest was reported by the authors.

References

Armstrong, Tim. "Social Credit Modernism." *Critical Quarterly* 55, no. 2 (2013): 50–65.
Bashford, Alison. *Global Population: History, Geopolitics, and Life on Earth*. New York: Columbia University Press, 2014.
Bayly, C. A. *Remaking the Modern World 1900-2015: Global Connections and Comparisons*. London: Wiley-Blackwell, 2018.
Carey, John. *The Intellectuals and the Masses: Pride and Prejudice among the Literary Intelligentsia, 1880-1939*. Chicago, IL: Academy Chicago, 2002 [1992].
Chakrabarty, Dipesh. "The Climate of History: Four Theses." *Critical Inquiry* 35 (Winter 2009): 197–222.
Chandra, Uday. "Liberalism and Its Other: The Politics of Primitivism in Colonial and Postcolonial Indian Law." *Law and Society Review* 47, no. 1 (March 2013): 135–168.
Coupland, Philip. "H. G. Wells's 'Liberal Fascism'." *Journal of Contemporary History* 35, no. 4 (2000): 541–558.
Craven, Josef Francis Charles. "Redskins in Epping Forest: John Hargrave, the Kibbo Kift and the Woodcraft Experience." PhD diss., University of London, 1998.
Dine, Philip. "The French Colonial Empire in Juvenile Fiction: From Jules Verne to Tintin." *Historical Reflections / Réflexions Historiques* 23, no. 2 (1997): 177–203.

Drakeford, Mark. *Social Movements and Their Supporters: The Green Shirts in England*. London: Macmillan Press, 1997.

Elwell-Sutton, L. P. "A History of the Kibbo Kift." Undated. Accessed April 4, 2016. http://www.kibbokift.org/kkkhist.html.

Esty, Jed. *A Shrinking Island: Modernism and National Culture in England*. Oxford: Princeton University Press, 2004.

Finlay, John L. *Social Credit: The English Origins*. Montreal: McGill-Queen's University Press, 1972.

Fleming, N. C. "Political Extremes and Extremist Politics." *Political Studies Review* 12 (2014): 395–401.

Fraser, W. Hamish. *Chartism in Scotland*. London: Merlin Press, 2010.

Fricke, Beate. "A Liquid History: Blood and Animation in Late Medieval Art." *RES: Anthropology and Aesthetics* 63, no. 64 (2013): 53–69.

Fryer, Peter. *Staying Power: The History of Black People in Britain*. London: Pluto Press, 1984.

Gagnier, Regenia. "Morris's Ethics, Cosmopolitanism, and Globalisation." *Journal of William Morris Studies* (Summer–Winter 2005): 9–30.

Gibson, Josh. "The Chartists and the Constitution: Revisiting British Popular Constitutionalism." *Journal of British Studies* 56 (January 2017): 70–90.

Gilroy, Paul. *The Black Atlantic: Modernity and Double Consciousness*. London: Verso, 1993.

Goodway, David. *Anarchist Seeds Beneath the Snow: Left-Libertarian Thought and British Writers from William Morris to Colin Ward*. Liverpool: Liverpool University Press, 2012 [2006].

Gould, Marty. *Nineteenth-Century Theatre and the Imperial Encounter*. London: Routledge, 2011.

Green, E. H. H., and D. M. Tanner, eds. *The Strange Survival of Liberal England*. Cambridge: Cambridge University Press, 2006.

Hale, Piers J. "Of Mice and Men: Evolution and the Socialist Utopia. William Morris, H. G. Wells and George Bernard Shaw." *Journal of the History of Biology* 43, no. 1 (2010): 17–66.

Hammond, J. R. *An H. G. Wells Companion*. London: Palgrave Macmillan, 1979.

Harrison, Royden. "Bertrand Russell: from liberalism to socialism?" *Russell* (Summer 1986): 5–38.

Hill, Christopher. *The Collected Works of Christopher Hill*. Vol. III. Amherst: Massachusetts University Press, 1986.

Hobsbawm, E. J. *Age of Extremes: The Short Twentieth Century, 1914-1991*. London: Abacus, 1995.

Hobsbawm, E. J. *Bandits*. London: Weidenfeld and Nicolson, 1969.

Hobsbawm, E. J. *Industry and Empire*. Middlesex: Penguin Books, 1980 [1968].

Hobsbawm, E. J. *Primitive Rebels: Studies in Archaic Forms of Social Movement in the 19th and 20th Centuries*. London: W. W. Norton, 1959.

Hobsbawm, E. J., and George F. E. Rudé. *Captain Swing*. New York: Pantheon, 1968.

Holland, Owen. *William Morris's Utopianism: Propaganda, Politics and Prefiguration*. London: Palgrave Macmillan, 2017.

Hutchinson, Frances, and Brian Burkitt. *The Political Economy of Social Credit and Guild Socialism*. London: Routledge, 1997.

Jeal, Tim. *Baden-Powell*. London: Hutchinson, 1989.

Kent, Eddy. "William Morris's Green Cosmopolitanism." *Journal of William Morris Studies* (Winter 2011): 64–78.

Martin, Wallace. *The New Age under Orage: Chapters in English Cultural History*. Manchester: Manchester University Press, 1967.

Masquelier, Charles, and Matt Dawson. "Beyond Capitalism and Liberal Democracy: On the Relevance of G. D. H. Cole's Sociological Critique and Alternative." *Current Sociology* 64, no. 1 (2016): 3–21.

Mazower, Mark. *Dark Continent: Europe's Twentieth Century.* London: Penguin Books, 1998.

McCarthy, Helen. "Parties, Voluntary Associations, and Democratic Politics in Interwar Britain." *The Historical Journal* 50, no. 4 (2007): 891–912.

McCarthy, Helen. "Whose Democracy? Histories of British Political Culture Between the Wars." *The Historical Journal* 55, no. 1 (March 2012): 221–238.

Mezaros, Istvan, ed. *Aspects of History and Class Consciousness.* London: Routledge, 1971.

Partington, John S. "H. G. Wells and the World State: A Liberal Cosmopolitan in a Totalitarian Age." *International Relations* 17, no. 2 (2003): 233–246.

Penny, Glen H. *Kindred by Choice: Germans and American Indians since 1800.* Chapel Hill: University of North Carolina Press, 2013.

Pollen, Annebella. *The Kindred of the Kibbo Kift: Intellectual Barbarians.* London: Donlon Books, 2015.

Qugana, Hana. "The Cultural Politics of Englishness: John Gordon Hargrave, the Kibbo Kift and Social Credit, 1920-1939." PhD diss., University College London, 2017.

Rediker, Marcus. "'Under the Banner of King Death': The Social World of Anglo-American Pirates, 1716-1726." *William and Mary Quarterly* 28 (1981): 203–227.

Rediker, Marcus. *Villains of All Nations: Atlantic Piracy in the Golden Age.* Boston: Beacon Press, 2004.

Rediker, Marcus, and Peter Linebaugh. *The Many-Headed Hydra: Sailors, Slaves, Commoners, and the Hidden History of the Revolutionary Atlantic.* Boston: Beacon Press, 2000.

Rosenfield, Israel. "How We Tried to Be Good." *New York Times*, 20 January 1985.

Ross, Cathy, and Oliver Bennett. *Designing Utopia: John Hargrave and the Kibbo Kift.* London: Philip Wilson, 2015.

Said, Edward. *Culture and Imperialism.* Vintage 1994 Edition. London: Chatto and Windus, 1993.

Sherwood, Marika. "Race, Empire and Education: Teaching Racism." *Race & Class* 42, no. 3 (January 2001): 1–28.

Smyth, Edmund, ed. *Jules Verne: Narratives of Modernity.* Liverpool: Liverpool University Press, 2000.

Starkey, David J., Jaap de Moor, and E. S. van Eyck van Heslinga, eds. *Pirates and Privateers: New Perspectives on the War on Trade in the Eighteenth and Nineteenth Centuries.* Exeter: University of Exeter Press, 1997.

Toye, Richard. "H.G. Wells and the New Liberalism." *Twentieth Century British History* 19, no. 2 (January 2008): 156–185.

Villis, Tom. *Reaction and the Avant-Garde: The Revolt Against Liberal Democracy in Early Twentieth-Century Britain.* London: I.B.Tauris, 2006.

Wood, John Cunningham. "J. A. Hobson and British Imperialism." *American Journal of Economics and Sociology* 42, no. 4 (October 1983): 483–500.

Imperial Liberalism and Institution Building at the End of Empire in Africa

Sarah Stockwell

ABSTRACT
This article discusses political liberalism at the end of empire in British Africa through analysis of British ideas about institution building below the level of parliamentary democracies. It suggests that while processes of institution-building have largely been discussed through the prism of development, they also constitute fruitful sites for the exploration of British ideas about the nature of politically-liberal systems. I argue that new articulations of an imperial liberalism during decolonisation had an energising effect on some Britons within domestic institutions whose expertise was called upon to assist with the development of successor institutions in emergent states. As they engaged in a process of institution-building, these individuals acted in ways that were not only determined by Western liberalism, but also by distinctive British ideas of the appropriate relationship of institutions to the state. I suggest, however, that while their approach to institution building in emergent states reflected deep rooted convictions about the kind of institutions that were essential to the operation of politically liberal systems, these ideals were in tension with more self-interested concerns which could in practice compromise efforts to replicate British institutions.

There can be few better illustrations of the reach of Western liberalism, as well as its contradictions and limitations, than developments associated with the end of the European colonial empires, including in Africa. They provide a powerful illustration of the extent to which in the twentieth century liberalism had become the dominant Western political ideology, transformed, in Duncan Bell's words, from a 'limited and contested position within political discourse' into 'the most authentic expression of the Western tradition or a constitutive feature of the West itself'.[1] Once European colonial powers were forced to retreat they aimed to transfer power to successor states fashioned along the lines of Western parliamentary systems that in the British case would take their place in the Commonwealth and help ensure, in the Cold War context, the preservation of British influence.[2] The wheel had come full circle: whereas in the nineteenth century liberalism once hostile to imperialism had become complicit in the imposition of colonialism,[3] so, in the twentieth, ideas of politically liberal systems underpinned efforts to transition back from 'formal' to 'informal' empire.[4] While managing this transition entailed the exercise of decidedly illiberal authoritarian powers, the British nonetheless sought to present decolonisation as the culmination of a liberal imperialism. In 1947 they even commissioned the historian Sir Reginald Coupland to produce a short historical account of the liberal nature of British imperialism to show that Indian independence represented the fulfilment of the liberal, civilising mission 'desired more than a century ago'.[5] For their part, colonial elites bought into and instrumentalised these liberal discourses to advance their own objectives.[6] They demanded independence within states and structures modelled along Western democratic lines, reflecting the ascendancy of discourses of self-determination and Western liberalism. This is despite the fact that as Emma Hunter has recently reminded us, alternative, conservative, forms of nationalism associated with chieftaincy had greater contemporary hold than historians, inclined to view nationalist politics through the lens of mid-twentieth-century liberalism, have sufficiently acknowledged.[7]

This article engages with the theme of liberalism through analysis of British ideas about institution-building below the level of parliamentary democracies in Anglophone African states at the end of empire. Processes of institution-building and transfer (through 'localisation' and the appointment of Africans to senior positions and the successful creation of parastatal institutions) were intimately related to the Westminster model. Sound institutions below the level of parliaments were crucial underpinning to the successful working of the Westminster system, and their political neutrality a fundamental aspect of Western, politically liberal systems (understood here as those in which executive power is balanced by that of the legislature and judiciary; the civil rights of individuals are protected by law; and in which institutions in civil society, such as the press, can operate free from state control).[8] Processes of institution-building have largely been discussed through the prism of development, including by scholars attentive to the striking parallels between discourses of 'good government' prominent during decolonisation and those associated with late twentieth and early twenty-first century humanitarian and neo-liberal interventions overseas.[9] There has been comparatively less attention to the ways in which institution-building served as a site for the articulation of political (as well as economic) liberalism.[10]

This article explores the views of academics on the development of higher education and public administration in emergent states, and of bankers in relation to the creation of new central banks in former colonies. It does not attempt to offer anything approaching a comprehensive survey of institution-building in these sectors. Moreover, while we focus here on British ideas, we should be clear that the reforming dynamic rested at least as much with African actors as with British, who throughout the colonial period had demanded the development of educational and other institutions, and the advancement of Africans within them, from colonial authorities that had resisted such calls, whether from self-interest or cultural and racial prejudice.[11] Even in a new climate of modernising development from the 1940s, as the British engaged in new processes of institution building they were generally still pushed into action by African, and sometimes international, pressure. A full discussion of the theme of institution building would also need to take in examples from other sectors, most obviously, legal. However, it is hoped that a focus on the quite different examples of higher education, administration and banking will serve to reinforce the case being made in this article about the pervasive influence of political liberalism on institution-building at the end of empire. It argues that, however instrumentally deployed, an imperial liberalism had an energising effect on some Britons within domestic institutions whose expertise was called upon to assist with the development of successor institutions in emergent states. Further, as these individuals engaged in a process of institution-building, they acted in ways that were not only determined by Western liberalism, but also by distinctively British ideas of state power. Nevertheless, while their approaches undoubtedly derived from deep rooted convictions about the kind of institutions that were essential to the operation of politically liberal systems, such considerations were in tension with more self-interested concerns which could compromise efforts to replicate British institutions.

Anglophone Africa offers rich scope for an exploration of this theme. In the transition to self-government even less progress had been made with institution building and localisation in Britain's African colonies than, for example, had been the case in South Asia. Not only did the movement to independence within a short period of time of so many colonies entail institution-building on an almost industrial scale, but this provided significant opportunity for Britons based in domestic institutions to deploy their expertise in the task. We should nevertheless be cautious about identifying any African particularity. One obvious reason for this is that the ideas and initiatives relating to institution-building discussed here principally through African examples were developed with reference to the dependent British empire in general. In some sectors, for example banking, British advisers also perceived their role as comparable to that they had earlier played in relation to the 'old' Commonwealth or—like Eric Ashby, an adviser on the establishment of African universities—consciously situated their activities in the longer history of the 'export' of British institutions that encompassed both settler colonies and India.[12] Equally pertinent, the circumstances in which institutions were developed or transferred varied across the continent according to local politics and were the product of distinct territorially-based processes of negotiation and implementation. Moreover, since a process of institution-building mostly accompanied or followed some element of self-government and was shaped by local elites (even though generally in contexts in which the British retained considerable influence), the sort of distinction drawn by several scholars (with reference to the Westminster system in Asia) between 'transplanted' institutions in settler states and those 'implanted' in non-settler states is too rigid to be fully applicable in the case of African countries.[13] In British eyes a variety of factors also applied according to African states' varying degrees of strategic and economic importance. But, perhaps less obvious, were distinctions of time. From our contemporary perspective it is easy to collapse the decolonisation of British African colonies into one short phase commencing with Ghanaian independence in 1957 and concluding (with the notable exception of Rhodesia, as well as the southern African high commission territories) in 1965 with that of the Gambia. But even as new institutions were being fashioned in some locations, others were being modified in those states that had already attained independence, influencing later British approaches.

* * *

A process of institution building began before but more frequently (especially in East and Central Africa) occurred at or after constitutional independence. But its origins can be dated to a series of shifts that occurred in British policy in response to developments in the late 1930s and in the first years of the Second World War. In the 1940s doctrines of 'trusteeship' and 'indirect rule' that had underpinned British approaches to administering Africa in the first half of the twentieth century were discarded in favour of new concepts of 'partnership' and 'development'. Rather than (as it had in the earlier twentieth century) seeking to preserve what the British identified as traditional African political institutions, British policy now aimed at the transformation of the colonies along British lines. The reasons behind this shift are well known and need not detain us long here: suffice to say that even before the war, problems with a system of colonial African governance based (theoretically) on hereditary claims to rule rather than meritocratic ones, and which vested authority in traditional rather than 'new', Western-educated, elites, were becoming apparent especially in increasingly urban societies. From 1947 British local government policy in Africa was reformed as a first step towards the development of fully-fledged parliamentary systems in Britain's colonies, although in practice the pace of political change in West Africa at least would mean that developments at the centre would soon after outstrip those at local governmental level.[14] Dismantling a system of 'native administration' based around the preservation of traditional African institutions and authorities that posited separate developmental routes had implications for other aspects of British colonial policy. For example, hitherto one objection to the appointment of Africans to senior positions in public administration had been that they would be unable to work effectively with the African chiefs and their advisers, in whom Britain had vested authority. This had led the British to resist the development of African higher education, demanded by African elites, in part because it was suspected that without jobs to enter (notably, in public administration) the creation of 'new' elites would ultimately foster colonial frustration and political instability. Upholding traditional systems had hence become one justification for Britain's failure to do more in relation to the expansion of higher education within Britain's African colonies.[15]

Even before the African local government reforms, the Colonial Office was already revising other aspects of colonial policy relating to development and welfare in response to widespread unrest in British colonies in the late 1930s and past policy failures, and to present British rule in a more progressive and constructive light. 'Partnership' and 'development' had become new ways of legitimising colonialism in the face of a variety of hostile forces and were very consciously used to promote an acceptable face of colonialism to audiences at home, within the empire, and internationally.[16] In summer 1943 the secretary of state for the colonies, Oliver Stanley, declared that the long-term objective of British policy was the gradual advancement of British colonies 'along the road to self-government within the framework of the British Empire'.[17] Paradoxically the actual process of creating liberal societies on British lines necessitated greater rather than less state intervention and Stanley's articulation of a new imperial mission was accompanied by other initiatives relating to colonial development, notably, as discussed below, in respect of colonial higher education. Conservatism, however, still characterised, and in some cases, compromised, British initiatives.

This imperial liberalism was also all too frequently accompanied by the exercise of illiberal powers.[18] Even as in London officials were advocating partnership and development, in wartime South Asia some 11,700 were imprisoned, including the most senior officials of the Indian National Congress, following the enactment of emergency legislation on the outbreak of war.[19] Whatever the British justification for such moves in terms of war and the defence of the Western liberal order, the enactment of emergency powers was illustrative of fundamental tensions in British political liberalism. Indeed as Terence Halliday and Lucien Karpik argue, while the British authorities had always insisted on the universality of the rule of law (a fundamental aspect of politically-liberal systems), this was compromised in colonial contexts by a rule of difference with parallel legal systems (in Africa, 'native courts'), and also, and most critically, by reserving the right to exercise power by sovereign decree and to declare states of emergency that abrogated normal law and gave the state unfettered coercive powers.[20] After the Second World War states of emergency were commonly used as the British sought to regain control in the face of insurgency or political disorder, most notably and for the greatest duration in Malaya, Cyprus and Kenya.[21] In this way rule by decree and the suspension of normal law was as much part of the political-legal inheritance of former British colonies on independence as liberal legal systems, with significant consequences for the colonies' post-colonial trajectory.[22]

However, to arrive at a richly-textured understanding of British decolonisation we need to incorporate a wide variety of dynamics, such as how ideas of the distinctively liberal identity of the British state and its relations with civil society helped shape the policies and responses of a range of British actors and institutions to the decolonisation process. As Emma Hunter observes,

> International thought was not characterised only by the assumption that the international political order would and should be based on nation-states and not empires. It was also characterised by a set of assumptions about what kind of political society should be contained within the building blocks of nations, defined in terms of parliamentary democracy, representative government and individual rights. [23]

In British eyes this required the relative autonomy of institutions from the state and from political interference, and the development of an African, professional, middle class to fill posts within them.[24]

These are features of any liberal political system, with the political neutrality of the judiciary or the army essential checks on the raw political authority of states. None the less, these features had assumed a distinct form within the British system. Patrick Joyce suggests that the British state was liberal not simply because it enshrined principles of political liberty, but because it also allowed designated bodies to operate comparatively independently.[25] We can see this in relation to British universities. In contrast to an American private model, British universities at the time were public institutions, but they had greater freedom from state control than public universities in most other European countries, where, Robert Anderson notes, the Napoleonic era left its 'stamp'. This is most obvious within the centralised and bureaucratic system of France but is evident too in the case of the older German universities whose financial independence was damaged by the effects of French conquest and occupation. Even though in the later nineteenth and the twentieth centuries the British state extended greater control over universities (for example as a result of the inauguration of student grants after the First World War), British universities still retained considerable autonomy.[26] Within British political culture a consensus had emerged about the desirability of limiting state control derived in part from the cultural capital of institutions like Britain's oldest universities, not least because those appointed to positions within the state had themselves generally been educated within them and bought into the same values. As Anderson further argues with reference to interwar Britain,

> politicians and bureaucrats belonged to a political culture which was suspicious of the power of the state, and really did believe that the independence of universities was an important liberal value, a tradition to be cherished, and that they worked best when left to determine their own policies.[27]

As they turned to the development of institutions in emergent states, those involved drew on the British examples they not only knew best but that they also deemed best practice. In so doing they incorporated their own distinctively

British ideas about the independence of institutions from the state. Some of the views expressed by British actors in institutions on the borders of the state relating to African institutional development need to be understood as also interventions in debates about the nature of the *domestic* state at a time at which—for all both individuals' and institutions' views on the nature of a politically liberal state —saw the emergence of new ideas about the state's place in the economy and society which challenged established assumptions about universities, the civil service, and about central banking. However, what might be thought of as disinterested concern with best practice—albeit that this was in itself a manifestation of an imperialism of knowledge derived from a presumption that the British knew best—was inextricably bound up with a set of other more selfish objectives. In their most benign form these aims embodied a vested interest in good governance, vital to the stability of new states within the Commonwealth and more broadly to Western interests in the Cold War. Engagement with institution-building overseas was crucial also to the British state's claims to be a source of modernising development along Western, liberal lines, and, through the dissemination of British models and Britishness, to the broader objective of securing influence at the end of empire.[28] But, whether consciously or unconsciously individuals based in British institutions also acted in ways that advanced their own narrower interests, even if they might also have conceived these as compatible with the best interests of emergent states.

*　*　*

British universities and academics were one obvious source of mid twentieth-century liberal ideas.[29] Many academics had been brought into advisory roles in relation to colonial policy both before the war and during it, exemplifying the state's growing recourse to 'experts' in the formulation and delivery of policy. They served on the committees and other specialist bodies that proliferated in the period and as advisers to the Colonial Office across a range of social and natural sciences.[30] Some of these academics were instrumental in the development of new policy initiatives in relation to colonial institution-building, including, as discussed, higher education and administration, and were energised by the state's articulation of a new liberal civilising mission. H.J. Channon, a professor of biochemistry at the University of Liverpool, and one of the most active members of the Colonial Office's education advisory committee, pressed on the Colonial Office in 1941 the importance of developing colonial universities as a crucial step towards enabling colonial peoples to 'stand on their own feet'.[31] At this date there were few universities anywhere in the colonial empire and none in Britain's African colonies, although there were several higher education institutions.[32] Margery Perham, reader in colonial administration at the University of Oxford argued that British universities now had a 'more important task than any handled by the Colonial Office itself' in 'the training of their [the emergent nations'] leaders and experts so that they may take back from us the control of their own affairs'.[33]

Channon and Perham both became central figures in metropolitan discussions around colonial universities. In 1943 Channon's intervention contributed to the Colonial Office's decision to appoint a commission chaired by Lord Justice Asquith to investigate higher education in the colonies;[34] as Tim Livsey has recently shown, developments in Africa also played a decisive role in the origins and shape of new initiatives relating to colonial universities.[35] Channon and Perham were both appointed to the new Commission, while Channon was also a member of a separate regional commission convened a few weeks earlier to give consideration to higher education in West Africa (the 'Elliot Commission').[36] When it reported in June 1945, the Asquith Commission recommended the formation of universities in the colonies and set out proposals to assist with the drafting of their founding constitutions. These recommendations remained the model for colonial universities until the late 1950s when there began to be greater reference to American experience as well as to the local conditions.[37] The Commission also proposed the creation of a new Inter-University Council for Higher Education in the Colonies (later Overseas) comprising members drawn from British and colonial universities to assist with these tasks.[38] A series of new university institutions followed. Via the secondment of academics to new colonial university colleges to facilitate their conversion to full university status, the creation of the IUC initiated a new and extended phase of British academic engagement with educational institutions in emergent states that Commission members hoped might generate close ties that would survive the colonies' transition to independence.[39] Margery Perham became one of the IUC's most longstanding and key members. Another was Ivor Jennings, initially as a representative of the University of Ceylon, and, from 1948 to 1961 co-opted to the Council.[40] Jennings' career straddled the worlds of democracy-building on the Westminster model and of sub-parliamentary institution building. He was the founding Vice-Chancellor of the University of Ceylon, as well as later Master of Trinity Hall in the University of Cambridge and Vice-Chancellor of the University of Cambridge from 1961 to 1963. He was also the foremost Commonwealth constitutional expert of the day and had advised on the Ceylon constitution as well as on constitutional issues in India, Pakistan, Malaya and Nepal.[41]

Of course, there was a complexity and diversity of views within Britain and within single institutions. For example, some, like Perham were excited by the prospect of assisting the colonies to eventual self-government, whereas others remained more committed to upholding empire. Equally, even among those who were most committed to empire within the universities, there were some who doubted the universities' capacity to participate in a latter-day civilising mission in this instance by making their academic staff available for secondment to new colonial institutions. Sir Douglas Veale, as the university's registrar the most senior administrative figure at the University of Oxford, and a committed 'empire man', reminded his long-term ally and director of colonial service recruitment at the Colonial Office, Sir Ralph Furse, in May 1943 in connection to proposals for the 'loan' of university staff for the service of empire, that 'the supply [of British academics] in fact is limited'. He feared, moreover, that 'not every eminent scholar' was 'suitable for this kind of missionary work'. It was no use, he warned, 'sending someone who suffers from ochlophobia', or who 'is exceedingly ill-mannered, or enjoys poor health', or even, he added, 'a disagreeable wife who insists on going with him'.[42]

As they engaged with the task of developing colonial universities, however, British academics agreed on the importance of replicating overseas the principle of academic freedom and university autonomy alongside other features of the British university system.[43] It was essential, the Asquith Commission noted, that the new institutions 'should have full freedom to manage their own affairs'.[44] According to Perham, reflecting retrospectively on the deliberations of the Asquith Commission, ensuring 'a form of university government which enshrined the academic freedom which we had developed in this country' had been one of two overriding principles that had guided the deliberations of the Commission, alongside the maintenance of standards by ensuring that admission to colonial universities was governed by the same high entry criteria as at home in Britain. Writing in the early postcolonial era, in the light of the transition away from these principles among some African universities, Perham wondered retrospectively if the Commission had been wrong. She concluded that 'we could give only what we knew & valued'.[45] As Tim Livsey argues in a discussion of the development of universities in Nigeria, British university freedom was relative rather than absolute, as was that of the new University of Ibadan in the late colonial era from the British authorities.[46] To an extent the Asquith recommendations had acknowledged the inevitability of this. 'Colonial universities', the Commission had proposed, 'should be autonomous in the sense in which the universities of Great Britain are autonomous'. Autonomy should not preclude a degree of public accountability nor some role for governments, including via the exercise of supervisory functions compatible with the award of state funding. Nevertheless, through appropriate checks and balances including a Senate which would be a purely academic body, as well as the judicious division of seats so that no external organisation could exercise a majority in a university's governing council, the Commission believed that academic freedom would prevail.[47] British academics had also secured for the IUC relative autonomy from the Colonial Office (which devolved to it considerable authority to act in relation to the development of colonial universities).[48] But Livsey's comments point to the distortions that could follow from the importation of British models into colonial contexts. There was one set of constraints which British academics would probably not initially have recognised, although Eric Ashby later acknowledged the tensions between academic freedom and the British role: the 'academic freedom' of new universities would be mediated by the supervision of British academics, for example via the inclusion of one or two representatives of the IUC on the governing councils of new universities and via special arrangements linking new universities to the University of London designed to ensure the maintenance of academic standards.[49] This wholesale adherence to British traditions and oversight by advisers who sought to instil their ideas of best practice was initially accepted, and even embraced, by elites in emergent states committed to the development of universities that should not in any way be regarded as 'second rate'. However, not only would the inbuilt safeguards prove no guarantee against future state interference, but the institutions' British complexion ensured that a subsequent decolonising phase would later follow, as independent states sought curricula and facilities better equipped to meet the needs of developing states.[50]

* * *

If we now turn from the development of higher education to that of public administration, we can see that the same understanding of the appropriate relationship of institutions to the state informed another aspect of the older universities' involvement with institution-building at the end of empire: training a first generation of overseas public servants to succeed British colonial officials within the public services of new states who should be free to act without political interference. Within the British system the traditions of public service (established in the 1854 Northcote-Trevelyan reforms, which recommended the creation of a permanent unified civil service recruited by competitive examination) included open entry by means of academic competition to positions within a service organised into grades according to function; a system of promotion based on merit and seniority; and adherence to a principle of political neutrality that meant officials retained their posts irrespective of their party political allegiances.[51] In practice, colonial public services had deviated from the British model in several important respects: they were organised on racial rather than meritocratic lines, and they did not realise the ideals of bureaucratic neutrality,[52] not least because until the advent of African self-government within Britain's African colonies British public servants exercised executive authority.

None the less while the Colonial Service differed from British public service traditions in this manner, we can again see ways in which British practice was distinct from continental European. Specifically, since 1926 new entrants to the Colonial Service had completed a training course at Oxford or Cambridge before taking up posts overseas in the service of individual colonies, rather than as in France or Belgium undergoing an initial training at dedicated colonial staff colleges.[53] In British eyes this less centralised system, in which responsibility for training was devolved by the imperial state to the universities, was preferable to the staff college model and crucial in the development of civil servants in the British tradition. As academics and administrators at Oxford and Cambridge argued in the early 1940s on the occasion of a major review of Colonial Service training,[54] this was best done via a broad university-based post-graduate course, one that privileged the academic rather than the practical, and the generalist rather than the specialist.[55] After the war the state sought to admit to these courses high-flying non-European students, especially Africans, who were initially destined for posts in the Colonial Service and later within bureaucracies in independent countries. In the 1950s British officials thought that studying at Oxbridge would be the best means of acculturating overseas civil servants to the values of a liberal education by broadening their outlook and horizons, and so shaping African middle-class entrants to administration along the lines of the generalists of the British civil service.[56] A nascent African administrative middle class was also perceived by some as vital not just to preventing administrative collapse in emergent states but to ensuring a pro-Western outlook.[57]

As overseas administrators were admitted to these courses, initially in only small numbers, but by the early 1960s comprising the majority of those enrolled on them, key figures involved in their delivery argued for the continuation of a form of administrative training at Oxbridge. Via tuition in a wide range of subjects as part of a liberal education, overseas students would be equipped with the skills necessary to act as key mediators between politicians and experts in ways that would help maintain the autonomy of civil servants from governments. By this date the manpower needs of new African states were considerable and urgent, and the priority for overseas governments was naturally the development of local training in public administration. The British acknowledged as much in a major review of British assistance in the training of overseas public administrators by a committee established under the chairmanship of Lord Bridges, former head of the home civil service.[58] Britain as well as other foreign countries and international organisations became one source of assistance in the development of new training institutes located in former colonies. A huge diaspora of British officials also remained in post in many former colonies or were seconded to new positions within the public services of new states under the auspices of the Overseas Service Aid Scheme, introduced in 1961 amidst fears that unless Britain did more to facilitate the continuation in post of British personnel there was a real danger of administrative collapse at least in East Africa.[59] But Oxford academics successfully defended the case for the continuation of some form of training for an elite few overseas administrators at Oxbridge, arguing in their evidence submitted to the Bridges committee that,

> An indigenous civil service cannot just have handed on to it, ready-made, high standards of impartiality, reliability, incorruptibility and so on; it must establish them afresh for itself. For this its officers need to learn how to read and to think; how to present a case and debate it; how to weigh conflicting arguments and reach a decision; how to apply that decision with realism and moderation; and how to recognise and use the lessons of experience. … nowhere can this be done better than in the older universities such as Oxford which, in effect, say to such students: 'We cannot give you the answers to your future problems; but we can help you to acquire for yourselves the equipment with which you can usefully tackle them.[60]

Through lectures on governance and British history overseas students were taught key aspects of British political culture, including the ways in which authority within the British system rested with institutions which had gradually evolved. The *gradual* evolution of British institutions of government might serve, as the Oxford course supervisor put it, as the perfect antidote to 'impatient and perfectionist political ambitions'.[61] Sir Ivor Jennings was among those lecturing to these administrative cadets at Cambridge in the 1950s; another means of educating students from a variety of African and other Commonwealth states in a British parliamentary and liberal tradition, which Jennings had already been instrumental in implanting in an Asian context.[62] In the 1950s, conscious of the burdens that delivering one-year courses imposed on the university, the authorities at Oxford debated whether they should continue to participate in administrative training. On balance they reflected that such courses represented an investment in the 'people in whose hands lay the future of large areas of the Commonwealth'.[63] Simultaneously at the request of several governments Oxford became involved from the 1950s in delivering bespoke courses for new diplomats within the new foreign services of Commonwealth states, which eventually developed into the University's Foreign Service Programme.

Nevertheless, such apparently disinterested statements of service and commitment to the emergent Commonwealth resided alongside individual and institutional self-interest. As Véronique Dimier argues, in the early and mid-twentieth century the association with the imperial services was a source of prestige for Oxford and Cambridge, and, until it was brought into the new post-war Devonshire training scheme, a source of resentment in London at the University of London's exclusion from this role.[64] There were material interests at stake too. For example, the universities received a stipend from first the Colonial Office, and later the Department of Technical Co-operation and the Ministry of Overseas Development, to deliver the colonial administrative service training and successor courses, generating income and funds to support academic specialisms. More abstractly, as academics and civil servants articulated a case in defence of the generalist tradition for the training, first, of Britain's colonial officials, and subsequently, overseas public administrators, it seems likely that they were—consciously or unconsciously—intervening in contemporary discussions about the nature of the home civil service as the value of the generalist-amateur tradition and emphasis on 'character' increasingly came under attack in the light also of persistent worries about elitism in a system in which Oxbridge graduates were over represented. The British generalist tradition was increasingly in tension with a growing reliance on specialist knowledge, as well as a Keynesian approach to economic planning.[65] In one of the most significant critiques Thomas Balogh expressly linked the home and overseas services, in arguing that a cultivation of 'powers of dialectical argument only' had had 'devastating effects' including in British colonies which lacked expertise in economic planning.[66] In the 1960s growing criticism led to the appointment of the Fulton Committee on the civil service.[67]

British discussions about training overseas public administrators hence occurred against a backdrop in which views of what constituted best practice were changing. Both Oxford and Cambridge continued to offer a form of the administrative training course, but the generalist tradition was increasingly a handicap as Whitehall officials began expressing greater preference for vocational training. State funding for the courses was finally withdrawn from Oxford in 1969, while the Cambridge course, reconfigured in the 1970s as a course on development, survived until 1981.[68] Africans who subsequently rose to the most senior positions within their own civil services were among course graduates. But even where they apparently subscribed to British administrative ideals, they might fall foul of governments hostile to a colonial inheritance and traditions of political neutrality.[69]

* * *

If the universities are an obvious place in which to locate the impact of imperial liberalism, it also registered in some less likely quarters. In summer 1943 a month after Oliver Stanley identified advancement towards self-government as the aim of British colonial policy, Montagu Norman, longstanding governor of the Bank of England, complaining to Stanley about Colonial Office proposals made in relation to colonial currency boards, turned Stanley's recent liberal rhetoric against him. 'I am especially disappointed', Norman wrote in response to Stanley's refusal to accept one of his proposals, 'because what I suggested seemed to me at best a step in the direction of democracy; and it is surprising to me to find such a step refused when you in particular are beating the democratic drum in the colonies'.[70] In question was whether there should be representatives with local business and financial knowledge on the London-based regional boards which issued and managed colonial currencies; Norman believed there should. Raymond Kershaw, an Australian economist, and since 1935 an adviser to the Bank's governors, deplored what he perceived as a Colonial Office tendency to 'neglect the view of local interest in the interests of alleged centralised efficiency'. In contrast the Colonial Office worried about the politics of selecting local representatives and feared also that this might entail the appointment of a 'native', at least in West Africa.[71] There was an ambiguity to Norman's words: whereas the Colonial Office saw the appointment of representatives of 'local' interests on the currency boards as likely to lead to the inclusion of African members, there is no evidence that Norman necessarily understood 'local' as anything other than the co-option of Britons engaged in business in the colonies. For our purposes what is most relevant here is what Norman's intervention reveals of his own understanding of the appropriate relationship of institutions to the state. As Norman had argued in correspondence a few weeks before with Sir George Gater, the permanent under-secretary of state at the Colonial Office, what the Colonial Office proposed seemed to 'foreshadow a condition in which there will be all State and no citizens, and certainly no citizens having a responsible share in the operations of the State'.[72] In private

Norman condemned the move as 'undemocratic—worthy of Nazi—although the Col. [sic] Office is waving the flag of democracy in most countries'.[73] Just as would later be the case with discussions over the generalist tradition and the public services, Norman's perspective was surely shaped by his own recent domestic experience of the gradual subordination of the Bank's control over monetary policy to the Treasury as ideas about the desirability of central bank autonomy shifted as a result of a Keynsian emphasis on the role of the state in economic management.

After the Second World War, this view of the importance of the independence of institutions from the state was reflected in the Bank's approach towards the establishment of new central banking institutions in Britain's colonies and former colonies. The Bank of England, like the universities, became involved in the provision of forms of technical assistance to new states, albeit in this instance as a result of its own initiative rather than under the auspices of any government department. Existing accounts of the Bank during decolonisation emphasise its resistance to developing new currencies and central banks, and focus on its priority of promoting the sterling area and sterling's role as an international trading and reserve currency.[74] But once in the mid-1950s it became obvious that the Bank could no longer profitably resist the development of institutions demanded by colonial politicians, as well as increasingly advocated by the World Bank,[75] the Bank sought to exercise as much oversight as possible over the creation of new financial institutions in emergent states. The Bank provided advisers who drafted founding statutes for some of the new African central banks, as well as seconding its own staff to fill senior positions in them, and also inaugurated a short training course for Commonwealth central bankers in London.[76] In these various activities what we might rightly see as a form of financial imperialism also resided alongside a more abstract and cultural understanding of what 'good banking' meant in the context of a British liberal tradition.

In 1946 the Bank of England had itself been nationalised.[77] But notwithstanding its change in status, Bank officials nevertheless remained committed to the principle of central bank autonomy and—just as with the universities and the civil service—distinct understandings of the state and its relation to civil society shaped the Bank of England's approach to its role in emergent states at the end of empire. A fundamental principle guiding the actions of their senior personnel as they advised on the statutes for which new central banks were based was that new banks should be as independent as possible of their governments.[78] Statutes for new banks in West and Central Africa drafted by Bank of England advisers therefore gave no powers to governments to direct the banks' affairs.[79] In East Africa, where the Bank was unable to exercise the same level of oversight over the development of new central banks as it had in West Africa, officials nevertheless also sought where they could to promote this model of central banking.[80]

In this respect the Bank's views increasingly collided with those of other international experts and reflect specific British approaches. After the war American experts attached to the Federal Reserve, who had previously cleaved to the same liberal financial orthodoxy as those at the Bank of England, prioritising external currency stability, now adopted an alternative approach, seeking to strengthen the capacity of national governments to pursue policies geared towards domestic monetary goals.[81] The American approach was premised on the idea that central banks could serve as engines of economic development in new states, including through their ability to advance money to their governments. The British on the other hand feared that if new governments had control over the banks they would raid them for funds to pay for expensive development projects, thereby fuelling inflation and damaging the prestige and stability of their currencies.[82] This had happened in the case of the Bank of Ceylon after the Ceylonese government turned to American experts to advise on the formation of their central bank as they sought to free themselves from what they saw (in many ways rightly) as the imperialism of the Bank of England. Opened in 1950, the Bank of Ceylon followed American models, and quickly became a source of credit to the government.[83] Similar concerns lay behind the Bank of England's preference to secure a separation of commercial and central banking functions; this also differed from American approaches since the latter anticipated that to facilitate economic development new banks in developing economies might have to be prepared to engage in direct lending.[84]

As English bankers engaged with questions of financial devolution within the emergent Commonwealth this adherence to what they perceived as 'best practice' co-existed with a set of more self-interested motives. As Peter Cain and A.G. Hopkins argue in relation to the interwar years, when the Bank had also been engaged in the development of new central banks, in this case in the dominions, India, and South America, central banks formed on an English model and permitted to function free from state interference were more likely to accept guidance from the Bank of England.[85] Most significantly, in the 1950s and early 1960s the Bank attached overriding importance to upholding sterling as a reserve currency and the mechanisms of the sterling area (to which African members were of increasing importance as older Commonwealth states began to draw down their sterling holdings).[86] Central banks under the control of independent African governments, elected to office amidst hopes that they would deliver ambitious development plans, were more likely to turn to sterling reserves to fund development schemes as well as to diversify their holdings away from sterling.

But rather than rely on such mechanisms Bank of England officials resorted to more direct ways of protecting the Bank's interests. For example, in drawing up the statutes of the new central banks of Ghana and Nigeria, the Bank of England's John Loynes built in a requirement that the banks keep a majority of their reserves in sterling, British government securities or gold held in

London.[87] In the Ghanaian case he even specified a fixed maximum fiduciary issue (that is, the limit to the issue of currency not backed by reserves) that could only be changed by the country's new parliament. In this and other ways he hoped to have created a bank that was not 'too dangerous'.[88] It seems likely that Loynes understood 'dangerous' not just in terms of a potential threat to British interests, but also in relation to the possible risks to the stability of Ghana's currency, and, by extension, to its ability to attract foreign investment that a departure from conservative approaches to monetary policy might entail. Even so, while the British sought to enshrine central bank independence from successor governments, they simultaneously sought to ensure the protection of British interests in ways that compromised the ability of the new banks to operate in an autonomous fashion and which were likely to generate tensions between the new banks and postcolonial African governments.

These more selfish objectives go a long way towards explaining the importance the Bank also attached to training a new class of Commonwealth central bankers and its willingness to second staff to fill posts in new banks.[89] By working with, and providing tuition to, Commonwealth bankers, it hoped to embed some attachment to sterling and the sterling area. But, in this instance too, these objectives are difficult to disentangle from a political liberal agenda. For via their training activities, Bank officials hoped to cultivate a class of African professional bankers who might take their place in international banking networks and contribute to the development of Western politically liberal systems. As one British banker seconded to work in Nigeria's new central bank observed, in relation to his Nigerian colleagues, 'once the middle class becomes sufficiently distinct to exercise an effect on public opinion and politics' it would help secure the country's future.[90] The Bank's Commonwealth course proved perhaps surprisingly durable, not least because of sustained demand from bankers in new states eager to make use of all training opportunities available to them. This was the case despite the fact that there was some suspicion of the Bank of England and British influence, particularly among their governments that in some instances encouraged a departure from the banking model British bankers were so keen to implant.

* * *

For a short period, then, as they engaged in an alternative form of constitution writing, drafting statutes and legal instruments for new institutions in Commonwealth African states, individuals acted in ways that reflected the traction that the liberal imperial idea had within sectors of British society. Although we need to see beyond individuals' sometimes self-justificatory and aggrandising claims about their commitment to, or role in, institutional development, liberalism was not simply a rhetorical device used to advance imperial objectives; rather it was also a conception of the British tradition that had been taught to individual Britons and which shaped their actions. In the eyes of Britons based in domestic institutions located on or beyond the borders of the state politically liberal systems entailed the construction of similar parastatal institutions similarly located, but not subordinated to, executive power. They perceived these as crucial accessories to the successful transfer of the Westminster model. These understandings of the appropriate relationship of institutions to the state reflected not just a broad Western liberal tradition but distinctive British ideas of the liberal state.

It quickly became apparent, however, that the British legacy fell short of these ambitions. A failure to institute processes of institutional development and transfer sufficiently early in Africa created states that were not properly institutionalised.[91] Even where some scholars judge British values had successfully been transferred in relation to institutions in different sectors, they conclude that the societies and cultures and the different circumstances in which different countries attained independence were crucial in determining the survival or otherwise of British values.[92] Furthermore, institutions that the British had conceived as crucial cogs in politically liberal states fell prey to political interference rather than serving as bulwarks against a transition away from a Westminster model. In the first of Britain's African colonies to attain independence, Ghana, the country's leader Kwame Nkrumah had instituted a one-party state and subordinated key institutions to it even as similar institutions were being constructed elsewhere in colonial Africa. Having first sought to circumvent the civil service by creating posts outside it (including a series of 'district commissioners' who would act as ministerial personal assistants), in 1960 he proceeded to change the public service commission as it had been established at independence. The following year he formed a branch of his party, the Convention People's Party in the Establishment Secretariat.[93] Between 1962 and 1963 both Ghana and Nigeria replaced the banking ordinances devised by a Bank of England adviser with new banking statutes that enabled them to diversify their holdings away from sterling.[94] In Ghana these new instruments enabled the Bank of Ghana to advance long-term credit to the government and gave the government greater control over it.[95] This was the very opposite of what the Bank of England had hoped, and the experience served as a salutary lesson that overseeing the founding statutes of new banks was no guarantee against unwelcome future developments.

These departures from British models occurred even as Britain's other African colonies were still progressing to independence and advisers adapted their approaches in the light of the West African developments.[96] As we have already seen, a similar trend in relation to new African universities was equally chastening for Margery Perham.[97] As Ian Maxwell later wrote, in these circumstances the IUC could do little more than 'give moral support' or occasionally attempt to bring some pressure to bear via informal channels. Developments in this sector nevertheless led Eric Ashby to reflect on the lessons to be learned if autonomy was to be restored or, in the case of future institutions, ensured. Sir Ivor Jennings offered one insight: speaking in 1948 he noted that Ceylonese experience suggested that—however counterintuitive—the inclusion of representatives of state legislatures on university governing bodies might in fact be the best means of ensuring university autonomy. Others also speculated as to whether the construction of institutions detached from the state in line with a British liberal tradition was not the problem rather than the solution. T.H. Silcock, drawing on his experience of universities in South-East Asia questioned whether the French model in which university staff were civil servants while still having academic freedom might not be better.[98]

More widely, although generalisation across so many countries and sectors is difficult, attempts to replicate the relative autonomy of institutions from the state and thereby to implant a distinctly British model of a politically liberal system, created institutions that might not only be viewed as 'colonial' but sometimes regarded with suspicion as alternative, and potentially competing, sources of power by governments that demanded political loyalty rather than neutrality. As we have also seen British ambitions to develop institutions on liberal lines were in tension with British self-interest, resulting in in-built distortions and ambiguities that (whether intentionally or not) departed from the British tradition. As Ashby reflected with reference to the derogation from freedom in institutions he had helped develop, 'The patterns we have exported are not in fact the patterns we practise'.[99] Contemporary Britons would probably not all have recognised this, but inevitably, institution building at the end of empire constituted a form of imperial liberalism rather than a liberal imperialism.

Notes

1. Bell, *Reordering the World*, 87.
2. On the transfer of the Westminster model, see Kumarasingham, *Political Legacy*.
3. Pitts, *Turn to Empire*; Koditschek, *Liberalism*; Conklin, *Mission to Civilize*.
4. On the transitions between formal and informal empires, see Louis and Robinson, "Imperialism of Decolonization"; and Gallagher and Robinson, "Imperialism of Free Trade".
5. The National Archives (TNA), Kew, London, FO 953/5A, Sir Reginald Coupland, 'The Goal of British Rule in India', attached to minute, 26 Sept. 1947, cited in Stockwell, "Britain and Decolonization".
6. As Cooper argues in relation to development: Cooper, "Modernizing Bureaucrats, Backward Africans". For a nineteenth-century Indian comparison, see Bayly, *Recovering Liberties*.
7. Hunter, "Languages of Freedom".
8. Based on Halliday and Karpik, "Political Liberalism," esp. 4.
9. See, e.g., Duffield and Hewitt eds., *Development and Colonialism*, esp. Hewitt, "Empire, International Development." For an earlier discussion of 'good governance' see Lee, *Colonial Development*.
10. Although it attracted more attention in some contemporaneous or near-contemporaneous studies: see, e.g., Hyden, Jackson, and Okumu eds., *Development Administration* or Symonds, *The British*.
11. For example, see Nwauwa, *Imperialism, Academe and Nationalism*, 1–28.

12. Stockwell, *British End*, 41; Ashby, *Universities. British, Indian, African*, x.
13. By Rhodes and Weller, "Westminster Transplanted," 3. For a critique, see Kumarasingham, "Eastminster," 6.
14. Extensively discussed in the 1980s, and on which see especially, Pearce, *Turning Point in Africa*.
15. See Nwauwa, *Imperialism*, 52–63.
16. Wolton, *Lord Hailey*; see also doctoral research being undertaken by Naima Maggetti of the University of Geneva.
17. Secretary of State for the Colonies Oliver Stanley: *House of Commons Debates*, Vol. 391, 13 July 1943, col. 48.
18. On which see, especially, Elkins, *Britain's Gulag*; Anderson, *Histories of the Hanged*; Huw Bennett, *Fighting the Mau Mau*.
19. De, "Emasculating the Executive," 59–90, esp. 62.
20. Halliday and Karpik, "Political Liberalism."
21. Grob-Fitzgibbon, *Britain's Dirty Wars*, 377.
22. Halliday and Karpik, "Political Liberalism." They offer possible explanations as to why some former British colonies were generally 'liberal-legal orders' (like India) and why others were 'despotic' (like the Sudan, Sri Lanka and Singapore) or 'volatile', oscillating between the two. See also Kumarasingham, "Eastminster," 23–7.
23. Hunter, "Languages of Freedom."
24. On the emergence of an African middle class see, esp., Lloyd ed., *New Elites*; West, *African Middle Class*; Melber, ed., *Rise of Africa's Middle Class*.
25. Joyce, *State of Freedom*, 3, 17–24, 188–93.
26. Anderson, *British Universities*, 28–30, 114, 189.
27. Ibid., pp. 114–15.
28. For my own contribution to this see Stockwell, "Exporting Britishness."
29. The following discussion about higher education and public administration draws on Stockwell, *British End*, 30–8, 62–3, 96–109, 122–3.
30. See, e.g., Hodge, *Triumph of the Expert*; Jöns, "University of Cambridge".
31. Ashton and Stockwell, eds., *Imperial Policy*, part II, doc. 148, 'Some observations on the development of higher education in the colonies', memo. by Professor H. J. Channon, Jan 1941, CO 859/45/2, no 1. However, there was a complexity to Channon's views, and Nwauwa argues that he saw the development of colonial universities as the key to colonial reform and a means of strengthening empire: Nwauwa, *Imperialism*, 117–18.
32. At Fourah Bay (Sierra Leone) established by the Church Missionary Society, the Prince of Wales College at Achimota (Gold Coast/Ghana), the Higher College at Yaba (Nigeria), and Makerere College, Kampala (Uganda) and Gordon Memorial College, Khartoum (Sudan): PP. 1944–45, Cmd., 6647, *Report of the Commission on Higher Education in the Colonies*. London: HMSO, June, 1945, 8–9.
33. Cited in Oliver, "Prologue," 24.
34. *Higher Education in the Colonies*; Ashton and Stockwell eds., *Imperial Policy*, part I, "Introduction," lxxix–lxxx.
35. Livsey, *Nigeria's University Age*, 19–20, 27–36.
36. *Higher Education in the Colonies*; PP. 1944–5, Cmd. 6655, *Report of the Commission on Higher Education in West Africa*. London: HMSO, June, 1945.
37. Ashby, *Universities*, 268–89.
38. Currently the subject of doctoral research at King's College London by Dongkyung Shin, and also discussed recently in Livsey, *Nigeria's University Age*. There is one major institutional history, written by a former secretary of the Council: Maxwell, *Universities in Partnership*.

39. *Higher Education in the Colonies*, 6, and esp. 30–4 (chapter VII).
40. Maxwell, *Universities in Partnership*, Appendix III. Jennings, *Constitutional Laws*; Nwauwa, *Imperialism*, 156.
41. On Jennings, see Kumarasingham, *Constitution-Maker*, 1–18.
42. Bodleian Library, Oxford University Archive (OUA), UR 6/Col/6/1, Sir D. Veale to Sir R. Furse, 25 May 1943. From 1949 Veale served on the IUC first as a representative of Oxford, and subsequently as a co-opted member.
43. Livsey, *Nigeria's University Age*; Nwauwa, *Imperialism*, 157.
44. *Higher Education in the Colonies*, 34–7.
45. Bodleian Library, Mss Perham 719/5, file on the work of the IUC 1950–69, ff. 1–2, notes on development of universities overseas, undated but probably written in the 1960s. For other testimony see the emphasis placed on autonomy by writers who were themselves participants in the process they discuss, although Ashby acknowledged the limits in practice to freedom: Ashby, *Universities*, 291, 306–43; Maxwell, *Universities in Partnership*, 31–4.
46. Livsey, *Nigeria's University Age*, 48.
47. *Higher Education in the Colonies*, 34–7.
48. Nwauwa, *Imperialism*, 157.
49. *Higher Education in the Colonies*, 34–7; Ashby, *Universities*, 307.
50. See Nwauwa, *Imperialism*, 212–18.
51. Tinker, "Structure of the British Imperial Heritage," 23–86, esp. 24.
52. As shown in Kuklich, *Imperial Bureaucrat*, 145.
53. Dimier, *Le Gouvernement des Colonies*; Dimier, "Three Universities."
54. By the 'Devonshire Committee'.
55. Archives of the University of Cambridge, Cambridge University Library, GB 760/939, Minutes of a meeting, 17 June 1942, between representatives from Cambridge including the VC and Sir Ralph Furse. On the British civil service, see Hennessy, *Whitehall*, 7, 74–5, 194–9, 123–5.
56. Stockwell, *British End*, 107–8.
57. CAB 134/1353, AF 1(59), 'The next ten years in Africa': minutes of Africa (Official) Committee meeting to discuss procedure for study, 14 January 1959, reproduced in Hyam and Louis eds., *Conservative Government*, part I, document 19.
58. *Department of Technical Cooperation. Report of the Committee on Training for Public Administration in Overseas Countries.* London: HMSO, 1963.
59. TNA, CO 1017/770, C (60) 116, 'Her Majesty's Overseas Civil Service', Cabinet Memorandum by the Secretary of State for the Colonies, 19 July 1960.
60. Bodleian, OUA, UR 6/Col 4/ file 13, COL/CP/789, 'The Future of Overseas Services Courses A and B at Oxford University' [undated, but 1961].
61. Bodleian, OUA, UR 6/Col 4/file 10, CCS, First and Second Courses Sub-Cttee. Supervisor's Report, 2 Jan. 1950.
62. Kumarasingham, "Eastminster."
63. Bodleian, OUA, CW1 /2, minutes CCS, 5 Mar. 1957.
64. Dimier, "Three Universities."
65. E.g., see evidence given to the 1929 Tomlin Royal Commission: Chapman, *Leadership*, 18.
66. Balogh, "Apotheosis of the Dilettante," esp. 12, 16, 27–8. First published in 1959 in Thomas ed., *The Establishment*.
67. It argued that the cult of the generalist 'is obsolete at all levels': PP. 1967–8, Cmd. 3638, *The Civil Service, Volume 1: Report of the Committee, 1966–68.* London: HMSO, 1968, para. 15.

68. Stockwell, *British End*, 130–7.
69. As the complicated career of one Zambian alumni of the Cambridge course from 1961–2 and a subsequent head of his country's civil service, Valentine Musakanya, exemplifies: Larmer ed., *Musakanya Papers*, 35–6.
70. Archive of the Bank of England (BoE), London, G1/202, no 77, Sir M. Norman to Oliver Stanley, 26 Aug. 1943.
71. Ibid., no 61, Sir M. Norman to Sir George Gater, 4 June 1943; no 63, Gater response, 18 June 1963; no 65, note by R. N. Kershaw addressed to Governor, 'London Currency Boards', 11 June 1943; no 76, Oliver Stanley to Sir M. Norman, 23 Aug. 1943; no 73, Confidential note on colonial currency boards, 19 July 1943.
72. Ibid., no 61, Sir M. Norman to Sir G. Gater, 4 June 1943.
73. Ibid., annotation by Sir M. Norman, 27 June 1943, on no 68, 'Colonial Currency Boards', 25 June 1943.
74. Uche, "Currency Board"; Uche, "Bank of England"; Schenk, "Origins of Central Bank," 409–31; Stockwell, "Instilling the 'Sterling Tradition.'"
75. Uche, "Bank of England."
76. Stockwell, *British End*, 166–86.
77. On the Bank's changing relationship to the British state, see Capie, *Bank of England*; Kynaston, *Till Time's Last Stand*.
78. Sayers, "Introduction," vii–xviii.
79. Basu, *Central Banking*, 71–2, 76, 96–7; Jucker-Fleetwood, *Money and Finance*, 58–9.
80. As I discuss in Stockwell, *British End*, 159–64.
81. Helleiner, "Southern Side."
82. BoE, OV 7/36, 'Some reflections on Currency Boards and Central Banks in the Colonial Context', paper by J. Fisher, 23 July 1958.
83. Gunasekera, *Dependent Currency*, 167.
84. Helleiner, "Southern Side," 253.
85. Cain and Hopkins, *British Imperialism*, 476–8.
86. Esp. Schenk, *Britain and Sterling Area*, 22, 417. On the importance of, and changing views towards, sterling's international role see also Schenk, *Decline of Sterling*.
87. Basu, *Central Banking*, 96–7.
88. BoE, OV 68/5, no 56A, J. B. Loynes to H. L. Jenkyns (Treasury), 18 February 1956.
89. This paragraph draws on Stockwell, *British End*, 171–90.
90. BoE, OV 68/7, no 183, personal reflections by P. B. Edgeley addressed to Messrs Heasman, Watson and Parsons, 25 Jan. 1961.
91. A full consideration of the reasons for institutional failure lies beyond the scope of this article and they have been discussed elsewhere including in an extensive near contemporaneous literature on institution-building, notably in relation to the military, as well as in later texts. See, for example, Chabal and Daloz, *Africa Works*.
92. Braibanti, *Asian Bureaucratic Systems*; Halliday, Karpik, Feeley eds., *Fates of Political Liberalism*.
93. Public Records and Archives Administration Department, Accra, Ghana, ADM 13/1/27, Cabinet Minutes, 9 September 1958, item 6; 16 September 1958, item 2; RG 3/1/622, various papers relating to the civil service; RG 2/4/27, Ohene Odame (Establishment CPP branch) to V. C. Crabbe (CPP headquarters), 27 September 1961.
94. Jucker-Fleetwood, *Money and Finance*, 58–9; Bangura, *Britain and Commonwealth Africa*, 99–102.
95. Basu, *Central Banking*, 97.
96. Stockwell, *British End*, 155.

97. On the different experiences of African universities and their relations to their governments, see Barkan, *An African Dilemma*, 21-2.
98. Ashby, *Universities*, 337-43; Jennings is quoted on 339, and Silcock on 341.
99. Ibid., 336.

Acknowledgements

This article brings together and develops material relating to the theme of political liberalism collected for Sarah Stockwell, *The British End of the British Empire* (Cambridge, 2018). I am grateful to the Leverhulme Trust for funding this research, to the Syndics of the University of Cambridge Library for permission to cite material in the Archives of the University of Cambridge, and to the Bank of England Archive and the Keeper of the Archives of the University of Oxford for permission to consult and cite material from their collections, as well as to staff at the Bodleian Library Oxford. An earlier version of this paper was presented at the 'Liberalisms within and beyond empire' workshop in Colombo, Sri Lanka, 17–19 December 2015. My thanks to the workshop organiser, Harshan Kumarasingham, for inviting me to participate and to other delegates for their comments as well as to Harshan and Arthur Burns for their helpful suggestions on an earlier draft of this article.

Disclosure statement

No potential conflict of interest was reported by the author.

References

Anderson, David. *Histories of the Hanged. Britain's Dirty War in Kenya and the End of the Empire*. London: Weidenfeld & Nicolson, 2005.

Anderson, Robert. *British Universities. Past and Present*. London: Hambledon Continuum, 2008.

Ashby, Eric. *Universities. British, Indian, African. A Study in the Ecology of Higher Education*. London: Weidenfeld and Nicolson, 1966.

Ashton, S. R., and S. E. Stockwell, eds. *Imperial Policy and Colonial Practice, 1925–1945*. British Documents on the End of Empire, Series A, Volume 1. London: HMSO, 1996.

Balogh, Thomas. "The Apotheosis of the Dilettante. The Establishment of the Mandarins." In *Crisis in the Civil Service*, edited by Thomas Balogh, Dudley Seers, Roger Opie, and Hugh Thomas, 11–51. London: Anthony Blond, 1968.

Bangura, Yusuf. *Britain and Commonwealth Africa: The Politics of Economic Relations, 1951–75*. Manchester: Manchester University Press, 1983.

Barkan, Joel D. *An African Dilemma. University Students, Development and Politics in Ghana, Tanzania and Uganda*. Nairobi: Oxford University Press, 1975.

Basu, S. K. *Central Banking in the Emerging Countries. A Study of African Experiments*. London: Asia Publishing House, 1967.

Bayly, C. A. *Recovering Liberties. Indian Thought in the Age of Liberalism and Empire*. Cambridge: Cambridge University Press, 2012.

Bell, Duncan. *Reordering the World. Essays on Liberalism and Empire*. Princeton: Princeton University Press, 2016.

Bennett, Huw. *Fighting the Mau Mau: The British Army and Counter Insurgency in the Kenya Emergency*. Cambridge: Cambridge University Press, 2012.

Braibanti, Ralph. *Asian Bureaucratic Systems Emergent from the British Imperial Tradition*. Durham, NC: Duke University Press, 1966.

Cain, P. J., and A. G. Hopkins. *British Imperialism, 1688–2016*. 3rd ed. Harlow: Longman, 2016.

Capie, Forrest. *The Bank of England 1950s to 1979*. Cambridge: Cambridge University Press, 2010.

Chabal, Patrick, and Jean-Pascal Daloz. *Africa Works. Disorder as Political Instrument*. Oxford: James Currey, 1999.

Chapman, R. A. *Leadership in the British Civil Service. A Study of Sir Percival Waterfield and the Creation of the Civil Service Selection Board*. London: Croom Helm, 1984.

Conklin, Alice C. *A Mission to Civilize. The Republican Idea of Empire in France and West Africa 1895–1930*. Indiana: Stanford University Press, 1997.

Cooper, Frederick. "Modernizing Bureaucrats, Backward Africans and the Development Concept." In *International Development and the Social Sciences: Essays on the History and Politics of Knowledge*, edited by F. Cooper, and Randall Packard, 64–91. Berkeley: University of California Press, 1997.

De, Rohit. "Emasculating the Executive, The Federal Court and Civil Liberties in Late Colonial India, 1942–44." In *Fates of Political Liberalism in the British Post-Colony. The Politics of the Legal Complex*, edited by Terence Halliday, Lucien Karpik, and Malcolm M. Feeley, 59–90. Cambridge: Cambridge University Press, 2012.

Dimier, Véronique. *Le Gouvernement des Colonies, Regards Croisés Franco-Britannique*. Brussels: University of Brussels, 2004.

Dimier, Véronique. "Three Universities and the British Elite: A Science of Colonial Administration in the UK." *Public Administration*, 84, no. 2 (2006): 337–366.

Duffield, Mark, and Vernon Hewitt, eds. *Development and Colonialism. The Past in the Present*. Woodbridge: Boydell and Brewer, 2009.

Elkins, Caroline. *Britain's Gulag, The Brutal End of Empire in Kenya*. London: Pimlico, 2005.

Gallagher, J. A., and Ronald Robinson. "The Imperialism of Free Trade." *The Economic History Review*, 2nd Series, 6 (1953): 1–15.

Grob-Fitzgibbon, Benjamin. *Britain's Dirty Wars and the End of Empire*. Basingstoke: Palgrave Macmillan, 2011.

Gunasekera, H. A. *From Dependent Currency to Central Banking in Ceylon: An Analysis of Monetary Experience, 1825–1957*. London: London School of Economics and Political Science, 1962.

Halliday, Terence C., and Lucien Karpik. "Political Liberalism in the British Post-Colony: A Theme with Three Variations." In *Fates of Political Liberalism in the British Post-Colony. The Politics of the Legal Complex*, edited by Terence Halliday, Lucien Karpik, and Malcolm M. Feeley, 3–55. Cambridge: Cambridge University Press, 2012.

Helleiner, Eric. "The Southern Side of 'Embedded Liberalism'. America's Unorthodox Money Doctoring during the Early Post-1945 Years." In *Money Doctors. The Experience of International Financial Advising, 1850–2000*, edited by Marc Flandreau, 249–275. Abingdon: Routledge, 2003.

Hennessy, Peter. *Whitehall*. London: Secker & Warburg, 1989.

Hewitt, Vernon. "Empire, International Development and the Concept of Good Government." In *Development and Colonialism. The Past in the Present*, edited by Mark Duffield, and Vernon Hewitt, 30–44. Woodbridge: James Currey/Boydell and Brewer, 2009.

Hodge, Joseph Morgan. *Triumph of the Expert. Agrarian Doctrines of Development and the Legacies of British Colonialism*. Athens, OH: Ohio University Press, 2007.

Hunter, Emma. "Languages of Freedom in Decolonising Africa." In *Transactions of the Royal Historical Society*, Sixth series, XXVII, 253–269. Cambridge: Cambridge University Press, 2017.

Hyam, Ronald, and Wm. Roger Louis, eds. *The Conservative Government and the End of Empire, 1957–1964*, British Documents on the End of Empire, Series A, Volume 4. London: The Stationery Office, 2000.

Hyden, Goran, Robert Jackson, and John Okumu, eds. *Development Administration. The Kenyan Experience*. Nairobi: Oxford University Press, 1970.

Jennings, Ivor. *Constitutional Laws of the Commonwealth*. London: Oxford University Press, 1957.

Jöns, Heike. "The University of Cambridge Academic Expertise and the British Empire, 1885–1962." *Environment and Planning*, 48, no. 1 (2016): 94–114.

Joyce, Patrick. *The State of Freedom. A Social History of the British State since 1800*. Cambridge: Cambridge University Press, 2013.

Jucker-Fleetwood, Erin E. *Money and Finance in Africa, The Experience of Ghana, Morocco, Nigeria, the Rhodesias and Nyasaland, the Sudan and Tunisia from the Establishment of Their Central Banks until 1962*. London: George Allen & Unwin, 1964.

Koditschek, Theodore. *Liberalism, Imperialism and the Historical Imagination. Nineteenth Century Vision of Greater Britain*. Cambridge: Cambridge University Press, 2011.

Kuklich, Henrika. *The Imperial Bureaucrat. The Colonial Administrative Service in the Gold Coast, 1920–1939*. Stanford: Hoover University Press, 1979.

Kumarasingham, Harshan. *Constitution-Maker - Selected Writings of Sir Ivor Jennings*. Cambridge: Cambridge University Press, 2015.

Kumarasingham, Harshan. "Eastminster – Decolonisation and State-Building in British Asia." In *Constitution- Making in Asia Decolonisation and State-Building in the Aftermath of the British Empire*, edited by Harshan Kumarasingham, 1–35. Abingdon: Routledge, 2016.

Kumarasingham, Harshan. *A Political Legacy of the British Empire. Power and the Parliamentary System in Post-Colonial India and Sri Lanka*. London: I.B. Tauris, 2013.

Kynaston, David. *Till Time's Last Stand. A History of the Bank of England 1694–2013*. London: Bloomsbury Publishing, 2017.

Larmer, Miles, ed. *The Musakanya Papers. The Autobiographical Writings of Valentine Musakanya*. Lusaka: Lembani Trust, 2010.

Lee, Michael. *Colonial Development and Good Government*. Oxford: Clarendon Press, 1967.

Livsey, Tim. *Nigeria's University Age: Reframing Decolonisation and Development*. Basingstoke: Palgrave Macmillan, 2017.

Lloyd, P. C., ed. *New Elites of Tropical Africa*. London: Oxford University Press, 1966.

Louis, W.R., and R. Robinson. "The Imperialism of Decolonization." *The Journal of Imperial and Commonwealth History*, 22, no. 3 (1994): 462–511.

Maxwell, C. M. *Universities in Partnership. The Inter-University Council and the Growth of Higher Education in Developing Countries 1946–1970*. Edinburgh: Scottish Academic Press, 1980.

Melber, Henning, ed. *The Rise of Africa's Middle Class. Myths, Realities and Critical Engagements*. London: Zed Books, 2016.

Nwauwa, Apollos O. *Imperialism, Academe and Nationalism: Britain and University Education for Africans 1860–1960*. London: Frank Cass, 1997.

Oliver, Roland. "Prologue: The two Miss Perhams." In *Margery Perham and British Rule in Africa*, edited by Alison Smith, and Mary Bull. London: Frank Cass, 1991.

Pearce, Robert. *The Turning Point in Africa. British Colonial Policy, 1938–1948*. London: Frank Cass, 1982.

Pitts, Jennifer. *A Turn to Empire. The Rise of Imperial Liberalism in Britain and France*. Princeton, NJ: Princeton University Press, 2005.

Rhodes, R. A. W., and Patrick Weller. "Westminster Transplanted and Westminster Implanted: Exploring Political Change." In *Westminster Legacies – Democracy and Responsible Government in Asia and the Pacific*, edited by Haig Patapan, John Wanna, and Patrick Weller. Sydney: University of New South Wales, 2005.

Sayers, R. S., ed. *Banking in the British Commonwealth*. Oxford: Clarendon Press, 1952.

Schenk, Catherine. *Britain and the Sterling Area. From Devaluation to Convertibility in the 1950s*. London: Routledge, 1994.

Schenk, Catherine. *The Decline of Sterling. Managing the Retreat of an International Currency 1945-1992*. Cambridge: Cambridge University Press, 2010.

Schenk, Catherine. "The Origins of a Central Bank in Malaya and the Transition to Independence, 1954-59." *The Journal of Imperial and Commonwealth History* 21, no. 2 (1993): 409-431.

Stockwell, Sarah. "Britain and Decolonization in an Era of Global Change." In *The Oxford Handbook of the Ends of Empire*, edited by Martin Thomas, and Andrew Thompson. Oxford: Oxford University Press, forthcoming.

Stockwell, Sarah. *The British End of the British Empire*. Cambridge: Cambridge University Press, 2018.

Stockwell, Sarah. "Exporting Britishness: Decolonization in Africa, the British State and Its Clients." In *The Ends of European Colonial Empires. Cases and Comparisons*, edited by Miguel Banderia Jerónimo, and António Costa Pinto, 148-177. Basingstoke: Palgrave Macmillan, 2015.

Stockwell, Sarah. "Instilling the "Sterling Tradition": Decolonization and the Creation of a Central Bank in Ghana." *The Journal of Imperial and Commonwealth History* 26, no. 2 (1998): 100-119.

Symonds, Richard. *The British and Their Successors. A Study of the Government Services in the New States*. London: Faber & Faber, 1966.

Tinker, Hugh. "Structure of the British Imperial Heritage." In *Asian Bureaucratic Systems Emergent from the British Imperial Tradition*, edited by Ralph Braibanti, et al. Durham, NC: Duke University Press, 1966.

Uche, C.U. "Bank of England vs the IBRD: Did the Nigerian Colony Deserve a Central Bank?." *Explorations in Economic History* 34 (1997): 220-241.

Uche, C. U. "From Currency Board to Central Banking: The Politics of Change in Sierra Leone." *African Economic History* 24 (1996): 147-158.

West, Michael O. *The Rise of an African Middle Class. Colonial Zimbabwe, 1898-1965*. Bloomington: Indiana University Press, 2002.

Wolton, Suke. *Lord Hailey, the Colonial Office and the Politics of Race and Empire in the Second World War. The Loss of White Prestige*. Basingstoke: Macmillan, 2000.

Index

academics, African end of empire 201
Africa: attitudes to 4; colonial universities 203; end of empire 195–219; public administration 204–7; self-government 207–10; state constitutions post-independence 210–11
Age of Extremes (Hobshawn) 187
The Aims of Labour (Henderson) 8–9
Alexandrowicz, C. H. 77
Alliance of Free Nations 11
All-India Women's Conference 130
Ambedkar, B. R. 66, 129–30
Amery, Leo 13
Amritsar Massacre 125
anarchism 178
Anderson, Robert 200–1
Angell, Norman 181, 183–4
Anglo–Boer war (1899–1902) 36
Anti-Corn-Law League 177
Antigua, republicanism 160
The Approach to Self-Government (Jennings) 69, 77
Arunachalam, Ponnambalam 73
Ashby, Eric 197, 203–4, 211
Ashton, S. R. 83
Asquith Commission (1945) 202, 203
Associated Overseas Trade (AOT) 23
At Suvla Bay (Hargrave) 178–9
Attack! (Front Line) 185
Attlee, Clement 16–17
Austin, Dennis 64, 81
Australia: Britishness, dwindling of 83; constitutional monarchy as 145; Dominions Office, interaction with 100; Indian-South African dispute 111–12; indigenous history 81–2; racism and 40; White Dominion as 9, 73
Australia and Britain – Studies in a Changing Relationship (Madden & Morris-Jones) 69
Authority in the Modern State (Laski) 125

Baden-Powell, Robert 173, 178–9, 181
Balfour Declaration (1926) 72, 147
Balogh, Thomas 206
Bank of Ceylon 209

Bank of England, African countries and independence 208–10
banners, Peterloo Massacre (1819) 176
Barbados 164; JCPC appeal abolishment 145; republicanism 160
Baring, Evelyn 97
Bayly, C. A. 4, 71–2, 76, 171
Beckett, Eric 101
Belize 164; JCPC appeal abolishment 145
Bell, Duncan 195
Beloff, Max 1–2
Bengal Famine 125
Bentley, Michael 62
Berkman, Alexander 178
Besant, Annie 46–7, 66
Beveridge, William 124
Bevin, Ernest 19–20, 101
Beyond a Boundary (James) 67–8
Bhownagree, Mancherjee 36
Blackburne, Kenneth 154
black flags: radicalism 170–94; Reform Bill (1831) 177
Black Power revolution, Caribbean countries 163–4
Boland, Frederick 84
Bonnerjee, W. C. 36
Bose, S. C. 135
Boy Scouts Association (BSA) 178–9; expansion of 179–81
Brahma Samej reformist movement, Ray 130
Brailsford, H. N. 18
Brasted, H. V. 81
Bridge, Carl 81
Bright, John 183–4
Britain and Indian Nationalism – The Imprint of Ambiguity (Low) 70
The Britannic Vision (McIntyre) 65
British Documents on the End of Empire 83
British Nationality Act (1914) 34
British Nationality Act (1948) 31
British Nationality and Status of Alien Act (1914) 41
Brock, Michael 69
bulk purchase agreements 13

INDEX

Burma: Chinese/Indian workers 34; grants for self-government 18; rapid decolonialisation 17
Burnham, Forbes 156
Burroughs, Peter 69
Bustmante, Alexander 149–50, 151–2
Butler, Uriah 146

Cabinet Government (Jennings) 68
Cain, Peter 209
Callaghan, James 24–5
Cambridge History of the British Empire 71
Canada: constitutional monarchy as 145; Dominions Office, interaction with 100; indigenous history 81–2; White Dominion as 9, 73
Cape Town Agreement (1927) 96, 98; India Office (IO) and 101
Capitalism and Slavery (Williams) 74
Caribbean countries 5, 144–69; coloured English gentlemen education 153–4; The Crown, loyalty to 154; Dominion Status 146–51; head of state 159–60; independence 146–51; Legislative Councils 146; nationalism 146, 151–5; non-English original settlers 145; political leaders 154; post colonies 155–63; refusal of self-government 146–8; republicanism 155, 159–60, 164
Caribbean Labour Congress (1949) 152
Carpenter, Edward 178
The Case for West Indian Self-Government (James) 67–8
caste system, Indian-South African dispute (1946) 98
Castle, Barbara 20–1
CDC (Colonial Development Corporation) 17
Ceylon: Chinese/Indian workers 34; constitutional and political history 73; independence 211–12; Muslims 78; rapid decolonialisation 17
Chagla, M. C. 113
Chamberlain, Joseph 10, 39–40
Chandra Pal, Bepin 49
Channon, H. J. 201–2
Charles, Eugenia 158
Chesterton, G. K. 184
Chinese indentured labour, South Africa 7
Chinese merchants, British naturalisation applications 35
Churchill, Winston 41
Cipriani, Arthur 146, 147, 151–2
citizenship 82
Citizenship, Social Service, Self-Governance for India 48
Civis Britannicus sum 3, 151–5; death of 32; racism and 40
Class Areas Bill (1938) 96
Closer Union Council (CUC) 147
Cockram, Ben 112

Cold War, Western interests 201
Cole, G. D. H. 8, 16, 184
Colley, Linda 81
Colonial Development Act (1929) 14
Colonial Development and Welfare Act (1940) 17
Colonial Development Corporation (CDC) 17
colonial independence 73
Colonial Office: academics and 201; African local government 199; Commonwealth Relations Office amalgamation 24; public administration in Africa 204–5
colour bar 15
colour question 41
Commonwealth: African state constitutions 210–11; America, co-operation against; Communism 19–20; EEC and 23–4; non-members, interest in 83–4; transition to from empire 19
Commonwealth Constitutional History 60–94; definitions 61–4; post-British 80–4; post-war/professional 76–80; pre-history 72–6; writers of 64–72
The Commonwealth Experience (Mansergh) 83
Commonwealth Labour Group of MPs 13
Commonwealth Relations Office 24
Communism, America–Commonwealth co-operation 19–20
Communist Party, empire, views on 13
complete political independence *(purna swaraj)* 51
Comradeship and Wheatsheaf 182–3
Congress and the Raj – Facets of the Indian Struggle (Low) 70
Congress Socialist Party (CSP) 137
Constitutional Decolonisation 81
constitutional factors: Commonwealth History 77; empire 11
constitutional history: England 63–4; teaching of 62–3
Constitutional History of India, 1600-1935 (Keith) 65
Constitutional Laws of the Commonwealth (Jennings) 68
Constitutional Problems in Pakistan (Jennings) 69
The Constitution of Ceylon (Jennings) 68
control, state power 61–2
Convention People's Party, Ghana 211
Cooper, Frederick 33
Coupland, Reginald 65, 67, 73–4, 196
Cowper, William 184–5
Creech Jones, Arthur 17–18, 19, 149
Cripps, Stafford 108
Cromwell, Oliver 186
Crossman, Richard 21–2
The Crown, Caribbean countries 154
Cruikshank, George 176
CSP (Congress Socialist Party) 137
CUC (Closer Union Council) 147

Cullen, Michael 77
Cunningham, George 21
Curran, James 83
Curtis, Lionel 10, 65, 74
Cyprus: independence problems 3; political disorder 199

D'Aguiar, Peter 156
Dale, William 64
Darwin, John 61, 69
Davidson, William 'Black' 176
Deakin, Alfred 40
Deane, Herbert 133
de Botha, Louis 40
de la Bastide, Michael 162
Delise Burns, C. 8
democracy: case for, Laski 132–6; disavowment of 172; nationalism and 135–6; reinvention of 172
Democracy in Africa (Jennings) 69
Democracy in Crisis (Laski) 126–7
Department of Technical Co-operation 206
de Smith, S. A. 64, 70
Destroyers for Bases Agreement (1940) 148
Dicey, A. V. 63, 73
Dimier, Véronique 206
disavowment of democracy 172
Dominica 158–9, 164; republicanism 145
Dominion Office (DO): Indian-South African dispute 97, 100–1, 105; India Office merge 112–13
Dominion Status, Caribbean countries 146–51
Douglas, C. H. 184
Drayton, Richard 52, 155
Dubow, Saul 83, 85
Dutt, R. C. 135

Eclipse of Empire (Low) 71
Economic Aid (Labour's Colonial Policy) 20–1
economic democracy 137
economic freedom, Soviet Union and 132–3
economics of empire 10–11, 15
Edward VII, India and 35–6
Elizabeth II: Dominica head of state 158; Jamaican visit 1953 154–5
Elliot Commission 202
Ellis, Havelock 181
empire: compartmentalisation of 12; economic integration of 15–16; economics of 10–11, 15; interconnected system as 8–9; land use 13; military dimension 14; military dimension of 14; rights of belonging to 33–6; social and constitutional factors 11
The Empire's New Clothes (Murphy) 144–5
England, constitutional history 63–4
Europe, anti-Indian measures 95–6
European Economic Community (EEC): Commonwealth and 23–4; Labour party and 22–3

Fabian Colonial Research Bureau 17–18
Fabian socialism 129
Fabrication of Empire – The British and the Uganda Kingdoms 1890-1902 (Low) 71
Facing the Flag (Verne) 174–5
Fawkes, Guido 186
February Revolution (1971), Trinidad and Tobago 157
federalism 82; imperial citizenship 46–50
Fieldhouse, D. K. 69
Fiji, Chinese/Indian workers 34
financial devolution, African countries independence 209
First World War: anti-Indian feeling 96; foreign university students 122; imperial citizenship test 46
Foot, Hugh 154
Foreign Office (FO): India, attitude to 113; Indian-South African dispute 101–2, 104
Forgotten Armies – The Fall of British Asia 1941-1945 (Bayly & Harper) 71
Forgotten Wars – The End of Britain's Asian Empire (Bayly & Harper) 71
Frame-Breaking Act (1812) 175
The Framing of India's Constitution – Select Documents (Shiva Rao) 67
Freeden, Michael 127
Freedom Party, Dominica 158
French West Africa, decolonisation of 33
Fulton Committee 206–7
Furse, Ralph 202–3

Gaitskell, Hugh 22–3, 25
Gambia, independence 145, 197
Gandhi, Mohandas 34, 96; imprisonment of 14; labour mobilisation 42; rights reclaiming in South Africa 36–9; support of Wilson Hunter 37–8
Gangadar Tilak, Bal 49
Gater, George 207–8
Geddes, Patrick 181
General Assembly, Indian-South African dispute 106–12
General Committee (UN), Indian-South African dispute 106–7
Georges, Telford 79
Ghana 81; central bank 209–10; Constituent Assembly 77; independence 145, 197; one-party system 211; Representational Assembly 77–8
Ghetto Act (1946) 97, 98, 100
Ghose, Lalmohan 36
Girvan, Norman 155
Gladstone, Herbert 40
Gokhale, G. K. 122–3
Gold Coast 81
Goldstone, Frank 9
Gopal, S. 75
Gore-Booth, Paul 105
Government of India Act (1919) 51

INDEX

Government of India Act (1935) 15, 75–6
The Government of the British Empire (Keith) 65
Great Britain (GB): Indian-South African dispute 99–102, 103–5, 107–8; international role under Labour 12–13; lascars in 34; withdrawal from empire 114
Green Shirts 173, 185–6
Grenada: nationalist movement 146; republicanism 159, 160
Grenadines, republicanism 160
Griffiths, James 22
Gullace, Nicoletta 50
Guyana: JCPC appeal abolishment 145; republicanism 145, 156

Haden-Guest, Leslie 13
Haksar, P. N. 135–6
Halliday, Terence 199
Hancock, Keith 65, 74–6
Hansen, Randal 34
Hardy, Keir 50
Hargrave, John Gordon 173, 178–9, 183
Harlow, Vincent 67
Harold Laski Institute of Political Studies (Ahmedabad) 121
Harper, Tim 71
Hatch, John 19
head of state, Caribbean countries 159–60
Healey, Joseph 176
Henderson, Arthur 8–9
Herenigde Nasionale Party (HNP) 97
Hickford, Mark 83
higher education, development of 196–7
Hobhouse, L. T. 123, 171–2
Hobsbawm, Eric 171, 187
Hobson, J. A. 8, 123, 184
Home Rule and Empire 48
Home Rule for India Campaign 46–50
Hopkins, A. G. 85, 209
Hopkins, Henry 31
Hopkinson, Harry 3
human rights denial, racism 99
Hunter, Emma 196, 200
Huxley, Julian 181
Hyam, Ronald 64

immigration, racially-incited violence 32
imperial citizenship: federalist visions 46–50; India and 32–3; radicalising agent as 50–3
Imperial Conference (1911) 41–2
Imperial Government (Madden & Robinson) 69
imperial liberalism 199
import boards, development of 16
independence, Caribbean countries 146–51
Independent Jamaica Council for Human Rights v. Attorney General Jamaica (1998) 162–3

India 31–59: Constitution 1950 77; constitutional history 77; establishment of republic 18–19; Foreign Office, attitude to 113; grants for self-government 18; Home Rule Campaign 46–50; imperial citizenship and 32–3, 42–6; imperial citizenship as radicalising agent 50–3; JCPC, right of appeal abolishment 161; payment to UK war effort 9; rapid decolonialisation 17; rights of belonging to empire 33–6; scholar-civil servants 76–7; South African racial policies and *see* Indian-South African dispute; 'superfluous' population re-distribution 34–5; *Towards Freedom* 83; women's suffrage 49
India League 112
Indian Home Rule League of America (1917) 49
Indian National Congress 81, 199
Indian Rebellion (1857) 35
Indian-South African dispute (1946) 4–5, 36–9, 44, 95–120; agreement failure 105–6; Britain's initial response 99–102; British delegation draft 103–5; Cabinet decision 106; conference initialization 102; Dominion Office and 100–1, 105; Foreign Office and 101–2, 104; General Assembly 106–12; impact of 112–13; Indian complaints 98–9; India Office 99–100, 104–5; open confrontation prevention 97–8
India Office (IO): Cape Town Agreement and 101; Dominion Office merge 112–13; Indian-South African dispute 99–100, 104–5
indigenous history 81–2
individual liberty, Marxism and 137
institution-building, Africa 196–8, 211
interconnected systems, empire as 8–9
International Court of Justice (ICJ) 107–8
international finance 184–5
International Relations theory 64
Inter-University Council for Higher Education in the Colonies 202
Ireland: Dominions Office, interaction with 100; JCPC, right of appeal abolishment 160; White Dominion as 73

Jagan, Cheddi 149, 156
Jamaica: British withdrawal from 81; Constitution (1944) 148–9; draft independence constitution 153; independence 2; JCPC, right of appeal abolishment 162; Queen Elizabeth's visit (1953) 154–5; republican status 145
Jamaican Independence Conference (1962) 150
Jamaican Labour Party (JLP) 149–50, 151
James, C. L. R. 63, 67–8
Jeffries, Charles 64
Jennings, Ivor 64, 68–9, 77, 202, 206
John, Patrick 158

Joint Committee (UN), Indian-South African dispute 109–10
Judicial Committee of the Privy Council (JCPC) 145; appeal abolishment 160–3, 164

Karpik, Lucien 199
Keith, Arthur Berriedale 65–6, 72–4, 160
Kenya: independence 145; political disorder 199
Kerr, John 80
Kershaw, Raymond 207
Khare, N. B. 96
Khilnani, Sunil 135
Kindred of the Kibbo Kift 179–80; Advisory Council 181; non-conformist syndicate 182; reform of 181–2
The King and the Imperial Crown: The Powers and the Duties of His Majesty (Keith) 65
King, Anthony 64
King, Michael 77
Kipling, Rudyard 8
Komagata Maru 42–6
Krishna Menon, V. K. 122, 124–5
Kropotkin, Peter 178

Labour and the Nation (1927) 12–13
Labour and the Nation (1928) 14
Labour and the New Social Order (1918) 10–11
Labour and the New Society (1950) 19
Labour in the Commonwealth (Cole) 8
Labour Party 7–30; Britain's international role 12–13; Commonwealth, transition to 19; land use of empire 13; military dimension of empire 14; racism and 15, 21–2; sustainable development promotion 20
The Labour Party in Perspective 16–17
Labour's Colonial Policy 20–1
Lahiri, Shompa 135
Lajpat Rai, Lala 46, 49, 50
Lanka Sama Samaja Party (Ceylon) 122
Lansbury, George 13, 14–15, 50
lascars, settlement in Britain 34
Laski, Harold 121–43; case for democracy 132–6; classical liberalism 134–5; lecture theatre 123–7; liberalism, limits of 136–8; Marxism and individual therapy 137; Masani, disagreement with 137–8; Mehta and Ray 127–32; radicalism 126; violence, aversion to 126–7, 134
Latham, R. T. E. 64
Laurier, Wilfred 41
The Law and the Constitution (Jennings) 68
Legislative Councils, Caribbean countries 146, 151–2
legislative independence, South Africa 9–10
legitimisation, state power 61–2
Lewis, Gordon 151, 153–4
liberal internationalism, Smuts 114
The Life of Captain Cipriani: An Account of British Government in the West Indies (James) 67

Lindsay, Louis 152
Lion Rampart – Essays in the Study of British Imperialism (Low) 71
Livsey, Tim 202, 203
London Colonial Conference (1897) 39–40
London School of Economics and Political Sciences (LSE) 121–2
Lonecraft (Hargrave) 178–9
Louis, W. Roger 74, 75
Low, D. A. 70–1, 80–1, 83
Lowry, Donal 79
Loynes, John 209–10
Luddites 175–6

MacDonald, Ramsay 12
Macpherson, C. B. 122, 126
Madden, A. F. 62, 63, 69, 84
Maitland, F. W. 63
Malan, D. F. 97
Malan, F. S. 41
Malawi, independence 145
Malaya: Chinese/Indian workers 34; external influences 3; political disorder 199
Malaysia, JCPC, right of appeal abolishment 161
Malinowski, Bronislaw 124
Malta, independence ideas 21, 75
The Man in the Moon (Cruikshank) 176
Manley, Norman 2, 149, 151–2
Mansergh, Nicholas 82–3
Maori Representation Act (1897) 78
Mara, Kamisese 79
Marshall, David 79–80
Marshall, Geoffrey 64
Marxism, individual liberty and 137
Masani, M. R. 137–8
Mauritius: Chinese/Indian workers 34; Muslims 78
Maxwell, Ian 211
McDermott, Geoffrey 24
McIntosh, Alastair 3
McIntosh, Simeon 161–2
McIntyre, W. David 65, 74
McLeod, Iain 150
Mehta, G. L. 122, 123, 124; Fabian socialism 129; Laski and 127–32
Menon, K. P. S. 112, 113
Miliband, Ralph 123, 138
military dimension, empire of 14
Mill, J. S. 48
Miller, J. D. B. 64
Miller, J. R. 82
Mills, Gladstone 124
Ministry of Overseas Development 206
minorities, exclusion of 82
Mintoff, Dom 21
Mohamad, Mahathir 78
Montagu, Edwin 52
Montgomery, Bernard 4
Moore, Barrington 51

Moreas, Frank 135
Morris-Jones, W. H. 69
Morrison, Herbert 148
Moyn, Samuel 52
Moyne Commission (1938) 147
Moynihan, Daniel Patrick 122–3
Muhammad, Ghulam 78
Mukherjee, Pranab 77
Mukherjee, Sumita 135
multi-racial conferences 22
Munrow, Trevor 81
Murphy, Philip 85, 144–5, 159–60
Muslim League 81

Naoroji, Dadabhai 36, 131
Narayanan, K. R. 122
Natal, Chinese/Indian workers 34
National Executive Committee (NEC) 22
nationalism: Caribbean countries 146; democracy and 135–6
National Joint Action Committee, Trinidad and Tobago 157
National Union of Freedom Fighters, Trinidad and Tobago 157
native administration, dismantling of 198–9
Navigation Act (1915) 34
Nehru, B. K. 135–6
Nehru, Jawaharlal 18–19, 113, 121, 122–3; interim government 102; Laski and 127–8; Ray, criticism by 132
Nevinson, Henry 180, 181
The New Commonwealth and its Constitution (de Smith) 70
Newfoundland: Dominions Office, interaction with 100; White Dominion as 9, 73
New Jewel Movement (NJM), Grenada 159
New Liberalism 171–2
New Zealand: constitutional history 83; constitutional monarchy as 145; Dominions Office, interaction with 100; EEC, objections to 23–4; imperial citizenship 41; indigenous history 81–2; Labour government 16; racism and 40; White Dominion as 9, 73
Nicholls, Heaton 109–10
Nigeria: central bank 209–10; independence 145; universities 203
Nkrumah, Kwame 23, 211
Noel-Baker, Philip 106, 113
non-conformist syndicate, Kibbo Kift 182
Northcote-Trevelyan reforms (1854) 204

Onslow, Sue 85
An Open letter to the British Public from the Hindustanis of North America 45
Ottawa system 15–16
overseas aid 19
Overseas Food Corporation (1948) 17
Overseas Service Aid Scheme 205
Owen, Nicholas 37

Oxford and the Idea of the Commonwealth (Madden & Fieldhouse) 69

Pacifico, David 35
pacifism, Hargrave 179
Pakistan 77; JCPC, right of appeal abolishment 161
Panday, Basdeo 162
Pandit, Vijaya Lakshmi 106, 109–10, 111
Parliament (Jennings) 68
People's National Congress (PNC) 152
People's National Movement (PNM), Trinidad and Tobago 149–50
Perera, N. M. 122
Perham, Margery 65, 70, 77, 201–2, 211
Persad-Bissessar, Kamla 163
Peterloo Massacre (1819) 176
Pethick Lawrence, Emmeline 181
piracy 173, 174
pirate flags 173
plenary vote (UN), Indian-South African dispute 110–12
The Plural Society (Labour's Colonial Policy) 20
political leaders, Caribbean countries 154
political neutrality 200
Ponnambalam, G. G. 79
Posnett, R. N. 158–9
post-war Commonwealth Constitutional History 76–80
post-war socialist reforms 136
'Princes, Chiefs and Peoples of India' Proclamation (1858) 35
public administration, Africa 204–7
public administration development 196–7
Public Order Act (1937) 186–7
purna swaraj (complete political independence) 51

racism 39–42; human rights denial 99; Labour Party and 15, 21–5; violence in immigration 32
radicalising agent, imperial citizenship as 50–3
radicalism, Laski 126
Ramanathan, Ponnambalam 2–3
Rau, B. N. 66
Ray, Renuka 122, 123; Laski and 127–32; Nehru, criticism of 132
Razak, Tun Abdul 80
Recovering Liberties – Indian Thoughts in the Age of Liberalism and Empire (Bayly) 72
Reform Bill (1831) 177
reinvention of democracy 172
Representational Assembly (Ghana) 77–8
republicanism: Caribbean countries 155, 159–60, 164; Grenada 159
Responsible Government in the Dominions (Keith) 65
Rhodes, Cecil 4
The Rise of European Literature (Laski) 125
The Road to Serfdom (Laski) 127

Robbins, Lionel 124
Roberts, Kenneth 64
Robin Hood 183–4
Robinson, Kenneth 69
Robinson, Patrick 144–5
Rockefeller Foundation 124
Roden Buxton, Charles 15
Rowlett Act (1919) 46, 51
Rowse, Timothy 123
Roy, Rammohan 130
Russell, Bertrand 129, 184

Samvidhaan: The making of the Constitution of India 77
Sartori, Giovanni 60, 85
satyagraha 42, 96
school children, constitutional history 62–3
Scott, James 51
Scouting for Boys (Baden-Powell) 181
Seaga, Edward 162
Second World War: Commonwealth after 4; foreign university students 122
Seeley, J. R. 48, 73
segregated empire 39–42
Select Documents on the Constitutional History of the British Empire 69
self-government: Africa 207–10; refusal in Caribbean countries 146–8
Shannon, Geoffrey 112
The Shape of Things to Come (Wells) 170–3
Sharett, Moshe 123
Shaw, George Bernard 50, 124
Shawcross, Hartley 100
Shiva Rao, B 66–7
Silcock, T. H. 212
Simmonds, David 161
Singapore 78–9: JCPC, right of appeal abolishment 161
Singh, Gurdit 42–6; imperial citizenship test 45
slavery 184–5
Sluga, Glenda 123
Smaller Territories (Labour's Colonial Policy) 21
Smartt, Thomas 40
Smith, John 81
Smuts, Jan Christiaan 96–7
Social Credit Party of Great Britain (SCP) 173, 186
social factors, empire 11
socialist reforms, post-Second World War 136
Some Characteristics of the Indian Constitution (Jennings) 69
sources, state power 61–2
South Africa: Burns 12; Chinese indentured labour 7; Dominions Office, interaction with 100; indentured labour termination 96; JCPC, right of appeal abolishment 160; legislative independence 9–10; Natal Provincial Council 96–7; post-Indian-South African dispute 114; racial policies, India's attacks on see Indian-South African dispute (1946); White Dominion as 9, 73
South African Indian Relief Act (1914) 42
Soviet Union, economic freedom and 132–3
Speeches and Documents of the British Dominions 1918-1931: From Self-Government to National Sovereignty (Keith) 65
Spry Rush, Anne 153
Sri Lanka 81; JCPC, right of appeal abolishment 161
Standard Oil rally (1914) 178
Standing Closer Association Commission (SCAC) 149
Stanley, Oliver 148, 199, 207
state power, sources/legitimisations/control 61–2
Stead, W. T. 50
Stockwell, Sarah 85
Stover, Leon 172–3
Stri Dharma (Women's India Association) 49
Stubbs, William 62–3
Studies in the Problem of Sovereignty (Laski) 125
St Vincent, republicanism 160
Survey of British Commonwealth Affairs (Toynbee) 74–5, 83
sustainable development promotion, Labour Party 20

Tagore, Rabindranath 181
Tanzania (Tanganyka), independence 145
Theosophical Society, Indian Home Rule 46, 47–8
Thomas, Ioan 13
Thomas, James 13
Thompson, E. P. 67
Thompson-Seton, Ernest 182–3
Thomson, George 25
Todd, Alphaeus 64
Towards Freedom 83
Toynbee, Arnold 74–5
Tracey, Bill 182
The Trail 180–1
Transfer of Power 83
Treaty of Berlin (1884), Treaty of Rome (1957) *vs.* 23
Trinidad and Tobago 78, 157–8; Chinese/Indian workers 34; general election 1956 153; Independence Conference (1962) 150; JCPC, right of appeal abolishment 162, 163; Legislative Council 151–2; nationalist movement 146; People's National Movement (PNM) 149–50; republicanism 145, 163–4
Trudeau, Pierre 122, 138
Turpin, Eugène 174

unfashionable independence 69
United Front, Guyana 156

United National Congress, Caribbean countries 163
United Nations (UN): Indian-South African dispute (1946); *see also* Indian-South African dispute (1946)
United States of America (USA), Commonwealth, co-operation against Communism 19–20
Universal Declaration of Human Rights (1948) 114–15
University's Foreign Service Programme 206

Veale, Douglas 202–3
Verne, Jules 174–5
Victoria: diamond jubilee (1897) 1–2; 'Princes, Chiefs and Peoples of India' Proclamation (1858) 35
violence, Laski, aversion to 126–7, 134
visions of kinship 173

Wallas, Graham 124
Walsh, Stephen 9–10
Ward, Joseph 40, 41
Ward, Stuart 83
Wavell, A. P. 96–7
Webb, Beatrice 124
Webb, Sidney 11–12, 50, 124
Wedgwood, Josiah 50

Wells, H. G. 170–3, 181
Western interests, Cold War 201
West Indian nationalists 147
Wheare, Kenneth C. 62, 64, 65, 69
White Dominions 9, 73
'White Man's Burden' 8
Whitlam, Gough 80
Wight, Martin 64
Williams, Eric 67, 74, 149, 152–3, 164
Williams, Francis 16–17
Wilson, Harold 18, 23–4
Wilson Hunter, William 37–8
Women's India Association (WIA) 49
women's suffrage, India 49
Wood, E. F. L. 2
Wooding Commission (1971), Trinidad and Tobago 157–8
World Bank 208
world government 75
World War I *see* First World War
World War II *see* Second World War

Yew, Lee Kuan 124
Young Men's Indian Association 52

Zachariah, Benjamin 136
Zimbabwe 85
Zimmern, Alfred 64, 65, 75
Zulu Rebellion (1906) 36